The BEGINNERS BIBLE™
BIBLE
Tells Me So

STANDARD PUBLISHING
Cincinnati, Ohio

Artwork: Copyright ©1998, James R. Leininger. The Beginner's Bible trademark is owned by James R. Leininger and licensed exclusively to Performance Unlimited, Inc. All rights reserved.

Project Editor: Christine Spence
Acquisitions Editor: Ruth Frederick
Lesson Writers: Peggy DaHarb (units 6, 12); Kathy Downs (units 2, 11); Cathy Falk (units 1, 9); Wanda Pelfrey (units 5, 7); Angela Smith (units 4, 8); Kristi Walter (units 3, 10)
Artist for Performance Unlimited, Inc.: Lisa S. Reed

Scriptures marked ICB are quoted from the *International Children's Bible, New Century Version,* copyright ©1986, 1988 by Word Publishing, Dallas, Texas 75039. Used by permission.

Scriptures marked NIV are quoted from the HOLY BIBLE—NEW INTERNATIONAL VERSION, copyright ©1973, 1978, 1984 International Bible Society. Used by permission of Zondervan Bible Publishers.

The Standard Publishing Company, Cincinnati, Ohio. A division of Standex International Corporation

©1998 by The Standard Publishing Company. All rights reserved.
Printed in the United States of America

Permission is granted to reproduce these pages
for ministry purposes only—not for resale.

04 03 02 01 00 99 98   5 4 3 2 1

ISBN 0-7847-0817-7

Table of Contents

The Bible Tells Me So 5
Time Line and Bible Activities 6

Unit 1: **God Created Everything** 7
Lesson 1: God Created Everything 9
Lesson 2: God Created the Sun, Moon, and Stars 13
Lesson 3: God Created the Animals 17
Lesson 4: God Created People 21
Unit 1 activity pages 25

Unit 2: **God Wants Me to Make Right Choices** 31
Lesson 5: God Wants Me to Tell the Truth 33
Lesson 6: God Wants Me to Follow Instructions 37
Lesson 7: God Wants Me to Work Hard 41
Lesson 8: God Wants Me to Keep My Promises 45
Unit 2 activity pages 49

Unit 3: **God Cares for Us** 55
Lesson 9: Out of Egypt 57
Lesson 10: A Dry Path Through a Wet Sea 61
Lesson 11: Where's the Water? 65
Lesson 12: Manna and Quail 69
Lesson 13: Ten Rules on Two Tablets 73
Unit 3 activity pages 77

Unit 4: **Celebrate Jesus' Birth** 83
Lesson 14: John's Parents Know Jesus Is Special 85
Lesson 15: Mary Sings Because Jesus Is Special 89
Lesson 16: Shepherds Tell People Jesus Is Special 93
Lesson 17: Simeon and Anna Thank God Because Jesus Is Special 97
Lesson 18: Wise Men Give Gifts Because Jesus Is Special 101
Unit 4 activity pages 105

Unit 5: **Jesus Is a Friend** 111
Lesson 19: Jesus Calls Four Special Friends 113
Lesson 20: Jesus Is a Friend to Children 117
Lesson 21: Jesus Is a Friend to a Leader 121
Lesson 22: Jesus Is a Friend to People Who Are Different 125
Unit 5 activity pages 129

Unit 6: **Jesus Is God's Son** 135
Lesson 23: Jesus Healed Peter's Mother-in-Law 137
Lesson 24: Jesus Raised a Widow's Son 141
Lesson 25: Jesus Fed More Than 5,000 People 145
Lesson 26: Jesus Healed Two Blind Men 149
Unit 6 activity pages 153

Unit 7:	**Jesus Teaches Us**	**159**
Lesson 27:	Jesus Taught Us to Pray	161
Lesson 28:	Jesus Taught Us to Share	165
Lesson 29:	Jesus Taught Us to Help	169
Lesson 30:	Jesus Taught Us to Be Thankful	173
	Unit 7 activity pages	177
Unit 8:	**Jesus Is Alive**	**183**
Lesson 31:	Jesus Is Praised	185
Lesson 32:	Jesus Is Alive!	189
Lesson 33:	The Disciples See Jesus	193
Lesson 34:	Breakfast with Jesus	197
Lesson 35:	Jesus Returns to Heaven	201
	Unit 8 activity pages	205
Unit 9:	**Tell About Jesus**	**211**
Lesson 36:	Peter Tells About Jesus	213
Lesson 37:	Peter and John Tell About Jesus	217
Lesson 38:	Philip Tells About Jesus	221
Lesson 39:	Paul Tells About Jesus	225
	Unit 9 activity pages	229
Unit 10:	**God Is Powerful**	**235**
Lesson 40:	God's Power Feeds Elijah	237
Lesson 41:	God's Power Feeds a Widow	241
Lesson 42:	God Shows the People His Power	245
Lesson 43:	God's Power Makes a Boy Live Again	249
Lesson 44:	God's Power Heals Naaman	253
	Unit 10 activity pages	257
Unit 11:	**God Hears Our Prayers**	**263**
Lesson 45:	Solomon Prays to Choose Right	265
Lesson 46:	Hezekiah Prays to Be Healed	269
Lesson 47:	Manasseh Prays When He Is Sorry	273
Lesson 48:	Jehoshaphat Prays When He Is Thankful	277
	Unit 11 activity pages	281
Unit 12:	**Do What Is Right**	**287**
Lesson 49:	Ezra and the People Learn God's Word	289
Lesson 50:	Josiah and the People Obey God's Word	293
Lesson 51:	Micaiah Tells the Truth	297
Lesson 52:	Samuel Chooses to Do Right All His Life	301
	Unit 12 activity pages	305
	Bible Time Line	311

The Bible Tells Me So

How Are the Lessons Organized?

The lessons are each built around three aims, which are printed at the beginning of the lesson. The *know* aim tells what Bible knowledge children will gain from the lesson. The *feel* aim tells how children should feel as a result of that knowledge. And the *do* aim tells what children should determine to do as a result of their knowledge.

Each lesson includes nine activities which accomplish the unit and lesson aims.

Activities 1 and 2 provide a foundation on which to build the lesson theme. Usually, one activity teaches children something about the Bible story, and the other activity introduces the application for the lesson. You may wish to set up these activities as learning centers, allowing children the choice of activities when they enter the room.

Bible Time contains the Bible story. Each story provides interesting visual ideas or ways to involve the children in the story time.

Application helps the children make a connection between the Bible knowledge and their lives.

They will learn ways to follow the example of the Bible person, such as praying, learning God's Word, or choosing right. Or they will discover ways to respond to what they have learned, such as worshiping God.

Bible Memory contains a variety of activities, that help children learn the unit Bible verse, which reinforces the unit theme.

Activity Time contains three choices for you to provide for the children as you have time in your schedule.

The **craft** section provides instructions for making a project which matches the lesson theme and can be a reminder for the children to take home.

The **snack** time suggests a simple, nutritious snack which coordinates with the Bible lesson.

The **game** section describes an active, fun game to involve your children in movement and further reinforce the lesson.

Wrap-up is a time for children to clean up and for you to sum up the lesson and encourage them to commit to doing what they have learned.

What Special Helps Are Provided for the Teacher?

Following each unit are six reproducible activity pages for use with the lessons. These pages include Bible visuals, crafts, games, puppets, and many other activities for the children.

A Bible time line is included on pages 311-318 of this book. The time line includes all 52 lessons in this book and contains pictures for the children to color and hidden objects for them to find.

Page 6 of this book contains several suggestions for using the time line. In addition, this page lists extra Bible activities that can be used when you have extra time in any lesson. The activities need no preparation, and the only materials you need to complete them are Bibles or children's Bibles.

Where Can I Obtain Extra Resources?

Each unit page provides a list of extra resources from Standard Publishing and The Beginner's Bible™. Stickers, books, puzzles, videos, and games are available which complement and reinforce your teaching. One advantage to using these resources is that the Bible scenes and characters will match the pictures in the materials and in the children's Beginner's Bibles. For more Beginner's Bible™ resource information, call your local Christian bookstore or look on the Internet under WWW.BEGINNERSBIBLE.COM.

Time-Line Activities

Stand-up Time Line

You will need copies of pages 311-318 on heavy paper, markers or crayons, and tape. If you cannot photocopy on heavy paper, have children glue the pages to construction paper.

Give each child a copy of pages 311-318. Assist them in laying out the pages in order. Then help them tape the pages together to make one long time line. When the pages are taped, help them fold the taped lines back and forth to accordion-fold between the pages, so that they can stand the time line up on the floor.

Provide a place in the classroom for children to store their time lines, so that they can work on coloring them and finding the hidden pictures each week. When the lessons are completed, the children can take their completed time lines home and stand them up on the floor in their rooms or hang them on their bedroom walls.

Time-Line Display

You will need copies of pages 311-318, crayons or markers, and tape or Plasti-Tak. If possible, enlarge pages 311-318 as you copy them, so that the pages will be easier for the children to see.

Color the photocopied pages and hang them in order on a wall or bulletin board in your classroom. Each week, show children the Bible story on the time line and allow them to search as a group for the hidden picture.

Weekly Time-Line Activity

If an extended project is not feasible in your situation, photocopy the time-line page that pictures the Bible story each week. Have children color the Bible-story picture for that day and find the hidden picture. They can take the time-line picture home each week to remind them of what they have learned.

Children's Bible Activities

The following Bible activities are intended to be used with children's picture Bibles, such as The Beginner's Bible™. Even though the children in your group are not reading well, they can begin to become familiar with the Bible stories and Bible books by looking at the pictures and hearing the stories in their children's Bibles.

These activities require no preparation and no materials, other than the children's Bibles. The activities may be used to: encourage children to read their Bibles; reinforce Bible-story facts; provide extra challenges for children who finish other activities early; or provide learning when you have extra time.

Children will not mind if you repeat the instructions from week to week. As they gain speed and skill and become more familiar with their Bibles, you can complete more instructions on the list.

1. Find today's Bible story in your Bible. (Give clues as needed: look near the beginning or end of your Bible; find page number ___.)

2. Find the first story in the Bible. Tell about it.

3. Find the last story in the Bible. Tell about the pictures.

4. Find a story about a boat. What do you think is happening in the story?

5. Find a story with a chariot in it. Who do you think is riding in the chariot?

6. Find a story about an animal. What does the animal do?

7. Find a story about a baby. Who do you think the baby is?

8. Find a story with fire in it. Where is the fire? What does it do?

9. Find a story with a bird in it. What does the bird do?

10. Find a story about Jesus as a baby. Look at the pictures and tell about the story.

11. Find a story about Jesus. Look at the pictures and tell about the story.

12. Find a story with a fish in it. Where are the fish? What do they do?

13. Find a story about a child. What does the child do?

Unit 1
Lessons 1-4

God Created Everything

By the end of this unit, the children and leaders will . . .
Know Name many things that God created.
Feel Feel amazed by the wonderful world God created.
Do Worship God because He created everything.

Unit Bible Words for Memory
"In the beginning God created the heavens and earth" (Genesis 1:1, NIV).

Unit Lessons

Lesson 1
God Created Everything
Genesis 1:1-13
Children explore the land, sky, and seas that God created.

Lesson 2
God Created the Sun, Moon, and Stars
Genesis 1:14-19
Children find reasons to worship God for the sun, moon, and stars: they give light and warmth; they determine the seasons; they help us tell time.

Lesson 3
God Created the Animals
Genesis 1:20-25
Children learn about the land animals, the sea animals, and the birds that God created.

Lesson 4
God Created People
Genesis 1:26-31
Children discover amazing ways God made our bodies. They find that God made human beings special—in His image.

Why Teach This Unit to Four-Year-Olds—Six-Year-Olds?

Four- to six-year-old children have a unique perspective on God's creation. Their sense of excitement and awe at their discoveries of the world around them can translate into worship for the Creator. God delights in praise from all His creation, but He must take special delight in the worship children offer to Him. As the children pray and sing praises to God, write poems and draw pictures, they will grow in a personal relationship with the God who loves them.

Bible Time Line

The stories for this unit are pictured on the time line, page 311. The time line will be used throughout all units in this book.

Provide the time-line page for children who arrive early, or plan time at the end of the Bible story during each session for children to color the time line and look for the hidden pictures.

See page 6 in this book for further instructions on using the time line and for suggested time-line projects.

Materials
All Lessons
  a Bible
  markers, colored pencils, crayons
  white paper, construction paper, poster board
  tape, masking tape
  Plasti-Tak
  glue
  scissors
  a stapler
  paper hole punch
  yarn or string

Lesson 1
  play dough
  one 36" circle made out of white poster board
  plants or pictures of plants God made, such as pinecones, pussy willows, leaves, grass, several kinds of flowers, nuts, apples, carrots, and so on
  a variety of flashlights
  bookmark
  9" white paper plates
  magazines, old picture calendars, and seed or pet supply catalogs
  6-9 bean bags

Lesson 2
  a length of black or dark blue bulletin-board paper (sold by the foot at teacher supply stores)
  pictures of some constellations from an encyclopedia or children's magazine
  flashlights
  a blanket, a flower and a piece of bread in a small paper bag, a clothes basket or box
  6" paper plates
  paper clips or beans
  rulers or wooden spoons

Lesson 3
  mural paper or bulletin-board paper
  old nature magazines
  pictures from magazines or books of many of the animals mentioned in the Bible Time
  paper grocery bags
  strips of heavyweight paper for headbands
  materials to decorate the headbands: feathers, synthetic fur, vinyl, and various colors and textures of paper

Lesson 4
  fabric scraps
  an apple and banana, a knife, and a blindfold
  enlarged pictures of the items from reproducible pages 25-27, other pictures from magazines of items God created
  a cassette player
  a cassette of a favorite worship song
  a blank cassette
  mobile bases (coat hangers, the top 6" of two-liter bottles, or pound margarine tubs)

The Beginner's Bible™ Resources

God's Amazing Animal Stickers, Standard Publishing, #22-01064, call 1-800-543-1353

God's Sea Creatures Stickers, Standard Publishing, #22-01065, call 1-800-543-1353

Adam and Eve Inlay Puzzle, Standard Publishing, #28-02700, call 1-800-543-1353

The Beginner's Bible™ Old Testament GeoSafari Bible Pack, Standard Publishing, #14-24001, call 1-800-543-1353

The Beginner's Bible™ Bible Lessons GeoSafari Bible Pack, Standard Publishing, #14-24005, call 1-800-543-1353

Creation Rubber Stamp Kit, Inkadinkado, call 1-617-938-6100

The Story of Creation, Sony Wonder Video Series, call 1-800-733-3000

Unit 1
Lesson 1

God Created Everything
(Genesis 1:1-13)

In the beginning God created the world. The earth was dark, wet, and bare. First, God made light. Then He made dry land by making mountains and valleys, oceans and lakes. Over the bare ground, God made trees and grass and plants of every kind.

Bible Words

"In the beginning God created the heavens and earth" (Genesis 1:1).

Goals

Tell about land, sky, and plants that God created.
Feel amazed by the wonderful world God created.
Worship God because He created everything.

ACTIVITY 1—What's in the World?

You will need play dough.

Before God made the world, it was very dark and wet and bare. There was no dry ground anywhere. There was no light anywhere. There was only a huge, dark ocean. Let's make pretend worlds out of play dough, and we will see what the earth might have been like before God created all the beautiful things that fill our world.

Give each child a lump of play dough, and show him how to roll it around in his palm to make a round pretend world. When all the children have made a round world, turn off the lights. **Our worlds are in the dark. Can you see your world? The first thing God did was make some light.** Turn on the lights. Now the beautiful things that God made could be seen.

---

children turn around and close their eyes while you remove one item. They can turn around and guess the item you removed. A child who guesses correctly may take the item home.

God Made Everything So Fine
(Tune: "This Old Man")

God created
Sky and earth,
Land and seas, and trees and plants.
In the very beginning of all time,
God made everything so fine.

Leaders' Evaluation

	Great!	OK!	More!	Oops!	Suggestions
Activity 1					
Activity 2					
Bible Time					
Application					
Bible Memory					
Craft					
Snack					
Game					
Wrap-up					

Next, God made some holes in the ground to collect the water—oceans and lakes, creeks and streams. Show the children how to push holes in their earths to make oceans and streams and lakes.

When God made the oceans and lakes to collect water, other parts of the land stood up high to make mountains and hills. The children can make bumps on their world for mountains and hills. **Tell us about your world. Where are the oceans? Where are the mountains?** Give children time to share about their creations.

Children should keep their worlds to display at the appropriate time during the Bible story.

ACTIVITY 2—World Puzzle

You will need a 36″ circle made out of white poster board, markers or crayons, and plants or pictures of plants God made, such as pinecones, pussy willows, leaves, grass, several kinds of flowers, nuts, apples, carrots, and so on. Before class, cut the circle into several large puzzle pieces.

God made plants and trees and grass to cover the mountains and valleys that He had created. Let's look at some of the plants God made. Encourage children to examine the plants you brought. Decide together which plant is the prettiest, the softest, the most prickly, smells the best, tastes the best, is the best food for animals.

Give each child or group of children one puzzle piece of the circle and ask them to draw a plant they are thankful God made on the piece. Encourage the children to use most of the paper and to make their drawings colorful. **When we draw pictures of things we are thankful God made, we are worshiping Him for what He created.**

After all the children have completed coloring their puzzle pieces, collect them and keep them to use during the Application section of the lesson.

WRAP-UP—Creation Litany

You will need poster paper, strips of plain paper, tape, and markers or colored pencils. Before class, print "God created everything" at the top of the paper. Then leave space and print the words several more times, leaving space between each line to add in the children's drawings.

Show the children the paper you have made. **We are going to write a litany about things God made. A litany is something we can write and say together to worship God. Let's name some of our favorite things that God created to include in our litany.** Encourage the children to name things God created.

Give each child or pair of children a strip of paper and ask them to draw a picture of something they are thankful God created. They can look at the world puzzle or the Creation Plates if they need ideas.

When the children have completed their pictures, ask them to explain them to the class. Then tape the strips of paper on the litany in the blank spaces. Say the litany as a class, pointing to each item the children drew as you name it. A sample litany follows:

God created everything.
God made flowers and God made trees.
God created everything.
God made apples and God made grapes.
God created everything.
God made lakes and God made mountains.
God created everything.
God made grass and God made pinecones.

After the litany, sing the words to "God Made Everything So Fine" from page 8 of this lesson. Conclude with prayer, thanking God for everything He created.

Until parents come, play a game with the nature items from Activity 2. Place the items on a tray or table. Then have the

BIBLE TIME—God Created the World

Before class, use the patterns found on pages 25-27 and draw simple pictures of many of the things mentioned in the first paragraph of the story. Also provide a variety of flashlights and the nature items used in Activity 2. Give each picture to a different child to stand and hold as you begin the story. As you mention each pictured item, ask that child to sit and place the picture facedown on the floor. Give flashlights to the children who do not have a picture to hold.

Let's imagine what it was like a very, very long time ago. There was no world. There were no stars or sky, no mountains or rivers, no trees or plants, no animals of any kind or people. But there was God. Step by step, God made our beautiful world.

He saw the darkness and the nothingness (Darken the room.) and He said, "Let there be light!" (Encourage the children to turn on their flashlights.) **And for the first time, there was light in our world.** God called the light *day*. He called the darkness . . . (Wait and let the children respond—"night.") The light was day and the darkness was called night and it was the first day.

On the second day God made the beautiful, blue sky. But the whole earth was still covered with water. There was no dry ground anywhere. So on the third day, God collected the water into streams, and rivers, and lakes, and huge oceans. He made dry ground and mountains and hills where the water had been. Ask children to display and explain their worlds from Activity 1.

But God saw that the mountains and valleys were bare, dry ground. So God made plants to cover the ground. Display the nature items used in Activity 2 and hold up each appropriate item as you mention it. God made soft grass that tickles our feet when we walk in it. God made big, strong trees with leaves that give us shade and wood that is used to make our houses. God made plants that were fun to touch, like pussy willows and pinecones. God made plants that smell and look

Lesson 1

3

---

following ingredients: nuts, coconut, sesame seeds, chopped dried fruit (such as raisins). Stir well.

In class, serve the granola in small paper cups. Offer children juice or milk to drink. **Our snack is made from many plants God made. Can you tell me any of the foods that are in your snack?** Allow children to respond. Explain where the foods come from: honey from the flowers where the bees feed, nuts from trees, raisins from grapes, oatmeal from oats.

You might assign children one ingredient to bring and add to the granola. If you bake the mix at church, play the following game while it is baking. Come back together to add the extra ingredients and enjoy the snack.

Option: Play a guessing game with the foods in the granola. Bring plants from which the foods in the granola come, and ask the children to guess which food goes with each plant. Examples follow: a flower for honey, a stalk of wheat for wheat germ, grapes for raisins, an uncut coconut for shredded coconut, an empty nutshell for nuts.

Game—Tell What God Made

You will need 6-9 bean bags, depending on the size of your group; Creation Plates made earlier; and masking tape. If you do not have bean bags, make them by putting dry beans in a sock and sewing or securely tying the end.

Arrange the Creation Plates on the floor. Make two or three target areas, each arranged in a triangular shape. Place pieces of masking tape on the backs of the paper plates to keep them from sliding on the floor.

Divide the children into two or three teams (one team for each target area). Give the first child in line three bean bags and let him toss each toward the target area. When the child retrieves the bean bags, he says, "God made . . ." and completes the phrase with the name of the picture each bean bag hit or came close to.

Unit 1

6

beautiful, like pink and red and yellow flowers. God made plants that were wonderful to taste, like carrots and apples and oranges and broccoli. God made each plant for a reason. **God made the world and everything in it.** Put pictures of these items back up as you mention them. God made mountains and the rivers. God made the stars in the sky. God made animals and people. God made the trees and the plants. God made animals and people. God is an awesome God!

APPLICATION—Worship God with Song

You will need the puzzle pieces made in Activity 2 and Plasti-Tak or tape.

We are going to sing a song about things God created. Teach the children the words to "God Made Everything So Fine" to the tune of "This Old Man" from page 8 of this lesson.

When we sing to God, we are worshiping Him for what He created. Let's use our puzzle pictures to worship God for things He created. Let children take turns displaying their puzzle pieces to the class and explaining what they drew. After each child shares, attach her puzzle piece to the wall or board, using tape or Plasti-Tak. Then sing "God Made Everything So Fine" again. After singing the song, ask, **What fine thing did God make?** Children can respond with the items pictured on the puzzle piece. Continue until each child has had an opportunity to share and the puzzle is completed.

BIBLE MEMORY—Act It Out

You will need a Bible and a bookmark. Before the session, mark Genesis 1:1 in your Bible with a bookmark.

Allow a child to help you open your Bible to Genesis 1:1. Point to the verse and allow each child to see it. **This part of the Bible is called the book of Genesis. Genesis tells us the story of how God created the earth. Our memory verse from the book of Genesis reminds us that God created everything in our world.** Read the words of the verse to the children. Then ask them to say the verse with you several times.

Use these simple movements to help children remember the Bible verse. Begin with all the children squatting. Children stand a little on each of the first three words of the verse, *In the beginning*. While they say the word *God*, children raise both hands straight overhead. Circle hands outward and stretch them out on the word *created*. Flutter fingers from left to right overhead on the word *heavens* and from right to left at waist height for the word *earth*.

ACTIVITY TIME

Do as many activities as time permits.

Craft—Creation Plates

You will need a 9" white paper plate for each child; scissors; glue; and magazines, old picture calendars, and seed or pet supply catalogs.

Ask the children to find a picture of something God has made. To save time, you might want to tear appropriate pictures from magazines in advance and let children choose from your selection. Have children cut out one picture they find and glue it to the paper plate. (A big picture will work better.) Letter on each paper plate "God Made" and the item pictured. Allow the glue to dry and use the paper plates in the bean bag toss later.

Snack—Earthy Granola

Mix together 4 cups oatmeal, 1 cup wheat germ, 1/2 teaspoon salt, 1/4 cup vegetable oil, and 1/2 cup honey. Preheat oven to 250°. Stir oatmeal, wheat germ, and salt together. Add vegetable oil and honey. Mix well. Spread mixture in a shallow layer on a baking sheet. Bake for 30 minutes. Allow to cool. Put baked granola into a large mixing bowl. Add 2 cups of one or more of the

Unit 1
Lesson 2

God Created the Sun, Moon, and Stars
(Genesis 1:14-19)

God made the sun to light the day and the moon to brighten the night. God also placed the sun and moon in the sky to help us keep track of the days, seasons, and years.

Bible Words

"In the beginning God created the heavens and earth" (Genesis 1:1).

Goals

Tell about sun, moon, and stars that God created.
Feel amazed by the wonderful world God created.
Worship God because He created everything.

Activity 1—Pictures in the Stars

You will need a length of black or dark blue bulletin-board paper (sold by the foot at teacher supply stores), stars made from the pattern on reproducible page 28, glue, crayons (white, silver, and gold), and pictures of some constellations from an encyclopedia or children's magazine.

Stars form patterns and make pictures in the sky. People have named many of the pictures the stars make, like the Big Dipper and the Little Dipper. Let's look at some pictures the stars make. Allow children to examine the different pictures of constellations in the encyclopedia or magazines. **If you go out and look at the night sky, you can probably find your own pictures in the stars God made!**

God Made Everything So Fine
(Tune: "This Old Man")

God created
Sky and earth,
Land and seas, and trees and plants.
In the very beginning of all time,
God made everything so fine.

God created
Moon and stars,
The sun to light the earth by day.
In the very beginning of all time,
God made everything so fine.

Leaders' Evaluation

	Great!	OK!	More!	Oops!	Suggestions
Activity 1					
Activity 2					
Bible Time					
Application					
Bible Memory					
Craft					
Snack					
Game					
Wrap-up					

Direct the children to glue the stars to the paper. Then have children draw a line between the stars with a white, silver, or gold crayon. As the children work, sing "Twinkle, Twinkle Little Star," substituting the words "God made you to shine at night" for "How I wonder what you are."

ACTIVITY 2—Many Suns

Ask children to bring a flashlight with them to class or gather as many flashlights as you can.

Talk about the sun and stars. **What gives us light during the day?** The sun. **What shines in the sky at night?** The moon and stars. **Did you know that the stars are really suns that are very far away?** Because they are millions of miles away they don't shine brightly but they look like they twinkle. **Do you know why we can't see the stars in the day?** It is because the sun is so bright we can't see the twinkling light from the stars. Let's do an experiment.

Give children the flashlights. Shut the door and close blinds or curtains at any windows, but leave the overhead light on. Help everyone turn on his flashlight in your lit room. Then turn off the overhead light. **Is it easier to see the flashlights when the overhead light is on or off?** Off. It's easier to see the flashlights when the room is dark. The stars twinkle in the sky all the time. We just can't see them because the sun is so bright.

Let's pretend our flashlights are stars that God made. What pictures can we make with our stars? Can we make our stars twinkle? Allow children to spend a few moments making light designs on the wall and ceilings with their flashlights.

BIBLE TIME—God Created the Sun, Moon, and Stars

Before class, trace the patterns of the phases of the moon from reproducible page 28 onto white paper and cut them out. Also

hold up the moon (do so), **you stop and pretend to sleep.** Demonstrate by resting your head on your hands. Children should leave their eyes open, so they can watch for the "sunrise." Alternate the sun and moon until the children have reached you. Play the game several times, changing the way the children move each time you play. They might skip, hop, tiptoe, gallop, or slide, depending on the amount of space you have.

WRAP-UP—Sing Praise to the Lord

Sing "God Made Everything So Fine" to the tune of "This Old Man" learned last week. The words are on page 8 of this lesson. Let the children shake their crescent moon noisemakers while they sing.

The Bible tells us it is good to praise God for the wonderful things He has done. We have been learning about one wonderful thing God did. Our memory verse tells us what that wonderful thing is. Ask children to say the verse with you, "God created the heavens and earth."

Until parents come, play a guessing game. Give each child or pair of children a flashlight. You will give the children clues. As soon as they know what you are describing, they should turn on their flashlights and call out the answer. Possible clues follow: I warm the earth. I am as big as a sun, but I am too far away to shine brightly. I make pictures in the night sky. I appear to be different sizes each night. I help you know each time a day has passed. Plants use me to make food. My light helps you see. (Moon, stars, or sun are acceptable answers.) The earth sticks close to me, so that it doesn't fly off into space.

cut a big sun from yellow construction paper.

Our Bible words say, "In the beginning God created the heavens and earth." God made the earth, the world we live in with its oceans and rivers and mountains. He also made the heavens—the sun, the moon, and the stars.

The sun is in the sky during the day and when it gets dark, the moon and stars appear. Each time the sun comes up it is a new day. We keep track of the days by counting the number of times the sun rises in the sky. Who would like to hold the sun? **Let's pretend to go through some days with the sun.** Give a volunteer the first opportunity to hold the sun. Ask him to hold it over his head and walk it from one side of the room to the other. Pretend to go through a day as the child progresses across the room—get up in the morning, eat lunch when the child is in the middle of the room, and lay down for bed when the child reaches the other side of the room. Repeat this process, giving each child a turn being the "sun" as you pretend to go through the days. Let the children pretend to go through a week, Sunday through Saturday.

The moon and stars appear at night. What are some of the special things we learned about stars? Let children share what they discovered in their activity time and display their star constellation pictures.

Have you ever watched the moon? Each night the moon's shape is a little different. When the moon is like a circle, we say there is a full moon. Ask one child to come forward and hold the full moon circle. The moon's shape changes a little each night. The full moon appears to get smaller until it is just a slim crescent and then each night after that, its shape gets fuller again. Have a child come forward and hold each phase of the moon in order.

There is a full moon about once every four weeks or once every month. A long time ago, people used the moon to help them tell time. These people didn't have clocks and calendars like we have in our homes. If children wanted to know how long it was until a special day, like Christmas, their moms and dads would say, "Christmas will be here after the moon is full

Lesson 2   3

---

color their moons. As they are coloring, move around the group and staple the two plates together. Be sure the tops of the plates are facing each other. Let children place several paper clips or beans inside before you finish stapling. Be sure staples are close enough together so the paper clips or beans will not slide out of the noisemaker.

We can use our noisemakers to praise God. When we sing, we can shake and rattle our noisemakers in time with our music. When we sing and play our noisemakers, we are worshiping God. Save the full moon noisemakers to use during the Wrap-up time.

Variation: For older children, make a crescent moon pattern out of a paper plate and allow children to trace and cut their plates to make "crescent moon noisemakers."

Snack—Sandwich Shapes

You will need bread, peanut butter or spreadable cheese, juice or water, knives, and cookie cutters in the shapes of moon, stars, and suns. (You could use a cup as a circle shape for the sun.)

Use cookie cutters to cut bread in the shape of crescent moons, stars, and suns. Help children spread peanut butter or spreadable cheese on top. Provide juice to serve with your open-face sandwiches.

What shape that God made did you cut out? Let's thank God for what He made. Say "Thank You, God, for . . . " and ask children to call out shapes they cut out.

Game—Sun for Day, Moon for Night

You will need white, blue or black, and yellow construction paper, scissors, glue or tape, and rulers or wooden spoons. Before class, make a large yellow sun and attach it to a ruler or wooden spoon. Also make a night scene on blue or black construction paper with a moon and stars. Attach the night scene to a ruler or wooden spoon.

Play this game outdoors or in a large, open area. Begin the game by having children line up 20-30 feet from you. **When I hold up the sun** (do so), **you start walking towards me. When I**

Unit 1   6

just three more times."

It's wonderful that God made the sun, moon, and stars beautiful to look at as they give us light, and that God made them help us tell time.

APPLICATION—Thanking God for His Creation

You will need a blanket, a flower, and a piece of bread in a small paper bag; a flashlight; glue or tape; a large container (a clothes basket or box). Before the session, place the items mentioned above in the large container.

Sing "God Made Everything So Fine" with the children several times. The words are on page 8 of this lesson. **What have you learned today about the stars? Why do they shine at night? Why don't they look as bright as our sun? I'm glad God made the stars so perfectly.** Sing "God Made Everything So Fine" again, stopping after you sing it each time and asking a child to thank God for something about the stars. Give suggestions as needed. "Thank You that the stars twinkle at night." "Thank You that the stars make pictures in the sky."

What have you learned today about the moon? How does the moon look on different nights? How does the moon act like a clock or calendar? Allow children to share. Then sing again, stopping and asking children to thank God for something about the moon. "Thank You that the moon helps us tell time." "Thank You that the moon shines brightly in the dark night."

What have you learned today about the sun? How does the sun help us tell time? Allow children to respond. **The sun helps our world in many ways.** Display the container filled with items. **This basket contains things that will remind us of ways the sun helps our world. Who wants to choose something from the basket?** Allow children to take turns drawing an item from the basket. As each item is discovered, talk about how the sun helps us in that way. The sun keeps us warm like a blanket. A flower can't eat food like bread. A flower's food is the sun. The sun gives us light like a flashlight. Just like glue or tape helps

things stick together, the sun makes our world stick close to itself. If it weren't for the sun, our world would just fly off into space.

Why are you thankful for the sun? Allow children to respond. Then sing "God Made Everything So Fine" again, allowing children to tell God why they are thankful for the sun.

BIBLE MEMORY—Your Turn, Our Turn

Review the Bible verse learned last week by repeating the actions with the verse. Begin with all the children squatting. Children stand a little on each of the first three words of the verse, *In the beginning*. While they say the word *God*, children raise both hands straight overhead. Circle hands outward and stretch them out on the word *created*. Flutter fingers from left to right overhead on the word *heavens* and from right to left at waist height for the word *earth*.

Next divide the class into two teams. **This time we are going to take turns saying the words of the verse with our team, and we aren't going to use the motions.** Team One begins by saying only the first word in the verse. Team Two then says the first and second word of the verse. Continue in this manner with each team repeating what has been said and adding the next word. Repeat the verse, letting the second team begin. If you would like to add movement, have each team stand when they say their word and sit when the other team speaks.

ACTIVITY TIME

Do as many activities as time permits.

Craft—Full Moon Noisemakers

You will need 6" paper plates, scissors, pencils, markers or colored pencils, a stapler, and paper clips or beans. Give each child two "moons" (6" paper plates). Have children

Unit 1
Lesson 3

God Created the Animals
(Genesis 1:20-25)

God created all the animals in the world. The Lord God made the bugs that creep, the birds that fly, the fish that swim, and each animal that walks on the earth.

Bible Words

"In the beginning God created the heavens and earth" (Genesis 1:1).

Goals

Tell about animals God made.
Feel amazed by the wonderful world God created.
Worship God because He created everything.

Activity 1—Animal Guessing Game

Gather the children in a group and play a guessing game. Give children one clue at a time until they have correctly named the animal you are describing. Children should guess the animal by saying, "God made (animal you are describing)." Begin with somewhat vague clues and then get more specific. Here are some examples.

• I have four legs and a tail. I am a kind of cat. I am very big. I roar. Some people call me the king of the jungle. (Lion.)
• I live in barns. I also live in houses and fields. I have eight legs. I eat insects. I make a web to be my home. (Spider.)
• I don't have any legs. I breathe through a hole in my head. I am one of the largest animals in the world. I live in the ocean. One of my kind may have swallowed Jonah. (Whale.)
• I don't walk; I fly. I have black and yellow stripes on my

God Made Everything So Fine
(Tune: "This Old Man")

God created
Sky and earth,
Land and seas, and trees and plants.
In the very beginning of all time,
God made everything so fine.

God created
Moon and stars,
The sun to light the earth by day.
In the very beginning of all time,
God made everything so fine.

God created
Birds and fish,
Dogs, and cows, and elephants.
In the very beginning of all time,
God made everything so fine.

Leaders' Evaluation

	Great!	OK!	More!	Oops!	Suggestions
Activity 1					
Activity 2					
Bible Time					
Application					
Bible Memory					
Craft					
Snack					
Game					
Wrap-up					

body. I make a buzzing sound. (Bee.)
- I am big and furry. I sleep through the winter, and I am very grumpy and hungry when I wake up. (Bear.)
- I make a growling sound. I live where it is extremely cold. I am white. (Polar bear.)
- I am a large, gentle animal. I stay in fields and barns. I chew my cud. I produce milk to drink. (Cow.)

Give clues for a variety of animals God created, such as a bear, a turkey, a donkey, an owl, a zebra, a frog. If you have older children in your class, allow them to take turns giving clues to the group. Assign each child an animal to describe.

ACTIVITY 2—Smallest to Tallest

You will need a long piece of mural paper or bulletin-board paper, markers or crayons, old nature magazines, scissors, and glue or tape. Before the session, tape the paper to the wall at the children's height, or lay it on the floor.

God made many different kinds of animals, birds, and fish. Some animals, like gnats, are so tiny you can hardly see them. Other animals, like elephants and whales, are almost as large as our room. Let's draw a picture of animals God made from the smallest to the tallest.

Ask children to look through the magazines and cut out pictures of all different sizes of animals, birds, and fish. When the children have found enough pictures, help them work as a group to place the pictures in order from the smallest to the largest. They can then attach the pictures to the mural in order. Children can use the crayons and colored pencils to draw other pictures of small and large animals on the mural. Encourage them to make their pictures large and to fill the space as much as possible. Offer suggestions and questions as children work.

What different colors are some of God's animals? What are some big animals, medium animals, and small animals? Which animals fly? Swim? Crawl? Hop? Run? What sounds do some of the animals make?

the volume of your voice. If you have time, allow children to take turns being the leader.

WRAP-UP—A Worship Prayer

Ask children to wear their headbands made earlier. They can pretend to be an animal God made as they clean up the room.

Sing the words to the three verses of "God Made Everything So Fine." The words are on page 8 of this lesson.

What animals that God made are you thankful for? Ask children to name animals. They can refer to the Smallest to Tallest Mural or the Bible-story pictures if they need help. **When we thank God, we show Him we love Him. Praying to God is a way to worship Him. Let's worship God for the animals He made. God, we are so thankful that You made so many different kinds of animals, birds, and fish. You are an amazing God. We worship You, God, for making _____.** Encourage children to call out different animals that they mentioned earlier. **We love You, God. Thank You for our world!**

Play a game until parents come. Ask children to wear their animal headbands and tell you what animal they are pretending to be. Then help the children make a live Smallest to Tallest Mural. **Who is pretending to be a tiny animal? Now who is pretending to be a medium-sized animal? Who is pretending to be a huge animal?** Help the children line up in order from the smallest animal to the tallest. Then help them line up in other ways as well: the slowest to the fastest, the least furry to the most furry, the smallest to the biggest ears.

BIBLE TIME—Amazing Animals

You will need the creation pictures from pages 25-27 and pictures from magazines or books of many of the animals mentioned in the story below.

Display the creation pictures from pages 25-27 as you mention each item. **When God made the world, He began by making light. He called the light** *day* **and the dark** *night.* **Then God made dry land appear and caused every kind of tree and plant to grow. In the sky God put the sun, the moon, and the stars.**

Then God made animals, birds, and fish. Let's pretend to be animals, birds, and fish. We will learn some motions. When I name a kind of animal, or a kind of bird, or a kind of fish, we'll make the right motion. Motions follow: animal—lightly slap the floor with open-palmed hands like a plodding animal; bird—flap arms, pretending to fly; fish—put hands together, thumbs up, and move hands from side to side to resemble swimming fish. Practice the motions several times with the children. Then encourage them to make the correct motion as you name animals, birds, and fish throughout the story.

First, God created every kind of animal. Show the pictures of animals from magazines or books as you mention them. **In the forest, God placed bears that plod and squirrels that scamper. He made rabbits that hop along and turtles that move so slow.** (Vary speed of hand slapping to reflect the various animals.) **God made all the jungle animals too: lions and tigers that roar and pounce, elephants, and giraffes with their long necks. He created farm animals like cows, horses, pigs, and dogs.**

God made soft, fuzzy animals like koala bears. God made wet, slippery animals like otters. He made prickly animals like porcupines. He made slow, stinky animals like skunks! He made animals that like cold like penguins and polar bears.

God even made creepy, crawly bugs. He made scuttling spiders and buzzing mosquitoes. God made ants and worms, and even roaches!

After God made the animals, He filled the oceans with fish

Lesson 3   3

---

the ears. Staple each child's ears to his headband. Fit the headbands to the children's heads and staple them together.

Let children use the materials to creatively decorate their headbands. Supervise the gluing of the materials on the headbands. If time permits, children can make a tail. **What animal that God made are you pretending to be? What sound do you make? Where do you sleep? What do you like to eat? How do you walk?** Allow children to wear their headbands and pretend to be the animal they chose.

Snack—Animal Crackers

You will need animal crackers, cream cheese, graham crackers, and juice or water.

Serve animal crackers and juice. Have children name each animal and make an animal-cracker display before they eat the snack. **What animal that God made do you have? What sound does your animal make? Let's make animal-cracker pictures on our graham crackers. Then we will thank God for the animals He made.** Help children make an animal-cracker display by spreading a thick layer of cream cheese on a graham cracker. Stand animal crackers in the cream cheese. Then pray and thank God for the animals He created.

Game—Animals, Birds, and Fish

Use the motions learned during the Bible Time and play a game. Motions follow: animal—lightly slap the floor with open-palmed hands like a plodding animal; bird—flap arms, pretending to fly; fish—put hands together, thumbs up, and move hands from side to side to resemble swimming fish.

Let children practice the motions first. Call out "animals," "birds," or "fish" and have the children do that motion until they are comfortable with the motions. Then call out some of the animals mentioned in the Bible Time and ask children to make the appropriate motion. Suggestions follow: dog, zebra, dolphin, squirrel, robin, elephant, donkey, whale, owl, bear, skunk, eagle, crow, shark, rabbit, kangaroo, cat, tuna, octopus. Give hints as needed. Vary the speed with which you name the animals and

Unit 1

6

and the sky with birds. God made sharp-toothed sharks and leaping dolphins. He made whales that shoot sprays of water high in the air and shiny trout that flip and splash in the streams. God made eagles and hawks that glide and dive in the sky. He made robins that dig in the grass for worms. He made crabs and eels and salmon. He made owls and cardinals and pigeons.

God's world sounded different now. Before, there were only the sounds of rushing, splashing water and leaves rustling in the wind. Now there were other sounds: chattering, chirping, squealing, squawking, purring, barking, roaring, growling, buzzing, snuffling, grunting, squeaking, and croaking. God's world was no longer a dark, wet, bare, quiet place! It was a beautiful, full, noisy world!

APPLICATION—Thank You, Thank You, God

Display the animal picture made in Activity 2. Sing a song to thank God for the animals He made that you have pictured. Sing to the tune of "Old McDonald Had a Farm," replacing bracketed words with different animals and sounds each time you sing.

Thank You, thank You, God.
God created [little lambs].
Thank You, thank You, God.
Yes, God created [little lambs].
With a [Baa!] here, and a [Baa!] there.
Here a [Baa!], there a [Baa!], everywhere a [Baa! Baa!]
Thank You, thank You, God.
God created [little lambs].

Other verses could include: God created furry mice (eek!); God created growling bears (grrr!); God created busy bees (bzzz!); God created pecking chicks (peep!); God created flipping fish (splash!).

When we sing about animals God created, we are worshiping God for His amazing creation!

4   Unit 1

BIBLE MEMORY—Walk Like an Animal

You will need paper grocery bags, markers, and masking tape. Before class, tear paper grocery bags into nine large irregular stepping-stone shapes. Print one word from the Bible verse on each stone. Make a path in your room by placing the "stepping-stones" close together. Tape the stones to the floor. Option: For carpeted rooms, cut the stones from felt so they will not slide.

Review the Bible verse with motions with the children. Begin with all the children squatting. Children stand a little on each of the first three words of the verse, *In the beginning*. While they say the word *God*, children raise both hands straight overhead. Circle hands outward and stretch them out on the word *created*. Flutter fingers from left to right overhead on the word *heavens* and from right to left at waist height for the word *earth*.

Next, lead the children along the stepping-stone path, saying one word as they step on each stone. Then lead the children in following the path and saying the verse several more times, walking like a different animal each time. For example, hop like a kangaroo, plod like an elephant, and gallop like a horse.

ACTIVITY TIME

Do as many activities as time permits.

Craft—Animal Headbands

You will need the ear patterns from reproducible page 29, strips of heavyweight paper for headbands, construction paper, scissors, a stapler, glue; and materials to decorate the headbands: feathers, synthetic fur, vinyl, and various colors and textures of paper. Before class, use the ear patterns found on page 29 to trace different types of ears onto construction paper. Make enough ears so that each child can have a set.

Give each child a headband. Let the children choose which ears they will use on their headbands. Help the children cut out

Lesson 3   20

Unit 1
Lesson 4

God Created People
(Genesis 1:26-31)

After God created a good and beautiful world, He made man and woman. God's last creation was made in His own image. When God looked at all that He had made, He saw that it was very good!

Bible Words

"In the beginning God created the heavens and earth" (Genesis 1:1).

Goals

Tell about special ways that God created me.
Feel amazed by the wonderful world God created.
Worship God because He created everything.

Activity 1—What Makes Me

You will need photocopies of the person figure on page 30 on heavy paper, scissors, crayons, fabric scraps, glue, a marker, a paper hole punch, and a long piece of yarn or string. If you have younger children in your class, cut out the figures before class.

What color hair do you have? What color are your eyes? What does your nose look like? What are your favorite clothes? What is your favorite food? Allow children to respond. God made each one of us special. You are like no other person in the world. Let's each make a person figure of ourselves. We will make our person look just like us.

Give children copies of page 30 and ask them to cut out the figure. They can draw a face and hair on the figure to make it look like themselves. Then they can cut and glue clothes (or

---

God Made Everything So Fine
(Tune: "This Old Man")

God created
Sky and earth,
Land and seas, and trees and plants.
In the very beginning of all time,
God made everything so fine.

God created
Moon and stars,
The sun to light the earth by day.
In the very beginning of all time,
God made everything so fine.

God created
Birds and fish,
Dogs, and cows, and elephants.
In the very beginning of all time,
God made everything so fine.

God created
You and me,
All the people that we see.
In the very beginning of all time,
God made everything so fine.

Leaders' Evaluation

	Great!	OK!	More!	Oops!	Suggestions
Activity 1					
Activity 2					
Bible Time					
Application					
Bible Memory					
Craft					
Snack					
Game					
Wrap-up					

draw their own clothes) on the paper doll to make it look like themselves. They can also cut and glue fabric over the clothes on the doll. Stress how God made each one of us different. As children color, move from student to student with a marker, printing something unique about each child on the paper doll—a physical characteristic, a personality trait, or something a child likes or dislikes.

When the children have completed their figures, punch a hole in the top of each figure. String the figures on a long piece of yarn or string and hang them in your classroom.

ACTIVITY 2—I Like to Eat Apples and Bananas

You will need an apple and banana, a knife, and a blindfold.

God made our bodies wonderfully. We are able to enjoy His beautiful world in many ways. Let's discover some ways we can enjoy God's world. Hold up an apple and a banana. **Which of these is an apple and which is a banana?** Let children respond. **How did you know?** They could see them. **But what if we couldn't see the apple or banana? We have some other ways of telling the difference. Do you know what they are?** Children can respond.

Play a game where you blindfold children and allow them to try to guess which is the apple and which is the banana. Let the first several children only touch the items to tell the difference. **How did you know which was the apple and which was the banana? How did they feel different?** Different shapes, skins feel differently.

Let the next children smell the items to try to guess the difference. **How did they smell differently?**

Let the next children listen as you peel and cut the apple and banana and try to guess the difference. **How did they sound differently?**

Let the last children taste the apple and banana to guess the difference. **How did they taste differently?**

When the last children have guessed, let all the children have

2 Unit 1

"God made us, and we can (action of their choice)." If the children need help coming up with actions, give them suggestions: wink, hop, bow, shrug, wave, march, smile, giggle, shake, squat, stretch, clap, turn around, bend, sniff.

WRAP-UP—We Love You, God

You will need the worship pictures made during Application.

Lead the children in this echo chant. The teacher says the line first and the children say the same thing back. Practice the chant a couple of times, then add a knee slap and a hand clap on the first word and a hand clap on the second. Alternate the clap and slap on each word of the chant.

Thank You, God, for making me.
Thank You, God, for my elbow and knee.
Thank You, God, for eyes that see.
Thank You, God, for making me!

Give the children their worship pictures. Sing the words to "God Made Everything So Fine" from page 8 of this lesson. Then ask the children to tell God about their pictures. Begin by explaining your picture. **God, I drew a picture of the sky and hearts, because I love You for making the beautiful blue sky.** Help children and offer suggestions as needed.

Play a game until parents arrive. Ask the children to stand in a circle. The teacher begins in the center of the circle, turning to see each child. He says, **I see someone God loves that has . . .** and completes the phrase by describing a physical characteristic or something the child is wearing. When a child guesses correctly who you are describing, that child takes a turn in the center of the circle. Continue until each child has had a turn.

22

Lesson 4 7

a taste of the fruit. **Isn't it wonderful that God made us able to see, touch, taste, hear, and smell His world!** If you know the song, sing "I Like to Eat Apples and Bananas!" Then sing the following verses: I like to touch apples and bananas; I like to smell apples and bananas; I like to hear apples and bananas; I like to taste apples and bananas.

Bible Time—God Created People

You will need the string of figures made in Activity 1.

Each day of creation God stopped and looked at what He had done. He was pleased with His work and thought it was good. God had made the earth and the heavens. The stars, the sun, and the moon were all in place. The earth had steep mountains and winding rivers. There were trees and flowers and plants of all kinds. Birds flew in the sky and fish swam in the oceans. Animals roamed the earth. But something was missing. There was no one to enjoy God's beautiful world. There were no people.

God saw that everything He had made was good, and He wanted someone to live in His beautiful world. So God made two people, a man and a woman, to care for His creation. God made them able to enjoy His beautiful world in many different ways.

In some ways God made man and woman just like He made the animals. He made us able to taste and smell and touch and hear His world. Ask children to share about their guessing game in Activity 2 and sing the song "I Like to Eat Apples and Bananas." He made us able to hop like bunnies. Ask children to do each action as you mention it. He made us able to run like cheetahs. He made us able to swim like fish. He made us able to wriggle like worms.

But God also made man very different from the animals. God made man in His image. Being made "in God's image" means that there are some special things we can do. We can feel sad and happy and mad. Animals don't cry or laugh or

Lesson 4   3

---fold---

Activity Time

Do as many activities as time permits.

Craft—Creation Mobile

You will need copies of the creation shapes on pages 25-27, a paper hole punch, scissors, markers or colored pencils, tape, string, and mobile bases (coat hangers, the top 6" of two-liter bottles, or pound margarine tubs). If you have younger children in your class, cut out the mobile pieces before the session.

Children can cut out the mobile shapes, then color the pictures. Tape a piece of string to each creation shape. You may want to vary the lengths for a more interesting mobile. Punch holes in the mobile bases and tie the other end of the strings to the base.

God created everything in our world! What things that God created do you see on your mobile? What things on your mobile are you thankful God created? Where can you hang your mobile at home to remind you to worship God for the world He created?

Snack—Happy-Face Muffins

You will need English muffin halves, cream cheese or peanut butter, and items to decorate the faces (raisins, sunflower seeds, carrot and celery sticks).

All of your faces look different. I'm glad God made each of us so differently. We are going to make faces on our muffins for our snack today. Give each child an English muffin half and help her spread it with cream cheese or peanut butter. Then help her use the items to decorate the muffin to look like a face.

When the children have completed their faces, pray to thank God for the special way He made each one of us.

Game—Wiggles and Winks

Stand in a circle with the children. Begin by saying, **God made us, and we can wiggle.** All of the children should wiggle with you. Then continue around the circle, letting each child say,

6   Unit 1

23

yell. But people can. Humans are made like God in a way that the rest of creation is not. Men and women, boys and girls were made to love God. We are all different. No two people **are exactly alike, even twins.** Display the string of figures made in Activity 1. Read the characteristic listed on each figure and allow children to guess who made each figure.

Humans are God's best creation. Nothing else God made can praise, thank, or worship Him like humans can. God created us, and He loves and cares for us all. God is pleased when we worship and thank Him.

APPLICATION—Worship Walk

You will need enlarged pictures of the items from reproducible pages 25-27, other pictures from magazines of items God created, blank paper, crayons or markers, a cassette of a favorite worship song, and a cassette player. Before the session, make a worship walk by placing the creation pictures you have collected on the wall around your classroom or in a hallway.

Option: If weather and time permit, plan a route for the children to walk outside that will showcase many items that God created.

God made us special. He made us able to worship Him. What are some ways we have worshiped God for what He created? Sung songs to Him; prayed; written and said a litany; drew pictures. **Today we are going to take a worship walk. We will find things on our walk that God made. Then we will worship God with our mouths, with our ears, and with our hands.** Lead the children on the creation walk you have prepared. Ask them to look for and name many items God created that they see on the walk.

When you are finished with your walk, return to the worship area. Give each child a blank piece of paper and markers or crayons. **What are some things we say to God when we worship Him?** We love you. Thank You. I'm glad You made (item God created). You are a great God. **What do you want to say to**

worship God for what He created? We are going to draw a picture to worship God for His creation. What could you draw to show God you love Him and you thank Him for His creation? Listen to children's ideas and offer suggestions. Besides drawings of items God created, children could draw colorful designs or shapes to express their worship. Play a tape of worship songs as the children work.

When the children have completed their pictures, sing the fourth verse of "God Made Everything So Fine" from page 8 of this session. If you have time, sing the first three verses as well. Keep the children's worship pictures to use during the Wrap-up.

BIBLE MEMORY—Do You Hear What I Hear?

You will need a cassette player and blank cassette.

Review the Bible verse for this unit with the children with the motions. Begin with all the children squatting. Children stand a little on each of the first three words of the verse, *In the beginning.* While they say the word *God*, children raise both hands straight overhead. Circle hands outward and stretch them out on the word *created*. Flutter fingers from left to right overhead on the word *heavens* and from right to left at waist height for the word *earth.*

Then record each child saying the words of the verse on a cassette player. Write down the order of children if you have a large group. After everyone has had a turn to say the verse into the recorder, rewind and play back the recording. Ask the children to tell you whose voice is saying the verse each time. Talk about how each voice sounds different. Children may not recognize their own voices on the tape, but gently assure them that that is what they sound like.

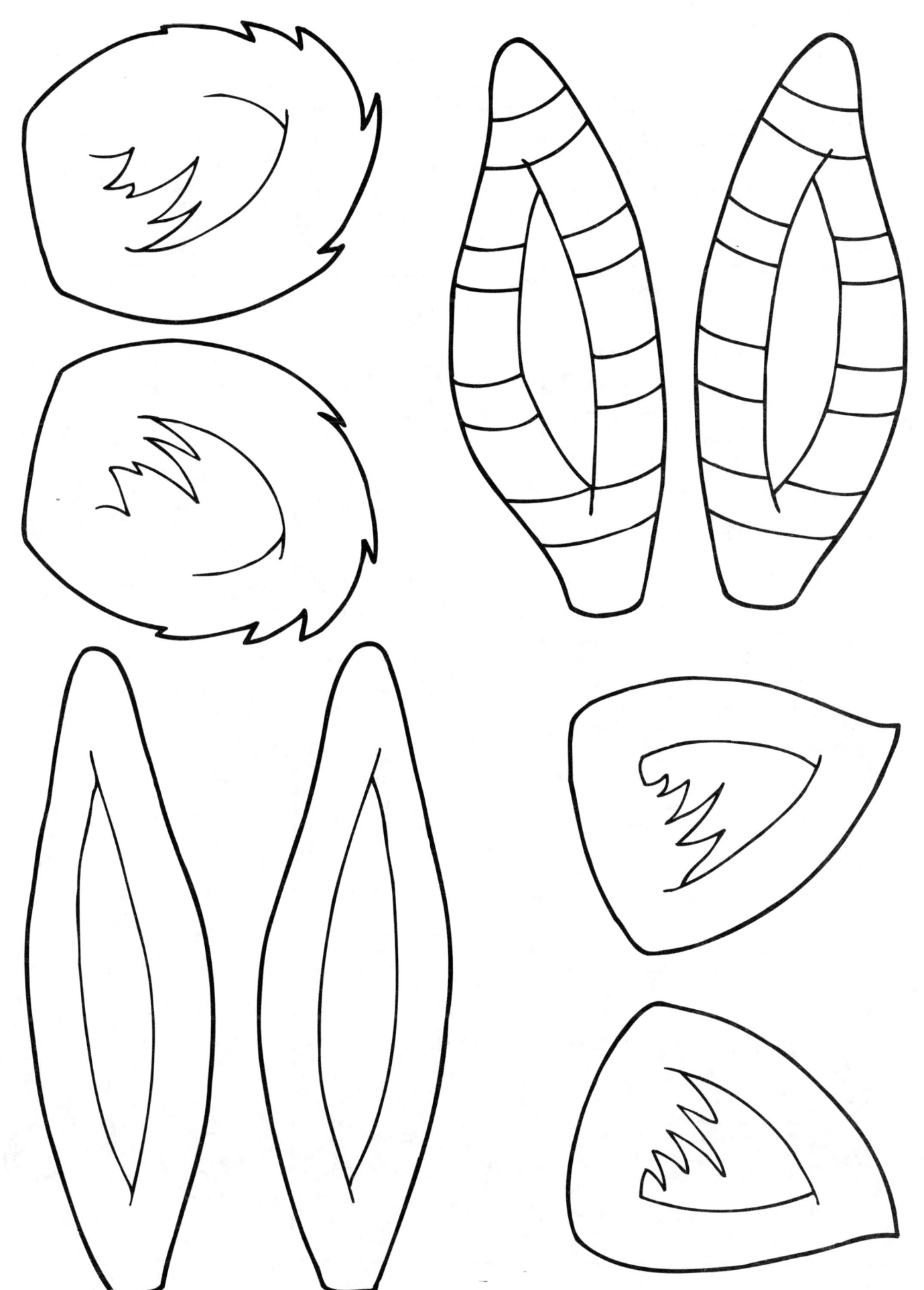

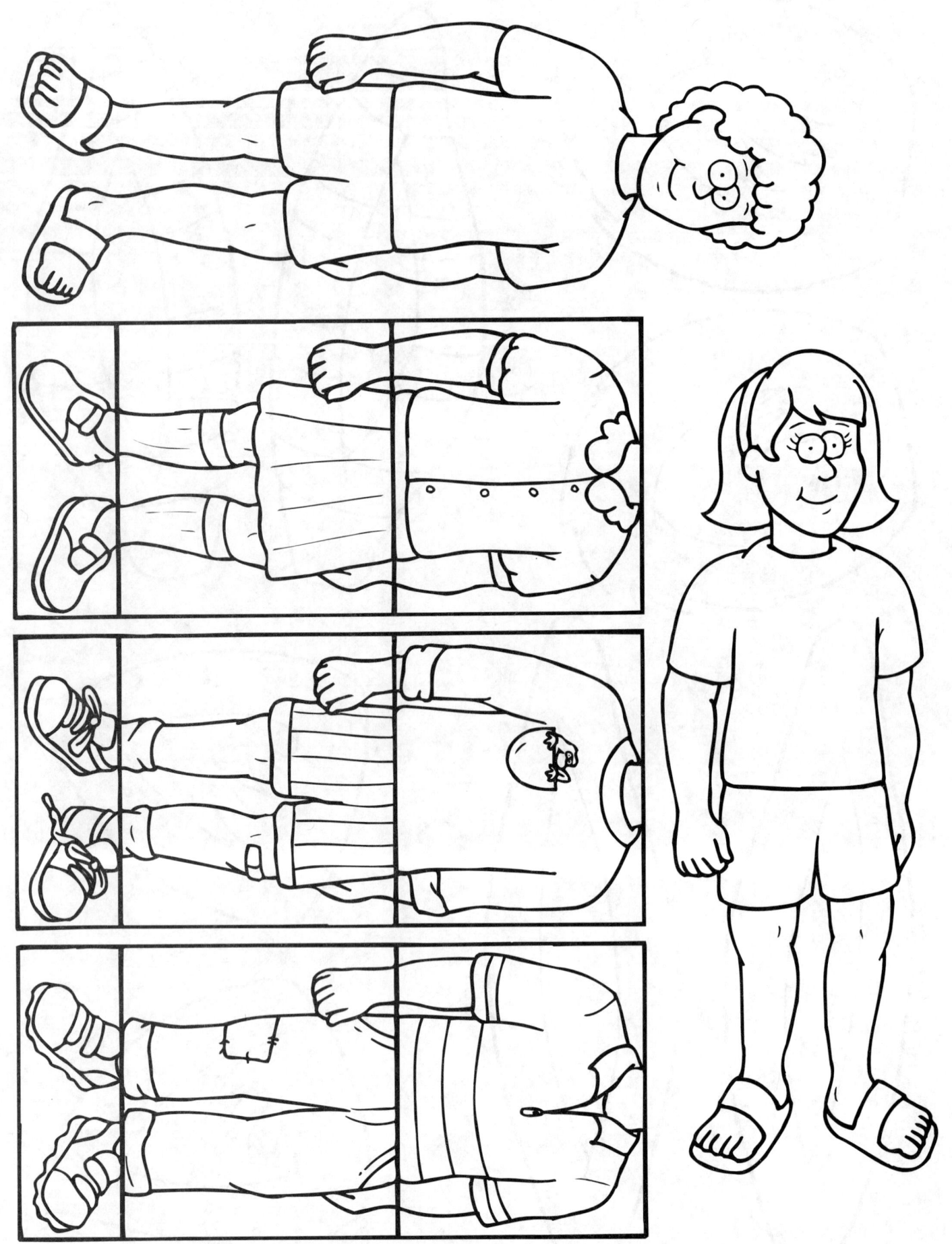

Unit 2
Lessons 5-8

God Wants Me to Make Right Choices

By the end of this unit, the children and leaders will . . .
Know Tell how five Bible people chose right.
Feel Feel willing to do what is right.
Do Choose to do what is right.

Unit Bible Words for Memory
"Help me obey your commands because that makes me happy" (Psalm 119:35, ICB).

Unit Lessons

Lesson 5
God Wants Me to Tell the Truth
Numbers 13; 14:5-9, 30, 34, 36, 37
Children will learn how Joshua and Caleb were not afraid to tell the truth about the land of Canaan, even when ten other men lied.

Lesson 6
God Wants Me to Follow Instructions
Joshua 5:13—6:20
Children will discover how the city of Jericho was overtaken because Joshua and the people of Israel followed God's instructions.

Lesson 7
God Wants Me to Work Hard
Ruth 1, 2
Children will find out how Ruth worked hard in the fields gathering grain to take care of herself and Naomi, her mother-in-law.

Lesson 8
God Wants Me to Keep My Promises
1 Samuel 1
Children will see how Hannah kept her promise to give her child to God, if He would give her a son.

Why Teach This Unit to Four-Year-Olds—Six-Year-Olds?

The lessons in this unit show examples of Bible people who dealt with the same kinds of choices that four- to six-year-old children make every day: telling the truth, following instructions, working hard, keeping promises. These choices touch every area of their lives: home, school, church, play. They can imitate the right choices the Bible people made by choosing right themselves.

Bible Time Line

The stories for this unit are pictured on the time line, page 313. The timeline will be used throughout all units in this book.

Provide the time-line page for children who arrive early, or plan time at the end of the Bible story during each session for children to color the time-line and look for the hidden pictures.

See page 6 in this book for further instructions on using the time line and for suggested time-line projects.

31

Materials
All Lessons
a Bible
markers, colored pencils, crayons
white paper, construction paper, poster board
tape, masking tape
Plasti-Tak
glue
scissors
a stapler
paper hole punch
yarn or string

Lesson 5
twelve empty toilet-paper tubes
two empty toilet-paper tubes for each child in your class
stickers
a yardstick
small or toy hammer
a set of keys
a toy car
a coin purse

Lesson 6
Invite someone to visit your class who makes something by following instructions, such as a carpenter, a cook, or a seamstress.
supplies to make cookies if you invite a cook to class, or ready-made cookies
simple costumes (plain colored T-shirts)
an overhead projector, a transparency with lines draw on it to look like a block wall
a clothes basket
clear adhesive-backed paper

Lesson 7
ants in a jar with a small piece of food
a book about ants from the local library
lunch-size paper bags
pieces of cloth
two sandwich bags and unpopped popcorn

Lesson 8
paper plates
paper clips and paper fasteners
two large paper grocery bags
a noisy baby toy for each team of five children
a cassette of favorite songs
a cassette player

The Beginner's Bible™ Resources
The Beginner's Bible™ Old Testament GeoSafari Bible Pack, Standard Publishing, #14-24001, call 1-800-543-1353

The Beginner's Bible™ Bible Lessons GeoSafari Bible Pack, Standard Publishing, #14-24005, call 1-800-543-1353

The Story of Joshua & the Battle of Jericho, Sony Wonder Video Series, call 1-800-733-3000

Unit 2
Lesson 5

God Wants Me to Tell the Truth

(Numbers 13; 14:5-9, 30, 34, 36, 37)

Moses sent twelve men to spy out the new land, Canaan. When they returned, ten of the men were afraid to trust in God's help to take the land. Only Joshua and Caleb told the truth about what they saw.

Bible Words

"Help me obey your commands because that makes me happy" (Psalm 119:35).

Goals

Tell how Joshua and Caleb chose to do right.
Feel willing to tell the truth.
Choose to tell the truth.

Activity 1—Do What's Right

Teach the first verse of "Do What's Right" to the tune of "Are You Sleeping?" with the hand motions. The words and motions are on page 8 of this lesson.

This tune will be used in all four lessons of unit 2. This is the first of four verses that will be taught. Because this is the first introduction to the song, sing the song slowly so the children can learn the words and motions.

Today we are going to learn about two men in the Bible who told the truth. Sometimes telling the truth is hard to do. Can you think of a time when you told the truth? Let children share their experiences. **The Bible says that when you tell the truth**

Do What's Right
(Tune: "Are You Sleeping?")

Verse 1:
Do what's right. *(Point with right hand.)*
Do what's right. *(Point with left hand.)*
Tell the truth. Tell the truth.
(Touch lips with pointing fingers.)
Always be honest. Always be honest.
(Clap hands as each syllable is sung.)
God will help. God will help.
(Point to Heaven.)

Leaders' Evaluation

	Great!	OK!	More!	Oops!	Suggestions
Activity 1					
Activity 2					
Bible Time					
Application					
Bible Memory					
Craft					
Snack					
Game					
Wrap-up					

you please God. Did you know God will help you tell the truth? Telling the truth is always the right thing to do.

ACTIVITY 2—"Uh-Oh!"

You will need a copy of the lips and the picture strip on page 49 for each child. Provide crayons or markers and scissors. Before class, make a sample strip to show the children.

While the children are coloring, talk about each picture on the strip. Ask the children to tell you what they think has happened. Picture #1: A father is upset because someone broke the new flower he was going to plant in the yard. Picture #2: A teacher found torn pages in a book. She wants to know how the pages were torn. Picture #3: Someone has eaten several cookies the mother had baked for dinner. She wants to know who ate them. Picture #4: A man has a broken window. He wants to know who broke it.

Help the children cut out the lips and the picture strip. Gently fold the lips in half so that you can cut a horizontal slit between the lips. Make the slit big enough for the picture strip to slide through. Put each child's name on his or her craft. Save for use after the Bible story.

BIBLE TIME—Two Who Told the Truth

You will need twelve empty toilet-paper tubes, reproducible page 50, scissors, glue, and markers. Before the session, use the reproducible page to make ten copies of wrapper #1 and two copies of wrapper #2. Color both halves of each wrapper the same, but color each man differently. Cut out and glue the 12 wrappers around 12 toilet paper tubes. Use these 12 puppets as sample binoculars during the story where indicated. Also place the 12 spies during the story where indicated. When you use the words "look" and "saw," bring the binoculars up to

---fold---

Game—Daddy, Daddy, Where's Your Hammer?

Provide a small or toy hammer, a set of keys, a Bible, a toy car, a coin purse, a box of crayons, and other small items.

Play a game similar to "Doggy, Doggy, Where's Your Bone?" **We are going to practice telling the truth. We are going to pretend we are a family member or a friend who has lost something.** Choose a child to sit in a chair in front of the class. Be sure he is sitting with his back to the class and his eyes hidden. Place the hammer under the chair. Silently choose someone to tiptoe to the chair, take the hammer, and tiptoe back to her place and put the hammer behind her back. All of the children should put their hands behind their backs too. Lead the class in saying: "Daddy, Daddy, where's your hammer?" Let the child in the chair have three guesses to see if he can find who took the hammer. Each child that is called upon must tell the truth and show his hands. The child with the hammer becomes the next person to sit in the chair. Repeat the game using the keys. Say, "Mommy, Mommy, where are your keys?" Continue playing using the following questions: "Teacher, Teacher, where's your Bible?" "Brother, Brother, where's your toy car?" "Sister, Sister, where's your coin purse?" "Friend, Friend, where's your box of crayons?"

WRAP-UP—To Tell the Truth

Ask the children to follow you around the classroom looking through their Truth Trackers for messy areas and trash. When the room is clean, gather in a circle and sing "Do What's Right." Pray with the children.

Until parents arrive, play an acting game. Name some commands from the Bible (i.e., love one another; be kind; obey your parents). Let the children take turns standing in the center of the circle and acting out a command. Tell the rest of the children to use their Truth Trackers to watch the child in the center.

your eyes.

Who remembers hearing Bible stories about Moses? Do you remember when God gave Moses and the Israelites the Ten Commandments? (Give some basic facts if needed.) After God gave the Ten Commandments, He led them next to the land He had promised to give to them. The land was called Canaan.

Then God told Moses to send some men to explore the new land. We will call these men "spies."

Moses chose twelve men. Line up the twelve paper-tube men in a row. Joshua and Caleb should be the last two in the row. Ask the children to count the number of men. Be sure the children see only the smiling-face side of each man. Have your Truth Tracker binoculars ready. He said, *"You are to spy out this new land. When you walk through Canaan, look at the land, look at the people, look at the towns, look at the dirt, look at the trees, and look at the food growing in the fields. Bring some of the food back for us to see."* March the twelve men off to your left. It will work best if the Joshua and Caleb tubes lead the way.

The twelve men did what Moses had said. They looked carefully at the new land. They saw many people living in large towns. They saw good soil for growing crops. They saw fields filled with grapes growing on vines. They saw trees filled with pomegranates (a sweet red fruit about the size of an apple) and figs. They cut a huge bunch of grapes to bring back to Moses. The grapes were so big and so heavy that two men had to carry them on a pole. The pole rested on their shoulders.

After forty days of exploring Canaan, the men returned to Moses. March the twelve men back to your right with their smiles showing. Be sure the Joshua and Caleb tubes are last. The twelve men said, *"This is what we saw. Canaan is a land where much food grows. Here is some of the food we found there."*

Then ten of the men said, *"The people are strong and their towns are big with strong walls all the way around to keep out their enemies."* As you tell about the report from the first ten

Lesson 5   3

Activity Time

Do as many activities as time permits.

Craft—Truth Trackers

Each child will need two empty toilet-paper tubes and an eighteen-inch piece of yarn. Provide crayons or markers, stickers, a stapler, and a paper hole punch.

Let the children color and decorate the tubes. Next, place the tubes side by side and staple at both openings. At one end punch a hole into each of the sides. Attach the yarn.

Put your Truth Trackers around your neck. Then hold them up to your eyes. Tell me what the twelve spies saw in Canaan. How many did not want to go into such a wonderful land? What did they see that made them afraid? How many spies wanted to go into the land? Why were they not afraid?

Snack—Tummy Yummy Snack

Provide green and red grapes, fig-filled cookie bars, and a yardstick. Show the children how grapes grow in bunches. Let several children help wash the grapes, while others pass out the napkins and the cookies. Hint: Cut the cookie bars into bite sizes. Encourage the children to at least taste the fig bars. If they like it, they can have a whole cookie. Let the children choose which color of grapes they want. Hopefully they will choose both! Pass the grapes out in small bunches.

Can you imagine one bunch of grapes so big that two grown-ups had to carry it on a pole? (Demonstrate by putting a yardstick on the shoulders of two children.) **Canaan had good land for growing food. God's people would have plenty to eat. Who remembers why God's people had to wait forty years before they could live there?** Ask a child to lead in prayer for the snack.

Unit 2   6

men, turn each tube around so that the children see each frowning face. "**The people are very big. Next to them we looked small. We felt as small as grasshoppers. We are not strong enough to take the land away from them.**"

Finally the last two men, Joshua and Caleb, told what they had seen. They said, "**We agree that the land is very good and the cities are strong, but we want to go into Canaan. We can do it! God wants us to live in that land. He will go with us and help us. He will keep us safe. Don't be afraid!**" Turn the last two men around and show that they are still smiling.

The people listened to all of the men. They chose to believe the ten men who were very afraid. Point to the frowning men. They did not want to go into the land God had promised them.

God was unhappy with the report given by the ten men. They had not told the truth. They had caused trouble. God said that everyone who believed the bad report and were afraid to go into the new land would not live there. Instead, they would live in the desert for forty years. Only their children would live in Canaan, the promised land.

Joshua and Caleb pleased God. They told the truth about the new land. God said Joshua and Caleb would live in Canaan.

APPLICATION—Truthful Lips

God wants us to choose to tell the truth too. He wants us to be like Joshua and Caleb who told the truth even though the other spies did not tell the truth. Let's look at the Truthful Lips we made earlier.

Pass out the lips and picture strips. Use the sample to demonstrate how to pull the strip through the slit. Put your fingers on the words "pull down" and pull the strip down through the lips so that only picture #1 shows. **Who in the picture broke the flower? What might the boy say if he chooses not to tell the truth? What would he say if he chooses to tell the truth? What** does God want the boy to tell his father? Allow children to respond. God wants the boy to tell the truth, because doing right will make the boy happy.

Discuss the remaining three pictures: God wants the child to tell the teacher the truth about how the pages were torn; God wants the child to tell the truth about who ate the cookies; God wants the child to tell the truth about how the window was broken. Sing "Do What's Right." **Let's pray and ask God to help us always choose to tell the truth.**

BIBLE MEMORY—Listening Echoes

Help the children memorize the verse as they pretend to be your echo. **Have you ever heard an echo?** (If not, explain what an echo is. Also explain that an echo is not louder than the original sound. It is softer.) **An echo repeats everything you say.** Remind the children to be good listeners and copy what you say.

Teacher: Help me obey
Children: Help me obey
Teacher: your commands
Children: your commands
Teacher: because
Children: because
Teacher: that makes
Children: that makes
Teacher: me happy.
Children: me happy.
Teacher: Psalm 119
Children: Psalm 119
Teacher: 35
Children: 35

You were good listeners. Now let's repeat the echo until you know this verse from memory. When you say the memory verse you are telling the truth, because every word in the Bible is true.

Unit 2
Lesson 6

God Wants Me to Follow Instructions
(Joshua 5:13—6:20)

God told Joshua that the city of Jericho was going to be given to him. But Joshua had to follow some very specific and unusual instructions in order to receive God's promise. When Joshua and the people of Israel followed God's instructions, He gave them the city of Jericho!

Bible Words

"Help me obey your commands because that makes me happy" (Psalm 119:35).

Goals

Tell how the people of Israel chose to do right.
Feel willing to follow instructions.
Choose to follow instructions.

◆◆◆◆◆

Activity 1—Follow the Instructions

Sing the first verse of "Do What's Right" learned last session. The words are on page 8 of this session.

God's people believed the ten spies who were afraid to move into Canaan. God said that they would have to live in the desert for a very long time (forty years). Finally God was ready for the people to go into the land of Canaan. God chose Joshua as their leader. God promised to help Joshua. All he had to do was listen to Him and follow the instructions. Let's sing another verse about doing what's right.

Teach the second verse to "Do What's Right" from page 8

1

Do What's Right
(Tune: "Are You Sleeping?")

Do what's right. (*Point with right hand.*)
Do what's right. (*Point with left hand.*)
Tell the truth. Tell the truth.
(*Touch lips with both pointing fingers.*)
Always be honest. Always be honest.
(*Clap hands as each syllable is sung.*)
God will help. God will help.
(*Point to Heaven.*)

Do what's right. (*Point with right hand.*)
Do what's right. (*Point with left hand.*)
Listen now! Listen now!
(*Touch ears with both pointing fingers.*)
Follow the instructions. Follow the instructions.
(*Clap hands as each syllable is sung.*)
God will help. God will help.
(*Point to Heaven.*)

Leaders' Evaluation

	Great!	OK!	More!	Oops!	Suggestions
Activity 1					
Activity 2					
Bible Time					
Application					
Bible Memory					
Craft					
Snack					
Game					
Wrap-up					

with hand motions. Sing the verses several times, until the children are comfortable with the song and motions.

ACTIVITY 2—A Recipe for Work

Invite someone to visit your class who makes something by following instructions, such as a carpenter, a cook, or a seamstress. Ask the person to bring the plans, recipes, or patterns she used and the finished product. (If a cook or baker visits, ask the person to help the children make cookies for today's snack.) Ask your guest to describe the materials and tools she uses. Also ask the guest to tell how she made the item. Be ready to ask questions that will help the children understand the process.

If a special guest is not available, make simple cookies with the children. Use an easy cookie recipe or a no-bake cookie recipe. Demonstrate how to follow the instructions given in the recipe. Involve the children in measuring, stirring, and shaping the cookies. (Be sure to include washing hands as the first step.) Prepare and bake the cookies. Involve the children in the cleanup process too. It will be helpful if you can have a parent bake the cookies while you continue with the Bible Time and Application.

What would have happened if (name of guest) had not followed the instructions? Did you know that God has given us instructions on how to do what is right? Who knows the name of God's instruction book? Hold up a Bible. **Yes, it's the Bible. It is always good to do what the Bible teaches.**

BIBLE TIME—When the Walls Fell Down

Provide simple costumes (plain colored T-shirts), props, and an overhead projector. On a blank transparency draw lines to look like a block wall with a fine-point permanent marker. Project the transparency onto a blank wall or a plain sheet tacked to a wall.

Game—"Joshua Says"

Play "Joshua Says" the same way "Simon Says" is played. Gather the children around and the adult who will be "Joshua." Tell the children to copy "Joshua's" movement only when they hear "Joshua says" first. Whenever they hear only the instructions, they should not follow. Practice a few times, then have the children sit down when they copy the action without hearing "Joshua says" first. Ask the children to jump up and down, pat their heads, blink their eyes, wiggle their ears, etc.

Did Joshua follow the instructions God gave him? Did the people follow the instructions Joshua gave them? Did you try to follow the instructions when you played the game? Sometimes it is hard to remember the instructions. God wants us to always try. He helped Joshua and the Israelites, and He will help you too.

WRAP-UP—Good Listeners

Before class, make a checklist of all the things that need to be done to clean up. Also copy the Good Listener headbands on page 51 on colorful paper. Cut more strips the same size from blank paper and staple them to the headband to make them fit.

Show the list to the children and assign each child a job to do. Sing the second verse of "Do What's Right" while the children help clean up the classroom. When the room is straightened, gather the children around the checklist. As you read each job on the list, ask the children who did that job to stand. Compliment them on following the instructions and place a Good Listener headband on each child. Place the headband around the child's head to measure where the final staple will go. Lead everyone in clapping.

Our memory verse reminds us that following instructions can be fun! Say the verse together. Then close with prayer.

Help the children dress in the costumes. Have the children stand in front of the wall and pretend to march around the wall as the story is told.

Who remembers how many men Moses sent into Canaan? Yes, there were twelve. Two of the men told the truth about Canaan. Joshua and Caleb said Canaan was a good place to live. The rest of the men were afraid because the people were strong and the cities were big. Joshua and Caleb knew God would help them, but the people didn't believe them. The people chose not to go into Canaan. This choice did not please God. God left them in the desert for a very long time. After forty years God chose Joshua to lead His people into Canaan.

Joshua led God's people near a city called Jericho. It had a very high wall around it with strong gates. The king of Jericho had heard about the Israelites. He had heard how God took care of them. The king said the gates must be kept closed. No one was allowed to come into Jericho and no one was allowed to leave. Everyone in Jericho was afraid.

Near Jericho, Joshua saw a man with a sword. He asked, "Who are you?"

The man answered, "I am the commander of the Lord's army. Take off your sandals. This ground is special. It is holy." Joshua did what the man said. Joshua knew this man was from God.

Joshua was given instructions on how to capture Jericho. Joshua listened carefully. He knew it was important to obey God's instructions.

Joshua called all of the people together. He said, "God has given us Jericho." Then he told them God's instructions.

Listen carefully, the way God's people did. Joshua said, "We will march around the walls of Jericho in a special way. First in line will be soldiers. Then seven priests will follow blowing trumpets. Next will be priests carrying the Ark of the Lord." (This was a special box. Inside it were the stone tablets on which Moses had written God's Ten Commandments.) "Behind the ark more soldiers will march. Then the rest of you will follow. It is important that you remember to march quietly."

Activity Time

Do as many activities as time permits.

Craft—Following Instructions Is "Sew" Fun!

You will need card stock paper, scissors, a paper hole punch, a marker, yarn with tape on both ends or shoestrings, and clear, adhesive-backed paper. Before the session, cut card stock paper into rectangular pieces to make sewing card "Bibles." Print "The Bible" on the front of each card and use a paper hole punch to punch holes around the edges. Make one for each child. To make it more durable, cover it with clear, adhesive-backed paper.

Provide each child with a length of yarn with tape on both ends, or shoestrings for sewing. (Determine length by sewing around the sample.) Demonstrate how to sew an over, under, and up stitch. If this is too difficult, do up and down stitches. **Before you sewed around your Bible today, did you think sewing was hard? When you follow the instructions, sewing can be fun. Look! You have sewn all the way around the Bible. The Bible is God's instruction book. It helps us do what is right. Will you choose to obey the Bible?** Sing verse two of "Do What's Right."

Snack—"We Did It!"

Provide two different colors of cups and napkins. Serve the cookies made earlier. Provide a fruit drink.

Let the children help set out napkins and cups. Give them instructions on how to arrange the colored cups and napkins in a special pattern. Demonstrate the pattern for them (e.g., red, blue, red, blue). Have the children copy the pattern with the napkins. Give help and encouragement as needed. **You did a great job following my instructions. When you follow instructions, God is pleased!**

Pray and thank God for the cookies that you made according to instructions. Also thank God for giving us His instruction book, the Bible.

Joshua and the Israelites obeyed the instructions. Every morning they lined up and marched around the wall one time. They did this for six days. Lead the children to march by the "wall" you have made.

On the seventh day Joshua said, "Today everyone is to march quietly around the wall six times. On the seventh time around the wall when the priests blow the trumpets everyone is to shout!"

Everyone obeyed the instructions. On the seventh time around the wall when the trumpets blew the people shouted loudly and the wall around Jericho fell down! Tell the children to shout and watch the wall. Pull the transparency so that the projected wall disappears.

Joshua and the Israelites captured the city because they had obeyed God's instructions. Sing verse two of "Do What's Right." Instruct children to leave their Bible costumes on for the next activity.

◆◆◆◆

APPLICATION—Giggle While You Work

Provide a basket. The children should still have on their costumes from the Bible Time.

I'm going to help you take off your costumes, fold them, and put them in a basket. That sounds like a lot to do, doesn't it? If you listen and follow the instructions, it will be fun and easy to do. Our Bible words tell us that obeying makes us happy. When I'm happy, I giggle. Do you? Get ready for a lot of giggling!

Hint: If your group is small, do the following all together. If your group is large, select children by shoe styles. First, those wearing shoes that buckle, etc.

First, stand and try to touch the ceiling. I'm going to help you take off your costume. When the costume is off, giggle while you turn completely around and sit down. Put the costume in the sitting child's lap.

Next, spread your costume flat on the floor. Demonstrate.

Giggle again when you have followed the instructions. Now take one side of the costume and fold it over so it touches the other side. Demonstrate. Giggle when you are done. Give help as needed.

We are going to make one more fold. This time take the top and fold it over to the bottom. Demonstrate. Giggle again. Help as needed.

The last thing we are going to do is pick up the costume and place it carefully in the basket. Demonstrate. Giggle when your costume is in the basket.

Help the children form a circle around the basket.

Now pat your neighbor on the back and say, "Good job!" Following the instructions makes everyone happy. Now you know how to fold clothes. You can be a helper for your family this week. I'm sure that will make them happy too. Sing verse 2 of "Do What's Right."

◆◆◆◆

BIBLE MEMORY—The Wall Came Tumbling Down

Form circles of no more than ten children. Have the children stand with their backs to the center of the circle. They are the wall around Jericho. They should stand up straight and tall and look very strong. Point to a child in the circle. Ask the child to say the first word, *Help*, and then sit down quickly. Point to the next child, ask him to say the second word, *me*, and sit down. Continue around the outside of the circle until the entire wall has "fallen down." If you have less than ten, ask some children to say two words before they sit down. Repeat until they can easily say the words and sit down. Then mix up the children and repeat. Do as long as they are interested.

When everyone followed the instructions, the wall of Jericho came tumbling down. If we hadn't followed the instructions, some of the wall would still be standing. Following God's instructions is always the best way.

Unit 2
Lesson 7

God Wants Me to Work Hard
(Ruth 1, 2)

Ruth loved her mother-in-law, Naomi, and took good care of her. Ruth worked hard picking up the leftover grain in the fields so that Naomi could make bread for them to eat.

Bible Words

"Help me obey your commands because that makes me happy" (Psalm 119:35).

Goals

Tell how Ruth chose to do right.
Feel willing to work hard.
Choose to work hard.

◆◆◆◆

Activity 1—Do What's Right

So far we have learned about telling the truth and following instructions. Sing the first two verses of "Do What's Right." The words are on page 8 of this lesson. Today we are going to learn about being hard workers. The Bible tells about a woman named Ruth who chose to do what's right by working hard. Teach verse 3 of "Do What's Right" along with the hand motions.

◆◆◆◆

Activity 2—Watch the Ants!

If possible, collect some ants in a jar with a small piece of food. Let the children observe what happens. Get a book from your local library about ants.

Do What's Right
(Tune: "Are You Sleeping?")

Do what's right. *(Point with right hand.)*
Do what's right. *(Point with left hand.)*
Tell the truth. Tell the truth.
(Touch lips with both pointing fingers.)
Always be honest. Always be honest.
(Clap hands as each syllable is sung.)
God will help. God will help.
(Point to Heaven.)

Do what's right. *(Point with right hand.)*
Do what's right. *(Point with left hand.)*
Listen now! Listen now!
(Touch ears with both pointing fingers.)
Follow the instructions. Follow the instructions.
(Clap hands as each syllable is sung.)
God will help. God will help.
(Point to Heaven.)

Do what's right. *(Point with right hand.)*
Do what's right. *(Point with left hand.)*
Work hard now. Work hard now.
(Pretend to hammer with fists.)
You are getting bigger. You are getting bigger.
(Clap hands as each syllable is sung.)
God will help. God will help.
(Point to Heaven.)

King Solomon, the son of King David, was a very wise man. In Proverbs he tells us to watch ants if we want to learn how to work hard. Read Proverbs 6:6-8. Use "lazy person" in place of "sluggard." Have you seen ants carrying food? Every ant works hard. Listen to this finger play about ants. Do the motions with me.

Here's a little anthill.
(Cup right hand on top of left hand, which remains flat.)
But where are the tiny ants?
(Shrug shoulders. Look puzzled.)
Winter is coming! (Cross arms and shiver.)
No time for growing plants. (Pretend to dig and plant.)

Watch them as they hurry. (Walk quickly in place.)
Look! Not one is standing still!
(Shake head "no" and stand still.)
Summer days are gone.
(Look sad and push with hands.)
They have tunnels to fill.
(Curl fingers of right hand to form a tunnel.
Poke pointing finger of left hand into the hole.)

Food crumbs are on their backs.
(Pretend you are carrying a sack on your back.)
See them marching in a line. (March in place.)
No ant is lazy,
(Shake head "no" while shaking pointing finger.)
and not one stops to whine.
(Put hands on hips and pretend to whine.)

When all the food is stored,
(Slap hands together as if you are finished working.)
the cold wind begins to blow. (Cross your arms and shiver.)
Their feast is ready, (Feed yourself.)
Even below the snow.
(Wiggle fingers as though they are falling snow.)

2 Unit 2

WRAP-UP—Hard Workers

Gather the children in the center of the classroom. Ask them to look around the room and choose an area to clean. Encourage them to work hard like ants. When the areas are almost clean, begin singing "Do What's Right." Sing all the verses until you have all the children gathered around you.

Review the "Watch the Ants" finger play and the memory verse. Remind the children to hang their "Be Like Ruth" pocket in a handy place when they get home. Pray with the children.

Play the memory-verse game "Gather Grain" while you wait for parents to pick up their children. As parents arrive, briefly explain the purpose of the paper plate pocket.

Leaders' Evaluation

	Great!	OK!	More!	Oops!	Suggestions
Activity 1					
Activity 2					
Bible Time					
Application					
Bible Memory					
Craft					
Snack					
Game					
Wrap-up					

Lesson 7

BIBLE TIME—A Hard-Working Woman

You will need photocopies of page 52, lunch-size paper bags, markers, scissors, yarn, tape, pieces of cloth, and glue. Cut out the puppets on page 52 and cut them apart at the line. Glue the top part of the face to the bottom of the paper bag, and glue the bottom part of the face on the bag right below the face, so that when you move the top part of the face, the puppet looks like it is talking. Decorate the puppets to look like different characters in the story: Naomi, Ruth, Orpah, Boaz. Use yarn to add hair and strips of cloth for head pieces. (Hint: If you want to involve all of the children in presenting the story, set up a third activity center. Help the children make puppets when they arrive. Additional characters could be: Naomi's husband and two sons; the farmer; workers in the field.) Select children to stand in front of the class holding the puppets while you tell the story. As you tell the story have the children step forward when their characters are mentioned.

Have you ever moved from one house to another house? Let children share. It can be fun to move, but sometimes it can be hard. Today our Bible story is about two women who had to move to new places.

First, Naomi had to move. She lived in Bethlehem with her husband and two sons. There wasn't enough food in Bethlehem for all of the people who lived there. Naomi's husband decided to move the family to another country named Moab.

Then something sad happened. Naomi's husband died. Her two sons, who had married women from Moab, also died.

Some good news finally came from Bethlehem. God had blessed the land. There was now plenty of food. Naomi decided to move again. This time she wanted to go back to Bethlehem. Her sons' wives, Orpah and Ruth, helped her pack her things. Then the three women started traveling to Bethlehem. On the way, Naomi stopped and said to Orpah and Ruth, "I want you to go back to your families. You have been very kind to me."

Lesson 7

---

paper plate. This is for hanging up the pocket holder.

Give each child a copy of the job slips. Older children can cut the slips themselves. If you have younger children, cut the slips before class. Demonstrate how to put the job slips in the pocket. At home their parents can reach in the pocket and pull out a job slip. The child will then do the job on the slip.

When you do a job for your family, you are being a hard worker like Ruth. Helping your family will make you happy. Who else will be happy?

Sing verse 3 of "Do What's Right."

Snack—Ants on a Log

Provide celery, peanut butter, cream cheese, raisins, napkins, juice boxes, and plastic knives. Before class, wash and cut the sticks of celery into three-inch pieces.

Have the children wash their hands. Let them spread the peanut butter or cream cheese on the celery. Show them how to place the raisins on the filling so that they look like "ants" on a log. Pass out juice boxes and napkins.

Why does the Bible tell us to watch ants? Yes, ants are hard workers. They are never lazy. Each ant has a special job to do. When we work hard we are choosing to do what is right.

Game—Underground Ants

Have the children divide into two teams. (If you teach a small group, use only one team.) Have the children form a line and stand close together. Next, ask the children to spread their legs far enough apart so a child can crawl through. The children are to pretend they are ants crawling though an underground tunnel. They are carrying food to be stored for winter. When a child comes to the end of the tunnel, he stands up and becomes the last person in the line. The first person in the line now crawls through. Start the line at one end of the room. As the children crawl to the end of the line, the line will move across the room.

Look! By working together we have tunneled across the room. Feel your muscles in your arms and legs. Strong arm and leg muscles help you do your best work.

Unit 2

Naomi kissed Orpah and Ruth good-bye. Orpah went back to her family, but Ruth would not leave Naomi. Ruth said, "I want to live where you live. I want to worship the one, true God. Please don't ask me to leave you." So Ruth and Naomi traveled together to Bethlehem.

When they arrived in Bethlehem, the fields were full of grain that was ready to be gathered. Naomi was old and gathering grain was hard work. Ruth said, "I will gather the grain. I will take care of you."

Ruth went to a farmer's field and asked if she could gather the leftover grain in the field. She worked all morning gathering grain. Soon the owner of the field came. His name was Boaz. He was a rich relative of Naomi. The workers told Boaz that Ruth was a hard worker. She was gathering the leftover grain so she could take care of Naomi.

Boaz told Ruth, "You can always come and pick the grain that is left in my fields." When it was time for lunch, Boaz invited Ruth to eat with him and his workers.

After lunch Boaz told the workers, "Leave some extra grain for Ruth to pick." Ruth worked all afternoon. That evening she went home with a full bag of grain. Naomi was happy to have grain to make bread.

Ruth went back to Boaz's fields every day until all the grain was picked. Choosing to work hard was the right thing to do. God took good care of Ruth and Naomi.

◆◆◆◆

APPLICATION—I Want to Work Hard

You will need one copy of the job slips from page 53. Cut apart the slips, fold them, and put them in a small basket. Ask children to come forward in pairs and draw a slip from the basket. They should then decide how to act out the job they drew. The other children will guess the job they are acting out. Give suggestions as needed. Continue until all the slips are drawn. Then talk about jobs the children can do.

What jobs do you do at your house? What new jobs would you like to learn how to do? How can you be a hard worker like Ruth? How does it feel to be a hard worker?

It pleases God when we choose to work hard. He wants us to always choose to do right and He will help us.

Sing verse 3 of "Do What's Right."

◆◆◆◆

BIBLE MEMORY—Gather Grain

Provide two small sandwich bags. Fill one bag half full of popcorn seeds. Use the second bag to "double bag" the popcorn. Use a twist tie to secure the opening.

Review the Bible words with the children. Then play a game similar to "Drop the Handkerchief." Have the children form a circle. Select a child to carry the bag of grain around the outside of the circle and drop it behind another child's back. When that child picks up the bag, he must say the memory verse to the child that dropped the bag. When the last word of the verse is said, the chase begins. If a child has difficulty saying the verse, give help as needed. Play until every child has said the verse from memory.

◆◆◆◆

ACTIVITY TIME

Do as many activities as time permits.

◆◆◆◆

Craft—Be Like Ruth

Provide paper plates, yarn, crayons or markers, stickers, copies of the job slips on page 53, scissors, and a stapler.

Give each child one half of a paper plate. Turn it over and decorate the bottom side with crayons or markers and stickers. Then give each child a whole paper plate. Print on the top half of the plate "Be Like Ruth." Staple the half paper plate to the full paper plate so that a pocket is formed. Children can color their pocket holders and decorate them with stickers. Cut a two-inch piece of yarn for each holder and staple it to the top of the full

Unit 2
Lesson 8

God Wants Me to Keep My Promises
(1 Samuel 1)

Hannah prayed for a baby. She promised God she would give the child back to Him. Samuel was born and when he was old enough, Hannah gave him to God.

Bible Words

"Help me obey your commands because that makes me happy" (Psalm 119:35).

Goals

Tell how Hannah chose to do right.
Feel willing to keep my promises.
Choose to keep my promises.

◆◆◆◆

ACTIVITY 1—Do What's Right

We have learned about ways to choose right. Do you remember who told the truth? Joshua and Caleb told the truth about the land of Canaan. Who followed instructions? Joshua and the people of Israel followed God's instructions when they marched around the walls of Jericho. Who worked hard? Ruth worked hard gathering grain in the fields to feed herself and Naomi. We can tell the truth, follow the instructions, and work hard just like these Bible people did. Let's sing "Do What's Right." Sing the first three verses from page 8 of this lesson. Today we are going to learn about keeping our promises. The Bible tells about a woman named Hannah who chose to do what was right by keeping her promise to God.

Do What's Right
(Tune: "Are You Sleeping?")

Do what's right. (*Point with right hand.*)
Do what's right. (*Point with left hand.*)
Tell the truth. Tell the truth.
(*Touch lips with both pointing fingers.*)
Always be honest. Always be honest.
(*Clap hands as each syllable is sung.*)
God will help. God will help. (*Point to Heaven.*)

Do what's right. (*Point with right hand.*)
Do what's right. (*Point with left hand.*)
Listen now! Listen now!
(*Touch ears with both pointing fingers.*)
Follow the instructions. Follow the instructions.
(*Clap hands as each syllable is sung.*)
God will help. God will help. (*Point to Heaven.*)

Do what's right. (*Point with right hand.*)
Do what's right. (*Point with left hand.*)
Work hard now. Work hard now.
(*Pretend to hammer with fists.*)
You are getting bigger. You are getting bigger.
(*Clap hands as each syllable is sung.*)
God will help. God will help. (*Point to Heaven.*)

Do what's right. (*Point with right hand.*)
Do what's right. (*Point with left hand.*)
O-bey God. O-bey God. (*Point to Heaven.*)
Always keep your promise.
Always keep your promise.
(*Clap hands as each syllable is sung.*)
God will help. God will help. (*Point to Heaven.*)

Teach verse 4 along with the hand motions. Use the same tune, "Are You Sleeping?"

◆◆◆◆

ACTIVITY 2—Promise Spinner Game

Make a copy of the spinner game on page 51 for each child. Cut out the circles. Provide card stock, markers or crayons, glue, paper clips, and paper fasteners. Prepare a sample.

Give each child a circle to color. While the children are coloring, discuss the four pictures. Ask them to say a promise that might go with each picture. Ask the children to tell about promises they have made. Ask them if anyone has ever made a promise to them. **Have you ever promised your mommy that you would go to bed when your baby-sitter says, "It is time for bed"? Was that a hard promise to keep? Has your daddy ever promised to take you to the park?**

As the children finish coloring, glue the circles onto card stock that has been cut a little larger than the paper circle. This will add stiffness to the game piece. Push the paper fastener through the center of the circle and spread apart the prongs on the back. Attach the paper clip to the round top of the fastener. Adjust the tension on the prongs so the paper clip will spin.

Show the children how to make the paper clip spin. Let them practice spinning the paper clip. Ask them to name the pictures their paper clips point to. Save the spinners until Wrap-up.

◆◆◆◆

BIBLE TIME—Hannah's Promise

You will need a paper grocery bag, markers, and a pair of scissors. As you tell the story, work on the bag. Use the markers to color designs on the bag. Use the scissors to cut openings for the front, neck, and arms. If the children ask what you are doing, just say, "I making something special." Or "You'll see soon." During the telling of the story, stop and ask a child to stand up. Pretend to be measuring the child and the "coat."

2 Unit 2

— fold —

◆◆◆◆

WRAP-UP—Promise Jobs

Gather the children around you while you sing verse 4 of "Do What's Right." Give each child a job to do. Before you send the child to do the job, ask the child to make a promise. ("I promise to pick up the paper on the floor.") Keep the jobs simple so that everyone is successful.

When all the jobs are done, gather the children around as you sing all the verses of "Do What's Right." Ask the children if it was hard or easy to keep the promises they had made for cleaning up the classroom. Briefly discuss.

Lead in a closing prayer or ask a child to do so. Distribute the spinner games made during Activity 2. Do the following activity until parents arrive. Have the children take turns spinning their paper clips. Ask the child to make a promise about the picture the clip is pointing to.

Jarred has made a good promise. He promises to pray when he gets up each morning. God will help Jarred keep his promise to pray.

Leaders' Evaluation

	Great!	OK!	More!	Oops!	Suggestions
Activity 1					
Activity 2					
Bible Time					
Application					
Bible Memory					
Craft					
Snack					
Game					
Wrap-up					

Lesson 8 7

Keep the children curious about what you are making while you tell the story.

Have you ever made a promise? Here is a promise all boys and girls have made. "I promise to pick up my toys." Did you keep your promise? That promise may be hard to keep, because picking up toys isn't as much fun as playing with toys. Should you keep promises you make? Keeping a promise is always the right thing to do. Today's Bible story is about a promise made by a woman named Hannah. She made a very special promise and she kept it, even though it must have been hard to do.

Our story begins when Hannah was very sad. She didn't have any children. Her husband loved her very much and wanted her to be happy. He gave her gifts, but nothing made her happy. She wanted a baby.

Every year Hannah and her husband would go to the house of the Lord and worship. Going to the tabernacle was a happy time for everyone, except Hannah. Hannah was always sad while they were there. Even when everyone was feasting she was too sad to eat. Her husband worried about her. He wanted her to be happy.

One time when Hannah was in the tabernacle praying, she began to cry. She said, "Oh God, please give me a baby boy. I promise to give him back to You so he can spend his whole life serving You."

Hannah prayed and cried a long time. Eli, the priest, watched Hannah. He knew something was wrong. He saw how sad she was. Finally, he said to her, "Go in peace. God will answer your prayer."

Hannah stopped feeling sad. She ate some food. The next day she and her husband prayed to God and then went home.

The most wonderful thing happened! God answered Hannah's prayer. She had a baby boy! Hannah and her husband took very good care of the promise she had made to God. She had asked God to give her a baby. She had promised

the directions on page 53 for cutting and folding the promise booklet. You may wish to let older children fold the booklet themselves in class.

When the children are finished coloring, direct their attention to each page. Ask the children to tell what promises they would make for each picture.

Making a promise can be easy to do. The most important part is keeping the promises you make. God wants us to do what is right. That means we should keep our promises, even if it is hard to do.

Snack—Baby Food

Provide foods toddlers would eat. Choose soft foods and finger foods (applesauce, vanilla wafers, crunchy cereals).

I wonder what kind of foods Hannah fed baby Samuel? What do babies you know like to eat? Here are some foods babies and toddlers like to eat. I like these foods too. Why do you think these foods are okay for babies to eat?

We have been making promises today. Did anyone promise to pray at mealtime? Let those children pray before the snack.

Game—Musical "Do What's Right" Chairs

Play the following game in groups of nine or less children. Gather the following supplies for each group: a chair for each child, a large paper grocery bag, music (a cassette of favorite songs and cassette player), a different color of construction paper for each child in the group.

Place the chairs for each group in a circle. Cut each sheet of construction paper in half. Tape one of the halves to a chair in the circle. Put the other half in the grocery bag.

Have the children stand in front of a chair. Tell them to walk around the circle of chairs while the music is playing. Then stop the music. All the children should find a chair and sit down. A teacher draws a color from the bag. The child, sitting on a chair that has the same color, stands up and tells something that is "right to do." (Tell the truth; keep my promises.) Continue until every color has been drawn out of the bag.

God that the child would always work for Him. This would be a hard promise to keep. Hannah loved Samuel very much.

When Samuel was big enough, Hannah and her husband took Samuel to the tabernacle. They took gifts to give to God too. This time Samuel was also given to God.

When Hannah and her husband went home, Samuel stayed at the tabernacle with Eli, the priest. Even though it was hard to do, Hannah kept her promise to God.

While Hannah was at home, she sewed a new coat for Samuel. She knew that little boys grow very fast. Put the final touches on the paper-bag coat. Hold the coat up for the children to see. Look very pleased with your work. Very carefully fold the bag. Each year, when it was time to go to the tabernacle, Hannah would take a new coat she had made to Samuel. Put the folded bag under your arm and smile. Hannah was not sad anymore. **She went happily to the tabernacle every year to pray and to give Samuel his new coat.** Ask a boy to stand by you. Put the paper-bag coat on him. Have him turn around so you can see if it fits. Pretend to make some adjustments. Let the child wear the coat for the rest of the story and application. Other children may want to try it on or wear it after Application.

God was pleased that Hannah chose to keep her promise. He blessed Hannah and her husband with three more sons and two daughters. Hannah did what was right. She kept her promise, even though it must have been very hard to do.

◆◆◆◆

APPLICATION—Stand Up and Promise

You will need the sample spinner used during Activity 2.

God is also pleased when we make good promises. Let's think about some promises you and I can make every day. Show the sample spinner. Move the paper clip so it points to the bed. **Stand up if you promise to make your bed every day.** Good! Parents like that promise. Have the children sit down. Point the spinner at the teeth. Now stand up if you promise to brush your teeth every day. Good! Your dentist will be happy

4 Unit 2

---

about that promise. Everyone sit down. Point the spinner at the toys. **Stand up if you promise to put your toys away when you are finished playing.** Great! I have seen children put toys away while they have been here in our classroom. Sit down. Now point the spinner at the praying hands. Now here's a promise that I have made to God. I have promised to pray every day. That promise is one that makes me happy and it makes God happy too. Would you like to make that promise too? **These are good promises to make.** Pray with the children and ask God to help them keep their promises.

◆◆◆◆

BIBLE MEMORY—Baby Relay

Provide a noisy baby toy for each team of five children. Line the children up on one side of the room. Place the baby toy on a chair across the room. The first child in line crawls to the chair as fast as she can. She recites Psalm 119:35. Then she picks up the baby toy and squeezes or shakes it to make noise. Then she puts the toy back on the chair and crawls back to the next person in line. Continue until everyone has had a turn.

Baby toys are made to make babies happy. Does a baby you know have a favorite toy? Why do you think the baby likes the toy? What does this Bible verse say makes us happy? Yes, obeying God's commands or rules. What commands has God given us? Review the commands learned in these four lessons: tell the truth, follow instructions, work hard, keep your promises.

◆◆◆◆

ACTIVITY TIME

Do as many activities as time permits.

Craft—My Book of Promises

You will need copies of the promise booklet on page 54, scissors, and crayons or markers. Before the session, carefully follow

Lesson 8 5

cut here

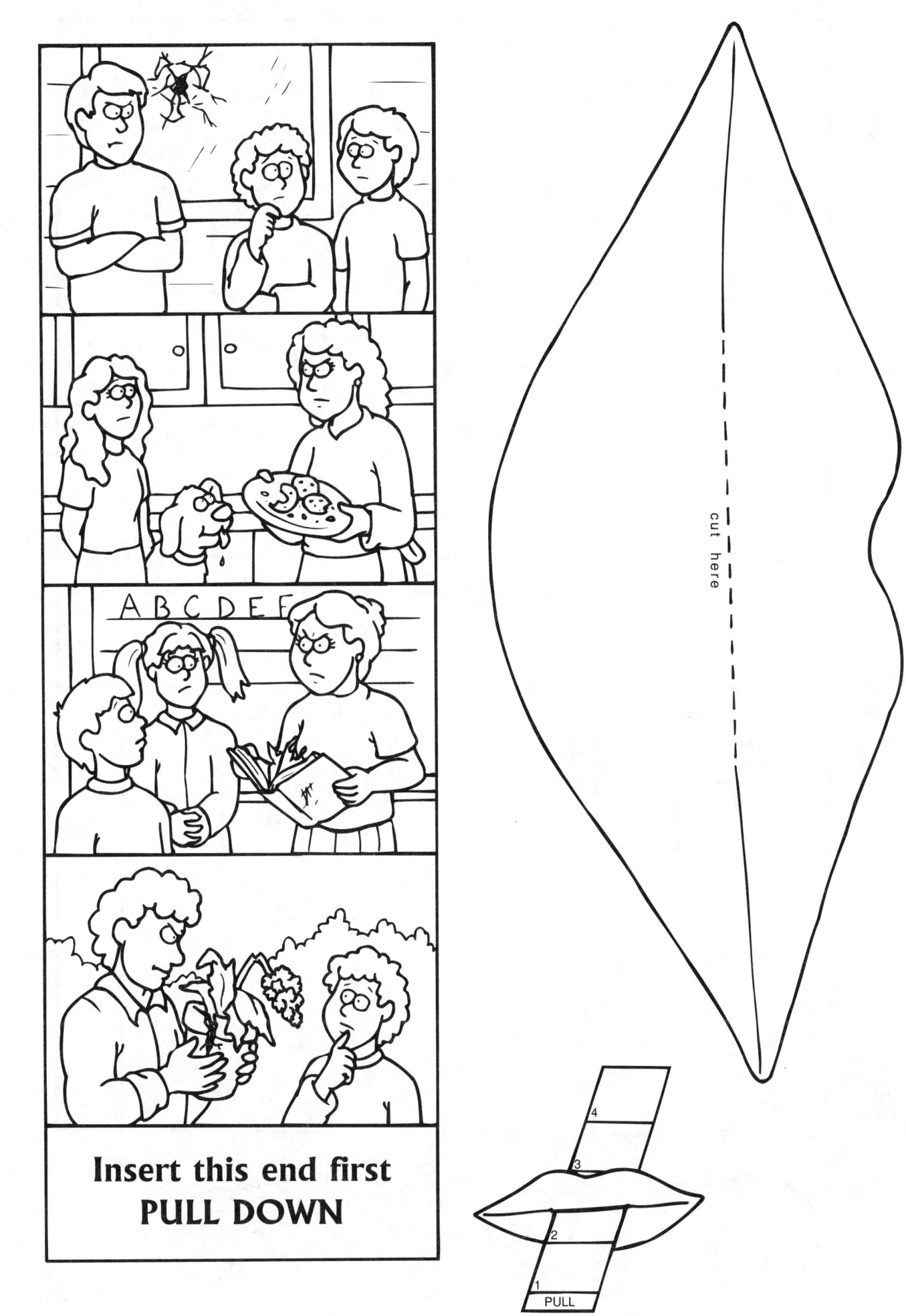

Insert this end first
PULL DOWN

PULL

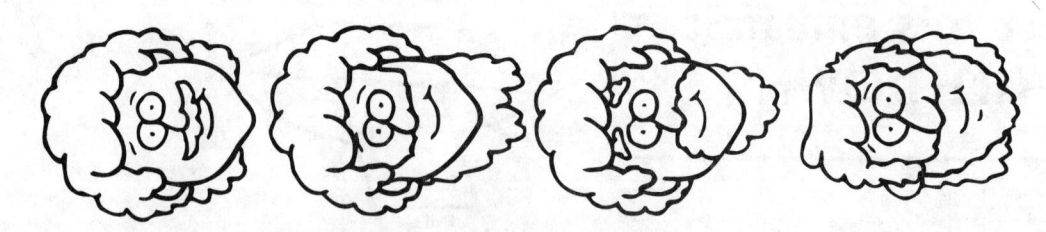

#1

#2

50

Good Listener

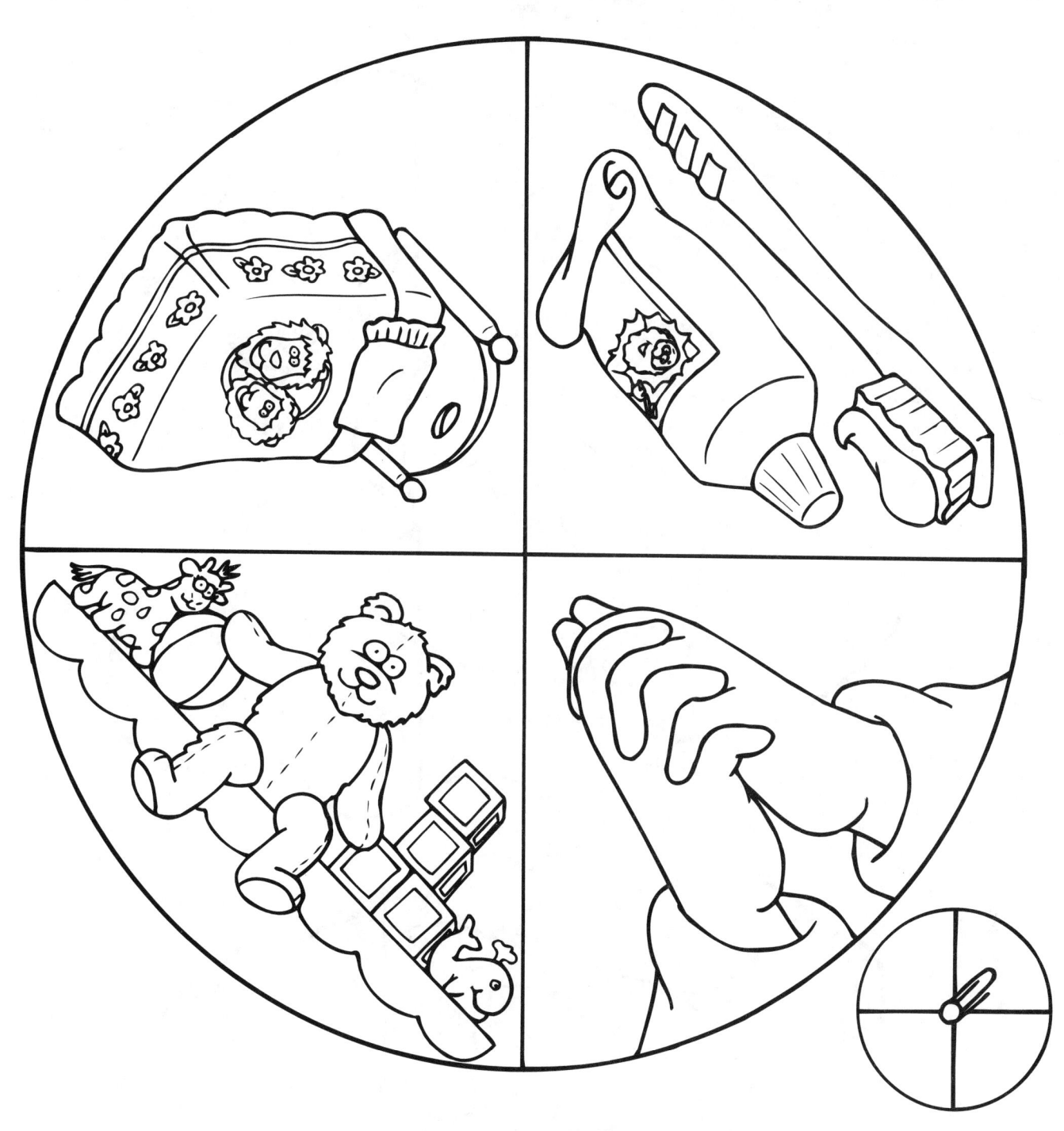

51

52

Set the Table	Empty Trash
Put Toys Away	Dust
Help Fold Laundry	Help Make Bed
Feed Pet	Rake Leaves

DIRECTIONS for PROMISE BOOK on page 54

Cut on the solid lines only. Crease the page in half horizontally and vertically. Crease the quarter folds. Fold the page in half vertically. The pictures will be on the outside of the folded page. Hold the two ends and push them to the middle so the quarter folds touch. Crease the booklet so the title page is first.

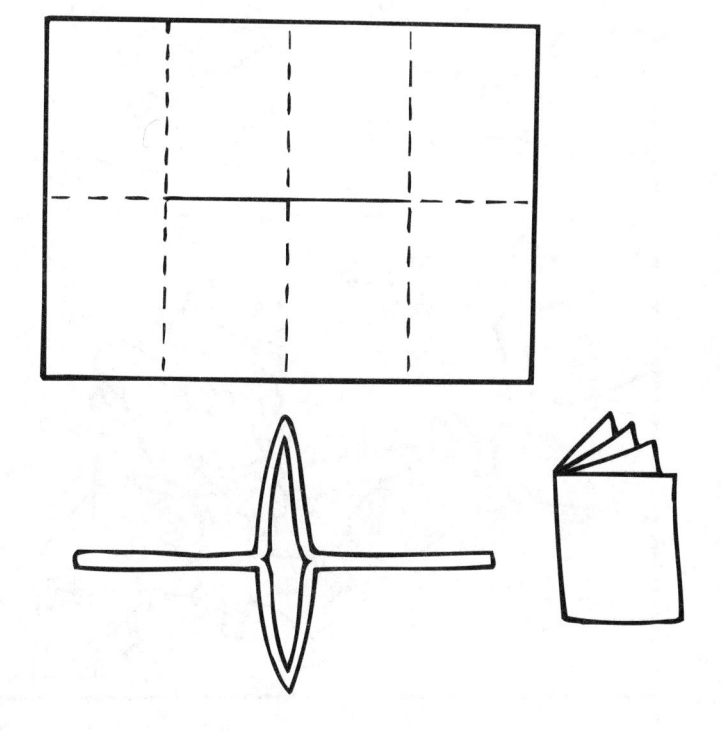

54

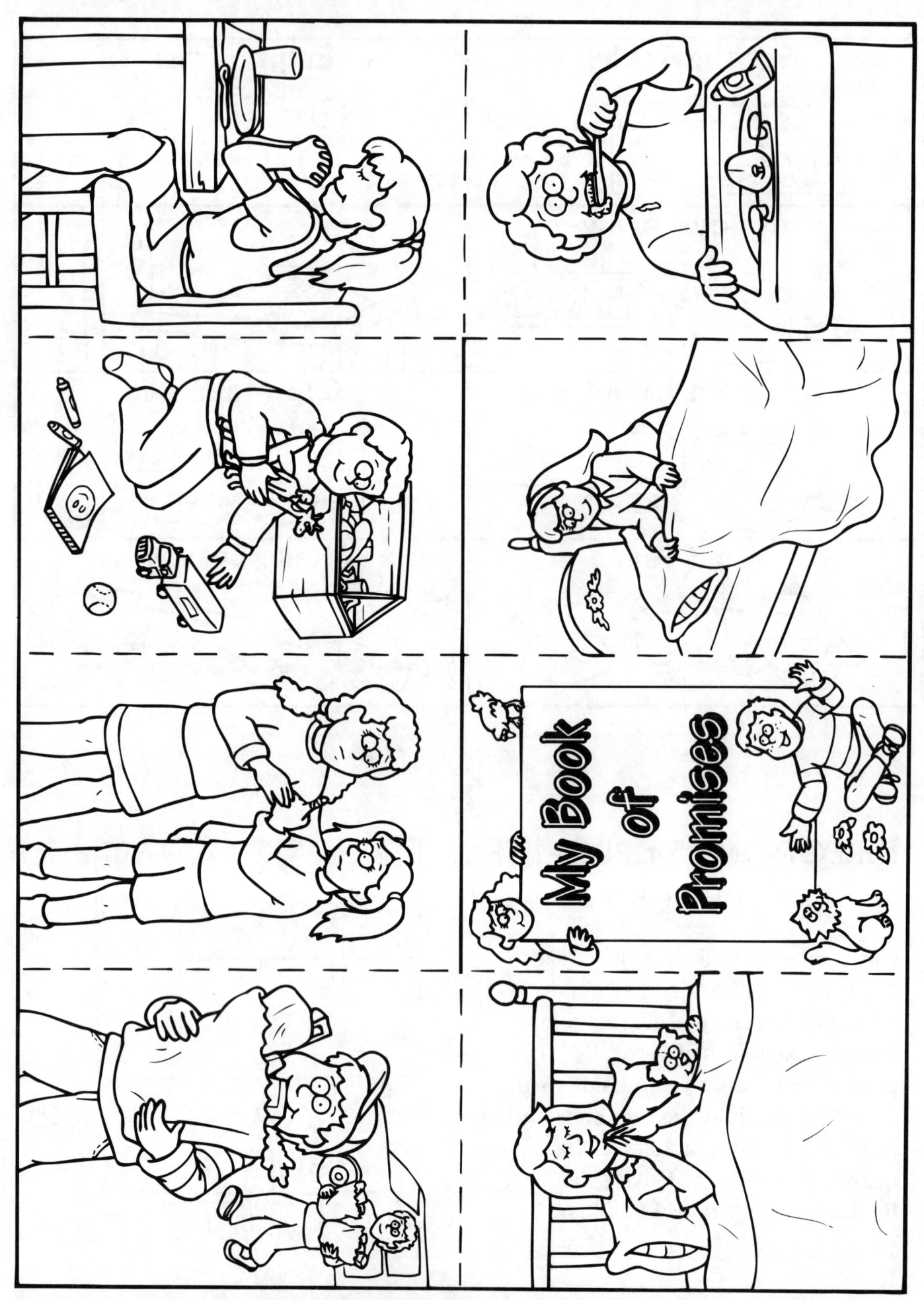

Unit 3
Lessons 9-13

God Cares for Us

◆◆◆◆◆

By the end of this unit, the children and leaders will . . .
Know Name ways God cared for His people.
Feel Feel thankful for God's care.
Do Worship God for ways He cares for us.

Unit Bible Words for Memory
"Come, let us bow down in worship, let us kneel before the Lord our Maker; for he is our God and we are the people of his pasture, the flock under his care" (Psalm 95:6, 7, NIV).

◆◆◆◆◆

Unit Lessons

Lesson 9
Out of Egypt
Exodus 12:31–13:22; Numbers 14:14b
Children will learn how God led His people away from Egypt by leading them with a pillar of cloud during the day and a pillar of fire during the night.

Lesson 10
A Dry Path Through a Wet Sea
Exodus 14:1–15:21
Children will discover how God helped His people escape the Egyptians by putting a pillar of cloud in their way and then making a dry path through the Red Sea for His people to walk across the sea.

Lesson 11
Where's the Water?
Exodus 15:22-25; 17:1-7
Children will find out how God made bitter water drinkable and made water flow from a rock.

Lesson 12
Manna and Quail
Exodus 16:1-36; Numbers 11:7-9
Children will see how God fed His hungry people manna and birds called quail.

Lesson 13
Ten Rules on Two Tablets
Exodus 19, 20
Children will learn ten rules God gave His people.

◆◆◆◆◆

Why Teach This Unit to Four-Year-Olds—Six-Year-Olds?

The Israelites faced fears of the unknown and fears for their safety, and God calmed those fears and took care of His people. Your children face fears and concerns, as well. Through this unit, they will discover that God cares for them, just as He cared for the Israelites.

◆◆◆◆◆

Bible Time Line

The stories for this unit are pictured on the time line, pages 311 and 312.

See page 6 in this book for further instructions on using the time line.

Materials

All Lessons
- a Bible
- markers, colored pencils, crayons
- white paper, construction paper, poster board
- tape, masking tape
- Plasti-Tak
- glue
- scissors
- a stapler
- paper hole punch
- yarn or string

Lesson 9
- a standard-size pillow
- backpacks, suitcases, and walking sticks—something for each child
- a working flashlight for each child
- ribbon

Lesson 10
- a tub at least the size of a dishpan, and towels
- tambourines and other noisemakers
- a small container and a staff (stick, yardstick, cane)

Lesson 11
- two large pitchers, lemon juice, and small cups
- a large rock and a tree branch
- a cooking pan, a washcloth, an empty shampoo bottle, a small watering can, a swimsuit, and laundry detergent
- two buckets of water, paper cups, two plastic pop bottles, two dishpans, and several dish towels

Lesson 12
- two different kinds of small dry items such as beans and popcorn or small pasta elbows and sunflower seeds and a small container for each child such as a Dixie® cup or a plastic sandwich bag
- old magazines with plenty of food advertisements
- dry beans, an inkpad, and wet wipes
- the following solution: two parts white glue, one part vinegar, a few drops of peppermint extract (optional)
- resealing plastic bags

Lesson 13
- tents that can be set up in the classroom or blankets that can be draped over tables
- other kinds of camping gear if available (blankets to sleep in, candles, sticks to make a "fire," cooking pot)
- small prizes, such as bubble gum or a small plastic toy

The Beginner's Bible™ Resources

The Beginner's Bible™ Old Testament GeoSafari Bible Pack, Standard Publishing, #14-24001, call 1-800-543-1353

The Beginner's Bible™ Bible Lessons GeoSafari Bible Pack, Standard Publishing, #14-24005, call 1-800-543-1353

Unit 3
Lesson 9

Out of Egypt

(Exodus 12:31–13:22; Numbers 14:14b)

When God led His people out of Egypt, He assured them of His care and His presence with a pillar of cloud by day and a pillar of fire by night. God's care for His people was constant. God's care for us is constant.

Bible Words

"Come, let us bow down in worship, let us kneel before the Lord our Maker; for he is our God and we are the people of his pasture, the flock under his care" (Psalm 95:6, 7).

Goals

Name a way God cared for His people day and night.
Feel thankful for God's care.
Worship God for ways He cares for us.

◆◆◆◆◆

ACTIVITY 1—Cloud by Day, Fire by Night

You will need a standard-size pillow, two sheets of poster board, and masking tape. From one sheet of poster board, draw, color, and cut out the shape of a pillar of cloud. Make it large to cover one side of the pillow. From the second sheet of poster board, draw, color, and cut out the shape of a pillar of fire. Use masking tape to attach the cloud to one side of the pillow and the fire to the other side.

In today's story, we are going to discover how God cared for His people in the day (show cloud side of pillow) and in the night (show fire side of pillow). God cared for His people by guiding them from the land of Egypt to the land He promised to give them. He gave them a pillar of cloud to follow during

---

God Cares for Me
(Tune: "Are You Sleeping?")

God cares for me.
God cares for me.
Praise to Him. Praise to Him.
He cares for His children.
He cares for His children.
Day and night! Day and night!

God cares for me.
God cares for me.
Praise to Him. Praise to Him.
He cares for His children.
He cares for His children.
In hard times. In hard times.

God cares for me.
God cares for me.
Praise to Him. Praise to Him.
He cares for His children.
He cares for His children.
He gives water. He gives water.

God cares for me.
God cares for me.
Praise to Him. Praise to Him.
He cares for His children.
He cares for His children.
He gives food. He gives food.

God cares for me.
God cares for me.
Praise to Him. Praise to Him.
He cares for His children.
He cares for His children.
He gives rules. He gives rules.

BIBLE TIME—Out of Egypt

You will need backpacks, suitcases, and walking sticks—something for each child. You will also need the pillow from Activity 1. Set up the room so that you may lead children around it as you tell the story. To begin, have the children stand around a table.

The children of Israel were excited. It was time for them to leave Egypt and to move to their new home. They had been living in Egypt for 430 years. During most of that time, they were the slaves of the Egyptians. They were tired from their

the day. Show cloud. He gave them a pillar of fire during the night. Show fire.

Let's follow the pillar of cloud. Stand and hold the pillow over your head with the cloud side facing the children. Lead the children around the room. **God cared for His people by giving them a pillar of cloud to follow.** Now, let's follow the pillar of fire. Turn the lights out and turn the pillow toward the children. Lead them around the room once again. **God cared for His people by lighting their way with a pillar of fire.** Turn the lights on.

ACTIVITY 2—God Cares for Me

❖❖❖❖

The Bible tells us that God cared for His people on their journey from Egypt to the promised land. He still cares for His people today. We are God's people. He cares for us.

Lead children in the song "God Cares for Me" from page 8 of this session. When the children are comfortable with the words of the song, add motions. Children can cross arms in front of them and hug themselves as they sing, "God cares for me." For "day," they can hold their arms over their heads like a sun. For "night," they can pillow their heads on their hands as though they are sleeping.

WRAP-UP—Snap and Clap, God Cares

❖❖❖❖

Instruct the children to straighten the room and clean up any items left from snack time. When children are finished, gather them in a circle and address each child by name. **Miranda, I am thankful for God's care! Are you thankful for God's care?** Lead students in this slap, clap, snap, snap rhythm: Slap legs with both hands and say, "God." Clap hands and say, "cares." Snap with right hand and say, "for." Snap with left hand and say, "me." Pause and say, "Day and night." Repeat several times. Then sing "God Cares for Me" from page 8 of this session.

NOTE: Keep the pillar of cloud and fire pillow for use in session 10.

Leaders' Evaluation

	Great!	OK!	More!	Oops!	Suggestions
Activity 1					
Activity 2					
Bible Time					
Application					
Bible Memory					
Craft					
Snack					
Game					
Wrap-up					

slavery, but they were happy because they were going to the land that God had promised to give them.

Distribute backpacks, suitcases, and walking sticks to students. Make sure each student has something to carry as you travel around the room.

The people were dressed and ready to leave Egypt. Their belongings were packed. They were waiting for word from Moses to leave. Soon after midnight, God's servant, Moses, announced that it was time to go. This was a special night, and God told His people to remember always the night they left their slavery in Egypt. God's people wanted to remember how God cared for them.

When everyone was ready, the children of Israel left Egypt and began their journey to the promised land. God led the way. Motion to students to follow you. Lead them around the room as you tell the rest of the story.

God went ahead of the people in a pillar of cloud by day. Hold up the cloud side of the pillow. **At night, God was ahead of them in a pillar of fire that gave them light.** Hold up the fire side of the pillow. **The people of God could travel by day or by night. Neither the pillar of cloud nor the pillar of fire left its place in front of the people.**

Day and night, the people could look at the pillar of cloud or the pillar of fire and see that God is mighty. Every time they looked, they could see that God cared for them. God was guiding their way to the promised land.

The same mighty hand of God that cared for the children of Israel cares for you and for me. The same God who put the pillar of cloud and the pillar of fire in the sky for the people of Israel cares for us. God may not use a pillar of cloud or fire to show His care for us today. Instead, He shows His care for us in other ways.

By the time you are finished with the story, have the children back at the table where you started. Ask them to remove their backpacks and to put down the suitcases and walking sticks.

Snack—Black and White, Day and Night

You will need any black and white snack such as Oreo® cookies, chocolate marshmallow pies, Little Debbie Ho Ho's®, or chocolate and vanilla pudding.

Ask a volunteer to offer a prayer for the snack. **Our snack will help remind us of two times that God cares for us. Look at your snack. What two times does God care for us?** He cares for us in the day and in the night. **The black color of our snack reminds us that God cares for us during the night. The white color of our snack reminds us that God cares for us during the day. If God cares for us during the day and during the night, then He cares for us all the time!**

Game—Follow the Pillar

You will need the cloud and fire pillow from Activity 1.

In today's story, God cared for His people day and night. How did God care for His people day and night? Discuss, then play this version of follow the leader. The leader uses the cloud/fire pillow. He begins by naming a way that God cares for us either during the day or at night. He holds the pillow over his head. If he named a way God cares for him during the day, he faces the cloud toward the followers. If he named a way that God cares for him at night, he faces the fire toward the followers. The followers follow the leader in single file. One at a time, each follower except the last one in line repeats what the leader named as a way that God cares for us. The last one in line says, "We thank You, Lord, for Your care." Then the first follower in line becomes the leader, and the leader goes to the end of the line. The pillar, however, must never leave its place in front of the people. Continue until all children have had a chance to be the leader and to name a way God cares. Give suggestions as needed. Encourage the children to be as personal and specific as possible. Examples follow: God cares for me by giving me my mommy and daddy, little sister or brother, grandma and grandpa. God cares for me by giving me chocolate chip cookies, macaroni and cheese, gummy bears, and hamburgers. God cares for me by giving me my warm bed.

APPLICATION—Flashlight Flash

You will need a working flashlight for each student. God cared for His children during the day and during the night. He cares for us during the day and during the night. I'll name a way that God cares for us. If it is a way that He cares for us during the day, keep your flashlights off. If it is a way that He cares for us during the night, turn your flashlights on. If it is a way that God cares for us both day and night, then turn your flashlights on.

Following are some suggestions of times that are specific to the children in your class. Include times that God cares. God cares for us by giving us a time to sleep. God cares for us by giving us good food to eat. God cares for us by giving us light during the day and night. God cares for us by giving us teachers. God cares for us with the beauty of the night sky. God cares for us by giving us water to drink. God cares for us by cooling the earth after a hot day. God cares for us by giving us friends. God cares for us by giving us families.

What are some other ways that God cares for you? If you have a way to share, turn on your flashlight. After each child shares, lead the group to pray, "Thank You, Lord, for Your care." As each child shares, have him turn off his flashlight and put it in a designated place such as a box. Share until all the flashlights are collected.

◆◆◆◆

BIBLE MEMORY—Act Out a Verse

We are thankful to God for His care. When we tell God thanks, we worship Him. Our memory verse will help us to thank God and to worship Him. Gather children around you and instruct them to repeat the following words to the memory verse and do the motions with you:

"Come"—motion with right arm as if asking someone to come here.

"Let us bow down in worship"—fold hands in prayer and bow head.

"Let us kneel before the Lord our Maker"—kneel on both knees.

"For he is our God"—point to Heaven.

"And we are the people of his pasture"—point to self with both hands then open arms wide.

"The flock under his care"—look and reach upward. "Psalm 95:6, 7."

Practice the verse and motions several times, until the children are comfortable with them. You may wish to start out saying the verse and add the motions as the children learn.

ACTIVITY TIME

Do as many activities as time permits.

◆◆◆◆

Craft—Times God Cares

You will need copies of the watches from reproducible page 77, ribbon, poster board, glue, scissors, and markers.

Students may choose to make a pocket watch, wristwatch, or a watch necklace. Have students color their watches. Glue the watches to poster board and cut them out. Use scissors to open the slits indicated on the watches. Thread ribbon through the slits and size to fit. Tie the wristwatches on the children's wrists. Attach the pocket watches to a belt loop. Provide safety pins to attach pocket watches to clothing without belt loops. Tie the watch necklaces around the children's necks.

Our watches will help us remember that God cares for us all the time. Whatever time it is when we look at our watches, it is a time that God cares for us. Look at your watch. **What time is it? God cares for us at** (name time). **If it is daytime when we look at our watches, then God cares for us. If it is nighttime when we look at our watches, then God cares for us. God cares for us day and night. God cares for us all the time.**

Unit 3
Lesson 10

A Dry Path Through a Wet Sea
(Exodus 14:1–15:21)

God's people were happy and excited when they left Egypt for the promised land. Their exciting time turned into a difficult time when they saw that they could not escape the Egyptians who were coming after them. God cared for His people when He provided a way for them to escape the Egyptians. God cares for us during difficult times as well.

Bible Words

"Come, let us bow down in worship, let us kneel before the Lord our Maker; for he is our God and we are the people of his pasture, the flock under his care" (Psalm 95:6, 7).

Goals

Name a way God cared for His people at the Red Sea.
Feel thankful for God's care.
Worship God for ways He cares for us.

◆◆◆◆

Activity 1—Part the Water

You will need a tub at least the size of a dishpan, and towels. Fill the pan one quarter with water and set it on a low table. Gather the children around the table. **In today's lesson, we will learn that God divided the water of the Red Sea to make a path for His people to cross over.** Ask the children to see if they can divide the water and make a path through it. They can try to divide it with their hands and by blowing on it. Let children take turns trying to divide the water. It is difficult for us to divide this little bit of water, but it is not difficult for God. The Bible tells us that God used a strong wind to divide the

---

God Cares for Me
(Tune: "Are You Sleeping?")

God cares for me.
God cares for me.
Praise to Him. Praise to Him.
He cares for His children.
He cares for His children.
Day and night! Day and night!

God cares for me.
God cares for me.
Praise to Him. Praise to Him.
He cares for His children.
He cares for His children.
In hard times. In hard times.

God cares for me.
God cares for me.
Praise to Him. Praise to Him.
He cares for His children.
He cares for His children.
He gives water. He gives water.

God cares for me.
God cares for me.
Praise to Him. Praise to Him.
He cares for His children.
He cares for His children.
He gives food. He gives food.

God cares for me.
God cares for me.
Praise to Him. Praise to Him.
He cares for His children.
He cares for His children.
He gives rules. He gives rules.

water of the Red Sea and to dry the land so that His children could cross from one side to the other.

♦♦♦♦

ACTIVITY 2—God's Mighty Hand Cares

Ask children to stand together in a circle. God's people were in a difficult situation at the Red Sea. The Egyptians were coming after them. God's people were trapped between the sea and the mountains. They had no way to escape. They were afraid, and they didn't know what to do. But God used His mighty hands to care for His people at the Red Sea. Ask the children to show you their hands. Tell them that they will use their hands to remind them of hard times when God cares for them. **Sometimes we have hard, scary things happen to us, just like the Israelites did. When we have to do something that is hard or that scares us, God cares for us.** Tell the children that you will all make a hand stack as you name times God cares. You will go around the circle twice, with the children putting in one hand each time. Start yourself so that you may be the base of the hand stack. Prompt children for ideas by asking, "What is a hard thing you had to do?" "When is a time that you were scared?" If a child cannot think of a hard time that God cares, give suggestions: in a thunderstorm, going to school alone, when a baby brother or sister was born, getting lost in the store. As each child names a way that God cares for him, he places one hand on top of the hands that are stacked in the center of the circle. Go around the circle twice until all the hands are in the stack. Then say a prayer of thanks for God's care.

♦♦♦♦

BIBLE TIME—A Dry Path Through a Wet Sea

You will need the pillar of cloud and pillar of fire pillow from session 9. Divide the students into two groups: God's people and the Egyptians. Seat them for the story with a space between the groups.

2 Unit 3

His people at the Red Sea? He parted the water and the people crossed to the other side. God cared for His people. God cares for us.

Sometimes we are afraid. We find ourselves in difficult situations. During those times, we can remember that God cared for His people during a difficult time. He will care for us during our difficult times. Remember how we tried to part the water in this tub? Demonstrate. It was difficult for us. We couldn't do it. But God could. He parted the water of the Red Sea. What seems difficult to us is not difficult for God. Let's worship God for His care. Lead students in the words and motions to the memory verse. Sing two verses of "God Cares for Me" from page 8 of this session.

62

Leaders' Evaluation

	Great!	OK!	More!	Oops!	Suggestions
Activity 1					
Activity 2					
Bible Time					
Application					
Bible Memory					
Snack					
Craft					
Game					
Wrap-up					

Lesson 10 7

God's people were happy. They were happy because they were no longer slaves in Egypt. Instruct God's people to cheer. The Egyptians had told God's people to leave Egypt. Instruct the Egyptians to tell God's people to go. God's people left Egypt and traveled to the Red Sea. A pillar of cloud guided them by day and a pillar of fire gave them light at night. Move the pillow in front of God's people. Instruct God's people to say, "God is leading us to the promised land."

When the king of Egypt found out that God's people had left Egypt, he knew he had made a mistake. Instruct Egyptians to say, "Oh, no! What have we done?" The king of Egypt thought about all the work that God's people had done for Egypt. He wanted them to come back and keep working for him. So the king of Egypt sent his army of chariots after God's people.

God's people were camped on the edge of the Red Sea. It wasn't long until the chariots of Egypt caught up with them. When God's people saw Egypt's chariots, they were afraid. God's people knew they were trapped. The Red Sea was in front of them. Mountains were on both sides of them. The only way to escape was being cut off by the Egyptian army. The excitement the people felt turned into fear. Instruct God's people to say, "Look! Egypt's army! We're going to die."

God told His people to stand firm, to be still, and to watch. They were going to see the power of God. The pillar of cloud moved from the front of the people and went behind them. It stood between the Egyptians and God's people and kept them away from each other. Move the pillow between the two groups of children. The pillar gave light to God's people and darkness to the Egyptians.

Then God told Moses to stretch out his staff over the Red Sea. The wind began to blow. The waters of the sea were divided. Between the two walls of water was dry ground. God's people crossed the sea on dry ground. Instruct God's people to say, "Awesome! Amazing! It's a miracle!"

The Egyptians followed God's people into the Red Sea. But God confused them and made their chariots difficult to drive.

Lesson 10 · 3

Moses' staff may have been a long straight stick shaped much like these pretzels. Distribute pretzels. **Was it Moses' staff that parted the water of the Red Sea?** No, it was God who parted the water. **God showed His power through Moses' staff. God showed His care for His people through Moses' staff.** Let's thank God for His care. Lead the children in a prayer of thanksgiving.

Game—Cross the Sea Walk

You will need a sheet of blue construction paper for each student, slips of paper, a small container, and a staff (stick, yardstick, cane). Before the activity, attach one sheet of blue construction paper to the floor for each student. Place them in a circular pattern. Number them beginning with the numeral 1. Write the same numerals on slips of paper and put them in a container.

Play a version of a cakewalk. Have students stand on a numbered sheet of construction paper. Raise the staff to signal students to walk the path of construction paper. Lower the staff to signal students to stop walking. Draw a number. The student standing on that number names a way God cared for His people at the Red Sea or he names a difficult time that God cares for him. The rest of the group responds by saying, "Thank You, God, for Your care." That student then leads the next round by raising and lowering the staff.

◆◆◆◆

Wrap-up—Part the Water

You will need the tub of water that the children tried to part during Activity 1 and paper towels to clean up any spills.

Instruct students to clean the room. Then gather them in a circle with the tub from Activity 1 in the center.

**When God's people saw the Egyptians coming after them, they were afraid. God's people were in a difficult situation. They had nowhere to go. The Red Sea was in front of them. Mountains were on both sides of them. And the Egyptians were blocking their only way to escape. How did God care for

6 · Unit 3

The Egyptians knew God was fighting for His people. Instruct Egyptians to say, "Let's get out of here!" Then God ordered Moses to stretch out his staff over the sea again. This time, the waters flowed back in place. The dry ground was gone. The path through the sea was gone. The sea flowed over the Egyptians and destroyed them. That day, God saved His people from the Egyptians! Instruct God's people to shout, "Hooray!" That day, God's people put their trust in Him and in His servant Moses.

◆◆◆◆◆

APPLICATION—He Is Worthy of Great Honor

You will need tambourines and other noisemakers.

After God's people safely crossed the Red Sea, they worshiped and praised God for His care. God cared for His people during a difficult time. He cares for us during difficult times too. We will use their song of praise to worship God for His care. Together, we will say, "I will sing to the Lord because He is worthy of great honor." Have students repeat this several times until they are familiar with it. Encourage them to use their tambourines and noisemakers as they say the words. Each time after you say the phrase together, ask one child to share a difficult time when God cares for us. Continue until each child who wishes to has had a chance to share. Remind children of difficult times they mentioned in Activity 2 if they need suggestions.

◆◆◆◆◆

BIBLE MEMORY—Worship God for His Care

Lead children through the memory verse using the motions from lesson 9. **Our memory verse tells us two ways that we can worship God for His care. What are those two ways?** Bowing and kneeling. **Let us bow and tell God thank-you for His care. Let us kneel and tell God thank-you for His care. What are some other ways we can worship God for His care?**

4 Unit 3

Have children name ways such as praying, singing, and raising hands. After each way is mentioned, use it to say thank-you to God for His care.

◆◆◆◆◆

ACTIVITY TIME

Do as many activities as time permits.

Craft—Fan-Fold Scenes

You will need copies of the fan-fold scene on page 78 and crayons.

Give each child a copy of the fan-fold scene. Instruct children to fold along the dashed and dotted lines. If the line is dashed, students fold toward the center of the paper. If the line is dotted, students fold away from the center of the paper. When finished, the paper will have two fan-folds that meet in the center of the paper. When students open the first set of folds, they will see God's people passing through the Red Sea. When students open the second set of folds, they will see God's people worshiping Him for His care.

Have students hold their papers so that all the fan folds are closed. **God cared for His people during their difficult time at the Red Sea. How did God care for His people?** Open the top fold on both sides. Have students tell how God cared for His people in the scene. **God's people were thankful for God's care. How did they say thank-you to God for His care?** Open the next set of folds. Have students name ways the people thanked God for His care. If time permits, have students color the two scenes.

Snack—Moses' Staff

You will need giant pretzel rods and cups of water.

In today's story, God gave Moses some very important instructions. What were those instructions? God told Moses to raise his staff over the waters of the Red Sea. **What happened?** The wind began to blow and the water in the sea separated.

Lesson 10 5

64

Unit 3
Lesson 11

Where's the Water?
(Exodus 15:22-25; 17:1-7)

As God's people traveled through the desert on their way from Egypt to the promised land, they became hot and thirsty. Water was scarce in the desert, and God cared for His people by giving them water to drink. God cares for us by giving us water to drink.

Bible Words

"Come, let us bow down in worship, let us kneel before the Lord our Maker; for he is our God and we are the people of his pasture, the flock under his care" (Psalm 95:6,7).

Goals

Name a way God cared for His people when they were thirsty.

Feel thankful for God's care.

Worship God for ways He cares for us.

◆◆◆◆

Activity 1—Water Taste Test

You will need two large pitchers, lemon juice, and small cups. Before class, prepare two large pitchers of water. Add a large amount of lemon juice to one of the pitchers so that the water tastes bitter.

Explain to the children that you are conducting a taste test. All students must taste the water from both pitchers of water and decide which water is better. Give all the students a cup of the bitter water. Wait for their reactions. Then give the children a cup of the good water. Wait for their reactions. Discuss which water tasted better and why.

God Cares for Me
(Tune: "Are You Sleeping?")

God cares for me.
God cares for me.
Praise to Him. Praise to Him.
He cares for His children.
He cares for His children.
Day and night! Day and night!

God cares for me.
God cares for me.
Praise to Him. Praise to Him.
He cares for His children.
He cares for His children.
In hard times. In hard times.

God cares for me.
God cares for me.
Praise to Him. Praise to Him.
He cares for His children.
He cares for His children.
He gives water. He gives water.

God cares for me.
God cares for me.
Praise to Him. Praise to Him.
He cares for His children.
He cares for His children.
He gives food. He gives food.

God cares for me.
God cares for me.
Praise to Him. Praise to Him.
He cares for His children.
He cares for His children.
He gives rules. He gives rules.

In today's story, God's people were thirsty. They were in the desert. They hadn't had any water to drink for three days. They were hot and thirsty. When they found water, it was bitter. They couldn't drink the bitter water. God cared for them by telling Moses what to do to make the water taste good. God cared for His people when they were thirsty.

ACTIVITY 2—Water That Takes My Thirst Away

Gather the children in a circle and teach them the words to the following song.

(Tune: "The ABC Song")

Thank You, God, for water to drink.
Thank You, God, for water to wash.
You give us water in many ways—
the rain, the rivers, and the seas.
Thank You, God, for water to drink.
Thank You, God, for water to wash.

Have you ever been thirsty? What did you do about your thirst? Have you ever wondered what you would do without water? Discuss. **When we think about life without water, then we realize how important water is to us. Thank You, God, for water.**

BIBLE TIME—Where's the Water?

You will need a large rock and a tree branch.

Divide the children into two groups and tell them they will learn something special to say when you point to them during the story. Group one will say, "Where's the water?" Group two will say, "This water's not good." Have the groups practice. Choose one person to play Moses. Moses will say, "Help, Lord!" Have the child practice.

Show children the rock and tree branch. **In today's story, God's people were hot and thirsty. God used these two**

the motions. Then sing "God Cares for Me" from page 8 of this session.

Until parents come, play a guessing game. Set the six objects from the Application section in front of the children and give clues about the objects. Children can guess which object you are describing and tell how it is used with water. Clues follow: I sit on a stove. I am fun to play in. I keep your clothes looking nice. You can find me in the bathtub (washcloth or shampoo). You can find me in the garden. You can find me in the kitchen. You use me when it's warm outside (swimsuit).

Leaders' Evaluation

	Great!	OK!	More!	Oops!	Suggestions
Activity 1					
Activity 2					
Bible Time					
Application					
Bible Memory					
Craft					
Snack					
Game					
Wrap-up					

things—a rock and a tree branch—to help them find water. Listen to find out how.

When God's people crossed the Red Sea, they saw how much God cared for them. They were amazed by God's miracle. God's people must have talked about this amazing event for a long time. After crossing the Red Sea, the people kept moving toward the promised land. They were traveling in the desert. They were hot and thirsty. They traveled for three days without finding water. They began to grumble. They said (point to group one and speak with them), "Where's the water?"

Finally, they came to some water and began to drink it. But the water was bitter. It wasn't any good. So the people grumbled (point to group two and speak with them), "This water's not good." So Moses prayed and asked for God to show His care for His people. Have student Moses say, "Help, Lord!" God showed Moses a tree and told Moses to throw the tree into the water. Moses obeyed. When Moses threw the tree into the water, the water became good to drink. God's people were reminded of God's power and of God's love and care for them.

God's people continued to travel through the desert. The people grumbled (point to group one and speak with them), "Where's the water?" Again, Moses asked God to care for His people. Have student Moses say, "Help, Lord!" This time God told Moses to strike a rock with his staff. Moses obeyed and water came out of the rock. The people had water to drink. Again, God showed His care and love for His people.

◆◆◆◆

APPLICATION—Water Ways

You will need a cooking pan, a washcloth, an empty shampoo bottle, a small watering can, a swimsuit, and laundry detergent. Before the session, place all the items in a bag.

We are thankful that God gives us water. We are thankful for water when we are thirsty. God cares for us by giving us water when we are thirsty. Water helps us in other ways too.

Lesson 11   3

---

need water. God showed care for His people by giving them water. God cares for us by giving us water. We are drinking water for our snack today because we want to remember that God cares for us by giving us water. Pour some water into each child's cup and distribute the crackers or cereal. Offer a prayer of thanks to God for water.

Game—Water Relay

You will need two buckets of water, paper cups, two plastic pop bottles, two dishpans, and several dish towels. Use the dish towels to clean up any spills. Set the plastic pop bottles in the dishpans. Set one bucket of water and one dishpan with one plastic pop bottle at each end of the table. Give each student a paper cup. Divide the students into two teams. Line teams up behind their bucket and plastic pop bottle. At the signal, the first player on each team runs around the table once, fills his cup with water from his team's bucket, pours his water into the plastic bottle, shouts "Thank You, Lord, for water," and tags the next player on his team. The first team to fill their plastic pop bottle with water wins.

Water is good to drink, it keeps us clean, and it is also fun to splash and pour and play in. I'm glad God cared for us by giving us water.

◆◆◆◆

Wrap-up—Thank You, God, for Water

Instruct students to clean up any spills and to straighten the room. Then gather them together.

Give children the cups they made to take home. What did God use to help give His people water to drink? A rock and a tree branch. Today, we can thank God because we have water all the time. Why are you thankful for water? Remind children of some of the uses of water mentioned during the Application. Give each child an opportunity to say a prayer of thanks to God for water. Encourage children to take their cups home and use them to remind them of God's care. Do the memory verse with

6   Unit 3

We are going to play an acting game to discover other times we can remember that God cares for us with water.

Allow groups of two or three children to take turns drawing an item out of the bag. Have one group at a time act out without using words how we use that item with water: cooking, taking a bath, washing hair, watering plants, swimming, washing clothes. The rest of the class will say the use for water. After each one say, "Thank You, God, for caring for us by giving us water."

When you have completed acting out all the uses for water, sing the words to the tune of "The ABC Song" learned in Activity 2.

◆◆◆◆

BIBLE MEMORY—Reasons to Worship God

Lead children through the memory verse using the motions described in lesson 9.

"Come"—motion with right arm as if asking someone to come here.

"Let us bow down in worship"—fold hands in prayer and bow head.

"Let us kneel before the Lord our Maker"—kneel on both knees.

"For he is our God"—point to Heaven.

"And we are the people of his pasture"—point to self with both hands then open arms wide.

"The flock under his care"—look and reach upward. "Psalm 95:6, 7."

Our memory verse tells us why we should worship God. Name the reasons why we should worship God. He is God. We are His people. We are the people He cares for. Ask for volunteers to offer prayers of thanks for each reason mentioned. **We are thankful to God because He is our God, and we are the people He cares for.** Again, lead children to say the memory verse along with the motions.

4 Unit 3

ACTIVITY TIME

Do as many activities as time permits.

◆◆◆◆

Craft—Water Cups

You will need one copy of page 79 for each student and scissors. If you have younger children in your class, cut and fold the cups before class. Then allow the children to use blue crayons or watercolor paints to color their cups.

Give children copies of page 79. Have children cut out the square along the wide black line.

Follow the picture instructions to make the cup. Demonstrate each step. Then have children repeat it to fold their own cups. Help children as needed before moving on to the next step.

1. Fold the paper in half diagonally. Make sure students fold their papers so the markings remain on the outside.
2. Fold the left corner so it touches the dot on the right side.
3. Fold the right corner so it touches the dot on the left side.
4. Fold the top right flap down on the right side. Fold the top left flap down on the left side.
5. Open the cup.

What can we do with a cup? Discuss. We can use it to get a drink of water. In today's Bible story, how did God care for His people? He gave them water. How did God give them water? He turned bitter water into sweet water. He gave them water from a rock. How do you think God's people drank the water? They probably used cups or cupped their hands to hold water.

Snack—Wonderful Water!

You will need ice cold water, the cups made during the craft or your own cups, and any selection of crackers or cereal.

In today's story, God's people had been traveling in the desert for three days. They were hot and thirsty. Have you ever been hot and thirsty? What did you want to do when you were hot and thirsty? You probably wanted to get a cold drink of water to cool off. That's what God's people wanted too. We all

Lesson 11 5

Unit 3
Lesson 12

Manna and Quail
(Exodus 16:1-36; Numbers 11:7-9)

On their journey to the promised land, God's people grumbled because they were hungry. God cared for them by providing them with manna and quail. God cares for us by giving us food.

Bible Words

"Come, let us bow down in worship, let us kneel before the Lord our Maker; for he is our God and we are the people of his pasture, the flock under his care" (Psalm 95:6, 7).

Goals

Name a way God cared for His people when they were hungry.
Feel thankful for God's care.
Worship God for ways He cares for us.

Activity 1—Gathering Manna

You will need two different kinds of small dry items such as beans and popcorn or small pasta elbows and sunflower seeds, a large sheet, and a small container for each child such as a Dixie® cup or a plastic sandwich bag. Spread the sheet on the floor. Mix the two dry items and spread them out on the sheet so that students can sift through them. Give each child a container.

God's people were in the desert, and they were hungry. They didn't have any food, and they didn't have a grocery store where they could buy food. So God provided food for His people. He gave them manna. The manna didn't fall on their doorstep. The people had to gather the manna. Manna was a small white seed, and God's people were in the desert.

— fold —

God Cares for Me
(Tune: "Are You Sleeping?")

God cares for me.
God cares for me.
Praise to Him. Praise to Him.
He cares for His children.
He cares for His children.
Day and night! Day and night!

God cares for me.
God cares for me.
Praise to Him. Praise to Him.
He cares for His children.
He cares for His children.
In hard times. In hard times.

God cares for me.
God cares for me.
Praise to Him. Praise to Him.
He cares for His children.
He cares for His children.
He gives water. He gives water.

God cares for me.
God cares for me.
Praise to Him. Praise to Him.
He cares for His children.
He cares for His children.
He gives food. He gives food.

God cares for me.
God cares for me.
Praise to Him. Praise to Him.
He cares for His children.
He cares for His children.
He gives rules. He gives rules.

So they had to pick out the small white seeds from the desert sand. We're going to pretend that we are gathering manna from the desert sand. Tell students which of the objects on the floor is the "sand" and which is the "manna." Have them gather the "manna" and then discuss. Did any of you gather any "sand" with your "manna"? Do you think it was easy for God's people to gather the manna when it was next to the sand? Do you think God's people were thankful for His care? Have students keep their "manna" until the Bible story.

❖❖❖❖

ACTIVITY 2—Many Kinds of Food

You will need old magazines with plenty of food advertisements and scissors (optional).

What are your favorite foods? Make a list. Are these the only foods you eat? No, we all eat lots of different foods. Let's find some pictures of our favorite foods along with any other kinds of foods in these magazines. When you find something, we will take it out. Have students cut or tear the food pictures out of the magazine. When they are finished, gather all the pictures together and lay them out on a table or the floor. Look at all this food! We could have a feast. When we sit at the dinner table, what do we do before we start to eat? We thank God for our food. It is important for us to thank God for our food. Our food comes from God. Giving us food is one of the many ways that God cares for us. I am thankful to God for food. Let's thank God for food. Say a prayer of thanksgiving.

❖❖❖❖

BIBLE TIME—Manna and Quail

God's people continued to travel toward the promised land. God had already shown them how much He loved and cared for them. He gave them a pillar of cloud to lead them by day and a pillar of fire to light their way at night. He opened the waters of the Red Sea so that they could cross on dry land and

2 Unit 3

In your game, how many of you were able to gather all of the manna cards before the sun got hot? Discuss. These manna cards say, **"God cares for me."** How did God care for His people when they were hungry? He gave them manna and quail. How does God care for us when we are hungry? He gives us food to eat. How did God's people feel about God giving them food to eat? They were thankful. How do we feel when God gives us food to eat? We feel thankful.

Lead students in this slap, clap, snap, snap rhythm: Slap legs with both hands and say, "God." Clap hands and say, "cares." Snap with right hand and say, "for." Snap with left hand and say, "me." Pause and say, "He gives us food." Repeat several times.

Let's say thanks to God for caring for us by giving us food. Allow any student who wishes to say a sentence prayer. Close by singing "God Cares for Me" from page 8 of this session.

Leaders' Evaluation

	Great!	OK!	More!	Oops!	Suggestions
Activity 1					
Activity 2					
Bible Time					
Application					
Bible Memory					
Craft					
Snack					
Game					
Wrap-up					

Lesson 12 7

get away from the Egyptians. God turned bitter water to sweet water, and He gave them water from out of a rock. God had already cared for His people in many ways on their journey to the promised land.

In spite of all this, the people began to grumble again. Do you know why they grumbled this time? Yes, they were hungry. They grumbled, "In Egypt, we had meat to eat. We had all the food we wanted. We will starve to death in this desert."

God heard the people grumble, and God told Moses that He would send food for the people to eat. God sent something that looked like small, white seeds. The food was on the desert floor every morning with the dew. The people called the food "manna." The word "manna" means "What is it?" The people used the manna to make bread. They baked and boiled it. When the manna was cooked, it tasted like bread made with honey.

For six days out of every seven days, God sent the manna. Have five children bring their containers of "manna" from Activity 1 forward and put them down in a row. On Sunday, Monday, Tuesday, Wednesday, and Thursday (point to a container of "manna" as you name each day), the people were to gather enough manna for that day and not keep any for the next day. Ask two more children to bring their containers of "manna" forward and pour them together. On Friday, the people gathered enough manna for that day and Saturday. The people rested from gathering on the seventh day, Saturday, because it was the day of rest.

God warned the people to follow His instructions. But some of the people did not obey. When they tried to keep manna for more than one day, it became full of worms and began to stink. Of course, this didn't happen to the manna gathered on the sixth day for the day of rest.

God also cared for His people by giving them meat to eat. He sent quail to their camp. Quail are small birds. The people probably baked and boiled the quail as well. They probably fixed it like we fix chicken. God cared for His people by giving them food to eat.

Lesson 12

How do we get the ingredients to make bread today? God gives it to us. Farmers plant the wheat and corn, but God causes it to grow. **God cares for us by giving us bread to eat.**

Look at all these different kinds of breads we have to eat. These breads were made by many different people, but they are all a gift to us from God. Let's thank God for giving us food, especially bread.

Game—Gather Manna Before the Sun Gets Hot

You will need copies of page 81, scissors, and tape.

Help children prepare the cube and cut out the game pieces. If you are short on time, do these preparations before class.

Children may play this game individually or in pairs. Children who want to play in pairs should use one set of manna cards, both sets of sun cards, and one cube.

When God sent manna to His people in the desert, He sent it with the dew. When the sun got hot and the dew disappeared, so did the manna. Tell the children that the object of this game is to gather as many manna cards as they can before they gather all of the sun cards. They should start by spreading all the cards faceup in front of them. Then they roll the cube to see which card they may take on each turn. When the cube matches a sun piece, they take the matching sun card. When the cube matches a manna card, they take a manna card and read it aloud. Each manna card says, "God cares for me." The game ends when a child gathers all four of the sun cards or all of the manna cards. Play the game once as a large group to demonstrate how it is done. Then allow children to play in groups of two or three.

◆◆◆◆◆

Wrap-up—Clap, Snap, God Cares

You will need resealing plastic bags.

Direct students to clean up the room. Provide resealing plastic bags for children to put their game pieces in. Then have children gather in a circle.

Unit 3

APPLICATION—How God Gives Us Food

You will need the pictures of foods gathered in Activity 2. Provide at least one picture for each child.

God cares for us by giving us food to eat. We don't have to go out each morning and gather enough manna for the day. We don't have to set a trap to catch quail. God provides our food through other ways. Let's think of some of those ways. Lead children to discuss. Some ideas might include the following. Farmers plant grain seeds and God causes them to grow. The farmers harvest the grain and sell it to a processor. The processors turn the grain into cereal, bread, and flour for sale in the store. Our parents work at jobs that God gives them to earn money to buy the cereal, bread, or flour at the store. Some families have vegetable gardens where they plant the seeds and God causes them to grow. Then when the vegetables are ready, they harvest them.

God cares for us; He gives us our food. I'm going to give each one of you a picture of some kind of food. Look at the picture to find out what food it is. Each of you will hold up your picture and say, "God gives us (name of food)." Then as a group we will say, "God cares for us; He gives us our food." Do this until all children have taken a turn. We are thankful that God gives us our food.

BIBLE MEMORY—Why Does God Care For Us?

Lead children in the motions to the memory verse learned in lesson 9. God cares for us. He cares for us during the day and at night. He cares for us by giving us food and water. He cares for us during difficult times. Our memory verse tells us why God cares for us. What does it say? We are the people of his pasture, the flock under his care. God cares for us because we belong to Him. Let's show our thankfulness to God for His care by saying the memory verse and doing the motions again.

4   Unit 3

ACTIVITY TIME

Do as many activities as time permits.

Craft—Open the Refrigerator

You will need a copy of page 80 and the thumbprint food on page 77 for each child, scissors, glue sticks, dry beans, an inkpad, and wet wipes. Make the thumbprint page into stickers by coating the back with the following solution and allowing it to dry: two parts white glue, one part vinegar, a few drops of peppermint extract (optional). If you have younger children in your class, cut out the thumbprint food before class. Also cut out and glue together the refrigerator.

In class, have students add their thumbprints in the large area of each food picture that is marked with an X. Help students roll thumbs across the inkpad starting with the inside of the thumb rolling to the outside. Apply the thumbprint to the art in the same manner. Instruct students to lift thumbs straight off the paper so they won't smear their prints. Provide wet wipes for students to wipe the ink off of their thumbs.

While the thumbprints are drying, have students prepare their refrigerators. Students should cut along the heavy lines on the top, right side, and bottom of both doors, leaving the left side uncut so that the doors may have a hinge. Use the glue sticks to glue around the outside edge of the refrigerator and glue over the illustration of the inside of a refrigerator. When they have completed their refrigerators, have students lick and stick their thumbprint food inside.

Snack—Bread Feast

Provide milk and butter along with a variety of breads such as sandwich bread, muffins, corn bread, cinnamon rolls, and homemade bread.

How did God's people get the manna that they used to make bread? God gave it to them. God sent the manna every morning with the dew. God cared for His people by giving them manna.

Lesson 12   5

Unit 3
Lesson 13

Ten Rules on Two Tablets
(Exodus 19, 20)

After three months of traveling through the desert, God's people arrived at Mt. Sinai. Here, God cared for them by giving them rules—the Ten Commandments. God cares for us by giving us rules.

Bible Words

"Come, let us bow down in worship, let us kneel before the Lord our Maker; for he is our God and we are the people of his pasture, the flock under his care" (Psalm 95:6, 7).

Goals

Name a way God cared for His people at Mount Sinai.
Feel thankful for God's care.
Worship God for ways He cares for us.

◆◆◆◆

Activity 1—Camping

You will need tents that can be set up in the classroom or blankets that can be draped over tables. Provide other kinds of camping gear if available (blankets to sleep in, candles, sticks to make a "fire," cooking pot).

For the past few weeks, we have been traveling with God's people. They left their home in Egypt where they were slaves. They traveled across the desert toward their new home—the promised land. God cared for them by giving them water and food. He protected them from the Egyptian army when He parted the Red Sea. God cared for them day and night by leading them with a pillar of cloud and a pillar of fire. Now, God's people have been traveling for three months. They have

---

God Cares for Me
(Tune: "Are You Sleeping?")

God cares for me.
God cares for me.
Praise to Him. Praise to Him.
He cares for His children.
He cares for His children.
Day and night! Day and night!

God cares for me.
God cares for me.
Praise to Him. Praise to Him.
He cares for His children.
He cares for His children.
In hard times. In hard times.

God cares for me.
God cares for me.
Praise to Him. Praise to Him.
He cares for His children.
He cares for His children.
He gives water. He gives water.

God cares for me.
God cares for me.
Praise to Him. Praise to Him.
He cares for His children.
He cares for His children.
He gives food. He gives food.

God cares for me.
God cares for me.
Praise to Him. Praise to Him.
He cares for His children.
He cares for His children.
He gives rules. He gives rules.

arrived at the desert of Sinai. Here, God's people set up camp at the foot of Mt. Sinai. We are going to pretend we are God's people. We are going to set up our camp. Set up the area so students can sit inside the tents and listen to the Bible story. We will come back to our camp in a minute. First we need to find out why God's people were camped at Mt. Sinai.

◆◆◆◆

ACTIVITY 2—Rock, Scissors, Paper, Name a Rule

Play this version of the classic game Rock, Paper, Scissors. Choose one student to begin as leader. He counts: one, two, three. On three, he and the class choose the motion for either rock (fist), paper (flat, open hand), or scissors (index and middle finger held out). All students whose motion matches the leaders choice step forward. The leader says, "God gives us rules because He cares for us." Then each person names a rule. Choose a new leader for each round. Play several times. If you wish, tell the children which kind of rules to tell you each time; for example, school rules, Bible rules, home rules, or game rules.

◆◆◆◆

BIBLE TIME—Ten Rules on Two Tablets

Have students gather at the campsite. Allow students to sit inside the tents as long as they can see you and hear the story. God's people were camped at Mt. Sinai for a very important reason. Who knows what that reason was? God was going to tell them His rules for living. We call God's rules the Ten Commandments. So we will call our camp *The Ten Commandments Camp*.

All of God's people waited at the camp while Moses went up Mt. Sinai to talk to God. God told Moses what to say to the people. So Moses returned to camp and told the people what God said. "God says, 'Obey me and keep my commandments. Then you will belong to me.'" The people answered, "We will

◆◆◆◆

WRAP-UP—Clap, Snap, God Cares

I have one more rule for you to follow. The rule is this: Clean up the room. When we follow this rule, we make the room nice for the next group who will use it. Let's clean up the room.

When students are finished, gather them in a circle. Lead them in this slap, clap, snap rhythm: Slap legs with both hands and say, "God." Clap hands and say, "cares." Snap with right hand and say, "for." Snap with left hand and say, "me." Pause and say, "He gives us rules." Repeat several times. Lead children in the motions to the memory verse.

Close by singing all verses of "God Cares for Me" from page 8 of this session.

Leaders' Evaluation

	Great!	OK!	More!	Oops!	Suggestions
Activity 1					
Activity 2					
Bible Time					
Application					
Bible Memory					
Craft					
Snack					
Game					
Wrap-up					

obey." Have students repeat, "We will obey." So Moses went back on the mountain and talked to God again. God gave Moses some more instructions. Moses came back down the mountain and gave the people God's instructions. The people were to get ready because in three days, they would receive God's commandments. In order to get ready, they had to take a bath and wash their clothes. They were not to touch the mountain because the mountain was holy. Do these sound like instructions that you could follow?

The third day came. A thick cloud came down on the mountain. Thunder and lightning came from the thick cloud. God was in the cloud. A trumpet sounded and the people gathered at the foot of the mountain.

When the people were gathered, God spoke His Ten Commandments. Do you know what any of those commandments were? Allow children to respond. Here are God's Ten Commandments:

1. Worship only me.
2. Don't bow down to idols.
3. Don't use my name in a bad way.
4. Keep a special day to worship me.
5. Obey and honor your parents.
6. Do not get angry and kill someone.
7. Husbands and wives must stay only with each other.
8. Do not steal.
9. Do not lie.
10. Do not wish for someone else's things.

God gave us these rules to protect us. He gave us rules because He knows what is best for us and what will make us happy. God gave us rules because He cares about us. These commandments are ten very important rules that help us follow God.

What did God's people say when Moses said, "Obey me and keep my commandments"? Yes, the people said, "We will obey." The people knew that God's commandments would help them to follow God and to live peacefully.

will help remind you that God cares for you by giving you rules!

Snack—Rules Help Us Feel Happy

You will need English muffins cut in half, cream cheese, raisins, and milk. Spread cream cheese on the muffins. Give each child a muffin and some raisins.

Rules are important to our lives. God's Ten Commandments are rules that show us how to treat God and how to treat others. When we follow them, we get along with God, and we get along with others. When we don't follow them, we have trouble with God, and we have trouble with others. Without rules, we would all be very sad because we wouldn't get along. Use the raisins to make a frown on your muffin. Allow children time to do so. This is how we feel without rules. When we turn our muffins around, we will see a smile. Tell children to do so. This is how we feel when we have rules. God shows His care for us by giving us rules. Have students add eyes and a nose to their faces. Ask a volunteer to pray and thank God for giving us rules. Then serve milk and have students eat their snacks.

Game—Follow the Rules Award

You will need copies of the certificate on page 77. Attach a small prize to each certificate such as bubble gum or a small plastic toy. Hide the certificate prizes around the classroom, one for each child. Create simple instructions for finding each prize. The instructions should contain only two steps. For example, Walk forward to the table and look underneath. All students should start from the same starting point.

Gather children together and tell them they will have a chance to follow some rules. Give them their instructions one at a time. What happened when you followed the rules I gave you? God cares for us, so He gave us rules to follow. God promises that following His instructions will make us happy!

APPLICATION—Bible Pledge

You will need a Bible.

All of God's rules for us are written in the Bible. The Bible is God's Word for us. It tells us all we need to know to follow God. The Ten Commandments are written in the Bible. Open the Bible to Exodus 20 and show the students where the Ten Commandments are written. God cares very much for us; He gave us His Word so that we would know His rules. We are going to worship God for caring about us by giving us rules. We are going to do this by pledging to follow God's rules that He has written in the Bible. We will say the pledge to the Bible. If students don't know the pledge from memory, have them repeat short phrases after you. When we say the pledge of allegiance to the Bible, God's Word, then we are telling God that we are thankful for His rules. We are pledging to obey God's rules. Ask for a student volunteer to hold the Bible. The volunteer should use both hands to hold the Bible open. Walk through the pledge process presented below to help students become familiar with it.

Begin by announcing the word "attention": At this word, children stand at attention. Announce the word "salute." Children place right hands over hearts. Announce the word "pledge." Children repeat the pledge. The pledge follows: "I pledge allegiance to the Bible, God's holy Word. I will make it a lamp unto my feet and light unto my path. Its words will I hide in my heart that I might not sin against God."

◆◆◆◆

BIBLE MEMORY—Bible-verse Leaders

Our memory verse helps us worship God for His care. We are all thankful for God's care. He cares for us in many ways. Let's name some ways. Discuss. He cares for us by giving us rules. Let's worship God for giving rules. By this time, most students should have the Bible verse and motions memorized.

4   Unit 3

---fold---

Allow volunteers to lead the class in saying the verse and doing the motions learned the last four sessions. Following are the motions to the verse:

"Come"—motion with right arm as if asking someone to come here.

"Let us bow down in worship"—fold hands in prayer and bow head.

"Let us kneel before the Lord our Maker"—kneel on both knees.

"For he is our God"—point to Heaven.

"And we are the people of his pasture"—point to self with both hands then open arms wide.

"The flock under his care"—look and reach upward. "Psalm 95:6, 7."

◆◆◆◆

ACTIVITY TIME

Do as many activities as time permits.

Craft—Ten Mobile

You will need a copy of page 82 for each student, colored poster board, scissors, a hole punch, and yarn. Before the session, use the spiral pattern on page 82 to make spirals out of colored poster board for each child. Use a hole punch to punch the hole in the top of each spiral.

Direct the children to cut out the shapes with numerals along the solid lines. The dashed lines are for folding. Tie a piece of yarn through the hole in the spiral for hanging the mobile. Tape various lengths of yarn to back sides of the numerals. Fold them over and attach them to the spiral at different places. Adjust yarn lengths as needed to balance the mobile.

Hang these mobiles in your room. The numbers one through ten will help remind you of God's Ten Commandments. They

Lesson 13   5

God cares for me.
God gives me rules.

78

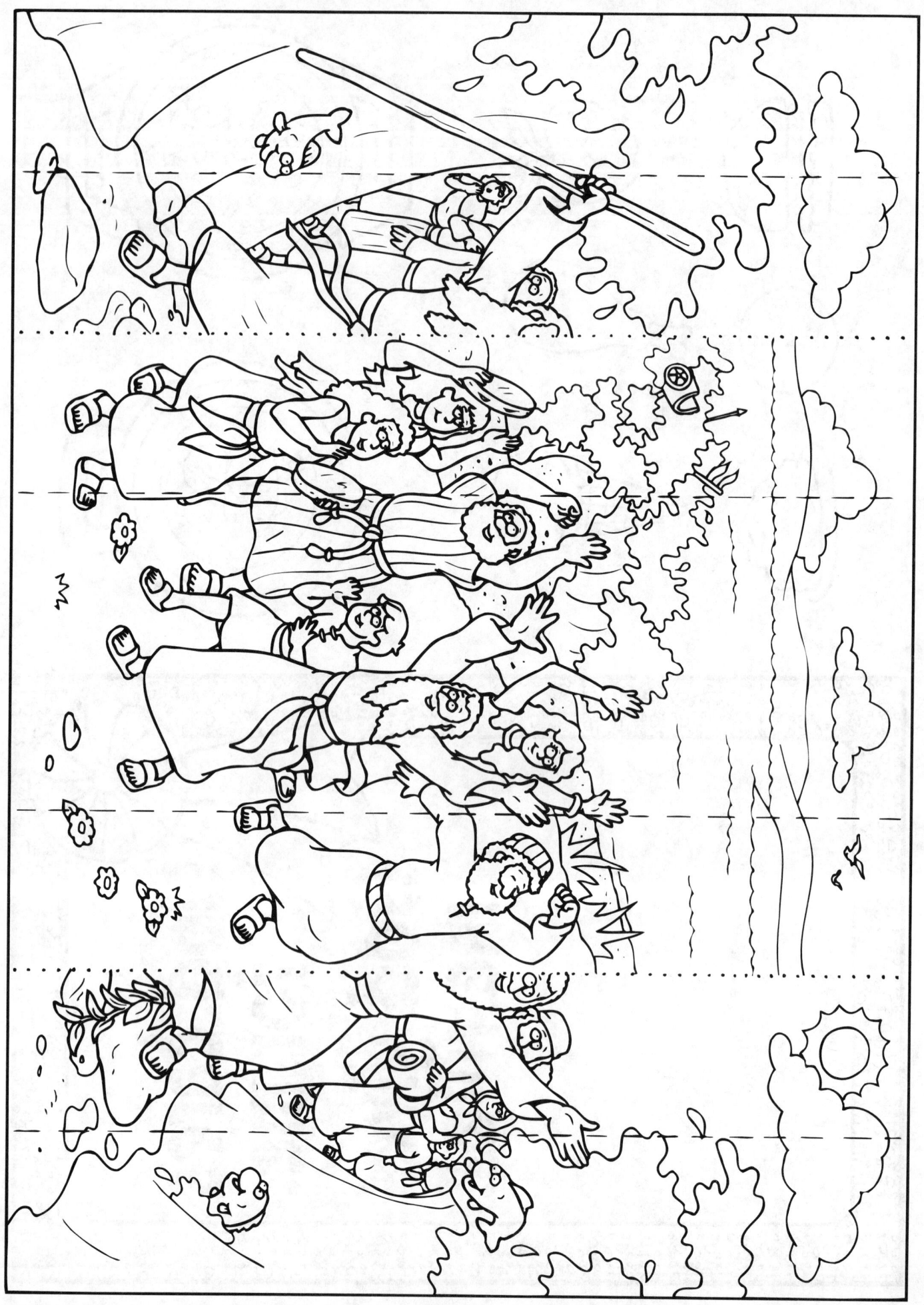

Water Cup

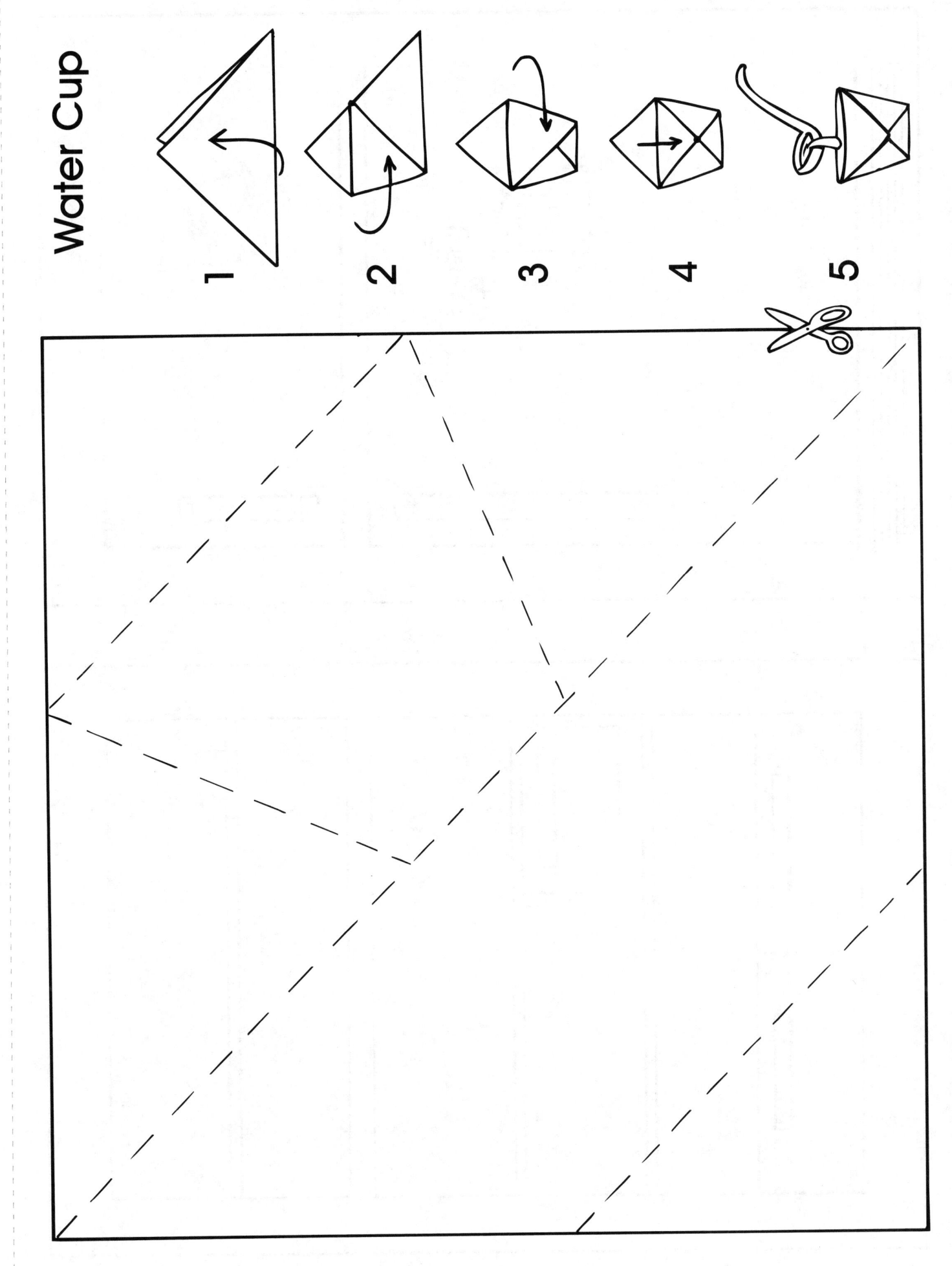

1
2
3
4
5

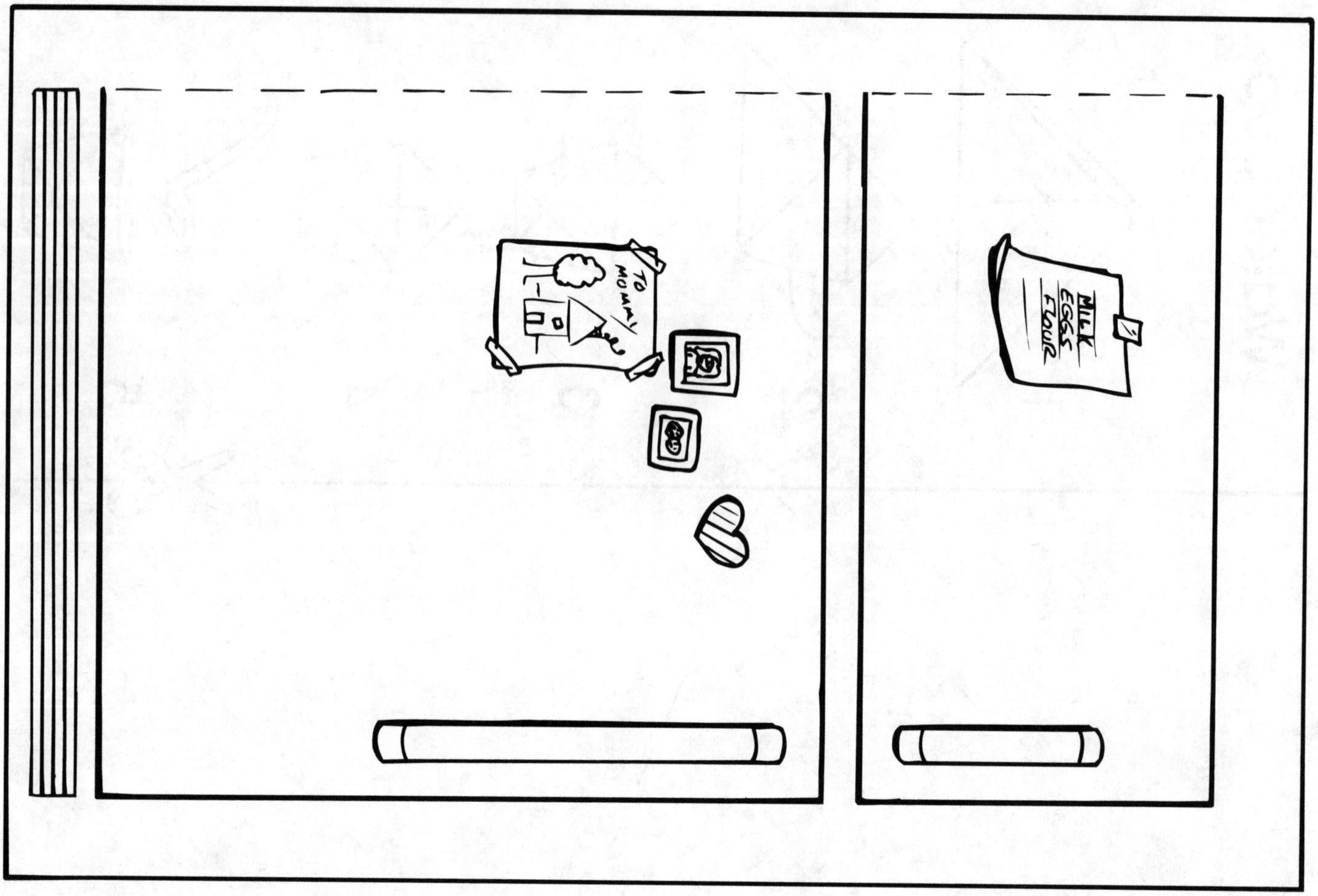
TO MOMMY
MILK
EGGS
FLOUR

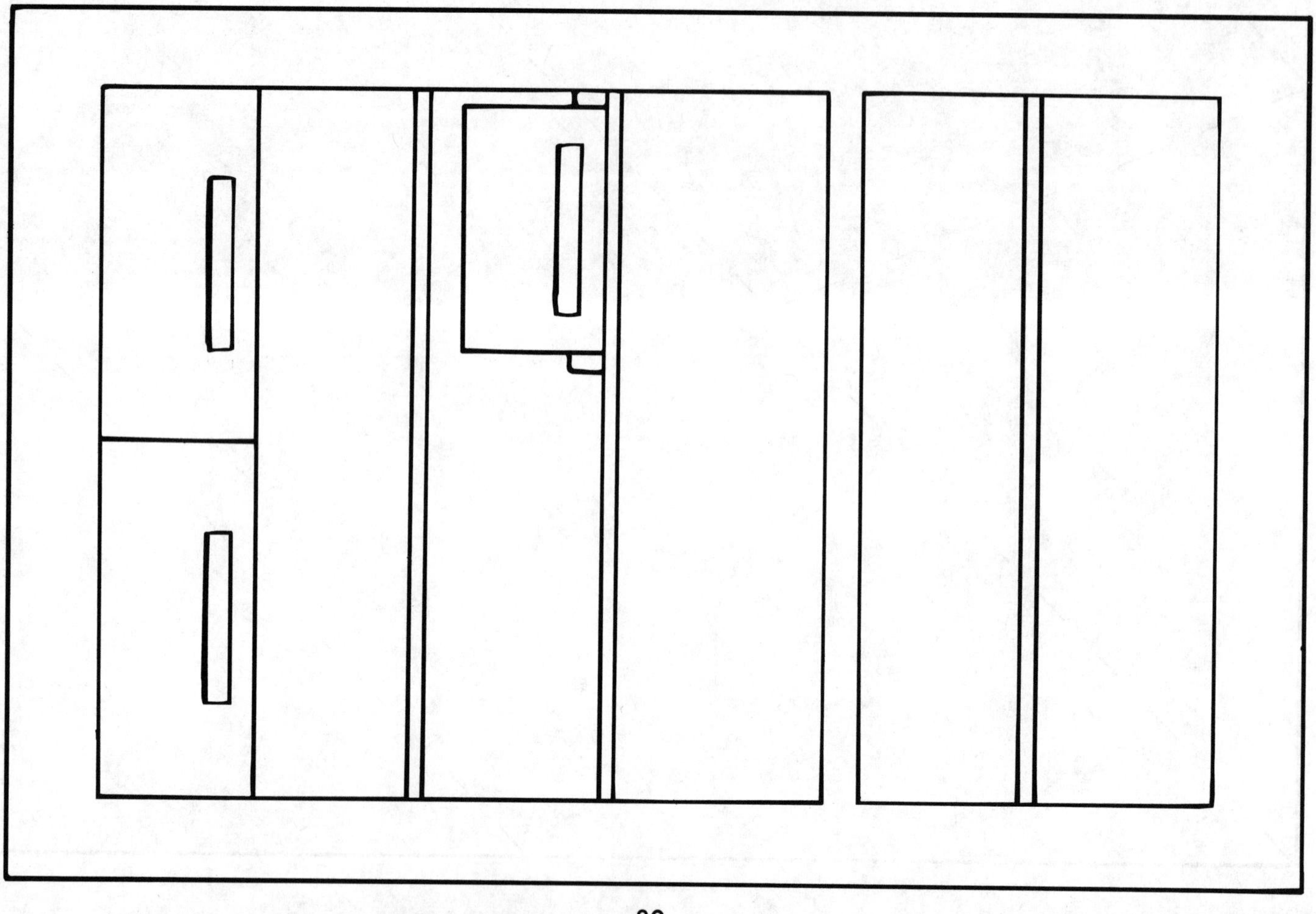

God cares for me

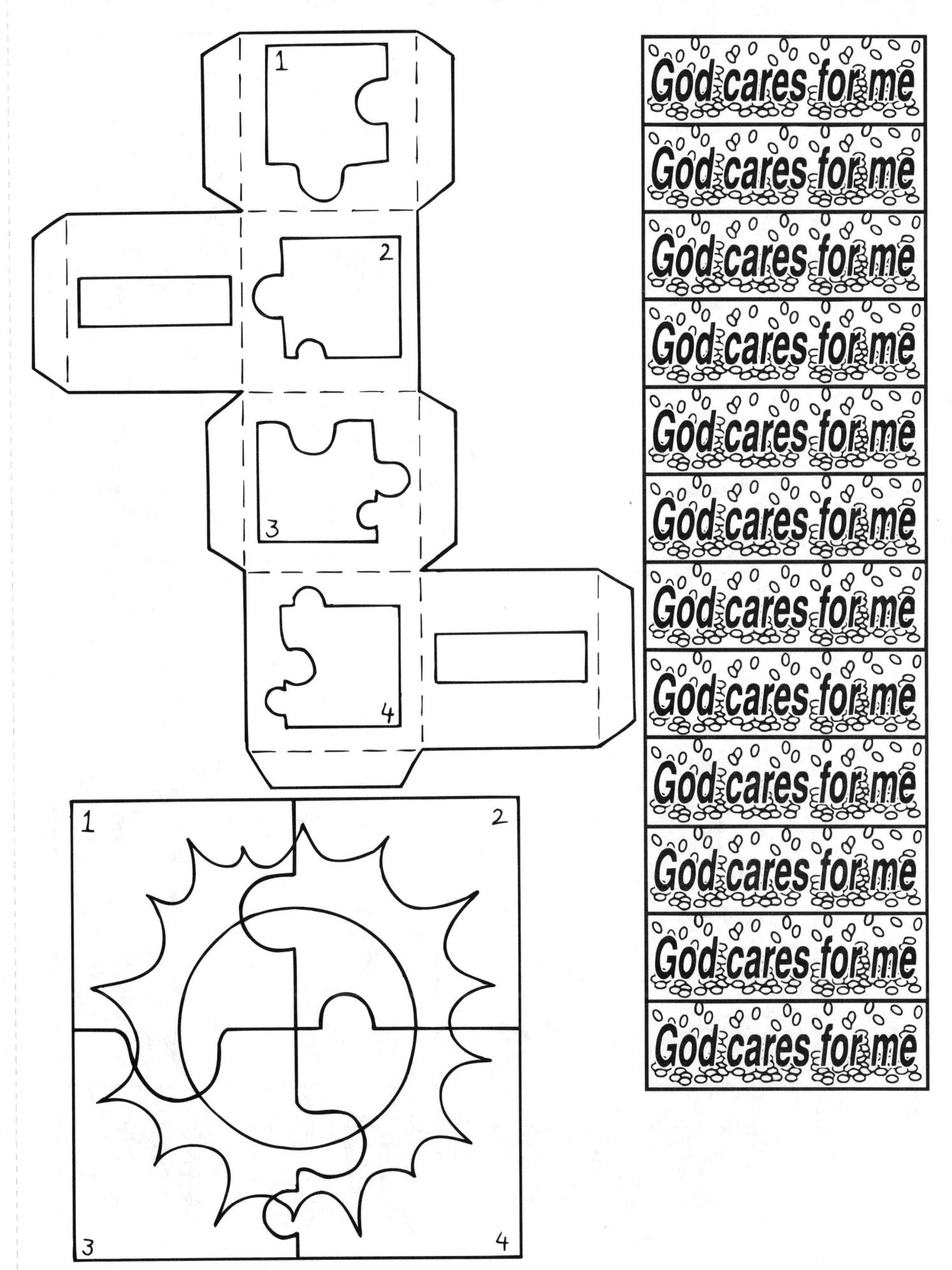

God cares for me

God cares for me

God cares for me

God cares for me

God cares for me

God cares for me

God cares for me

God cares for me

God cares for me

God cares for me

God cares for me

82

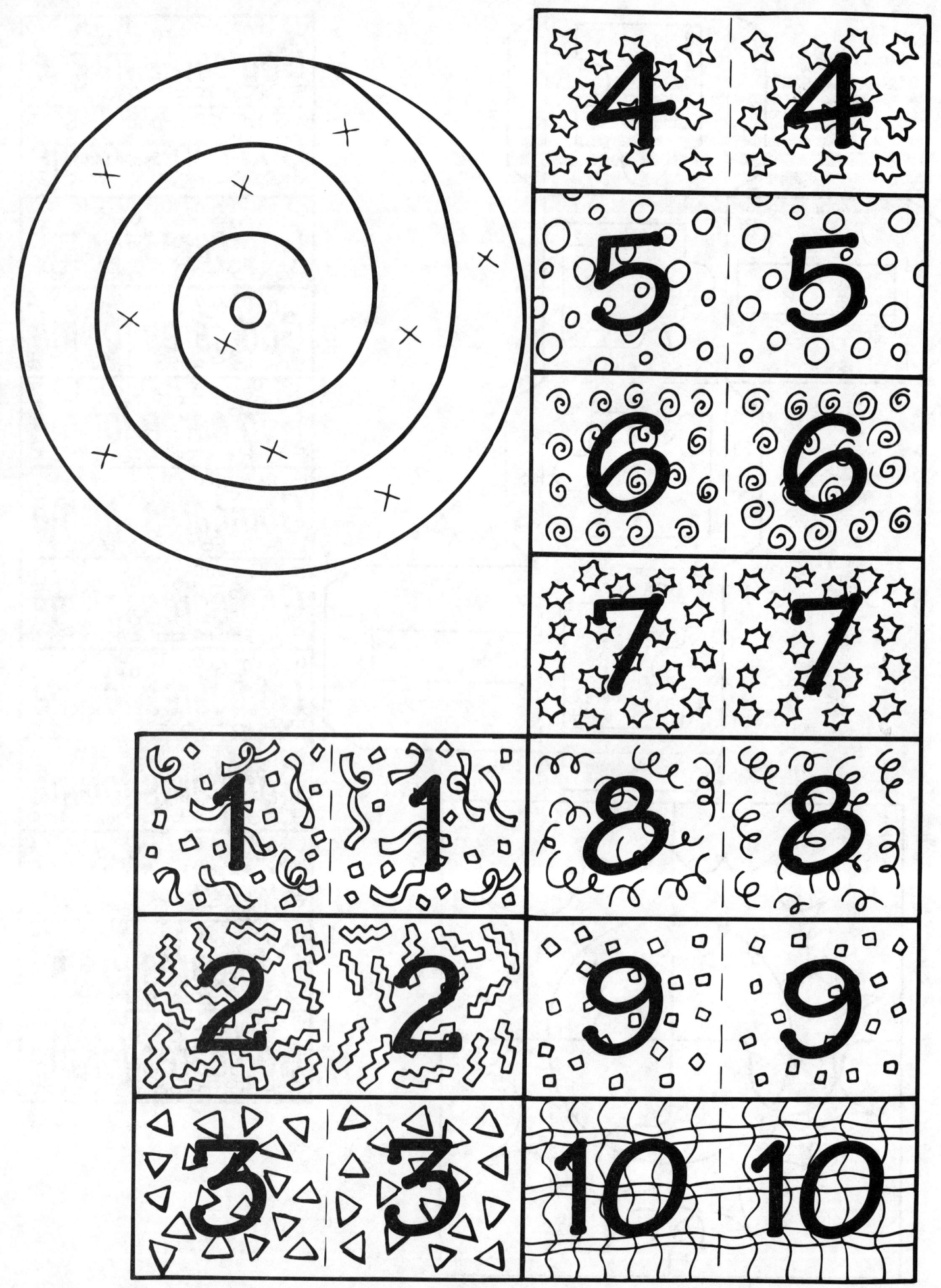

Unit 4
Lessons 14-18

Celebrate Jesus' Birth

◆◆◆◆◆

By the end of this unit, the children and leaders will . . .
Know Name five ways they know that Jesus was a special baby.
Feel Feel eager to show that Christmas is Jesus' birthday.
Do Celebrate the birth of Jesus.

Unit Bible Words for Memory
"Do not be afraid. I bring you good news. A Savior has been born to you; he is Christ the Lord" (Luke 2:10, 11, NIV).

◆◆◆◆◆

Unit Lessons

Lesson 14
John's Parents Know Jesus Is Special
Luke 1:5-24, 39-45, 57-80
Children hear that an angel told Zechariah about the birth of Jesus.

Lesson 15
Mary Sings Because Jesus Is Special
Luke 1:26-56
Children learn that an angel appeared to Mary to tell her about Jesus' birth, and she sang a song of praise to God.

Lesson 16
Shepherds Tell People Jesus Is Special
Luke 2:1-20
Children find out that angels told shepherds about Jesus' birth. When the shepherds found Jesus as the angels had said, they told everyone they met about the special baby.

Lesson 17
Simeon and Anna Thank God Because Jesus Is Special
Luke 2:22-38
Children discover that Simeon and Anna had waited for years to see the baby Jesus. They praised God for Jesus when they saw Him in the temple.

Lesson 18
Wise Men Give Gifts Because Jesus Is Special
Matthew 2:1-15
Children learn that wise men followed a star on a long journey from the East to bring gifts to the baby King, Jesus.

◆◆◆◆◆

Why Teach This Unit to Four-Year-Olds—Six-Year-Olds?

The story of Jesus' birth may already be familiar to your children, but through the example of the Bible people, they can discover new ways to celebrate Jesus' birth.

◆◆◆◆◆

Time Line

The stories for this unit are pictured on the time line, page 315.

Provide the time-line page for children who arrive early, or at the end of the Bible story.

Materials

All Lessons
- a Bible
- markers, colored pencils, crayons
- white paper, construction paper, poster board
- tape, masking tape
- Plasti-Tak
- glue
- scissors
- a stapler
- paper hole punch
- yarn or string
- cassette of Christmas songs
- cassette player

Lesson 14
- gold garland, a step stool
- old newspapers
- craft sticks
- Fruit Loops® cereal, paper or plastic bags
- a bag of solid-colored Christmas package bows

Lesson 15
- a variety of rhythm instruments (see Activity 1)
- large cups, straws, liquid dish detergent, red or green food coloring
- Christmas decorating items, such as bows, stickers, pieces of wrapping paper, old Christmas cards
- large paint brushes, red and green tempera paints, paint smocks

Lesson 16
- bathrobes and towels for shepherds' clothing, large sticks for staffs, large cardboard blocks
- a grocery sack or laundry bag, birthday streamers, party hat, birthday candle, party favor kazoo, and unbreakable nativity scene figures
- stickers about Jesus' birth (see resources below)
- empty toilet-paper tubes cut in various lengths
- pictures of stable animals (see the Game section)

Lesson 17
- many different baby dolls, including some multicultural ones
- items for taking care of the babies: clothing, blankets, towels, bottles, diapers
- strips of cloth
- magazines, catalogs, and ads that contain pictures of toys or other items that children might want for Christmas
- a package of Christmas bows
- red and green balloons
- red and white play dough (buy or make your own using the recipe in the Craft section)
- paper clips
- wax paper
- gold garland and strips of cloth

Lesson 18
- glitter and aluminum foil
- donated clothing and toys for a needy family
- Christmas wrapping paper, ribbons and bows
- a doll wrapped in a blanket
- various textured materials (corrugated cardboard, burlap, felt, sandpaper, needlepoint, plastic)
- a yardstick
- craft sticks and letter-size envelopes

The Beginner's Bible™ Resources

Jesus' Birth Stickers, Standard Publishing, #22-01034, call 1-800-543-1353

Christmas Carols Play-a-Sound Book, Standard Publishing, #24-03867, call 1-800-543-1353

Christmas Story Play-a-Sound Book, Standard Publishing, #24-03868, call 1-800-543-1353

Jesus Is Born Inlay Puzzle, Standard Publishing, #28-02704, call 1-800-543-1353

The Beginner's Bible™ New Testament GeoSafari Bible Pack, Standard Publishing, #14-24002, call 1-800-543-1353

The Story of Nativity, Sony Wonder Video Series, call 1-800-733-3000

The Nativity Rubber Stamp Kit, Inkadinkado, call 1-617-938-6100

The Birth of Jesus, Brighter Child Interactive CD Roms, call 1-614-818-7030

Unit 4
Lesson 14

John's Parents Know Jesus Is Special
(Luke 1:5-24, 39-45, 57-80)

Zechariah and Elizabeth had given up hope of having a child. It was a miracle when an angel spoke to Zechariah and God sent the elderly couple a son. This son, John the Baptist, grew up to tell the world of Jesus' coming.

Bible Words

"Do not be afraid. I bring you good news. A Savior has been born to you; he is Christ the Lord" (Luke 2:10, 11).

Goals

Name two people who told others Jesus was special.
Feel eager to show that Christmas is Jesus' birthday.
Celebrate the birth of Jesus by telling.

◆◆◆◆

Activity 1—Little Angels

You will need gold garland, scissors, tape, and a step stool. Before the session, cut pieces of gold garland and tape the ends of each together to make a halo the size of an average child's head.

In our story today and in other stories we will hear later, there are lots of angels. Do you know what an angel is? An angel is a messenger from God. He tells people news that God wants them to hear. Let's pretend to be angels telling good news from God.

Give each child a "halo" to wear. Have children sit in a circle. Put a step stool in the center. One child at a time can stand on

---

Do You Know the Good News?
(Tune: "Mary Had a Little Lamb")

Do you know the good news?
good news? good news?
Do you know the good news?
Jesus Christ is born.

Baby Jesus Christ
(Tune: "O My Darlin' Clementine")

I will tell, I will tell,
I will tell the good news.
Baby Jesus Christ was born.
I will tell the good news.

Leaders' Evaluation

	Great!	OK!	More!	Oops!	Suggestions
Activity 1					
Activity 2					
Bible Time					
Application					
Bible Memory					
Craft					
Snack					
Game					
Wrap-up					

the step stool. Lead the class in singing, "Do You Know the Good News?" to the tune "Mary Had a Little Lamb" from page 8 of this session. At the end of the song, the "angel" in the middle can answer loudly, "Jesus Christ is born!"

◆◆◆◆◆

ACTIVITY 2—Christmas Cards

You will need photocopies of page 105, old newspapers, red and green construction paper, scissors, washable markers, and glue. Before the session, fold pieces of construction paper in half to make cards.

Give each child a photocopy of reproducible page 105 and a folded construction-paper card. Children should cut their photocopies in half and glue the "EXTRA! EXTRA!" page to the front of the construction-paper card. Let children cut out pieces of newsprint to glue to the front of their cards. Have children color the picture of Jesus in the manger from the bottom half of the reproducible page, and glue it inside the card. Children can finish decorating their cards as time permits.

There is a lot of news in the newspaper. But we know the very best news. We have Christmas because baby Jesus was born! Let's tell people the good news by making them a card. Do you know somebody who needs to hear the good news? You can give them this card about the good news of Jesus' birth.

BIBLE TIME—Good News

You will need copies of the Bible figures from pages 106-108 on heavy paper, scissors, markers, craft sticks, and tape. Before the session, color and cut out the Bible figures from pages 106-108. Attach the figures to craft sticks to make stick puppets. You will use some of the figures during each session of this unit. For today's story, you will need the stick puppets of Zechariah, Elizabeth, and the angel.

angel used during the Bible Time, and the step stool used during Activity 1.

Today we have learned that Jesus was born on Christmas. He was a very special baby. While we clean up today, let's say those words.

As children clean up, encourage them to say "Jesus is special!" each time they pick up a toy or push in a chair.

When cleanup is finished, gather children and show them the figures of Zechariah, Elizabeth, and the angel. Review the story and Bible verse. **An angel told Zechariah good news about Jesus. Whom will you tell the good news this week? What will you tell that person?** Ask children to name people they can tell and what good news they will tell that person. If they need suggestions, remind them of the good news they told during the game.

When you decorate your tree or make special cookies, you are celebrating Jesus' birth. When you tell other people the good news about Jesus, you are celebrating Jesus' birth. Sing the first verse of "Baby Jesus Christ" from page 8 of this session, inserting the name of the person they will tell. "I will tell, I will tell, I will tell (my mom); baby Jesus Christ was born. I will tell (my mom)." Children can take turns standing on the step stool used during Activity 1 and the Bible Time as you sing about the person they will tell. At the end of the song, they can say the good news that they will tell that person.

◆◆◆◆◆

WRAP-UP—E-special-ly Clean

You will need the figures of Zechariah, Elizabeth, and the

Snack—Christmas Wreath Bagels

You will need bagels, a soft tub of cream cheese, green food coloring, maraschino cherries, and plastic knives. Before class, mix a few drops of green food coloring in a tub of soft cream cheese. Carefully drain and cut up a number of maraschino cherries. Cut bagels (either large or mini-sized) in half if they are not pre-cut.

Why do we decorate our houses at Christmas? It is Jesus' birthday. Jesus is special so we hang decorations for His birthday. One of the decorations that we sometimes put up is a Christmas wreath. **How many of you put up Christmas wreaths at your house? What do they look like?** Allow children to share. **We will make a Christmas wreath for our snack. But we won't hang our wreaths to celebrate Jesus' birthday. Instead, we'll eat them for our snack. We can thank God for the good news about Jesus' birth as we eat.**

Let children spread the cream cheese on their bagels, then decorate the "Christmas wreaths" with red maraschino cherries to look like berries. Say a prayer, then let the children enjoy their snacks.

Game—Celebrate Jesus!

You will need a bag of solid-colored Christmas package bows. Have children put their chairs in a circle facing one another.

Let each child choose a bow to put on. When you call out a color, the children with that color of bow should run to the middle, shake hands and tell the good news ("Jesus is special!") to each other, then run back to a chair. **What other good news can we tell about Jesus?** Have children offer suggestions, and play the game several more times, choosing different good news to tell about Jesus each time you play. (An angel told about Jesus. Christmas is Jesus' birthday. Jesus is God's Son.) To vary the game, you may call more than one color at a time or have children switch bows.

Whose birthday do we celebrate at Christmas? We can celebrate Jesus' birthday by telling people the good news. Jesus is special, and Christmas is His birthday.

Unit 4

Let children wear their halos from Activity 1 during the story. The teacher can wear one too. Put the step stool used for the first activity and a chalkboard nearby.

We learned today that angels tell news from God. Let's see if you angels remember what the good news is. Sing, "Do You Know the Good News?" and wait for the children's response. **Good! Now listen and tell me what news the angel brings in this story.**

Zechariah and Elizabeth were sad. Let's all make sad faces to show how Zechariah and Elizabeth may have felt. Encourage children to do so. **They had been married for many, many years. Now they were old, but they still did not have any children.**

Zechariah was a priest. He worked every day in the temple-church. One special day it was Zechariah's turn to go inside the temple alone to pray to God. All the people waited outside the temple for Zechariah to come out. They waited and waited (tap your foot, shrug your shoulders), **but Zechariah did not come. Do you know why? Because Zechariah had a big surprise! When he was in the temple, an angel came to him with good news! The angel said** (stand up on the step stool and give the good news), **"Zechariah, God sent me to tell you that your wife is going to have a baby. You will name him John. He will grow up and tell people about Jesus."**

Zechariah could not believe what the angel told him. The angel said (stand on the stool again), **"Since you do not believe, you will not be able to talk until the baby is born."**

When Zechariah came out of the temple-church, the people wondered what had happened. But Zechariah could not tell them, because when he tried to talk it came out like this. Imitate by mouthing words and gesturing.

Elizabeth had a baby, just like the angel said. When it was time to name the baby, Zechariah couldn't talk. So they brought him a tablet to write on. Zechariah wrote, "His name is John." Write the words on the chalkboard as you say them. **As soon as he wrote the words, Zechariah's mouth started working again. He could talk!**

Lesson 14

Zechariah and Elizabeth knew that their son John was important, because he would tell people about Jesus. They sang songs to tell people that Jesus is special.

Ask children if they heard what the good news was that the angel gave Zechariah.

◆◆◆◆

APPLICATION—Whose Birthday?

You will need copies of the eight "Celebrate His Birthday!" picture cards from pages 109 and 110, scissors, markers, and tape or Plasti-Tak. Before the session, color the pictures and cut them out.

Hang pictures facedown on a wall or board. Have one child at a time come up and choose a picture. All the children can help decide if the picture shows something we should do to celebrate Jesus' birthday. The children can divide the pictures into two stacks: one stack that shows ways to celebrate Jesus' birthday; another stack that shows whose birthday it is. What can we do to show people why we have Christmas? Whom can you tell that Christmas is Jesus' birthday?

All birthdays are special. But the day Jesus was born is the most special. Most people like to have Christmas, but sometimes they forget whose birthday it is. What can we do to show people why we have Christmas? Whom can you tell that Christmas is Jesus' birthday?

Lead children in singing "Baby Jesus Christ" (Tune: "O My Darlin' Clementine") from page 8 of this session.

◆◆◆◆

BIBLE MEMORY—Share the News

You will need two pieces of poster board, scissors, markers, glue, and a Bible with the Bible verse marked. Before the session, write the Bible words in large letters on one piece of poster board. Cut the poster board into several pieces to make a puzzle. Have children work to put the puzzle together. Children can glue the Bible-verse puzzle to the other piece of poster board

and decorate it with markers. Choose a prominent place to hang the Bible-verse poster throughout this unit.

Open the Bible and read the Bible verse to the children. Say the verse together several times. Say it in a whispered voice, then shout it out loud. Children will like to point to the words and "read" the verse by themselves.

An angel said the words of our memory verse to some shepherds when Jesus was born. *Savior, Christ,* **and** *Lord* **are all names for Jesus. Do you think the angel said the words in a whisper or a shout?**

◆◆◆◆

ACTIVITY TIME

Do as many activities as time permits.

◆◆◆◆

Craft—Tree Chains

You will need long pieces of yarn or string, tape, Fruit Loops® or a similar cereal, bowls, and paper or plastic bags. Before the session, cut long strings or pieces of yarn for each child. Tape one end of each piece for stringing. Knot the other end.

Do you decorate your house at Christmastime? What do you do? Decorate a tree, hang lights and wreaths, set up a nativity scene. **We decorate our houses at Christmas to celebrate Jesus' birthday. Let's make something to hang up in our houses.**

Give each child a length of yarn or string. Put the cereal in bowls where children can reach. Let children string cereal on the yarn. Children may wish to make a sequence of colors (red, green, red, green). When children are finished, knot the end and put the chain in a paper lunch sack or large freezer bag with the child's name on it. If you have a tree in the classroom, show the children how to hang a chain.

You can hang this pretty chain on your Christmas tree or someplace else in your house. It will remind you that Christmas is Jesus' birthday.

Unit 4
Lesson 15

Mary Sings Because Jesus Is Special
(Luke 1:26-56)

God sent an angel to tell Mary that she would be the mother of Jesus, and that He would be the Son of God. Mary was undoubtedly somewhat scared and unsure of her circumstances, but she chose to trust God concerning this special baby that would be born to her. Mary sang a song of praise to God.

Bible Words

"Do not be afraid. I have good news. A Savior has been born to you; he is Christ the Lord" (Luke 2:10, 11).

Goals

Name someone who sang because Jesus was special.
Feel eager to show that Christmas is Jesus' birthday.
Celebrate the birth of Jesus by singing.

◆◆◆◆

Activity 1—Happy Songs

You will need a variety of rhythm instruments: tambourines, drums, cymbals, rhythm sticks/blocks, xylophones, bells. They can be toy instruments or ones that you make yourself, such as the following. Pots and pans with wooden spoons or empty oatmeal boxes with pencils can make drums. Wooden blocks can be tapped together or covered with sandpaper and swished together for an interesting sound. Paper plates stapled together with beans or pasta in the middle can be shaken as tambourines. Use empty toilet paper tubes to make kazoos by covering one end with wax paper and holding it in place with a rubber band.

Do You Know the Good News?
(Tune: "Mary Had a Little Lamb")

Do you know the good news,
good news, good news?
Do you know the good news?
Jesus Christ is born.

Christmas is His birthday,
birthday, birthday.
Christmas is His birthday.
Jesus Christ is born.

His mother Mary sang a song,
sang a song, sang a song.
His mother Mary sang a song.
Jesus Christ is born.

I will tell the good news,
good news, good news.
I will tell the good news.
Jesus Christ is born.

Baby Jesus Christ
(Tune: "O My Darlin' Clementine")

I will tell, I will tell,
I will tell the good news.
Baby Jesus Christ was born.
I will tell the good news.

I will sing, I will sing,
I will sing the good news.
Baby Jesus Christ was born.
I will sing the good news.

Let children choose the instrument they would like to play. They can trade between songs for more variety. Show children how to play their instruments as they sing the songs to God. Lead children in singing "Baby Jesus Christ" and "Do You Know the Good News?" from page 8 of this session. Children may also choose Christmas songs that they know.

Mary, the mother of Jesus, sang a song to show that Jesus is special. We can show that Jesus is special by playing our instruments and singing songs to Him.

◆◆◆◆

ACTIVITY 2—Bubbling Over with Joy

You will need large cups, straws, liquid dish detergent, red or green food coloring, and paper towels for cleanup.

Give each child a large cup and a straw. Have the children practice blowing out through their straws. Pour a small amount of water in each child's cup. Let them blow bubbles in the water. Add a drop of liquid dish detergent to each cup of water, and let them blow again. You can add a tiny drop of red or green food coloring to make it more festive. The bubbles will overflow, and there will be a lot of smiles and laughter.

I can tell that you are happy, because you are laughing and smiling. What other things make you happy? Prompt the children's thinking if needed: playing with Dad, visiting grandma, and so on. **Mary was happy when she heard that she would have baby Jesus. She may have laughed and smiled too. But the Bible tells us one thing Mary did when she was happy. Mary sang a song. Why are we happy at Christmas? Jesus was born. We can sing happy songs, just like Mary did.**

◆◆◆◆

BIBLE TIME—A Happy Song

You will need the stick puppets of Mary and the angel made last week from pages 106-108.

WRAP-UP—Happy Helpers

Lead children in singing "Baby Jesus Christ" while they clean up. Ask children to show the group the paintings they made earlier and explain their Christmas pictures. Mary showed Jesus is special when she sang her song. **We show Jesus is special when we sing and when we paint.** Close with prayer thanking God for His special Son, Jesus.

Until parents come, play another game with the pictures from pages 109 and 110. Ask the children to stand in a circle. Place all the pictures in the middle of the circle. Call out pictures to find and have children see how quickly they can find that picture. Suggestions follow:

- Everyone who is wearing something blue find a blue picture.
- If you have a hair bow, find a picture of someone singing about Jesus' birth.
- If you are wearing boots, find a picture of someone eating Christmas cookies.
- If you love Jesus, find a picture of someone celebrating Jesus' birth.

Leaders' Evaluation

	Great!	OK!	More!	Oops!	Suggestions
Activity 1					
Activity 2					
Bible Time					
Application					
Bible Memory					
Craft					
Snack					
Game					
Wrap-up					

What do you do when you are happy? Smile, laugh, wiggle, jump, sing. **Show me what you do when you are happy.** Let children take turns showing you something they do when they are happy. **What are some things that you told me earlier make you happy?** Review ideas the children mentioned in Activity 2.

Last week we talked about Zechariah and Elizabeth. They were happy because they had some good news. **Do you remember what their good news was?** They had a baby, John. They knew Jesus was special.

Our story today is about a girl who was happy. Her name was Mary. Hold up the stick puppet of Mary. Mary loved God very much. One day Mary had a surprise! An angel came to her and started talking to her. Hold up the stick puppet of the angel. At first, Mary was scared. **Show me how you would look if you were scared.** Bend down, cover head or eyes with hands, shake. The angel said, "Don't be afraid, Mary. God is pleased with you. You are going to have a special baby. His name will be Jesus. He will be the Son of God."

Mary was very surprised! **Show me how you would look if you were surprised.** Jump up and down. Clap your hands. She said to the angel, "I am happy to do what God says."

After the angel left, Mary sang a song. She sang, "I am happy because God is good." She knew that her baby would be very special to all of us.

◆◆◆◆◆

APPLICATION—Christmas Caroling

You will need a poster board or large sheet of mural paper; markers; scissors; glue or tape; and Christmas decorating items, such as bows, stickers, pieces of wrapping paper, old Christmas cards, and so on. Before the session, letter "Jesus is born!" in very large, open block letters on the poster board or paper. Arrange to visit one or two other classrooms to carol.

At Christmas, sometimes people get together and sing for each other. They even go to other houses and sing. This singing is called "Christmas caroling." Mary sang about Jesus'

Lesson 15

3

Thank You, God, for sending Jesus, a special baby. Thank You for smiles and laughter. Thank You that we can sing happy songs like Mary. Talk about the story as the children eat their snacks.

Game—Treasure Hunt

You will need several copies of the eight "Celebrate His Birthday" cards from pages 109 and 110. Make each copy of the cards on a different color of paper. Or use a crayon or marker to make each set of pictures a different color. Before class or while children are eating their snacks, hide the pictures around the room.

Divide children into teams and assign each team one color set of cards to find. When each group has found all eight of their cards, play a guessing game where you call out a description of a card and have each group see how quickly they can find that card.

1. What did Mary do to celebrate Jesus' birth? I'm looking for a picture of children celebrating Jesus' birth like Mary. (Children singing Christmas carols.)

2. Last week you made a card to give someone that told about Jesus' birth. I'm looking for a picture of a girl giving a card about Jesus' birth.

3. I'm looking for a picture of someone who is eating too many Christmas cookies.

4. I'm looking for a picture of a girl who is telling God "thank-You" for Jesus' birth. (Girl praying.)

5. I'm looking for a picture of a boy taking all the presents from under the Christmas tree.

6. I'm looking for a picture of a girl giving someone a gift.

7. I'm looking for a picture of a girl who is NOT saying "thank-you" for a gift.

8. I'm looking for a picture of someone who is putting up a nativity scene to celebrate Jesus' birthday.

There are lots of ways to celebrate Jesus' birthday. Which of these pictures show ways we can celebrate? How are you going to celebrate Christmas?

Unit 4

6

birthday. We can celebrate Jesus' birthday by singing too. We are going to go Christmas caroling. But first we will make a banner to take with us to tell the good news about the birth of Jesus, God's Son.

Allow children to use markers to color the banner. They can glue and tape the Christmas decorations in and around the letters "Jesus is born." When the children have completed the banner, practice singing "Baby Jesus Christ" from page 8 of this session and other familiar Christmas songs. Then let two or three volunteers carry the banner at the front of your group as you march as a group to the classrooms you have arranged beforehand to visit.

Explain to the other classes that you are here to celebrate Jesus' birthday by singing or "caroling." Encourage children to sing out.

BIBLE MEMORY—Action Words

You will need the Bible-verse poster made last week.

See if any children can remember what the Bible words are. Refer the children to the Bible-verse poster made last week. Review the verse by saying it several times with the children. **Sometimes it helps us to remember our Bible words if we put actions with them. What kinds of actions could we use to help us remember the words of our Bible verse?**

Have children suggest actions for the Bible verse. Here are some ideas:

Start the verse sitting down.
"Do not (*shake head back and forth*) be afraid (*bow head and cover eyes*). I have good news. (*Jump up and smile.*) A Savior has been born to you (*stretch arms out to everyone*). He is Christ (*pretend to hold a baby*), the Lord (*point up to Heaven*)."

ACTIVITY TIME

Do as many activities as time permits.

Craft—Painting to Music

You will need large pieces of heavy paper, large paintbrushes, liquid dish detergent, red and green tempera paints, paint smocks, a cassette of familiar Christmas songs, and a cassette player.

Give children paper and paintbrushes. Mix the liquid dish detergent with red and green tempera paints. Make sure every child has a paint smock on.

We can celebrate Jesus' birthday with music and singing. Let's listen to the Christmas songs and paint a Christmas picture. Play the cassette of Christmas songs. Children can sing along if they like. Show the children how to paint in time to the music. **This music is happy music. What happy things about Jesus' birth and Christmas does this music help you remember? What shapes make you think of happy things? What colors make you think of happy things? You can draw those colors and shapes on your paper to make a happy picture.**

Option: Use markers or crayons instead of paints.

Snack—Show Me Your Smile

You will need rice cakes, peanut butter in small bowls, popsicle sticks or plastic knives, and various items to make faces (raisins, mini-marshmallows, M&M®'s, various shapes of cereal).

Give each child a rice cake and a popsicle stick or plastic knife. Set the peanut butter and items to make faces on the table. **Let's make a happy face for our snack today. Why was Mary happy?** She was going to have the baby Jesus. **What did Mary do because she was happy?** She sang a song to God.

Show children how to spread the peanut butter on the rice cakes. Then allow them to make faces on the cakes by arranging the raisins and marshmallows.

Unit 4
Lesson 16

Shepherds Tell People Jesus Is Special
(Luke 2:1-20)

When Jesus was born in Bethlehem, Mary laid Him in a manger because all the inns were full. Angels appeared to shepherds in a field nearby and told them about the special baby. After the shepherds saw the baby, they wanted to tell the good news to everyone they met.

Bible Words

"Do not be afraid. I bring you good news. A Savior has been born to you; he is Christ the Lord" (Luke 2:10, 11).

Goals

Name people who told others Jesus was special.
Feel eager to show that Christmas is Jesus' birthday.
Celebrate the birth of Jesus by telling.

◆◆◆◆

ACTIVITY 1—Shepherds and Sheep

You will need bathrobes and towels for shepherds' clothing, large sticks for staffs, and large cardboard blocks.
Let's pretend that we are shepherds taking care of our sheep. Let's build a stable with a manger inside. A stable is a barn. A manger is a big feeding box. Animals eat out of the box. Make sure the children understand what the words *stable, manger,* and *shepherd* mean.

Let children build a stable and a manger with large cardboard blocks. Some children can be shepherds and some can be sheep. The shepherds can lead the sheep around the room to find food

---

Do You Know the Good News?
(Tune: "Mary Had a Little Lamb")

Do you know the good news,
good news, good news?
Do you know the good news?
Jesus Christ is born.

Christmas is His birthday,
birthday, birthday.
Christmas is His birthday.
Jesus Christ is born.

His mother Mary sang a song,
sang a song, sang a song.
His mother Mary sang a song.
Jesus Christ is born.

I will tell the good news,
good news, good news.
I will tell the good news.
Jesus Christ is born.

Baby Jesus Christ
(Tune: "O My Darlin' Clementine")

I will tell, I will tell,
I will tell the good news.
Baby Jesus Christ was born.
I will tell the good news.

I will sing, I will sing,
I will sing the good news.
Baby Jesus Christ was born.
I will sing the good news.

and water, make sure no sheep get lost, and help the sheep find a safe spot to sleep.

Option: Bring stuffed animals that will be the children's "sheep." Use a cane to show the children how the shepherd used the curved end of his staff to keep the sheep from wandering away and to rescue sheep.

ACTIVITY 2—Mystery Bag

Before the session, place the following items in a grocery sack or laundry bag: birthday streamers, party hat, birthday candle, party favor kazoo, and unbreakable nativity scene figures (Mary, Joseph, animals, manger, shepherd, angel). If you do not have a nativity set, make stand-up figures of Mary, Joseph, baby Jesus, shepherds, and the angel from the figures on pages 106-108. See the Craft activity in this lesson for instructions on making the figures.

We have Christmas to celebrate Jesus' birthday. When you draw something out of the Mystery Bag, hold it up and tell us if it was part of Jesus' birthday or not.

Allow children to take turns drawing items out of the bag. The group can decide together if the item was part of Jesus' birthday.

Jesus is special. His birthday is different from any other birthday.

◆ ◆ ◆ ◆

BIBLE TIME—The Best News of All

Use the unbreakable (wood or plastic) nativity scene from the last activity to tell the Bible story. Set the figures on a table as you talk about each one.

I have very exciting and happy news to tell you! Do you know what it is? What special day is coming soon? Christmas. Do you know why we have Christmas? To celebrate Jesus' birthday. Two weeks ago, we learned about a man that an

2   Unit 4

---

stable animal. The rest of the class can guess which animal the child is pretending to be. Then ask the children to stand on the circle of animal pictures, each child on one picture. Play a tape of Christmas music while the children walk from picture to picture. When the music stops, the children should stop on a picture and make the noise of the animal they are standing on.

◆ ◆ ◆ ◆

WRAP-UP—Stable Cleanup

Let's pretend that our room is a stable that needs to be cleaned up. Assign children specific tasks to do. When the room is clean, gather the children together. Sing all the verses to "Do You Know the Good News?" and "Baby Jesus Christ" from page 8 of this lesson.

Play a game until parents come using the nativity scene from the Bible Time. Set all the figures out where the children can see them. Have children close or cover their eyes. Take one figure away and hide it behind your back or under the table. **Can the children tell you what is missing?**

94

Leaders' Evaluation

	Great!	OK!	More!	Oops!	Suggestions
Activity 1					
Activity 2					
Bible Time					
Application					
Bible Memory					
Craft					
Snack					
Game					
Wrap-up					

angel visited in the temple-church. Who was the man? Zechariah. What good news did the angel tell Zechariah? He would have a son, John, who would tell people about Jesus, God's Son. Last week, we learned about a woman that an angel visited. Who was the woman? Mary. Set out the figure of Mary. What good news did the angel tell Mary. She would have a special baby, God's Son. The baby's name would be Jesus. Mary was so happy that she sang a song. She knew that this baby was going to be a very special baby, because He was the Son of God.

When it was time for Mary to have her baby, she and her husband, Joseph, had to take a long trip to a town called Bethlehem. Add the figure of Joseph. When they got there, do you know where they stayed? Was it in a hotel? Was it in a hospital? No, they had to stay in a stable because there wasn't any other room. Do you remember what a stable is? Set up the nativity scene stable and animals. A stable was a very cold, dark, dirty place. There were probably spider webs in the corner and dirt on the floor. The stable probably didn't smell very good. But the stable protected Mary and Joseph from the wind and kept them dry.

While they were in the stable, the time came for Mary's baby to be born. She named Him Jesus. She wrapped Him up in strips of cloth. Do you know where she laid Him? Was it in a crib? Was it in a bed? No, she laid him in a manger full of hay. Do you remember what a manger is? Set up the manger with the baby. The feeding box made a soft bed for the new baby.

That night there were shepherds in the field near Bethlehem watching their sheep. The shepherds didn't even have a stable to sleep in. They were sleeping outside under the night sky. They had to watch their sheep all night to be sure none of them got lost or wandered away. Set out shepherds and sheep. It was probably very quiet, and dark, and cold out in the field. But suddenly something made the shepherds come wide awake. The field was no longer dark. It was no longer quiet. There was an angel in the sky. Hold up angel. The shepherds

Lesson 16

---

tubes cut in various lengths. If you wish to save time, cut out the figures on the pages before class.

Children can color and cut out the figures. Then they can tape the tubes to the backs of the figures to make them stand up. Write the child's name on each figure to avoid confusion later. **Now you have a nativity scene that you can use to tell people about Jesus' birthday. Who told the good news in our story today? Who knew that Jesus was special?**

Let children practice using their nativity scenes to tell the Bible story.

Snack—Shepherd Staff Kabobs

Provide large wooden kabob sticks and several types of fruit (grapes, strawberries, pineapple chunks, mandarin oranges) for this snack. Let children stick fruit on their kabobs. Older children might want to sequence their fruit (e.g., grape, strawberry, pineapple, grape, strawberry, pineapple). **Shepherds came to see the baby Jesus. Shepherds often carried "staffs," or large wooden sticks with them. What did they use their staffs for?** Guiding the sheep, helping them walk over rough places.

Say a prayer, then allow children to eat their snacks.

Game—Stable Animal Charades

You will need a cassette of Christmas songs and a cassette player, construction paper, masking tape, and pictures of animals that would have been in a stable: cows, donkeys, horses, chickens, sheep, pigeons, rooster. Before the session, tape pictures of animals that would have been in a stable to pieces of construction paper. Make enough pictures for every child in your class. You should have several pictures for each animal. Tape the pictures in a circle on the floor.

Today babies are usually born in a hospital. Where was baby Jesus born? Stable. **A stable is a barn where animals stay. What kinds of animals might have been in the stable? Let's take turns pretending to be different animals in the stable.**

Let children come up one or two at a time and pretend to be a

Unit 4

were scared! They covered their eyes and fell down on their faces because they were so scared. But the angel said, "Do not be afraid. I bring you good news. A Savior has been born to you; He is Christ the Lord." The angel told the shepherds to look for this Savior, baby Jesus, wrapped up in strips of cloth and lying in a manger. Suddenly the sky grew even brighter. Many angels filled the sky, singing songs about Jesus!

The shepherds didn't wait until the next day. They ran into Bethlehem right then, in the middle of the night. They may have searched in several feeding boxes and stables before they found little baby Jesus wrapped in strips of cloth just like the angel had told them. Take shepherds and sheep to the stable. They were so happy to see the special baby Jesus.

When the shepherds left the stable, where do you think they went? Allow children to guess. They didn't go right back out to their quiet field. No, the shepherds went and told every person they saw about what the angel had said. They told everyone about the special baby Jesus.

◆◆◆◆

APPLICATION—What's Missing?

You will need a pen, a basket, and stickers about Jesus' birth (see unit page 84 for suggestions). Before the session, cut the stickers apart.

Jesus' birthday was different from most birthdays. He was a very special baby. **Who told people that He was special?** Shepherds. **Whom can we tell?** Family members, friends, neighbors. As children name people to tell, write the names on the backs of the stickers you cut apart before class and place the stickers in the basket. **What are some things we can tell people about Jesus?** Accept children's answers. Mary saw an angel; Zechariah told the good news; shepherds came to see Him; angels sang about Him; Jesus is the Son of God.

Let children take turns drawing a sticker from the basket. Sing "Baby Jesus Christ" from page 8 of this session, inserting that person's name in the song. After you sing the song each time,

— fold —

sing it again, stopping at the phrase "Baby Jesus Christ was born" and asking one child to name something we can tell about Jesus at Christmas.

Dear Jesus, we know that Christmas is special because it is Your birthday. Help us to tell others about Your birthday. Make sure every child gets at least one sticker. Encourage the children to take their stickers home. They can keep them to remind them to celebrate Jesus' birth or they can give to someone to remind them to tell them about Jesus' birth.

◆◆◆◆

BIBLE MEMORY—The Shepherd Walk

Read the Bible words from Luke 2:10, 11. Have the children say the words together with the motions learned last week. Start the verse sitting down. "Do not (*shake head back and forth*) be afraid (*bow head and cover eyes*). (*Jump up and smile.*) I have good news. A Savior has been born to you (*stretch arms out to everyone*). He is Christ (*pretend to hold a baby*), the Lord (*point up to Heaven*)."

Show the children how to walk in time to your clapping. Let's pretend to be the shepherds telling people about baby Jesus. **Listen to my clapping. If I clap slowly, then you walk slowly. If I clap fast, then you walk fast. When I stop, you should freeze and we will repeat the words that the angel said.** After children have become comfortable with the game, allow volunteers to take turns being the leader.

◆◆◆◆

ACTIVITY TIME

Do as many activities as time permits.

Craft—Nativity Scenes

You will need copies of the figures of Mary, Joseph, baby Jesus, the angel, and shepherds from pages 106-108 on heavy paper, scissors, crayons or markers, tape, and empty toilet-paper

Unit 4
Lesson 17

Simeon and Anna Thank God Because Jesus Is Special
(Luke 2:22-38)

After baby Jesus was born, Mary and Joseph went to present Him at the temple. Two elderly servants of God were there waiting to see the new King. Simeon and Anna thanked God for baby Jesus.

Bible Words

"Do not be afraid. I bring you good news. A Savior has been born to you; he is Christ the Lord" (Luke 2:10, 11).

Goals

Name two people who thanked God because Jesus was special.

Feel eager to show that Christmas is Jesus' birthday.

Celebrate the birth of Jesus by thanking God.

◆◆◆◆

ACTIVITY 1—Babies Are Special

Provide many different baby dolls, including some multicultural ones. You will also need items for taking care of the babies: clothing, blankets, towels, bottles, diapers, and so on. Also provide strips of cloth to show how baby Jesus was wrapped. **All babies are special. Mothers and fathers show that their babies are special by taking good care of them. Let's pretend to be moms and dads, and take care of our babies.**

Lead the children in pretending. They can wrap their babies warmly in blankets, pretend to give their babies a bath, put diapers on their babies, feed their babies bottles.

Do You Know the Good News?
(Tune: "Mary Had a Little Lamb")

Do you know the good news,
good news, good news?
Do you know the good news?
Jesus Christ is born.

Christmas is His birthday,
birthday, birthday.
Christmas is His birthday.
Jesus Christ is born.

His mother Mary sang a song,
sang a song, sang a song.
His mother Mary sang a song.
Jesus Christ is born.

I will tell the good news,
good news, good news.
I will tell the good news.
Jesus Christ is born.

Baby Jesus Christ
(Tune: "O My Darlin' Clementine")

I will tell, I will tell,
I will tell the good news.
Baby Jesus Christ was born.
I will tell the good news.

I will sing, I will sing,
I will sing the good news.
Baby Jesus Christ was born.
I will sing the good news.

Then show them how Mary took care of her baby by wrapping Him in strips of cloth. Let children try to wrap their babies like Mary wrapped baby Jesus.

Who was the most special baby ever born? Jesus. Who thought Jesus was special? Angels, shepherds, Zechariah and Elizabeth, Mary and Joseph.

◆◆◆◆

ACTIVITY 2—Christmas Wish List

You will need a large piece of butcher paper; magazines, catalogs, and ads that contain pictures of toys or other items that children might want for Christmas; glue sticks or paste; scissors; a marker. Before class, sketch a simple Christmas tree on a large piece of butcher paper. Leave ample space at the bottom for "gifts." Hang the tree on the wall of the classroom.

Have children look in the magazines to find picture of things they like, cut them out, and paste them under the tree on the wall (use glue sticks or paste, not glue, which will run down the wall). Leave the tree on the wall to use later in the lesson.

These toys you chose are fun presents, but do you know what the very best Christmas present was? God gave us baby Jesus!

◆◆◆◆

BIBLE TIME—A Very Special Baby

You will need the stick puppets of Simeon, Anna, Mary, Joseph, and baby Jesus from pages 106-108. Hold them up at the appropriate times during the story.

We have been talking about a very special baby. Do you remember Who that special baby is? Jesus. I will need your help with the Bible story today. You will have to listen carefully. When I say the word "baby," you will say "Jesus is special." Let's practice first. We are going to talk about a baby. (Jesus is special.) He is a very important baby. (Jesus is special.) Great! You are ready to listen to the story.

2 Unit 4

◆◆◆◆

WRAP-UP—Thankful Helpers

Simeon and Anna thanked God for baby Jesus. Let's thank God as we clean up the room. Thank You, God, for our toys. Thank You for our books. Thank You for our church.

As children clean up, encourage them to thank God for things that they see. Then gather for a prayer and sing all the verses to "Do You Know the Good News?" from page 8 of this session. Until parents arrive, play "Pin the Star on the Christmas Tree." Use the Christmas tree picture and Christmas bows from the Application section, or cut simple stars out of construction paper and place tape on the back of them. Use the shepherd's headband from the game as a blindfold. Give each child a star or bow and let children take turns trying to pin the star on the top of the Christmas tree. Blindfold each child and turn him in a circle several times before he takes his turn.

Leaders' Evaluation

	Great!	OK!	More!	Oops!	Suggestions
Activity 1					
Activity 2					
Bible Time					
Application					
Bible Memory					
Craft					
Snack					
Game					
Wrap-up					

Lesson 17 7

Mary had her baby (Jesus is special.) in a stable. She laid Him in a manger full of hay. She and Joseph loved the new baby. (Jesus is special.) Lots of people knew that Jesus was special!

When Jesus was only a little more than one month old, Mary and Joseph took the baby (Jesus is special.) to the temple-church. The temple-church was not in the town of Bethlehem. It was in the city of Jerusalem, nearby Bethlehem. Mary and Joseph had to take a short trip to Jerusalem. They must have been proud and happy to take little Jesus with them. Mommies like to show everyone their new babies. They like other people to tell them how special and wonderful and beautiful their babies are. But Jesus was not just a wonderful baby (Jesus is special.); He was the Son of God. God had already sent an angel to Zechariah, to Mary, and to some shepherds to show how special Jesus was. Once again, God was going to show that Jesus was His Son.

When Mary and Joseph went into the temple-church, a man named Simeon saw them. God had told Simeon that before he died, he would get to see Jesus. When Simeon saw Mary and Joseph and the baby (Jesus is special.), he was so happy. He held Jesus in his arms and praised God!

There was another person in the temple-church who wanted to see the baby. (Jesus is special.) Her name was Anna. Anna was an old woman who stayed in the temple, serving God. When she saw the baby (Jesus is special.), Anna knew that He was special. She told everyone about the important baby. (Jesus is special.) Simeon and Anna both knew that Jesus was a special baby. (Jesus is special.) We know that Jesus is special too.

◆◆◆◆◆

APPLICATION—Thanking God

You will need a package of Christmas bows.

Refer back to the Christmas gifts under the tree that the children made earlier. Talk about the gifts that they chose and why they chose them.

Lesson 17

"Happy Birthday" to Jesus and thank God for sending us a special baby.

After saying a prayer, light a candle in one cupcake and lead the children in singing "Happy Birthday" to Jesus. Then children can eat their snacks.

Game—Halos and Headbands

You will need halos made of Christmas garland and headbands made of strips of cloth. Make approximately the same number of halos and headbands. Make enough so that each child in the class can have either a halo or a headband.

Ask the children to stand in a circle. **In this game, you will be either an angel** (hold up a halo) **or a shepherd** (hold up a headband). **When I put on a halo, those of you wearing halos will say, "We bring good news!"** Have children say the words with you. **When I put on a headband, those of you wearing headbands will say, "Jesus is born!"** Have children say the words with you. Practice switching between the halo and the headband several times. **When I say "go," I want you to go to the center of the circle, put on a halo or a headband, and return to your place.** Allow children time to do so. Then put on your halo or headband, leading the appropriate children in saying the words with you. After several switches, have the children put their halos and headbands back in the center of the circle and start again. When the children become familiar with the game, let volunteers take turns being the leader.

Option: Before class, gather costumes for an angel (halo made of garland, white robe, cardboard wings) and a shepherd (bathrobe, towel, and headband for headpiece). Use your imagination to come up with items for the costumes, but they should take equal time to put on. Divide costumes into separate bags.

Divide children into two groups and show them how each costume works. When given the word to start, children will go one at a time to dress in the costume, remove it, and return to their group for the next person to go. If time permits, children may want to switch costumes.

Unit 4

When you open a gift at Christmas, what do you say? Thank you. All gifts are special and we should say "thank you" when we get them. Jesus is the best Christmas gift ever. We celebrate Christmas when we say "thank-You" to God for Jesus. **What could you say to God to thank Him at Christmas?** Encourage children to respond. Offer suggestions as needed. Thank You, God, for sending baby Jesus. Thank You, God, for sending angels to sing. Thank You, God, for telling shepherds about baby Jesus. Thank You, God, for sending Your Son.

Sing "Baby Jesus Christ" from page 8 of this session. Then ask children to pray thank-You prayers to God. For each thank-You that is said, the child should attach a Christmas bow to the tree and packages made in Activity 1.

Look at all the thank-You's we've given to God. God is so pleased and happy when we thank Him at Christmas.

Option: Use candy canes instead of Christmas bows. Put a small piece of tape on the back of each candy cane to attach it to the tree.

BIBLE MEMORY—Keep it Up!

You will need your Bible with the Bible words marked and red and green balloons. Before class, blow up enough balloons so that each child can have one, plus extras in case some of the balloons pop.

Read Luke 2:10, 11 from the Bible. Say the verse with the motions used the last few weeks. Start the verse sitting down. "Do not (*shake head back and forth*) be afraid (*bow head and cover eyes*). (*Jump up and smile*.) I have good news. A Savior has been born to you (*stretch arms out to everyone*), the Lord (*point up to Heaven*)." He is Christ (*pretend to hold a baby*), the Lord (*point up to Heaven*)."

Give children the balloons and show the children how to keep them in the air, saying one word of the verse with each hit. **An angel told these words to some shepherds. What was the good news?** Jesus is born! **Let's practice saying the Bible words while we keep our balloons in the air.**

Unit 4

4

♦♦♦♦♦

ACTIVITY TIME

Do as many activities as time permits.

Craft—Candy Canes

You will need red and white play dough (see instructions below), paper clips, and wax paper.

Mix your own play dough before class, using the following ingredients: 1 cup of flour, 1/2 cup of salt, 2 tsp. cream of tartar, 1 Tbsp. cooking oil, 1 cup water. Cook the ingredients over low heat on the stove, stirring constantly until the mixture forms a ball. Separate the dough in half. Add several drops of red food coloring to one half and knead in, along with two drops of peppermint oil and 1/2 Tbsp. of glitter. You may also add peppermint oil and glitter to the white half of the dough. Make a sample candy cane to show the children.

Let children play with the dough, then show them how to make candy canes by rolling a red and a white "snake" and twisting them together. Remember that the children's work will not be perfect. A paper clip can be pushed into the back of each candy cane to make a hanger for the ornament. Lay candy canes out on wax paper to dry.

Do you have candy canes on your Christmas tree at home? Many people knew that Jesus was special. Can you name those people? Zechariah and Elizabeth, Mary, shepherds, Simeon and Anna. **Take your candy cane home with you. It will remind you that Jesus' birthday is special.**

Snack—Birthday Cake

Before class, make enough cupcakes for each child. Provide red and green icing in small bowls, popsicle sticks or plastic knives, sprinkles, a birthday candle, and matches or a lighter.

Give each child a cupcake and let children ice their cupcakes with red or green icing and then decorate them with sprinkles. **Whose birthday do we celebrate at Christmas? Let's sing**

100

Lesson 17

5

Unit 4
Lesson 18

Wise Men Give Gifts Because Jesus Is Special
(Matthew 2:1-15)

When a new star appeared in the sky, wise men from the East followed it to see the young King. After finding the baby Jesus, they worshiped Him and gave Him gifts of gold, frankincense, and myrrh.

Bible Words

"Do not be afraid. I bring you good news. A Savior has been born to you; he is Christ the Lord" (Luke 2:10, 11).

Goals

Name people who gave gifts to Jesus because He was special.
Feel eager to show that Christmas is Jesus' birthday.
Celebrate the birth of Jesus by giving gifts.

Activity 1—Reach for the Stars

You will need white or yellow construction paper, scissors, glitter, glue, aluminum foil, and tape or Plasti-Tak. Cut various sizes of small stars and one very large star. Decorate the large star with glitter and glue or aluminum foil.

Give each child a star or several stars. Let children put tape or Plasti-Tak on the backs of the stars and see how high they can place them on the wall. First, they can see how high they can place stars by reaching with one hand on tiptoe. Then they can try jumping and placing stars on the wall. The teacher can place the "special star" high on the wall surrounded by the smaller stars the children have placed.

Do You Know the Good News?
(Tune: "Mary Had a Little Lamb")

Do you know the good news,
good news, good news?
Do you know the good news?
Jesus Christ is born.

Christmas is His birthday,
birthday, birthday.
Christmas is His birthday.
Jesus Christ is born.

His mother Mary sang a song,
sang a song, sang a song.
His mother Mary sang a song.
Jesus Christ is born.

I will tell the good news,
good news, good news.
I will tell the good news.
Jesus Christ is born.

Baby Jesus Christ
(Tune: "O My Darlin' Clementine")

I will tell, I will tell,
I will tell the good news.
Baby Jesus Christ was born.
I will tell the good news.

I will sing, I will sing,
I will sing the good news.
Baby Jesus Christ was born.
I will sing the good news.

In our Bible story today, we will be talking about some men who followed a special star. It would lead them to a King. Do you know Who the King was? Let children guess. Tell them the King was Jesus.

Which star on our wall is the biggest and brightest? If you were looking for Jesus, which star would you follow?

Option: If you have time, allow children to decorate their stars with glue and glitter or aluminum foil before they attach them to the wall.

◆ ◆ ◆ ◆

ACTIVITY 2—Giving Gifts

Before class, find out from your church's benevolence committee if there is a family with children in it who are in need of help. Ask parents, teachers, children, or the church to donate several items of clothing and/or toys for these needy children. You could also use items from the food pantry. Also provide Christmas wrapping paper, tape, ribbons and bows, construction paper, scissors, and markers. On the construction paper, print "Here are some gifts for Christmas, because it is Jesus' birthday."

What ways have we learned to celebrate Christmas? We can tell others about Jesus' birthday; we can thank God for Jesus; we can sing songs about Jesus' birth. **Another way that we can celebrate Jesus' birthday is by giving gifts.** Explain to the children that the toys (clothing, food, etc.) are for some children who don't have any presents for Christmas. The children can show them the true meaning about Jesus' birthday by giving gifts to them.

Let children choose gifts, then wrap them in Christmas paper and decorate them with ribbons and bows. The gifts do not have to look perfect. Have children sign and decorate the construction-paper card for the children, telling why they are giving them gifts.

Note: Even if Christmas is already past, plan to wrap and deliver gifts to someone in need.

WRAP-UP—Heads Up!

While children straighten up the room, encourage them to look up at the special star from Activity 1 on the wall. While we clean up, let's pretend we are the wise men following the star. We will start cleaning up the corner, and then move toward the star.

We have learned a lot about Jesus' birthday. Let's see what you remember. Can you name some people who thought Jesus was special? Told other people about Him; thanked God; sang songs; gave gifts. **What can we do to celebrate Jesus' birthday?** We can do the same things the Bible people did. We can thank God. We can sing to Jesus. We can tell others about His birth. We can give gifts. **Today we made a gift that we can give to celebrate Jesus' birth. To whom will you give your stick puppets?** Encourage children to share. Sing all the verses of "Baby Jesus Christ" from page 8 of this session.

Leaders' Evaluation

	Great!	OK!	More!	Oops!	Suggestions
Activity 1					
Activity 2					
Bible Time					
Application					
Bible Memory					
Craft					
Snack					
Game					
Wrap-up					

BIBLE TIME—Special Christmas Gifts

You will need a doll, the large star on the wall from Activity 1, and a crown. Before the session, choose one teacher to be King Herod. Place a chair in the corner of the room and have King Herod sit in the chair and wear the crown. Place the doll under the large star on the wall from Activity 1.

The children will go on a "journey" with you during this story. Start the story in the farthest corner of the room from the star on the wall and the baby.

We are going to go on a journey today to find the baby Jesus. After baby Jesus was born, a special star appeared in the sky. Wise men who lived far, far away from Jesus saw that star. There were lots of stars in the sky, but this star was the biggest and brightest of all! Point to the star. The wise men spent a lot of time studying the stars. They knew that this star meant that a new King had been born. They wanted to see the new King, so they packed their bags and started on a long journey. Have children pretend to "pack their bags" and follow you around the room.

The wise men traveled for days and days and days. They must have been very tired. Slow your walk, stretch, and yawn. But they just kept following that special star. Point to the star again. Finally, the wise men got to a big city. They went to see the king in the city, whose name was Herod. Knock on the door or wall where "King Herod" is sitting. They said, "Where is the new baby King? We are following His star." Herod was angry, because he wanted to be the ONLY king. He went out to ask his helpers about this King. Have "King Herod" leave the room for a moment, then return and say, "The new King should be in the town of Bethlehem. When you find Him, let me know, so I can worship Him."

The wise men left king Herod. Do you think that they would go back and tell him where baby Jesus was? No way! An angel would warn them to go home another way! They

Lesson 18

---

can be used to make a collage.

In our story today, who followed a special star to find a special child? Three wise men who studied the stars. Who was the child? Can you make stars on your paper?

Snack—Star Sandwiches

You will need slices of American cheese, white bread, and star cookie cutters.

Let children put the cheese slices between the bread. Then they can use the cookie cutters to cut star-shaped sandwiches. If the cookie cutters will not cut through the sandwiches, cut the stars from the bread and cheese separately before making the sandwiches. Lead the children in prayer, then join them in eating their snacks. Dear God, thank You for sending a star to show the wise men the way to the child Jesus. Thank You that they gave Jesus special gifts. Thank You that we can give gifts to others and to You to celebrate Jesus' birthday at Christmastime.

The wise men followed a star to find Jesus. What did the wise men give Jesus? They gave Jesus gold, frankincense, and myrrh. **They knew that Jesus was a very special child. Who else knew that Jesus was special?** Children can refer to their stick puppets if they need help. Zechariah and Elizabeth, Mary, shepherds, Simeon and Anna.

Game—Follow the Star

You will need yellow poster board, scissors, tape, and a yardstick. Before the session, cut a large yellow star out of poster board and use tape to attach it to the yardstick.

The wise men saw the star in the sky and followed it to find a new King. Who was the King? Let's pretend to be the wise men and follow the star.

Hold the star up ahead of you. Have the children line up behind you and follow, imitating the actions that you do (marching, skipping, tiptoeing, hopping, galloping). When children understand the game, let them take turns being the leader.

Unit 4

knew King Herod would hurt the baby King if he found out where Jesus was.

The wise men followed the star to Bethlehem. It stopped over a house. Do you know Who was in the house? Stop under the big star and knock on the wall. Pretend to go inside and find Jesus. They saw the child Jesus with Mary and Joseph. They bowed down and worshiped Him. Then they gave Him very expensive gifts. They gave Him gold. They gave Him precious and expensive perfumes: frankincense and myrrh. The wise men knew that Jesus was very special!

APPLICATION—Christmas Presents

You will need copies of pages 106-108 on heavy paper, scissors, craft sticks, tape, markers, and letter-size envelopes. If you have young children, cut out the figures on the pages before class.

The wise men brought gifts to baby Jesus. We can celebrate Jesus' birthday by giving gifts too. What gifts did the wise men bring? Gold is a precious metal. Frankincense and myrrh are special perfumes. What kinds of gifts could you give? Let children think of ideas of things they could give. Remind them a gift can be something that they "do" for someone.

We are going to make some puppets of people who knew Jesus was a special baby. You can give your puppets to someone you know. Tell that person you are giving them a gift because Jesus is special. Guide children to cut out the figures from pages 106-108, color them, and tape a craft stick to the back of each puppet. If time is limited, children may choose only three or four puppets to make.

Sing all the verses of "Do You Know the Good News?" from page 8 of this session. As the children sing, have them hold up the stick puppets they are singing about.

When you are finished, give each child an envelope to hold the stick puppets.

BIBLE MEMORY—Musical Stars

You will need yellow and black paper, scissors, a cassette of Christmas songs, and a cassette player. Before the session, cut out a number of large black circles, along with two large yellow stars. Cut enough circles and stars for each child in the class. Lay the circles and stars on the floor in a circle. You may wish to tape them to the floor to hold them in place.

Practice saying the Bible verse together, using the motions learned the last several weeks. Start the verse sitting down. "Do not (*shake head back and forth*) be afraid (*bow head and cover eyes*). (*Jump up and smile.*) I have good news. A Savior has been born to you (*stretch arms out to everyone*). He is Christ (*pretend to hold a baby*), the Lord (*point up to Heaven*)."

Then have each child stand on a circle or a star. As you play a cassette of Christmas songs, children will move around the circle stepping from one circle/star to the next. When you pause the tape, children should freeze. The two children who are standing on stars can say the Bible verse together. Help the children with the words of the verse as needed.

ACTIVITY TIME

Do as many activities as time permits.

Craft—Star Rubbings

You will need white paper (not construction paper or other heavy paper), crayons, scissors, and various textured materials (corrugated cardboard, burlap, felt, sandpaper, needlepoint, plastic). Before the session, cut different sizes of stars from the textured materials.

Give children white paper and crayons. Show children how to lay a star under their paper and color over it to make a rubbing. For best results, hold the star in place and use the side edge of the crayon. Many different colors of crayons and sizes of stars

EXTRA! EXTRA! GOOD NEWS!

DECEMBER 25   **VOL. IX**

THE BIRTH OF THE BABY JESUS

"Jesus Christ, the Son of God, was born today in a stable in Bethlehem," reported the innkeeper who owns the stable. Because of the census, all other available housing was already full when the parents of the baby, Mary and Joseph, arrived in Bethlehem. The baby was wrapped in swaddling clothes and put in a manger. The couple reported that they were very excited and honored to be the parents of the Christ. Two local shepherds were also interviewed at the stable. They were eye-witnesses to an unusual appearance of a host of angels as they were watching their sheep late last night. The angels told them that the Savior had just been born.

JESUS IS BORN!

Angel

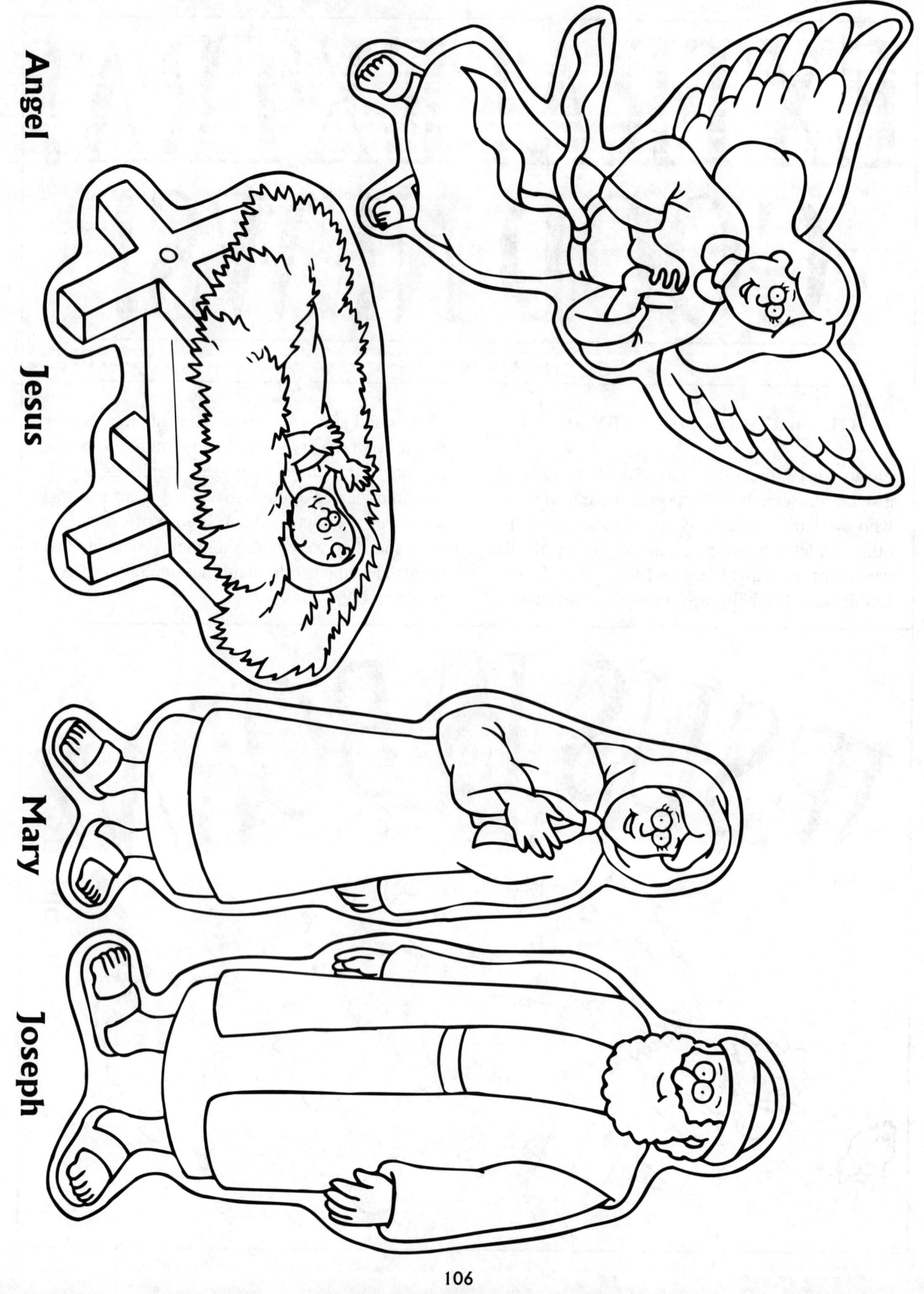

Jesus

Mary

Joseph

Elizabeth

Zechariah

Shepherds

Wise Men

Simeon

Anna

108

109

110

Unit 5
Lessons 19-22

Jesus Is a Friend

◆◆◆◆◆

By the end of this unit, the children and leaders will . . .
Know Tell about four times Jesus was a friend.
Feel Feel eager to be a friend like Jesus.
Do Follow Jesus' example by being a friend.

Unit Bible Words for Memory
"You are my friends" (John 15:14, NIV).

◆◆◆◆◆

Unit Lessons

Lesson 19
Jesus Calls Four Special Friends
Mark 1:16-20; Luke 5:1-11
Children will learn how Jesus helped four fishermen catch many fish and called them to become His friends.

Lesson 20
Jesus Is a Friend to Children
Mark 10:13-16
Children discover how Jesus took time to talk and play with children, even when His followers thought He was too busy.

Lesson 21
Jesus Is a Friend to a Leader
John 3:1-21
Children find out how Jesus talked to Nicodemus at night and answered his questions about who Jesus was.

Lesson 22
Jesus Is a Friend to People Who Are Different
John 4:4-26
Children see how Jesus showed He was a friend to a Samaritan woman by talking to her and asking her for a drink.

◆◆◆◆◆

Why Teach This Unit to Four-Year-Olds—Six-Year-Olds?

Jesus was a friend to everyone, whether they were poor or rich, influential leaders or simple working fishermen, playing children or grandmas and grandpas. Children can follow Jesus' example. In this unit, they will practice ways of being a friend. And they will find people they know who need them to be a friend like Jesus. Their habits of acceptance and friendship will grow with them.

◆◆◆◆◆

Bible Time Line

The stories for this unit are pictured on the time line, pages 316 and 317. The time line will be used throughout all units in this book.

Provide the time-line page for children who arrive early, or plan time at the end of the Bible story during each session for children to color the time line and look for the hidden pictures.

See page 6 in this book for further instructions on using the time line and for suggested time-line projects.

Materials

All Lessons
a Bible
markers, colored pencils, crayons
white paper, construction paper, poster board
tape, masking tape
Plasti-Tak
glue and glue sticks
scissors
a stapler
paper hole punch
yarn or string

Lesson 19
a waterproof drop cloth
a child's wading pool or baby bathtub
fishnets or pieces of fabric netting to use as nets
some floating fish (purchase reusable drink coolers shaped like fish or cut fish from plastic lids using the pattern on page 130)
envelopes, stamps, and a phone book
a kitchen timer
one clear two-liter plastic bottle per child, small seashells (available in a craft store), sand, net, and a hot glue gun
measuring cups, buckets, and towels

Lesson 20
sugar cookie dough, waxed paper, a rolling pin, boy and girl cookie cutters, candy decorations, cookie sheets
plain paper sacks of different sizes, stickers (see resources below), tissue paper

small, inexpensive gifts: coloring or activity book, stickers, pencils or decorative erasers, play dough (purchase yourself or ask several parents to purchase)
a watch or clock for each child (they do not need to be working)
a large grocery sack filled with toys, clothes, and snack foods
small paper bags or plastic baggies
a snapshot of each child brought from home or an instant camera with film
three cardboard boxes, a large ball

Lesson 21
a broom and dustcloth, two mats or towels, two cups, an oil lamp or a candle
a world map or a globe; pictures of local, national, or world leaders cut from newspapers and magazines
tempera paint, a shallow basin, and hand washing supplies, and a picture and information about a leader you have chosen (see Application)

Lesson 22
Through a missionary, locate a class of children close in age to the class you are teaching.
enough wooden blocks in a variety of colors for each child to hold one
a stick of gum
baby-food jar, a brown paper bag, a bowl of many different kinds of beans, rubber bands
an English/another language dictionary

The Beginner's Bible™ Resources

Jesus and the Children Stickers, Standard Publishing, #22-01035, call 1-800-543-1353

Jesus and the Children Floor Puzzle, Standard Publishing, #28-02717, call 1-800-543-1353

Jesus and the Children Inlay Puzzle, Standard Publishing, #28-02703, call 1-800-543-1353

The Beginner's Bible™ New Testament GeoSafari Bible Pack, Standard Publishing, #14-24002, call 1-800-543-1353

The Beginner's Bible™ Bible Lessons GeoSafari Bible Pack, Standard Publishing, #14-24005, call 1-800-543-1353

Unit 5
Lesson 19

Jesus Calls Four Special Friends
(Mark 1:16-20; Luke 5:1-11)

Even though He had specific work for them to do, Jesus chose His special friends for what He could do for them, not for what they could do for Him. Jesus knew following Him would raise their lives to standards they had never dreamed.

Bible Words
"You are my friends" (John 15:14).

Goals
Tell how Jesus was a friend to fishermen.
Feel eager to be a friend like Jesus.
Follow Jesus' example by being a friend.

◆◆◆◆

Activity 1—Go Fishin'

You will need a waterproof drop cloth, a child's wading pool or baby bathtub, fishnets or pieces of fabric netting to use as nets, and some floating fish (purchase reusable drink coolers shaped like fish or cut fish from plastic lids using the pattern on page 130).

Fill the pool with three inches of water. Add the fish. Give the children the net and challenge them to catch the fish with the net without touching the fish with their hands.

Have you ever gone fishing? What did you use to catch fish? How many fish did you catch? Allow children to share their fishing experiences. Tell them about times when you have gone fishing. **When Jesus lived on earth, many men were fishermen. They did not fish for one fish at a time with a pole. They used nets and worked together to catch many fish at once.**

Oh, Jesus Was a Friend
(Tune: "Did You Ever See a Lassie?")

Oh, Jesus was a friend,
A friend, a friend.
Oh, Jesus was a friend
To four fishermen.

Oh, Jesus helped them catch fish.
Then they followed Him.
Oh, Jesus was a friend
To four fishermen.

Leaders' Evaluation

	Great!	OK!	More!	Oops!	Suggestions
Activity 1					
Activity 2					
Bible Time					
Application					
Bible Memory					
Craft					
Snack					
Game					
Wrap-up					

Encourage children to work together to catch the fish in the tub, using the nets and not touching the fish with their hands.

In our story today, Jesus gave four fishermen a more important job than catching fish.

◆◆◆◆

ACTIVITY 2—What Is a Friend?

You will need the person pattern from reproducible page 129, scissors, poster board or butcher paper, markers or colored and pencils, and tape or Plasti-Tak. Before the session, enlarge the person pattern on page 129. Cut the person from poster board or butcher paper. Attach the figure to the wall or an easel using tape or Plasti-Tak. Provide markers or colored pencils.

Who are your friends? Ask the children to draw pictures of their answers on the figure. Give suggestions as needed. They can draw pictures of their friends. They can draw pictures of places they like to play with their friends, such as the playground, their yards, with their toys at home, at preschool. **What do you like to do with your friends? How do you choose your friends?**

When the children have completed their pictures, teach the words to "Oh, Jesus Was a Friend" (Tune "Did You Ever See a Lassie?") from page 8 of this session.

Jesus chose four friends in our story today. Listen to see who Jesus' friends were and what Jesus did with His friends.

◆◆◆◆

BIBLE TIME—Four New Friends

You will need the net from Activity 1, 10 or more poster-board fish made from the patterns on page 130, and a Bible. Place the poster-board figures in your Bible. Have the children sit around the net holding the edges as you tell the story.

We talked earlier about times that we've gone fishing. Throw a poster-board fish into the net. **Fishing for fish is fun.** Throw in another fish. **Fishing for fish feeds people.** Throw in another fish. **Fishing for fish can even be a good full-time job.**

---

dip as much water from the pool as possible. Give them towels to dry the drop cloth.

Fishing is hard work. Being a friend like Jesus is hard work too. I can tell you can do hard work because of the way you are cleaning the water up. How will you work hard to be a friend like Jesus this week? To whom will you be a friend? Allow children to tell to whom they will be a friend and how they will be a friend like Jesus. Give suggestions as needed. They can be a friend like Jesus by helping (helping their friend clean up, helping them with schoolwork) and by telling their friends about Jesus.

When you help your friends and tell them about Jesus, you are being a friend like Jesus.

Lead the children in prayer, asking God to help them be friends like Jesus. Review the Bible verse with the children. Sing the song, "Oh, Jesus Was a Friend." The words are on page 8 of this session. Be sure children have their Bible Memory Fish Strips and the invitations from the Application time as they leave.

NOTE: Ask parents to send a snapshot of their child to the next class. You may also want to ask them to send a small inexpensive gift. See Activity 2 of Lesson 20.

◆◆◆◆

WRAP-UP—A Friend Like Jesus

Provide measuring cups and buckets for the children to help

Throw in another fish.

The Bible tells us that one day Jesus met two families of fishermen. Simon and Andrew were brothers, and James and John were brothers. They made their living fishing on the lake of Galilee. Throw in another fish. They probably knew the best places on the lake to catch fish and the best times to look for fish. But on the day that they met Jesus, they had no fish. They had been working all night, and they hadn't caught even one fish. Remove all the fish from the net. They probably were very tired; they probably wanted to get home and rest up so they could try again the next night. But when they met Jesus, He said, "Take your boat out into the deep water, and let down your nets for a catch."

Simon, Andrew, James, and John had already fished all night. They could have said, "Why should we go out again? There's no fish to catch out there today. If there were fish, we would have already caught them. Besides, what does this teacher guy Jesus know about catching fish?" Do you think that's what the four fishermen said about Jesus? Allow children to respond.

Simon, Andrew, James, and John knew that Jesus was special. Jesus wasn't a fisherman, but He is the Son of God. Simon told Him, "We've worked hard all night and haven't caught anything. But because You say so, we will let down the nets."

When Simon and Andrew let down their nets as Jesus had said, they caught so many fish that their nets began to break. Throw all the fish back into the net. They called for their partners, James and John, to bring their boat and help them. The four men filled both boats so full of fish that they began to sink. They were amazed and a little bit afraid at what Jesus could do!

When they got back to the shore with their boats full of fish, Jesus was waiting. "Don't be afraid!" He said. "From now on you will catch men." Simon, Andrew, James, and John left their boats and their nets. Drop the net and fish on the floor. They left everything to follow their new friend Jesus.

Lesson 19 Unit 5 3

---

white cloth. Children can make a picture by gluing the boat to a piece of construction paper. They can glue a craft stick on the boat to make a mast, and glue a piece of cloth to make a sail. They can decorate and color the picture with crayons.

Snack—Eat an Ocean

You will need individual cups of blue gelatin. If possible, use five-ounce paper cups with fish designs. Also serve 1/2 fish stick per child.

As the children eat, focus the conversation on fishing and the four fishermen who followed their friend Jesus. **This gelatin reminds me of the ocean or a large lake where fish can be caught. What kinds of fish are on your cup? Many people eat fish often. Have you tasted your fish stick yet? Fishermen provide us with fish to eat. Fishing is an important job. Can you think of a more important job? Do you remember the names of the four fishermen Jesus called to become fishermen of men?**

Game—Fish and Men Hunt

You will need construction-paper people and fish cut from the patterns on pages 129 and 130 and two baskets. Make an equal number of fish and people. Before the session, hide the figures in your classroom. As an option, hide the figures in an unused classroom if one is available.

Divide the children into two groups. Give each group a basket. One group will look for fish. The other group will look for people. Show each group an example of what they are looking for. When the children find the figures, they should place them in the basket.

Before Simon, Andrew, James, and John met Jesus, they spent their lives looking for fish. After they met Jesus, they spent their lives looking for people to tell them that God loved them. How was Jesus their good friend? He helped them catch fish. He gave them special work to do.

6 Unit 5 115

APPLICATION—Fishin' Time

You will need the invitation from reproducible page 131, envelopes, stamps, colored pencils, and a phone book. Before the session, copy and cut out the invitations from page 131. Put stamps on the envelopes.

Who were Jesus' four friends? Simon, Andrew, James, and John. **Why did they leave their fishing nets and follow Jesus?** Jesus asked them to follow Him and fish for men. **Whom could you ask to follow Jesus and become His friend?** Encourage children to name people they could tell about Jesus. They can name friends or other adults they come in contact with, such as a neighbor or bus driver.

Let the children color the invitations you prepared before class and fill them out. Help the children as needed, by printing what they dictate to you and telling them how to spell words. Help the children print the name of the person to whom they are sending the invitation on the outside of the envelope. If the address is available, print it on the envelope too. (Check the phone book for addresses.) If not, write a short note to parents, asking them to provide the address. Send the invitations home with the children with instructions that they be mailed early in the week.

When you invite other people to follow Jesus, you are being a friend like Jesus.

◆◆◆◆

BIBLE MEMORY—Memory Fish Match

You will need 4" x 17" pieces of blue construction paper, copies of the fish on page 130, a glue stick, and a kitchen timer. Before class, cut and mount in order one set of the memory fish on one 4" x 17" strip of blue construction paper. Cut out one set of fish for each child.

Show the children the sample Bible-verse strip that you made before class. Ask the children to say the words of the verse with you. Demonstrate how to place another blue strip below the control one and match the fish in order according to the control. Let each child race the timer to see if he can match the fish in one minute. If you have a young class, you may want to increase the time accordingly. Read the verse aloud with each child as she glues her fish in order on a blue construction-paper strip. **Our memory fish have Jesus' words, "You are my friends," swimming in order. See if you can place yours in the same order before the timer rings. Jesus wants to be your friend. He wants you to help others become His friend.**

Option: Provide blue plastic wrap. Cover the construction-paper strips with the wrap and tape it in the back. When the fish are glued onto the strips, it will look as if they are swimming in water.

◆◆◆◆

ACTIVITY TIME

Do as many activities as time permits.

◆◆◆◆

Craft—Verse in a Bottle

You will need one clear two-liter plastic bottle per child, small seashells (available in a craft store), sand, net, black and blue permanent markers, and a hot glue gun. Before the session, cut a slit along one side of each bottle. On the back half of the bottle, trace the boat found on page 129. On the front half of the bottle, print the Bible words, "You are my friends."

In class, spread glue along the inside bottom of the bottles. Let the children move the bottles from side to side to spread the glue more. Let them spoon in shells, net, and sand. Have another teacher take the completed bottles to another room and seal the opening with a hot glue gun.

When you look at your bottle, you can remember that Jesus was a friend to four fishermen: Simon, Andrew, James, and John.

Option: Copy and cut out the boats from page 129. Provide glue, construction paper, crayons, craft sticks, and squares of

Unit 5
Lesson 20

Jesus Is a Friend to Children
(Mark 10:13-16)

Children have a natural need for attention. They will do things to receive negative attention to avoid receiving no attention at all. Today's Scripture shows Jesus' desire to spend time with and give attention to children.

Bible Words

"You are my friends" (John 15:14).

Goals

Tell how Jesus was a friend to children.
Feel eager to be a friend like Jesus.
Follow Jesus' example by being a friend to children.

◆◆◆◆

Activity 1—Cookie Children

Bring sugar cookie dough (ready-made refrigerated dough would work well), waxed paper, a rolling pin, boy and girl cookie cutters, candy decorations, and cookie sheets. Make arrangements to have the church oven preheated and ask an adult or teen to take the cookie sheets to the kitchen after the activity and bake the cookies before Snack time.

Roll out dough onto waxed paper. Let each child cut out at least one cookie and decorate it with candy eyes and colored sugar clothes. When a cookie sheet is filled, let the children admire their handiwork.

Look at all the boys and girls! They all look special just as you all are special. Every boy and girl is special to Jesus. Jesus is a friend to children like you. We will each enjoy a cookie at Snack time.

Oh, Jesus Was a Friend
(Tune: "Did You Ever See a Lassie?")

Oh, Jesus was a friend,
A friend, a friend.
Oh, Jesus was a friend
To four fishermen.

Oh, Jesus helped them catch fish.
Then they followed Him.
Oh, Jesus was a friend
To four fishermen.

Oh, Jesus was a friend,
A friend, a friend.
Oh, Jesus was a friend
To little children.

He smiled and hugged them,
And spoke kind words to them.
Oh, Jesus was a friend
To little children.

ACTIVITY 2—Friendship Gifts

You will need gifts (see the explanation below), plain paper sacks of different sizes, items to decorate the sacks (markers, colored pencils, stickers), and tissue paper. See unit page 112 for suggested stickers. Find out the name of a child in your community who is confined to home or in the hospital because of illness or injury. Purchase several gifts or contact the parents of your children and ask them to each send one inexpensive, age-appropriate gift for the child. Suggested gifts are: coloring or activity books, stickers, pencils or decorative erasers, play dough, and so on.

Ask the children to decorate the sacks and place their gifts inside. Then place crumpled-up tissue paper in the top of the sack. Arrange to deliver the gifts during the following week. **(Name of child) is sick right now and cannot play with friends or go to school. I am sure these gifts will make her feel that you care about her. Doing nice things for people helps them know that we are their friends. Jesus once showed some children that He was their friend.**

◆◆◆◆

BIBLE TIME—Jesus' Time for Children

You will need an assortment of watches and clocks (one for each child) in a sack. They do not have to be working. Place the sack in your lap with your Bible until the appropriate time in the story.

We just talked about how giving people gifts can let them know we want to be their friends. We like it when people give us gifts. What are some gifts that you have received at Christmas or on your birthday? Allow children to share. There is one thing we all like to receive. When someone gives us that thing, we know we are important to them. Ask each child to reach inside the sack and draw out one item. What did you draw from inside the sack? What does it help you do? Clocks and

WRAP-UP—Teamwork

One way we can be friends to each other is to help one another. Our room needs to be cleaned. Can we work in teams? Assign two or three children to each task.

Sing all four verses of "Oh, Jesus Was a Friend" from page 8 of this session. Have children show their memory-verse puzzle pieces and share who they will be a friend to in the coming week. **How will you be a friend like Jesus?**

Then have the children join hands one more time and lead them in a closing prayer thanking God by name for each child present.

Be sure children have their cookies, puzzles, and Jesus and the Children pictures to take home.

Until parents come, play a guessing game. Say, "I see a friend of Jesus who . . ." and give a description of a child in the group. Let children guess whom you are describing.

◆◆◆◆

Leaders' Evaluation

	Great!	OK!	More!	Oops!	Suggestions
Activity 1					
Activity 2					
Bible Time					
Application					
Bible Memory					
Craft					
Snack					
Game					
Wrap-up					

watches help us tell time. Time is what we all like to receive from people we care about. We like for them to spend time with us. Hold on to the watch or clock I have loaned you. Let's hear about some friends that Jesus gave time to.

Jesus was busy when He was here on earth. He was busy teaching people. He was busy making sick people well. He was busy spending time with God. Jesus did not wear a watch (Hold up watch.)**, but He knew how much He had to do every day.**

Jesus' followers knew how busy Jesus was. We learned about four of them last week. Do you remember the names of Jesus' four fishermen friends? Simon, Andrew, James, and John. Jesus' friends may have worried that He was too busy. They probably encouraged Him to rest more. They may have felt that He should save His time (Hold up watch.) for important people. Let's name some people that Jesus' friends might have thought were important. Encourage children to think of people —Jewish leaders like the Pharisees, leaders of countries and cities like the Romans, leaders in the temple-churches and synagogues like the rabbis or teachers.

One day some parents decided to bring their children to see Jesus. They wanted Jesus to touch them and give them His blessing. Jesus' special friends knew Jesus was busy teaching grown-ups. They told the parents that Jesus did not have time (Hold up watch.) **to be bothered with little children. The parents must have felt sad.** The children must have felt disappointed.

But wait! Jesus stopped His followers from sending away the parents and children. Jesus said, "Let the little children come to me. Don't stop them." Jesus stopped what He was doing with the grown-ups and spent time (Hold up watch.) **with the children. Jesus probably smiled at the children, gave them warm hugs, and spoke kindly to them.** The children knew they were special to Jesus. They knew Jesus was their friend.

Lesson 20

We are friends like Jesus when we give others smiles, kind words, and hugs.

Snack—Cookies and Milk

Bring milk to serve with the cookies the children cut out and decorated during Activity 1. If each child made more than one cookie, place the extra ones in sandwich bags for them to take home and share with other children.

It is always fun to have cookies and milk with our friends. Wouldn't it be fun to have cookies and milk with Jesus?

As the children eat, review the story. **What did the parents want Jesus to do for their children? Who did not want to let the children see Jesus? What did Jesus say?**

Game—Friends in Deed

You will need three cardboard boxes, a marker, masking tape, and a large ball. Before the session, label one box, "Smiles." Label the second box, "Kind Words." Label the third box, "Hugs and Handshakes."

In class, place the three boxes at one end of the room. Place a masking-tape line on the floor behind which the children will stand to throw the ball in the boxes.

Divide the children into two groups. Let children from each group take turns trying to throw the ball in a box. (If children are unsuccessful after several tries, you may need to move the masking-tape line closer to the boxes.) When a ball lands in a box, the children from that group must do the "friendly" action on that box to the other group. Tell the children they may substitute handshakes for hugs if they wish. If they choose the box labeled "Kind Words," they should decide as a group what they will say to the other group. Give them suggestions if needed, such as "You look great today," "We're glad you're here," "You are our friends," "We like you."

Option: Use poster board and a bean bag. Divide the poster board into three sections and label them with the three ways to be a friend.

Unit 5

APPLICATION—Friend Tools

You will need a large grocery sack filled with toys, clothes, and snack foods.

How was Jesus a friend to the children in the Bible story? Allow children to respond. He spent time with them. He talked to them and hugged them. **Let's sing a song about ways Jesus was a friend to the children.** Sing verses three and four of "Oh, Jesus Was a Friend" from page 8 of this session. Sing the song several times until children are familiar with the words. **How does this song say Jesus was a friend to the children?** He smiled, hugged them, and spoke kind words to them.

We can be a friend to children like Jesus was. We can use smiles, kind words, and hugs to be a friend. Let's practice. Practice smiles, kind words (say a nice thing about the person next to you), and hugs.

Hold up the sack of items you brought to class. **This bag has some things you probably have at your home. I want you to draw an item from the bag and decide how you can use that item to be a friend.** Let the children take turns exchanging their watches or clocks for one of the items in the sack. When each child has taken an item from the bag, let them share ways they can use the items to be a friend. Offer suggestions as needed. Suggestions follow: They could spend time with their friends playing with toys; they could share toys or food with their friends; they could say kind words about a friend's new dress or shirt.

◆◆◆◆

BIBLE MEMORY—Puzzles

You will need a copy of the Bible-verse puzzle on page 132 for each child, scissors, markers or colored pencils, and small paper bags or plastic baggies.

Review the Bible verse with the children. Then ask children to cut apart their puzzles and practice putting the pieces back together as they practice saying their Bible words.

Jesus was a friend to four fishermen and some children. Today Jesus is still a friend to children. Turn your puzzle pieces over. Write or draw a picture of people to whom Jesus was a friend on two of your puzzle pieces. Simon, Andrew, James, John, or children. **Draw a picture of yourself on one of the pieces.** Then think of someone to whom you can be a friend like Jesus. **Draw a picture of that person on a puzzle piece.** Have children put their Bible-verse puzzles in small paper or plastic bags to take home.

◆◆◆◆

ACTIVITY TIME

Do as many activities as time permits.

◆◆◆◆

Craft—My Friend Jesus

You will need a piece of construction paper or an 8 1/2" x 11" piece of poster board for each child, a snapshot brought from home or an instant camera with film, tape, glue, scissors, copies of page 133, and markers or colored pencils. Before class, use the pattern above the picture on page 133 to cut out the square on the top left corner of each piece of construction paper or poster board to make a built-in frame for the photos. If you have younger children in your class, cut and glue the picture of Jesus and the children onto the construction paper before class.

Let the children cut along the heavy lines of the picture of Jesus and the children. Help them glue the picture in place with the right angle corner of the picture and the lower right corner of the rectangle matching. Help each child glue or tape his photo behind the frame opening. If you brought an instant camera, take the children's pictures in class. After children have attached their photos behind the frame, they may color the picture of Jesus and the children.

Jesus is our friend. He shows us how to be friends to others.

Unit 5
Lesson 21

Jesus Is a Friend to a Leader
(John 3:1-21)

Jesus knew important people like Nicodemus needed Him just as much as humble fishermen and children needed Him. He was willing to take the time to meet the needs of an important leader like Nicodemus and to be His friend.

Bible Words

"You are my friends" (John 15:14).

Goals

Tell how Jesus was a friend to a leader.
Feel eager to be a friend like Jesus.
Follow Jesus' example by being a friend to a leader.

◆◆◆◆

ACTIVITY 1—A Rooftop Meeting

You will need masking tape, a broom and dustcloth, two mats or towels, two cups, an oil lamp or a candle, dark construction paper, tape, and white and yellow crayons or star stickers. Before the session, mark off a square area in one corner of the room with the masking tape. Coming off one side of the square area, put several short strips of masking tape that will be the stairs. Place the other items you have gathered outside the marked-off area.

Our Bible story today is about an important leader named Nicodemus. Nicodemus had a nighttime meeting with Jesus. Jesus probably met with Nicodemus on the roof of the house where He was staying. Point to the masking-tape area you have made. This is the roof of our house. We are going to prepare our rooftop for Nicodemus' visit with Jesus. Point to the

---

Oh, Jesus Was a Friend
(Tune: "Did You Ever See a Lassie?")

Oh, Jesus was a friend,
A friend, a friend.
Oh, Jesus was a friend
To four fishermen.

Oh, Jesus helped them catch fish.
Then they followed Him.
Oh, Jesus was a friend
To four fishermen.

Oh, Jesus was a friend,
A friend, a friend.
Oh, Jesus was a friend
To little children.

He smiled and hugged them,
And spoke kind words to them.
Oh, Jesus was a friend
To little children.

Oh Jesus was a friend,
A friend, a friend.
Oh, Jesus was a friend
To important leaders.

masking-tape "stairs" you made. **These are the stairs leading up to our roof. It's important that we remember always to climb the stairs to get to our roof.**

Guide children to use the items you brought to prepare the roof for Nicodemus. They should carry the items up the "stairs." They can sweep and dust the area. They can spread mats or towels on the floor as seats for Jesus and Nicodemus. They can fill cups with water and place them near the seats. They can place a lamp or candle on the roof to provide light. Since the meeting took place at night, they can draw or stick stars on the dark construction paper and tape it to the wall behind the roof to make a nighttime scene.

You worked hard. Now we are ready for Nicodemus' visit on the rooftop with Jesus.

◆◆◆◆◆

ACTIVITY 2—Leaders Who Need Jesus

You will need a world map or a globe; pictures of local, national, or world leaders cut from newspapers and magazines; and Plasti-Tak or tape. Picture of leaders to include could be: the leader of the country; your governor, your city or town mayor, ministers or elders in your church, schoolteachers and Sunday-school teachers.

A leader is someone who guides a group of people, a city, a state or a country. **Our church has leaders. Our town has leaders. Our state,** (name state)**, has leaders. Our country has leaders.** Ask children to name some leaders they know. **We think of leaders as important, but they need Jesus to be their friend just as much as we do.** Show children the pictures of leaders that you have brought to class and discuss who the leaders are and what they do.

Let the children use Plasti-Tak or tape to attach the pictures onto the globe or map. You may want to guide the children to place the pictures near the place where the person pictured is a leader.

in a closing prayer. Remember again to pray for the leader you have chosen. Be sure to send each child's prayer reminder home.

Until parents come, play a game about people who were and are Jesus' friends. Have children sit down in a circle. Give clues and have children stand up when they know the person you are describing. Alternate between clues concerning Bible people and clues concerning children in the classroom. Possible Bible clues follow:

- **Jesus' followers didn't want to let these people see Jesus.** Children.
- **These people worked all night before meeting Jesus.** Four fishermen: Simon, Andrew, James, and John.
- **This man came to see Jesus at night.** Nicodemus.
- **These people were in a boat when Jesus spoke to them.** The four fishermen.
- **Their parents brought these people to Jesus.** The children.
- **This person was a Jewish leader.** Nicodemus.

Leaders' Evaluation

	Great!	OK!	More!	Oops!	Suggestions
Activity 1					
Activity 2					
Bible Time					
Application					
Bible Memory					
Craft					
Snack					
Game					
Wrap-up					

BIBLE TIME—A Friend for Nicodemus

Tell the story around the rooftop area that the children prepared earlier. You stand on the rooftop as you tell the children the story.

Last week, we learned about some people to whom Jesus gave smiles, and gentle words, and hugs. Do you remember who Jesus was a friend to in last week's story? Jesus was a friend to children. Jesus took time for the children, even though His followers didn't think they were important enough. Jesus was a friend to everyone He met, whether they were old or young, rich or poor, important leaders, or working fishermen. This week, Jesus spends some time with an important leader of the Jews.

Earlier you prepared our rooftop for the leader's visit to Jesus. The man's name was Nicodemus. He was a Jewish leader. Nicodemus came to see Jesus one night. He may have sneaked in to see Jesus when it was dark so that none of the other leaders could see him. Or maybe Nicodemus wanted a quiet time to talk to Jesus because he had so many questions.

Jesus was probably tired. He had been talking to people and helping people all day. But Jesus knew Nicodemus needed a special friend. He knew Nicodemus needed answers to his questions about Jesus and about God.

Nicodemus told Jesus, "We know you are a teacher who has come from God." Nicodemus knew that Jesus could make blind people see, make lame people walk, make deaf people hear, and make dead people come alive again. Only the Son of God would be able to do these things.

But Nicodemus wanted to know more about who Jesus was and why God had sent Him to earth. Jesus answered Nicodemus' questions. Jesus said, "God loved the world so much that He sent His Son to the world. If you believe in God's Son, you will have eternal life. God sent His Son to save the world!"

When he left, Nicodemus knew Jesus cared about him. Jesus

---

whole family might like to pray for this leader. **What will you tell them about our leader and why he needs prayer?** Have children review facts about the leader and items you listed for which he needs prayer.

Snack—Patriotic Treat

Early in the week, freeze paper cups half full of red fruit juice. Just before the juice freezes, insert a plastic spoon into each cup. When the juice is completely frozen, pour in blue fruit juice. Allow the cups to freeze for at least twenty-four hours before serving. To serve, tear away the paper cups and provide white napkins.

Red, white, and blue are the colors in our flag. (If you live in a country whose flag has different colors, please adapt.) **The flag can help remind us that the people who lead our country need our prayers. They need Jesus to be their friend.**

Game—Follow the Leader

You will need a large open area. A hall will do if it can be used without disturbing other classes.

Play "Follow the Leader." Ask the children to follow you and imitate whatever you do. Do actions such as hopping up and down, tugging your ear, blinking your eyes, wiggling your fingers over your head, flapping your arms like a chicken, and so on. Then let the children take turns until each child who wishes to do so has had a turn.

What makes a good leader? Do good leaders need any help? How can you help? Remind the children they can always pray for leaders.

WRAP-UP—Leaders' Friends

Lead the children in cleaning the room. A good leader sets a good example. Praise noticeably good efforts.

Sing the song "Oh, Jesus Was a Friend" from page 8 of this session, adding a fifth verse for this week. Then lead the children

cared enough to spend time with him. Jesus cared enough to answer his questions.

Jesus was a friend to Nicodemus because He listened to him, spent time with him, and answered his questions.

◆◆◆◆

APPLICATION—Prayer Gram

You will need a large piece of paper or cloth, tempera paint, a shallow basin, hand washing supplies, and a picture and information about the leader you have chosen.

Before the session, print, "We have prayed for you" in the center of the paper or cloth. Write the name and address of your class and church on the bottom right corner. Choose a leader to whom you will send your prayer gram. Bring a picture and information about that leader.

Show children the picture you brought and tell them about the leader you chose. **Today we will pray for** (name of leader). **We will make a picture to help** (leader) **remember that we are praying.** Place the tempera paint in a basin. Help children place their hands one at a time in the basin and then make a handprint on the paper or cloth you prepared before class. As soon as each child makes his handprint, he should wash and dry his hands. While the handprints are drying, talk about things the leader might need prayer for. For example, if you chose a minister, your list might include opportunities to tell people about Jesus; help in teaching people God's Word; time to spend with family. For a government leader, you might pray for help in making good decisions; that their personal lives would be pleasing to God. When you have decided what to pray for, ask volunteers to pray for each item on your list.

After your prayer is completed and the handprints are dry, help each child print his name beside his handprint. Hang the paper or cloth outside the room for parents to see. During the coming week, mail the message to the leader you have selected.

BIBLE MEMORY—Memory Handshakes

Have the children stand in a circle. Demonstrate the proper way to shake hands. Show the children how to take turns shaking hands one at a time around the circle.

Review the words of the verse by saying them several times aloud with the children. Then explain how to do the activity. **I will turn and shake hands with the person next to me and say the first word of the verse. Then he will turn and shake hands with the person next to him, and say the next word, and so on. When you finish the verse, begin again. If you forget the next word, look at me. I will help you.** Include the Scripture reference, John 15:14, in the reciting of the verse.

Let the game continue until the children can say the verse smoothly and as long as they are interested in the activity. If the children become comfortable with the game, play variations, such as shake hands behind your back, do high fives with the person next to them, and so on.

◆◆◆◆

ACTIVITY TIME

Do as many activities as time permits.

Craft—Prayer Reminder

You will need copies of the prayer reminder on page 134 on construction paper or tagboard, scissors, and crayons or colored pencils. Fill in the leader's name used in the Application time before making copies. Be sure to have enough copies plus extras for each child.

Let each child cut out, color, and decorate his prayer reminder with crayons or colored pencils. Show him how to fold it in half so it can stand on a table.

Where will you put your prayer reminder? Let the children share. Suggest prominent places, such as the kitchen table, beside the bed, on a table in the living room. **Perhaps your**

Unit 5
Lesson 22

Jesus Is a Friend to People Who Are Different
(John 4:4-26)

Jesus was comfortable with all types of people. Because of His caring friendship, He was able to draw many types of people to God. We can do the same when we recognize that being different can be positive and interesting rather than negative.

Bible Words

"You are my friends" (John 15:14).

Goals

Tell how Jesus was a friend to a Samaritan woman.
Feel eager to be a friend like Jesus.
Follow Jesus' example by being a friend to a person who is different.

◆◆◆◆◆

Activity 1—Stay Away from Samaritans

You will need construction paper, markers, a paper hole punch, yarn, masking tape, a cup, a nearby area to wash hands. Before the session, print "Samaritan" on several pieces of construction paper. Print "Judea," "Galilee," and "Samaria" on other pieces of construction paper. Print "Jew" on all the other pieces of construction paper. Divide your room or area into three sections with masking tape lines. Label the top and bottom sections "Galilee" and "Judea." Label the middle section "Samaria." Punch two holes in the top of each paper and string yarn through the holes. Tie the yarn to make a loop big enough to hang around a child's neck. Make enough signs for each child in

---

Oh, Jesus Was a Friend
(Tune: "Did You Ever See a Lassie?")

Oh, Jesus was a friend,
A friend, a friend.
Oh, Jesus was a friend
To four fishermen.

Oh, Jesus helped them catch fish.
Then they followed Him.
Oh, Jesus was a friend
To four fishermen.

Oh, Jesus was a friend,
A friend, a friend.
Oh, Jesus was a friend
To little children.

He smiled and hugged them,
And spoke kind words to them.
Oh, Jesus was a friend
To little children.

Oh Jesus was a friend,
A friend, a friend.
Oh, Jesus was a friend
To important leaders.

Oh, Jesus was a friend,
A friend, a friend.
Oh, Jesus was a friend
To those unlike Him.

your class to have one. Choose another teacher or helper to be a "Samaritan" along with the other children who choose a Samaritan sign.

Give the children the signs and ask them to put them around their necks. **Are you a Jew or a Samaritan?** Help children decide which group they belong in and stand with their group. **Jews lived in Judea and Galilee.** Point out those sections and have the Jews stand in Judea. **Samaritans lived in Samaria.** Point out Samaria and have the Samaritans stand there. **Jews hated Samaritans. Samaritans hated Jews. Jews didn't talk to Samaritans; they didn't even touch Samaritans. Let's pretend we are Jews going on a journey from Judea to Galilee. Let's see what it would have been like between the Jews and the Samaritans.** Have the Jews walk through Samaria. They should stay as far away from the Samaritans as possible and not look at them. When the Jews reach Galilee, tell them they must all go wash their hands in case they got anything from Samaria on them. **Now let's go back to Judea. But I have an idea. It's too much trouble to be around those Samaritans. This time, we'll just have to take the long way around.** Return to Judea, but this time, don't go through Samaria. Make a wide path around Samaria to get to Judea. Explain that many Jews would go far out of their way to avoid even being in the country of Samaria.

How do you think it felt to be a Samaritan? Let children respond. **How do you think it felt to be a Jew?** Let children respond. **In today's story, Jesus meets a woman. Jesus is a Jew. The woman is a Samaritan. What do you think happens between the Jew and the Samaritan? Listen to find out.**

◆◆◆◆

ACTIVITY 2—Pen Pals

Through a missionary, locate a class of children close in age to the class you are teaching. Describe those children to your class. Let them dictate a letter to you. Mail the letter to the class. Encourage your children to draw a friendship picture to enclose. **The children to whom we are writing are different from us**

2   Unit 5

— fold —

bles, and grains. You could offer miniature egg rolls, taco shells, and a small slice of a fruit or vegetable which is not familiar to your children. Encourage the children to taste, but do not insist. **People who live in different parts of the world eat different foods. It is fun to try different foods. It is one way to learn about people from other parts of the world.**

Game—Duck, Duck, Goose International

Using an English/another language dictionary or a personal resource, find out the words for duck and goose in another language. Have the children sit in a circle. Demonstrate the game using the words in the different language. (Most of your children will be familiar with this game.) Lightly touch the head of each child you pass behind and say the word for duck. At some point as you walk behind the circle, substitute the word for goose and say it with emphasis. That child you were touching will try to catch you before you run around the circle and reach her vacated space. Repeat until each child has had a turn and as long as interest continues.

◆◆◆◆

WRAP-UP—Different Friends

Remind the children that friends help one another work as they clean their room. **We are probably all different in how we do chores and which chores we like to do. When we work together as friends, we get every job done.**

Ask children to share how they will be a friend to a person who is different this week, using the pictures they drew in Application. Talk about the many ways people can be different from one another: different color skin, different likes and dislikes, different language, different abilities (such as people in wheelchairs, and other people with disabilities).

Sing "Oh, Jesus Was a Friend" from page 8 of this session.

Lesson 22   7

in some ways. **How do you think they are different?** Allow children to respond. Then describe some ways the children are different—different language, different clothing, different food, different types of houses, and so on. **They are like us in other ways. How do you think they are like us?** Allow children to name ways. Offer suggestions. They love their families. They have moms and dads, and brothers and sisters. They like to play, though their games may be different. They probably like animals. They have favorite foods. They giggle and laugh. The most important way they are like us is that they need Jesus as a friend just as much as we do.

◆◆◆◆◆

BIBLE TIME—A Woman at a Well

You will need a blue circle 18" in diameter and enough wooden blocks in a variety of colors for each child to hold one. Place the circle in front of you. Give each child a block. Tell the children that you will point to each of them at sometime during the story. When you point to a child, she should bring her block and put it where you point to around the circle. (You will be building a well.)

Jesus and His friends were traveling through the country of Samaria. Jesus and His friends were Jewish. The people who lived in the country of Samaria were Samaritans. Most Jewish people and Samaritan people did not get along. They would not talk to each other. They would not touch each other. They were different from each other. They even worshiped God in different places. Ask children to describe what they learned in Activity 1.

Begin pointing to children and building the well. **The Bible tells us that one day Jesus decided to rest beside a well. His friends went into town to buy food. While Jesus was resting, a Samaritan woman came to the well. She was different from Jesus in two ways. She was a Samaritan and she was a woman. According to what the Jews said, Jesus should not look at the woman; He should not speak to the woman; He should not

---

down. It was a piece of gum. The mean girl wasn't mean anymore. She was my friend!

◆◆◆◆

BIBLE MEMORY—International Doll Verse

You will need the paper-doll pattern from page 134, scissors, and markers or colored pencils. Before the session, cut a chain of four paper dolls for each child. Print each word of the Bible verse on a different doll in order. Older children may print the words on the dolls themselves.

Ask the children to color each one of their dolls differently, with different color skin, hair, and eyes.

As you color, would anyone like to say the Bible verse by himself? Let each child who wishes to do so say the Bible verse.

◆◆◆◆

ACTIVITY TIME

Do as many activities as time permits.

Craft—Bean Jar

Each child will need a baby food jar with a lid. Cut 3" circles from a brown paper bag and print the Bible words in the center. You will also need a bowl of many different kinds of beans and rubber bands.

Point to the bowl of beans. **God made many different kinds of everything, including people!** Ask the children to fill their baby-food jar with beans and put the lid on it. Then they should use a rubber band to hold the paper with the Bible words on it on the lid of the jar. **Put this jar where you can see it at home and let it remind you that Jesus created all people, even those who are different from us.**

Snack—Different Food

Serve small samples of foods from around the world. Many supermarkets now have sections of international fruits, vegeta-

touch the woman. **What do you think Jesus did?** Let children respond. Jesus talked to the Samaritan woman. He said, "May I please have a drink of water?"

The woman was surprised when Jesus asked her for a drink of water. She was surprised that a Jewish man would talk to her. She was surprised that He would want to drink from a pitcher that she had touched. She asked Jesus some questions about God.

Jesus knew the Samaritan woman needed to know about Him. She needed to know that God loved her, and that Jesus would be her friend. Jesus knew that Jewish people, Samaritan people, and all people needed to know about Him. They all needed Jesus to be their friend.

After talking to Jesus, the woman knew that Jesus was different from anyone she had ever met. She knew it was a good difference. She thought that Jesus was probably the Messiah that the Jewish and Samaritan people knew had been promised by God. She was right! She ran home to tell all her friends and neighbors about this man sent from God, Jesus.

❖❖❖❖

APPLICATION—Different Kinds of Different

You will need paper, colored pencils, and a stick of gum. Earlier we drew some pictures and wrote a letter to some children who are different from us. **Do you remember how the children were different?** Allow children to respond. The children were different because they live in a different country.

Some people are different because they speak a different language from us or eat different foods. But some people are different from us in other ways. Listen to a story about a girl who found a way to be a friend to a person who was different.

Gather the children around you as you tell them the story "A Stick of Gum" printed below. Hold up the stick of gum as it is mentioned in the story. Ask the children to listen carefully, since they will be asked to draw a picture of the story when it is over. When you are finished with the story, give the children the paper. Ask them to fold their papers in half. **How was the person in the story a friend to the mean girl?** Help children remember ways. On one half of the paper, ask them to draw a picture of how the person was a friend to the mean girl. **Jesus was a friend to a person that everyone expected Him to hate. Whom do you know who is different? Maybe no one else is nice to that person. Maybe that person isn't nice to you. How could you be a friend to that person?** On the other half of the paper, ask children to draw how they will be a friend this week to the person they chose. Children will share about their pictures during the Wrap-up time.

A Stick of Gum

This story is about a stick of gum that taught me about being a friend like Jesus.

When I was six years old, a mean girl sat in the row next to me at school. Her desk was one row back from mine. During rest time, when I folded my hands on the desk, the mean girl would stick her tongue out at me and I would stick mine out right back. During recess, the mean girl would make fun of me and make faces at me. I didn't like that mean girl.

At home, I asked Mom, "What do I do about that mean girl? I don't like her."

My mom said, "Jesus was a friend to everyone, even people who were mean. If you want to be like Jesus, you need to be a friend to the mean girl. You need to do nice things for her."

Yuck! I didn't feel like being nice to the mean girl, but I really wanted to be like Jesus.

The next day at rest time, when the mean girl stuck out her tongue at me, I just smiled. When we got into line to go to lunch, I said to the mean girl, "Would you like to get in line ahead of me?" When we drew a picture, I shared some of my colored chalk with the mean girl. I was nice to the mean girl all week.

One day, I was walking home from school. The mean girl was walking in front of me. Suddenly she turned around and threw something at me. She called, "Hey, that's for you." I looked

129

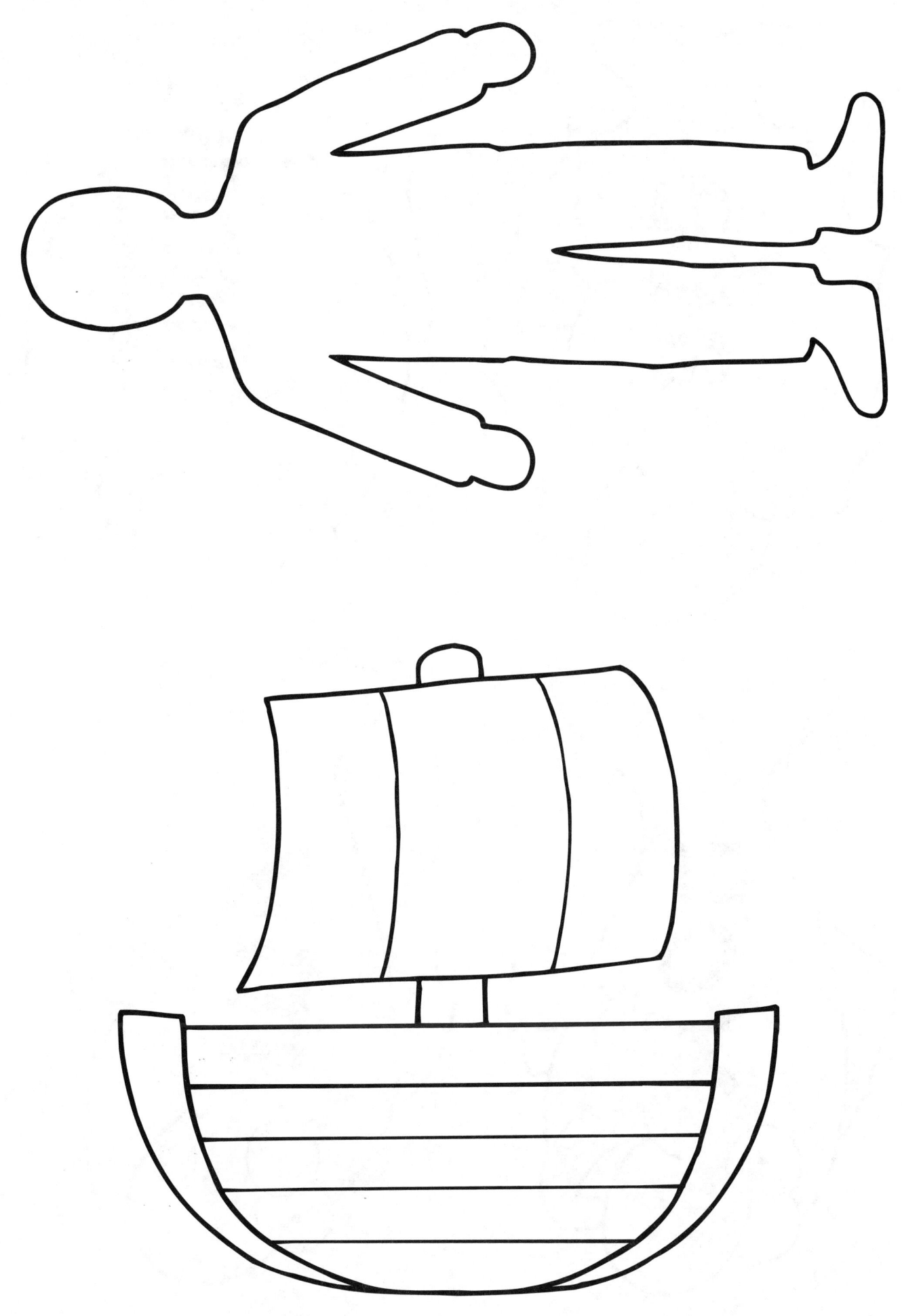

are

friends
John 15:14

You

my

Dear _____,

Please come to _____
(name of church)
to learn more about my friend Jesus.
My family and I will be glad to have you
come with us. Class time is _____.

Love,

"You are my friends" John 15:14

133

Pray for _____

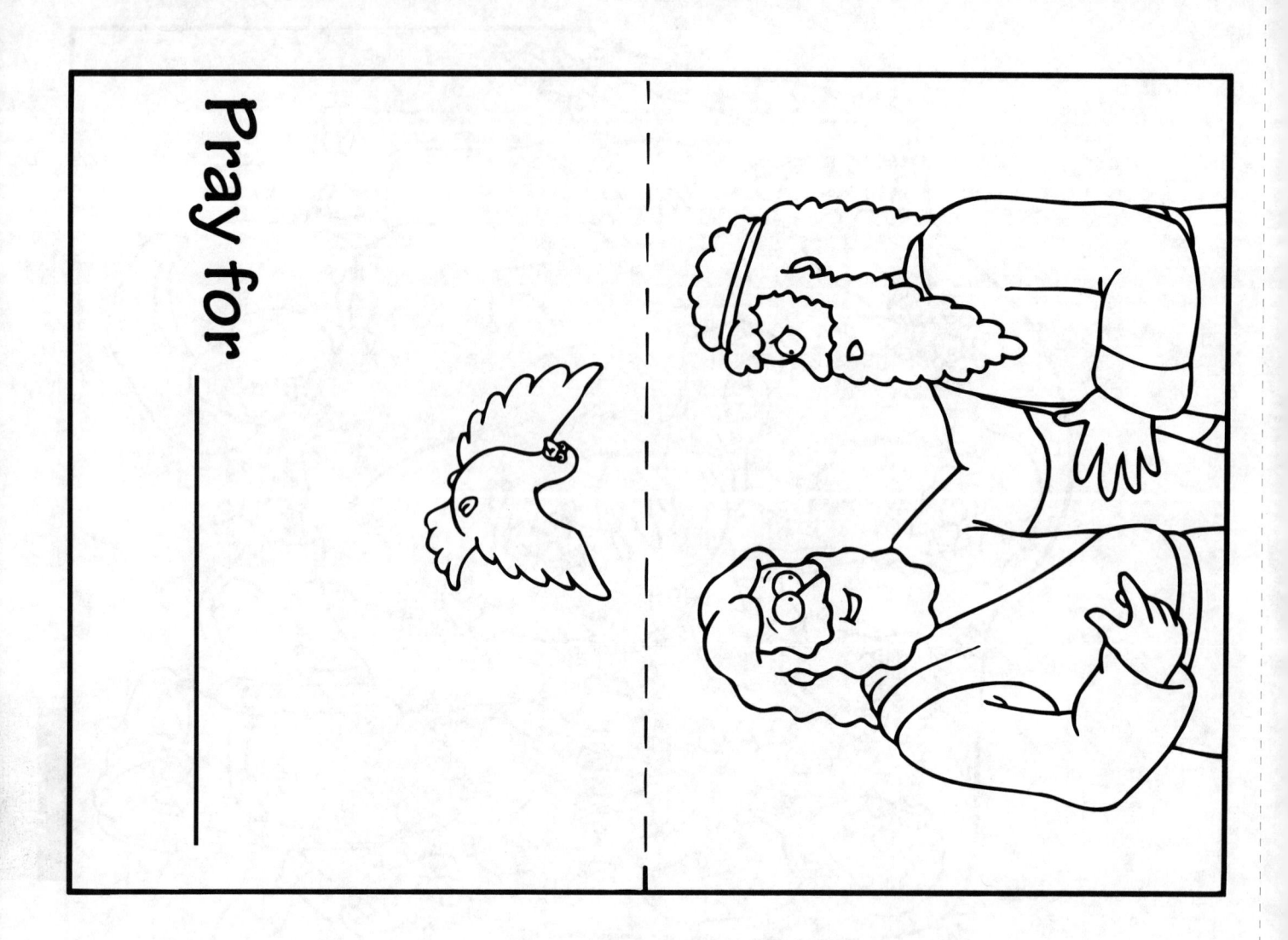

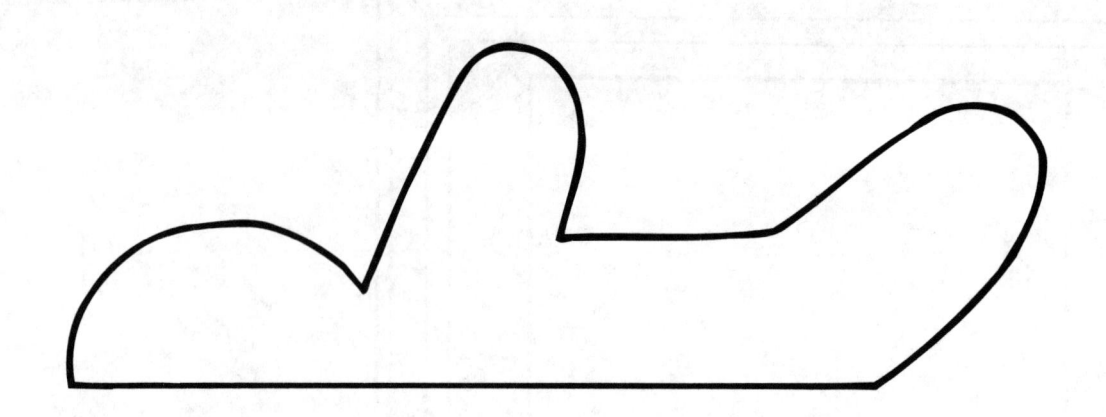

Unit 6
Lessons 23-26

Jesus Is God's Son

◆◆◆◆◆

By the end of this unit, the children and leaders will . . .
Know Learn four special things Jesus did that show He is the Son of God.
Feel Feel eager to talk about Jesus.
Do Tell others that Jesus is God's Son.

Unit Bible Words for Memory
"Jesus is the Son of God"
(1 John 4:15, NIV).

◆◆◆◆◆

Unit Lessons

Lesson 23
Jesus Healed Peter's Mother-in-Law
Mark 1:29-34, 40-45
Children will learn that Jesus healed a woman who had a fever. She felt so well that she was able to get up and fix a meal for her guests.

Lesson 24
Jesus Raised a Widow's Son
Luke 7:11-17
Children will find that Jesus not only heals the sick, He can also make a dead person come back alive.

Lesson 25
Jesus Fed More Than 5,000 People
Mark 6:30-44
Children will discover that only Jesus could make five loaves of bread and two small fish feed a crowd of over 5,000 people.

Lesson 26
Jesus Healed Two Blind Men
Matthew 20:29-34; Mark 10:46-52
Children will learn that Jesus made two blind men able to see again when they called out to Him and asked for His help.

◆◆◆◆◆

Why Teach This Unit to Four-Year-Olds—Six-Year-Olds?

In unit 4, children discovered why Jesus' birth was special. In this unit, they will discover special things that Jesus did that prove He is the Son of God. When children understand that ONLY Jesus could make a person come back alive or make a little food into a whole lot of food, they will be excited about telling the people they meet about Jesus, the Son of God.

◆◆◆◆◆

Bible Time Line

The stories for this unit are pictured on the time line, pages 315 and 316.

Provide the time-line page for children who arrive early, or plan time at the end of the Bible story during each session for children to color the time line and look for the hidden pictures.

See page 6 in this book for further instructions on using the time line and for suggested projects.

135

◆◆◆◆◆

Materials

All Lessons
a Bible
markers, colored pencils, crayons
white paper, construction paper, poster board
tape, masking tape
Plasti-Tak
glue
scissors
a stapler
paper hole punch
yarn or string

Lesson 23
old nylon hose and scraps of quilt batting
paper plates, plastic knives, small cups, oranges, and a hand juicer
popsicle sticks, a paper fastener
items used with sick people: a thermometer, a box of Band-aids, some children's liquid medicine, a container of children's pills, some cream to put on cuts or rashes, rolled bandages and tape
empty toilet-paper tubes
sticker solution: two parts white glue, one part vinegar, a few drops of peppermint extract (optional)
a cassette of familiar music, a cassette player

Lesson 24
nature items (see Activity 1)
paper plates, red rubber bands, two small circles for eyes (film canister lids, milk carton lids, pop bottle lids, or cut circles out of heavy cardboard), dry red beans (nose), cotton swabs
pennies
wood blocks or cardboard boxes
a very lightweight washcloth or 11" x 11" piece of terry cloth for each child; a small (1—1 1/2") plastic egg or mini ziplock bag for each child; small pompoms, buttons, or markers; hair gel

old flannel shirts and blouses with sleeves and collars cut off
old ties for belts and headbands
a large doll or a rolled blanket on a bath towel
a toy microphone or something to use as a microphone (pencil, rolled-up piece of paper)

Lesson 25
red, yellow, and green liquid tempera paint; foil pans; aprons or smocks; a hand washing pan or sink for cleanup; and various cut pieces of vegetables (broccoli, cauliflower, carrot, celery, an ear of corn cut into two-inch lengths, a pepper, a potato, a radish)
items to set up a grocery store (see Activity 2)
a picnic basket, a blanket, tiny baskets or lunch-size paper bags, croutons, and gummy fish
several fishing poles (children's are best, but adult-size will work too), small pieces of strip magnet, paper clips, a blue sheet or shower curtain
a potato
a margarine tub with a slit in the bottom and a craft stick for each child

Lesson 26
a large mirror or several smaller mirrors (or purchase mirror tiles and let each child use one)
a spray bottle filled with water
textured items (bubble wrap, foam, fur, sandpaper, grass, carpet, plastic, wood, aluminum foil) and a cane (optional)
a large box, a pillow, thermometer, stethoscope, orange, rocks, plastic fish, hard roll, basket, boo-boo bunny, carrot, potato, radish, glasses, binoculars, spy glass, money
a hopscotch board, a bean bag
craft sticks, envelopes, and an X-acto knife or other sharp knife

◆◆◆◆◆

The Beginner's Bible™ Resources

Feeding 5,000 Stickers, Standard Publishing, #22-01036, call 1-800-543-1353

The Beginner's Bible™ New Testament GeoSafari Bible Pack, Standard Publishing, #14-24002, call 1-800-543-1353

The Beginner's Bible™ Bible Lessons GeoSafari Bible Pack, Standard Publishing, #14-24005, call 1-800-543-1353

Unit 6
Lesson 23

Jesus Healed Peter's Mother-in-Law
(Mark 1:29-34, 40-45)

Jesus went to Peter and Andrew's home. Peter's mother-in-law was in bed with a fever. Jesus took her hand and helped her up. The fever left her and she began to wait on them. Only the Son of God could have healed as Jesus did.

Bible Words

"Jesus is the Son of God" (1 John 4:15).

Goals

Tell what Jesus did for Peter's mother-in-law because He is the Son of God.

Feel eager to talk about Jesus.

Tell others that Jesus is God's Son—He made sick people well.

◆◆◆◆

Activity 1—Stuff a Pillow

You will need old nylon hose and scraps of quilt batting. Before the session, cut 11" to 12" off the toe end of old nylon hose. You will need enough hose for each child in your group to have one.

Do you remember some times when you were sick? Where were you? How did you feel? Did you have a fever? Let children tell about times that they were sick. Discuss what a fever is. In our Bible story Jesus was in the home of a sick woman. She was very hot because she had a fever. Because Jesus is the Son of God, He had the power to do something very special for Peter's mother-in-law. Ask children if they know any special

---

Tell, Tell to All
(Tune: "Row Your Boat")

Tell, tell, tell to all
Jesus is God's Son.
Telling, telling, telling.
Tell to everyone.

Tell, tell, tell to all
Jesus is God's Son.
Jesus makes sick people well.
Tell to everyone.

Jesus Is the Son of God
(Tune: "London Bridge Is Falling Down")

Jesus is the Son of God,
Son of God, Son of God.
Jesus is the Son of God.
First John four fif-te-en.

things only the Son of God can do. **I'm glad you are telling about Jesus.**

Give children the pieces of nylon hose and ask them to stuff the hose with the quilt batting. Finish their "pillows" by tying a knot in the open end.

◆◆◆◆◆

Activity 2—Juice Oranges

Provide paper plates, plastic knives, small cups, oranges, and a hand juicer. Allow half an orange for each child. **When you are sick, what makes you feel better? Are there some special things that your parents or friends do for you that make you feel better?** Let children share. Some suggestions follow: give you medicine; make a bed on the couch for you; read you a book; watch your favorite movie with you; bring you a drink.

Today we are going to practice something that we could do for a sick friend. We are going to make some fresh juice. Have children take turns cutting their oranges in half and squeezing the juice with a hand juicer. Discuss other ways they could help a sick friend. **The best way to help a sick friend is to tell them about Jesus. What could you tell a sick friend about Jesus?** Have children name friends and something they can tell about Jesus as they work.

◆◆◆◆◆

Bible Time—Jesus Heals a Sick Woman

You will need a copy of page 153, cardboard or heavy paper, popsicle sticks, a paper fastener. Before the session, follow the instructions on page 153 to assemble the Time to Tell Clock.

Hold up the Time to Tell Clock and say the rhyme to introduce the Bible Time.

Have children sit on their pillows made in Activity 1. **Pillows are soft and make us feel good when we are sick. Listen to our** today's story? Point to the right face as I review the story. Who came to visit Peter and Andrew's home? (Jesus.) **Who told Jesus about the sick woman?** (Sad servants.) **How did the woman feel when Jesus made her well?** (Happy.)

Ask the children to use their Telling Tube to help them choose someone to tell about Jesus this week. They can give that person their stickers and tell them the story about Jesus.

Until parents come, play a game using the Telling Tubes and a Beginner's Bible™ or other children's Bible with pictures. Turn to familiar stories about Jesus in the Bible and ask children to use their Telling Tubes to say what they could tell about Jesus from that story. Suggested stories follow: The birth of Jesus; shepherds come to see Jesus; wise men worship Jesus; Jesus makes a lame man walk; Jesus stops a storm; Jesus walks on water; Jesus makes a blind man see.

Leaders' Evaluation

	Great!	OK!	More!	Oops!	Suggestions
Activity 1					
Activity 2					
Bible Time					
Application					
Bible Memory					
Craft					
Snack					
Game					
Wrap-up					

Bible story. When you hear about a sick person, pick up your pillow and lay your head on it. If the person gets well, lay the pillow in your lap.

Jesus had just done some amazing things at the synagogue church. Everyone wanted to see this amazing person. People were probably saying, "Have you seen this man Jesus? He does amazing things. No one else can do these things. Let's go and tell our friends about Him."

Jesus was with His new helpers Peter, Andrew, James, and John. Peter may have said, "Come with my brother Andrew and me to our house. You must be tired after having all those people around you. My wife's mother will fix us something to eat."

When they came to Peter and Andrew's home, the servants ran to Jesus and said, "Peter's wife's mother is very sick." Wait for children to get pillows. "She is very hot with a high fever."

Put finger to lips and speak softly. Jesus went quietly to her bed. Jesus took her hand and helped her up. The fever left her and she was well. Wait for the children to put their pillows in their laps. Peter's mother-in-law felt so good that she got out of bed and began to fix their food.

"Amazing!" That's probably what the servants and Jesus' helpers said. They knew only the Son of God could make the sick (head on pillow) woman well (pillow on lap).

That night many sick (head on pillow) people came to Jesus. Jesus made them well (pillow on lap). I think the people said, "This man is amazing. I'm going to tell my friends what He did."

◆ ◆ ◆ ◆

APPLICATION—Tell, Tell to All

You will need items used with sick people: a thermometer, a box of Band-aids, some children's liquid medicine, a container of children's pills, some cream to put on cuts or rashes, rolled bandages and tape, and so on. Before the session, place all the items in a paper bag.

---

did the servants tell Jesus? What will you tell about Jesus with your mouth?

Game—Telling Chairs

You will need the Telling Tube art from page 156, scissors, tape, a cassette of familiar music and a cassette player. Before the session, enlarge, color, and cut apart sticker squares from the Telling Tube. Set the chairs in a circle and tape the six pictures to different chairs. Set up enough chairs for each child to have one.

Play a version of musical chairs. Children will walk around the chairs while you play the music. When the music stops, children should sit in a chair. The children with pictures on their chairs will name someone whom they will tell about Jesus. **Who is your friend at school? Who is your doctor? Do you have a baby-sitter? Does the person who brings your mail know Jesus?**

Option: To make the game more fun, provide the music by singing "Tell, Tell to All" or other familiar songs into your Telling Tube.

◆ ◆ ◆ ◆

Wrap-up—Food Letter

You will need the Time to Tell Clock used during Bible Time and copies of the letter and stickers from page 154. Before you copy the letter, fill in the information for your class. Also, coat the backs of the three stickers with the following solution: two parts white glue, one part vinegar, a few drops of peppermint extract (optional). Paint lightly, making sure you reach the corners of the paper. Allow the solution to dry.

Say "How to tell" as you hold up the Time to Tell Clock to gather the class.

Give children the letter to take home. Read and explain the letter. **We will put our canned food in a big basket.** Have the children fold their letters.

Give each child a sticker of Jesus, a sad face, and a glad face. **These stickers can help you tell about Jesus. Who was sick in**

Today we learned something we can tell about Jesus. What can we tell? Allow children's responses. They can tell people that Jesus is the Son of God; He makes sick people well. Teach children the two verses to "Tell, Tell to All" from page 8 of this session.

Ask children to sit in a circle. Show them the bag you brought. **This bag contains items that we use to help us feel better when we are sick or hurt.** Tell the children that you will pass the bag around the circle. Each child or pair of children should draw out an item. When each child or pair has an item, sing "Tell, Tell to All" again. After each time singing the song, a child or pair should tell what item they drew and how it is used to make sick people better. Then they should say, "But Jesus makes sick people well." You begin. Help children as needed. Continue until each child or pair has had a chance to share.

◆◆◆◆

BIBLE MEMORY—Sing a Verse

You will need a copy of the Telling Tube cover art from page 156 and a Bible. Before class, use the Telling Tube art to mark the Bible words, 1 John 4:15, in the Bible.

Our Bible words help us remember who Jesus is. Let's play a game as we sing the words from our Bible. Ask a child to find the place in your Bible marked with the Telling Tube art. Read the words and say them together. Then sing "Jesus Is the Son of God." The words are on page 8 of this session.

When the children know the song well, divide the class into groups of five by saying, **"Jesus had four helpers: Peter, Andrew, James, and John."** Touch heads as you say a name. Two children will be partners for the bridge as they sing the Bible words. The other three children in each group will walk under the bridge as they sing. As they sing "First John four fifteen," the two children making the bridge will lower their arms to catch one child. Different pairs of children may take turns being the bridge.

Unit 6

4

— fold —

ACTIVITY TIME

Do as many activities as time permits.

◆◆◆◆

Craft—Telling Tube

You will need empty toilet-paper tubes, copies of the Telling Tube cover on page 156, markers, colored paper, glue, and scissors. Before class, copy and cut out the Telling Tube covers. Make stickers by coating the backs of the Telling Tube covers with the following solution: two parts white glue, one part vinegar, a few drops of peppermint extract (optional). Paint lightly, making sure you reach the corners of the paper. Allow the solution to dry. You may wish to make the stickers for the Wrap-up at the same time.

We are going to make a Telling Tube to help us tell about Jesus. Children will color and cut apart the stickers. Then they may decorate their tubes by gluing colored paper on their tubes and then putting the stickers on the tubes.

Who are some people you can tell about Jesus? Use your Telling Tube to remind you. Grandparents, doctor, friend, mail carrier, baby-sitter. **What can you tell about Jesus?** Jesus is the Son of God. Jesus makes sick people well.

Option: Younger children can color the stickers and then glue them in one piece to the tubes, instead of cutting apart the stickers or gluing colored paper on the tubes.

Snack—Apple Mouth Sandwich

You will need apples, peanut butter, miniature marshmallows, and a knife.

Wash and cut apples into ½" slices. Spread with peanut butter. Let children place miniature marshmallows on the bottom slice for teeth and add the other slice to make a sandwich. Say a prayer before the snack. **Thank You for mouths to tell about Jesus. Thank You that Jesus makes sick people well.**

As the children eat their snack, talk about telling about Jesus. **How did the people in our Bible story use their mouths? What**

Lesson 23

140

5

Unit 6
Lesson 24

Jesus Raised a Widow's Son
(Luke 7:11-17)

When Jesus saw a widow lady walking with her dead son's funeral procession, He felt great compassion. Jesus spoke to the woman and then brought her son to life.

Bible Words

"Jesus is the Son of God" (1 John 4:15).

Goals

Tell what Jesus did for a widow's son because He is the son of God.

Feel eager to talk about Jesus.

Tell others that Jesus is God's Son—He made dead people live again.

◆◆◆◆

ACTIVITY 1—Dead or Alive

You will need nature items that are dead and alive (butterfly, moth, worms, sea horse, starfish, leaves, flowers, bugs, frog, frozen fish), magnifying glasses, and containers for collecting if you take a nature walk (plastic tubs or paper sacks). If some of the nature items are fragile, place them in greeting card boxes with plastic tops, so they are protected.

If possible, plan to take a nature hike. Give each child a container in which to collect items. **Let's look for things on our walk that are dead or alive.** Have children check with the teacher before taking any items they see. When the children return to class, allow them to use magnifying glasses to examine the specimens you brought to class and the items they collected on the walk.

---fold---

Tell, Tell to All
(Tune: "Row Your Boat")

Tell, tell, tell to all
Jesus is God's Son.
Telling, telling, telling, telling.
Tell to everyone.

Tell, tell, tell to all
Jesus is God's Son.
Jesus makes sick people well.
Tell to everyone.

Tell, tell, tell to all
Jesus is God's Son.
Jesus made a dead man live.
Tell to everyone.

Jesus Is the Son of God
(Tune: "London Bridge Is Falling Down")

Jesus is the Son of God,
Son of God, Son of God.
Jesus is the Son of God.
First John four fif-te-en.

Which things are dead? Which things are alive? How can you tell what is dead and what is alive? Discuss the differences. Things that are alive move and grow. Dead things don't move or grow. **Can dead things live again? Dead things do not come back alive again.**

ACTIVITY 2—Glad/Sad Face

◆◆◆◆

You will need paper plates, red rubber bands, two small circles for eyes (film canister lids, milk carton lids, pop bottle lids, or cut circles out of heavy cardboard), dry red beans (nose), yarn (hair), scissors, glue, cotton swabs, and a stapler. Before class, staple a red rubber band (mouth) to a small plain paper plate for each child. Provide two film can lids (eyes), a red bean (nose), and yarn (hair) to glue to the face.

Give children the paper plates and help them glue the eyes, nose, and hair to the plate to make a face. Place glue in small lids and apply with cotton swabs to limit amount and facilitate quick cleanup. **Can you make your face look glad?** Pull rubber band down. **Can you make your face look sad?** Pull rubber band up. **How would your face look if someone died? How would your face look if they came back alive?**

Option: If your time is limited, draw the eyes and noses on the plate with a marker, rather than gluing objects.

BIBLE TIME—Jesus Brings a Dead Man to Life

◆◆◆◆

You will need the Time to Tell Clock used last week, the Glad/Sad Faces made in Activity 2, and a Bible with Luke 7:11-17 marked and highlighted.

Use the Time to Tell Clock and rhyme to signal children for Bible story. Have children bring their Glad/Sad Faces to Bible Time. **I have some glad news to tell you.** Show your paper plate face with a glad mouth. **Jesus is the Son of God. When you hear glad news in our Bible story, show a glad face. When you

2 Unit 6

---

tell about Jesus last week? What did you tell? Whom did you tell? Allow children to share their experiences.

Sing the three verses of "Tell, Tell to All" from page 8 of this session. After the third verse is sung, ask children to take turns using the microphone to say something they will tell about Jesus this week. When each child has had a turn to share, sing the song again.

Let's sing our Bible words one more time before we leave. Sing "Jesus Is the Son of God" from page 8 of this session. Ask for volunteers to say the Bible words from memory.

NOTE: Remind children that you are collecting food. If children brought canned goods to class, direct them to put the food in the box or container you have provided. See the Wrap-up for lesson 23.

Leaders' Evaluation

	Great!	OK!	More!	Oops!	Suggestions
Activity 1					
Activity 2					
Bible Time					
Application					
Bible Memory					
Craft					
Snack					
Game					
Wrap-up					

142 Lesson 24 7

hear sad news, show a sad face. Let's practice using our sad and glad faces. Jesus loves you. (glad) A friend did not share. (sad) Jesus is our friend. (glad)

Have a child help you find the Bible story as it is marked in your Bible. Today's story is about a man who was no longer alive. He had died. What did we learn about dead and alive things? Ask children to share some of their observations from Activity 1. Dead things do not come alive again. But listen to what happens when Jesus, the Son of God, comes to visit.

Remind the children to listen for glad/sad news.

Jesus was traveling around to many towns. One day as Jesus entered a town, He heard a very sad sound. (sad) The sound was people crying. Jesus looked ahead at the town gate. He saw a sad (sad) sight. A woman was walking behind a dead man being carried out of town. The dead man was her son. Her husband was already dead. Now her son had died. She was very sad. (sad)

Jesus was sad (sad) because this woman had no one to take care of her. Jesus said to the widow woman, "Don't cry." Then Jesus walked over to the men carrying the dead man. They stopped walking. They may have wondered, "What is Jesus doing?"

Jesus said, "Young man, I say to you, get up!" (glad) What do you think they saw next? Allow children to tell what they think happened next. The man who was dead sat up. (glad) Then the man began to talk. (glad) Jesus took him back to his mother. (glad)

Nobody was sad (sad) anymore. Everyone was amazed and praised God. (glad) Everyone was glad (glad), for they knew God's power had made the dead man live. (glad) Only Jesus, the Son of God, could make a dead man live. (glad)

The people began thanking God and hurried to tell everyone they saw about Jesus, God's only Son.

Let's make our puppet mouths say, "Jesus is the Son of God." Now everyone should have a big smile!

Lesson 24

3

---

ask each child which cracker they want the happy face on and which one the sad face. They can help add the eyes and nose. **Let's close our eyes and fold our hands and talk to God today. Thank You for Your love. Thank You for Jesus, Your Son. Thank You for Your Word, the Bible. When did the people have sad faces in our Bible story? When did they have happy faces? Tell what makes you happy.**

Game—Acting Rhyme

Cut sleeves and collars off old flannel shirts and blouses. Provide old ties for belts and headbands. Dress the children like Bible-times people. Place a large doll or a rolled blanket on a bath towel to carry. Choose the following actors: Jesus, carriers, live man, mother, friends.

Read the following rhyme as children act out the parts. You may have a child act as the storyteller and hold the Bible.

Jesus walked into the town (*Jesus walks in.*),
Saw the people sad with frowns. (*Carriers, women, friends walk and cry.*)
On that day the dead He raised (*Carriers lay down towel, Jesus touches dummy. Move it and have live man sit up.*),
"He's God's Son," the people praised. (*Jesus walks man to mother. Everyone smiles, hugs, folds hands in praise.*)

If you have time, choose new actors and repeat acting out the story.

♦♦♦♦

WRAP-UP—Ways to Help

You will need the Time to Tell Clock and a toy microphone or something to use as a microphone (pencil, rolled-up piece of paper).

Look around your room for cleanup jobs. Give each child two choices. Stack chairs, wash tables, straighten block or bookshelf, pick up paper scraps, close windows, or put away supplies.

As children are finishing the cleanup, signal them with the Time to Tell Clock and rhyme to gather together. **Did anyone**

Unit 6

143

6

APPLICATION—Time to Tell About Jesus

You will need photocopies of page 153, scissors, crayons or markers, and pennies. If you have younger children, cut out the Time to Tell Clocks before class.

Children should decorate and cut out their clocks. Discuss the times to tell that are pictured on the clock. **Whom could you send a letter about Jesus? What could you tell someone on the phone about Jesus? Do you know someone at school you could tell about Jesus? What have we learned that we can tell about Jesus?** He is the Son of God. He made sick people well. He made a dead man live again.

Play a game in groups of three or four. Children will take turns tossing a penny onto the clock. They will say what they will tell about Jesus at the place or to the person that the penny lands on.

◆◆◆◆

BIBLE MEMORY—Word Block

You will need paper, wood blocks or cardboard boxes, a marker, and tape or Plasti-Tak. Before the session, write the words and Scripture reference for the memory verse on separate pieces of paper and tape or Plasti-Tak them to the blocks or boxes.

Sing "Jesus Is the Son of God" from page 8 of this session.

As you sing the Bible words song, show each word of the verse on the blocks. See if children can recognize the words Jesus, Son, or God. **Does anyone's name start with J, S, or G? Who knows the first word of our Bible words? Who sees that word?** Have children point out each word of the verse, as they help you put the blocks in order. Then mix up the words again and have children help you sequence them.

For variety, have a child mix up the words and choose someone to put them in order. Younger children will need help. Always have the class sing or say the Bible words when the word blocks are in order.

ACTIVITY TIME

Do as many activities as time permits.

◆◆◆◆

Craft—Little Bunny Boo-boo

Provide each child with a very lightweight washcloth or 11" x 11" piece of terry cloth; a small (1 to 1 1/2") plastic egg or mini ziplock bag; a copy of the bunny song from page 155; small pompoms, buttons, or markers; and hair styling gel. Before class, use the instructions on page 155 to fold the washcloths into bunnies and secure with rubber bands. Make a completed sample bunny with eyes, nose, and a tail.

Have any of you ever fallen down or bumped your head? Bumped or scraped. Today, we will make a bunny that will help our boo-boos feel better. Show children the folded bunny washcloths and the completed bunny. Assist them in gluing buttons or drawing with markers to make the bunnies' faces. They can glue on pompoms for the bunnies' tails.

Give children the plastic eggs or ziplock bags. Each child will place a tablespoon of hair styling gel in the egg or bag, and then put it in bunny. See the instructions on page 155. **You can keep your bunny in the freezer. When you get a bump or scrape, Little Bunny Boo-boo can make it feel better.** Sing or say the "Little Bunny Boo-boo!" song several times with the children.

Bunny Boo-boo can make our bumps feel better. But when someone dies, he cannot help himself feel better. Only Jesus can make a dead person come back alive! You might want to give your bunny to someone that doesn't know Jesus. What could you tell them about Jesus? Jesus is the Son of God. Only Jesus could make a dead person come back alive. Only Jesus could heal a sick woman's fever.

Snack—Happy/Sad Face Crackers

Serve two sizes of round crackers. With a can of squirt cheese,

Unit 6
Lesson 25

Jesus Fed More Than 5,000 People
(Mark 6:30-44)

Jesus had been teaching the people all day. The people were hungry and far from a town, so Jesus told His disciples to feed them. They could not. But with only two small fish and five loaves of bread, Jesus, the Son of God fed everyone and had His disciples collect the twelve baskets of leftovers.

Bible Words

"Jesus is the Son of God" (1 John 4:15).

Goals

Tell what Jesus did for more than 5,000 people because He is the Son of God.

Feel eager to talk about Jesus.

Tell others that Jesus is God's Son—He made a little food feed more than 5,000 people.

Activity 1—Vegetable Painting

You will need large sheets of newsprint; red, yellow, and green liquid tempera paint; foil pans; aprons or smocks; a hand washing pan or sink for cleanup; and various cut pieces of vegetables (broccoli, cauliflower, carrot, celery, an ear of corn cut into two-inch lengths, a pepper, a potato, a radish). You may wish to provide plastic corncob holders to make handles for the vegetables for painting.

Place one or two tablespoons of red, yellow, and green liquid tempera paint in foil pans. Have children put on an apron or

---

Tell, Tell to All
(Tune: "Row Your Boat")

Tell, tell, tell to all
Jesus is God's Son.
Telling, telling, telling, telling.
Tell to everyone.

Tell, tell, tell to all
Jesus is God's Son.
Jesus makes sick people well.
Tell to everyone.

Tell, tell, tell to all
Jesus is God's Son.
Jesus made a dead man live.
Tell to everyone.

Tell, tell, tell to all
Jesus is God's Son.
Jesus fed 5,000 people.
Tell to everyone.

Jesus Is the Son of God
(Tune: "London Bridge Is Falling Down")

Jesus is the Son of God,
Son of God, Son of God.
Jesus is the Son of God.
First John four fif-te-en.

smock and choose a vegetable. They should dip the vegetable in the paint and press it onto the newsprint to make a pattern. Let children trade colors and vegetables. Encourage them to fill the newsprint with their vegetable painting.

What food are you painting with? What food do you like to eat? Have you ever been hungry? More than 5,000 people in our Bible story were hungry, and they had no food. But Jesus was there. We'll find out how the Son of God helped some hungry people.

◆◆◆◆

ACTIVITY 2—Grocery Store

Use the following items to set up a grocery store: cash registers, money (strips of paper and buttons), sacks, purses, billfolds, pictures of food on meat trays and in berry baskets, plastic food, food boxes stuffed with paper to make them sturdy, spice cans, food cans, cartons, tubs, butcher aprons, and hats. A real frozen fish adds great interest. Set up food departments with shelves or cardboard boxes. Arrange tables or furniture like checkout lines.

With whom do you go to the store? How do you help your mom or dad at the store? Who are some people you see at the store? Checkout person, friends or neighbors, store workers.

In our story today, Jesus made a tiny bit of food feed many, many people. That's a good thing to tell people about Jesus. Let's tell the people at our pretend store about Jesus. Children can practice telling the pretend workers and their friends at the store about Jesus.

◆◆◆◆

BIBLE TIME—A Little Food and a Lot of People

You will need the Time to Tell Clock used in the last two sessions, a Bible, a picnic basket, a blanket, tiny baskets or lunch-size paper bags, croutons, and gummy fish. Before class, prepare a "lunch" for each child by putting five croutons and two

---

WRAP-UP—Counting Food

You will need the Time to Tell Clock and the canned foods brought in the last two sessions.

Guide children as they clean up the room. Have children work in pairs and give each pair a specific task to do. When cleanup is complete, hold up Time to Tell Clock and use the "Who to Tell" rhyme to call children to the large group area.

Have the children get their canned food and bring them to the story area. **Let's build a pyramid with our food cans.** Name the foods as cans are added. Stop after two cans. **What did Jesus use two of in our Bible story?** Stop after five. **What were there five of in our story?** Stop after twelve. **Why did we stop at twelve?**

Close by singing the four verses of "Tell, Tell, Tell to All" from page 8 of this session. **Whom will you tell about Jesus this week? What will you tell?** Encourage children to share.

Leaders' Evaluation

	Great!	OK!	More!	Oops!	Suggestions
Activity 1					
Activity 2					
Bible Time					
Application					
Bible Memory					
Craft					
Snack					
Game					
Wrap-up					

gummy fish in each container. Mark the page the lesson Scripture is on in your Bible (Mark 6:30-44).

Hold up the Time to Tell Clock used in the last two sessions and say the rhyme.

Have children help as you prepare for Bible Time. **Come on, everybody, let's get a picnic ready. What shall we take?** Put the lunches you prepared before class in the basket. Pretend to put other items they mention into your basket. **What shall we sit on?** Hold up the blanket. **We're going to talk about Jesus on our picnic. Where can we read about Jesus?** Have a child get the Bible and place it into the basket. You may want to put on pretend hats in case it is sunny. Walk outdoors, around the room, or to a quiet sunny place in your building. Ask for helpers to spread out the blanket. Have everyone sit down.

You are sitting and listening just like a group of people in Galilee might have listened in our Bible story. Choose a helper to find the Scripture in the Bible. Jesus and His disciples had been teaching and helping people. Jesus said, "Come with Me and we'll find a quiet place to rest." They got in a boat and rowed to a quiet hillside by themselves. But many people, more than 5,000, saw the boat and hurried around the lake to meet them. Jesus felt sad because they did not know He was the Son of God. So He started teaching them again. The people listened to Jesus. All morning. All afternoon. All evening, until it was late. Jesus kept teaching, and the people kept listening. His disciples said, "Jesus, the people are hungry. Send them to get some food."

Jesus said, "You feed them."

But the disciples said, "We don't have that much food or money to buy food for more than 5,000 people."

Jesus asked, "How much food do you have?" Who knows what the disciples had? Wait and see if the children remember. That's right! Two little fishes and five loaves of bread.

Jesus said, "Have everyone sit down on the green grass in groups." We might be like one group waiting to see what Jesus would do. It probably got very quiet. Then Jesus took the five loaves and two fish, looked up to Heaven, thanked

Let children choose pieces of vegetables to dip and eat. See if the children can name the vegetables before they taste them. Offer water to drink.

What did Jesus do before He broke the bread and fish into pieces? He looked to Heaven and thanked God. **Who would like to stand and thank God for our food?** Guide the volunteer as she thanks God. **Thank You, God, for Jesus. Thank You, God, for food.**

Game—One Basket, Two Basket

You will need a basket.

Have the children stand in a circle. As you say the rhyme below, give them a basket to pass around the circle. Continue through the second verse, pausing at "four" and "more" for the child who is holding the basket to tell something about Jesus. Continue until each child has had a chance to tell. Help the children as needed. **What did we learn today that you can tell about Jesus?** He made a little food feed more than 5,000 people. **What other things about Jesus can you tell?** Children can name things from past lessons: an angel told about His birth; He made a dead man come back alive; He healed a sick woman.

Verse 1:
1 basket, 2 baskets, 3 baskets, four—
5 baskets, 6 baskets, 7 baskets, more!
8 baskets, 9 baskets, 10-11-12;
Jesus did a miracle,
For all to see once more!

Verse 2:
1 tells, 2 tell, 3 tell, four—
5 tell, 6 tell, 7 tell, more!
8 tell, 9 tell, 10-11-12;
Jesus did a miracle,
So tell to all once more.

God, and started breaking up the bread and fish. Begin giving children their croutons and fish. Have the other teachers help if your class is large.

The disciples passed the food out, and passed the food out, and passed the food out until more than 5,000 people were fed. That's more people than our whole neighborhood or church or even some of our towns. But Jesus did not let them run out of food. My basket is empty, but Jesus had lots of food left over. The disciples brought one basket, two baskets, three baskets (have children help you count, using fingers too), four baskets, five baskets, six baskets, seven baskets, eight baskets, nine baskets, ten baskets, eleven baskets, twelve baskets. TWELVE BASKETS of food left over! It was a miracle. Only Jesus could make five loaves of bread and two fish feed over 5,000 people. Jesus really is the Son of God.

◆◆◆◆

APPLICATION—Fish and Tell

You will need several fishing poles (children's are best, but adult-size will work too), small pieces of strip magnet, several copies of the fish from page 157 photocopied onto heavy paper, paper clips, tape, a blue sheet or shower curtain. Before the session, cut out the fish on page 157 and tape a paper clip to the back of each fish. You may wish to laminate the fish to make them more durable. Tie or tape a strip magnet to the end of the fishing line on each fishing pole. If you do not have access to fishing poles, make poles from 20" dowel sticks with 15" of string tied to the end. Put a drop of glue on the end of each dowel rod to hold the string to the rod.

Lay a blue sheet or shower curtain in the middle of the floor and put the fish on it. Have the children take turns using the fishing poles to catch fish. When a child catches a fish, he should say what he will tell about Jesus from the picture on the fish and name whom he will tell. **What does the picture on your fish show Jesus doing? What could you tell someone about Jesus? Whom could you tell about Jesus?**

4 Unit 6

BIBLE MEMORY—Potato Pass

You will need the Bible-verse blocks used in lesson 24 and a potato.

Have the children set up the Bible-verse blocks from session 24. Sing "Jesus Is the Son of God" from page 8 of this session as you play the following game. Have the children form a circle and sit down. **We are going to pass a potato as we say our Bible words. When you get the potato, you say the next word or number to our Bible words. Let's go slowly at first and then try to go faster next time.**

◆◆◆◆

ACTIVITY TIME

Do as many activities as time permits.

◆◆◆◆

Craft—Counting Baskets

Each child will need a margarine tub with a slit in the bottom, a craft stick, scissors, glue, markers or colored pencils, and a copy of the food and basket cover from page 156.

Have the children color the food and basket. Cut out the food and glue it to the top of the craft stick. Glue the basket to the side of the tub. Insert stick into tub and slit. As the children answer the following questions, have them move their sticks up and down to show the food. **How many baskets did Jesus start with?** (one) **How many fish were in the basket?** (two) **How many loaves of bread?** (five) **More than how many people were fed?** (5,000) **We don't have time to count to 5,000 and more!! When everyone was finished eating, how many baskets of food were left?** (twelve) **Why could Jesus do a miracle?** (He is the Son of God.)

Snack—Veggie Pieces

You will need small pieces of vegetables (carrot and celery sticks, broccoli and cauliflower, radishes, or leftover vegetables from Activity 1) and a vegetable dip.

Lesson 25 5

Unit 6
Lesson 26

Jesus Healed Two Blind Men
(Matthew 20:29-34; Mark 10:46-52)

Jesus was leaving Jericho with His disciples when He heard two blind men calling loudly to Him. The men asked to be given their sight, and Jesus touched their eyes and healed them. They praised God.

Bible Words

"Jesus is the Son of God" (1 John 4:15).

Goals

Tell what Jesus did for two blind men because He is the Son of God.

Feel eager to talk about Jesus.

Tell others that Jesus is God's Son—He made two blind men see.

◆◆◆◆

Activity 1—Mirror Tiles

You will need a large mirror or several smaller mirrors (or purchase mirror tiles and let each child use one), washable markers, a spray bottle filled with water, and paper towels for cleanup.

Let children draw freely with markers as they look with their eyes at and in the mirror. Use water bottles to squirt the mirrors and wipe with a paper towel. Then ask the children to close their eyes and draw a design on the mirrors with their eyes closed. **Would you know what color to pick up if you could not see? Try drawing a design with your eyes closed. Two blind beggars in our Bible story asked Jesus to make them see. We will find out what Jesus did for them.**

---fold---

Tell, Tell to All
(Tune: "Row Your Boat")

Tell, tell, tell to all
Jesus is God's Son.
Telling, telling, telling, telling.
Tell to everyone.

Tell, tell, tell to all
Jesus is God's Son.
Jesus makes sick people well.
Tell to everyone.

Tell, tell, tell to all
Jesus is God's Son.
Jesus made a dead man live.
Tell to everyone.

Tell, tell, tell to all
Jesus is God's Son.
Jesus fed 5,000 people.
Tell to everyone.

Tell, tell, tell to all
Jesus is God's Son.
Jesus made two blind men see.
Tell to everyone.

Jesus Is the Son of God
(Tune: "London Bridge Is Falling Down")

Jesus is the Son of God,
Son of God, Son of God.
Jesus is the Son of God.
First John four fif-te-en.

149

ACTIVITY 2—Blind Man Walk

You will need textured items for the children to feel (bubble wrap, foam, fur, sandpaper, grass, carpet, plastic, wood, aluminum foil) and a cane (optional).

Lay the textured items on the floor. Ask the children to take off their shoes and walk across each item with their eyes closed. If they wish, they may practice using a cane one at a time to help them find their way. Talk about how each object feels. **What did you feel and hear while you could not see? Which things felt scratchy? Soft? Which things tickled your feet? Poked them? Which things sounded loud when you walked on them? Which didn't make any noise?**

The men in our Bible story could not see, but then they met Jesus!

BIBLE TIME—Jesus Makes Two Blind Men See

You will need the Time to Tell Clock used the last three sessions and a Bible with Matthew 20:29-34 marked.

Before the session, practice the Bible-story rhyme with actions several times, until you are comfortable saying it.

Signal the Bible story with the Time to Tell Clock and rhyme used in the last three sessions.

You are going to help me tell the Bible story today. Ask a volunteer to find the lesson Scripture that you have marked. We will open the Bible and lay it right here while we do the story actions. Close your eyes and do what I say. Stay in place and walk with your feet and legs. Do actions as you say the story in rhythm and give directions.

Jesus was walking from Jericho, (Keep walking.)
A large crowd followed wherever He'd go. (Now open your eyes and do what I do. Walk sideways, walk back, walk front.)
Two blind men were begging that day (Kneel down, hold out your hands.)

different areas of the room and let children guess which job you are describing. Then send children to do each task as they guess it.

Sing the five verses of "Tell, Tell to All" from page 8 of this session.

Say 1 John 4:15 together and close with prayer. Let each child who wishes ask God to help him tell about Jesus this week.

Teach children motions to help them remember the things they learned about Jesus that they can tell. Ask children to touch their foreheads. **Jesus healed a woman who had a fever.** Ask children to point to their eyes. **Jesus healed two blind men see.** Ask children to point to their mouths. **Jesus fed over 5,000 people with five loaves of bread and two small fish.** Ask children to put their hands over their hearts. **Jesus made a dead man come back alive.**

Now, you do the motions and ask children to tell you what they mean. Children can practice doing the motions and telling what they learned about Jesus until parents arrive.

Leaders' Evaluation

	Great!	OK!	More!	Oops!	Suggestions
Activity 1					
Activity 2					
Bible Time					
Application					
Bible Memory					
Craft					
Snack					
Game					
Wrap-up					

When they heard Jesus was on His way. (Put hands to your ears.)

"Lord, Son of God, have mercy on us." (Cup hands around mouth.)

The crowd said, "Quiet! Don't make such a fuss." (Put finger to mouth, Sh-h-h-h.)

Louder and louder they called to Him (Put hands to mouth, wave hands over head.),

"Lord, Son of God, have mercy on us." (Start walking in place.)

Jesus stopped and called back to the two (Stop and look to side, with hands to mouth.),

"What do you want me to do for you?" (Hands out like a question.)

"Lord, give us our sight—we want to see!" (Put your hands over your eyes.)

Jesus touched their eyes, and the men believed. (Put one finger on each eye.)

They could see and they followed immediately! (Put your hand above eyes. Look around.)

And so they praised God. (Look up and fold hands in prayer.)

Just like you and me. (Point to children and self.)

Ask the children to sit down. **Do you remember what it felt like not to be able to see? What was it like to paint? What was it like to walk?** Ask children to share what they experienced in Activities 1 and 2. **What did the blind men do when Jesus made them able to see? What do you think the blind men wanted to look at first?** Allow children to share things the blind men might have wanted to look at first, such as their family members and friends, the blue sky, Jesus' face. **The blind men praised God. The blind men probably couldn't wait to tell all their friends and everyone they met what Jesus had done. Only Jesus, the Son of God, could make blind men able to see again.** If you have time, do the rhyme with motions again.

Lesson 26

Snack—Blind Man's Snack

Mix together a variety of snack items, such as cereal, fish crackers, pretzels, raisins, butterscotch chips, peanuts, marshmallows, or animal cookies. Place a small portion in a lunch bag for each child and fold the bags shut. **We cannot see our snack today, but we want to thank God.** Ask for a volunteer. **Thank You, God, for tongues to taste and hands to feel. Thank You, God, for eyes to see.** Have children eat the snack without looking. **How can you tell what you are eating?** Feel and taste. **How does it feel? How does it taste?** Soft, crunchy, sweet, salty. **What is it?** See if children can name the foods.

Game—I Spy

Let's use our eyes to spy someone we can tell about Jesus. Describe the people in your room and let the children guess. **I spy someone wearing black shoes that tie. I spy someone with a blue hair clip.** Then give clues concerning people the children might know that they can tell about Jesus.

• **I work on a cash register. I help you when you buy your food.** Grocery store clerk.

• **I watch you when your parents go somewhere.** Baby-sitter.

• **I like to play with you and talk to you.** Friend.

• **I love you and give you hugs.** Mother, Father, Grandma, Grandpa.

• **I like to go sledding with you.** Friend.

• **I see you at school. I help you learn new things.** Teacher.

When a child guesses correctly, let that child tell something special about Jesus. Include teachers and compliment children on using their eyes and mouths for Jesus.

◆◆◆◆

Wrap-Up—Touch and Tell

Hold up the Time to Tell Clock and have the children gather as they say the rhyme.

Continue playing "I Spy" to help the children clean up. "Spy"

Unit 6

APPLICATION—Touch and Tell Box

You will need a large box, scissors or a knife, and items to help children remember things to tell about Jesus (pillow, thermometer, stethoscope, orange, rocks, plastic fish, hard roll, basket, boo-boo bunny, carrot, potato, radish, glasses, binoculars, spy glass, Bible, money). Before the session, cut two large holes in the side of the box, large enough for the children's hands to reach in the box. Place the items in the box.

Who is Jesus? He is the Son of God. **What things have we learned that Jesus did that show He is the Son of God?** Ask children or pairs to take turns reaching in the box and feeling an item. They should guess what the item is and tell something about Jesus having to do with that item. Help children by asking questions and offering clues. Things to tell about Jesus learned this unit include: He is the Son of God; He makes sick people well; He made a dead person live again; He made a little food feed over 5,000 people; He makes blind people see. After the child tells about the object, he should take it from the box. Continue until each child or pair has had a turn and all the objects have been discussed.

Gather objects from the box that the children could choose to take home, such as the food, the rocks, plastic fish, and so on. Let children choose an object to take home to remind them of something to tell about Jesus. **Whom will you tell about Jesus? When do you see that person? What will you tell that person about Jesus?** Encourage children to choose a specific time when they will tell the person, and a specific thing they will tell.

BIBLE MEMORY—Hopscotch

You will need a hopscotch board, masking tape, and a bean bag. Before class, print instructions concerning how to say the Bible verse in each square of the hopscotch board: loud, soft, fast, slow, two times in a row, clap hands, stomp feet. Tape the board to the floor. Tape a starting line about six inches from the board. Line chairs by the side of the board. If you don't have a hopscotch board, make one on the floor with masking tape. Review the Bible words by singing "Jesus Is the Son of God" from page 8 of this session.

Have a child stand on the starting line and toss the bean bag. The child will hop in the squares and pick up the bean bag. Then lead the group in saying the verse according to the instructions on the square. Continue until everyone has had a turn. **What did Jesus do that shows He is the Son of God?** Made a dead man live; healed a woman with a fever; made a little food feed 5,000 people; made a blind man see. **To whom will you tell your Bible words this week?** Encourage children to decide whom they will tell this week.

ACTIVITY TIME

Do as many activities as time permits.

Craft—Stick Puzzle

You will need copies of page 158, markers or colored pencils, glue, craft sticks, envelopes, and an X-acto knife or other sharp knife.

Give each child a copy of page 158. Let them color their pictures, then glue craft sticks closely together on the back. Give each child an envelope to decorate while you cut in-between the craft sticks with an X-acto knife.

Ask questions about the Bible story as the children practice putting together their puzzles. **Who asked for Jesus' help in today's story?** Two blind men. **What did Jesus do for them?** He touched their eyes, and they were able to see. **Why could Jesus make blind men see?** He is the Son of God.

When the children have completed their puzzles, they can put the pieces in the envelope they decorated to take home.

**Tic-toc, tic-toc,
Time✶ to tell
Time✶ to tell
Tic-toc, tic-toc,**

**Time✶ to tell
about Jesus.**

✶Use How or Who in place
of Time for other verses.

DIRECTIONS:
Copy, enlarge, color, and laminate or mount on cardboard. Make hands by punching holes in popsicle sticks and attaching with a 1 1/2" paper fastener.

Dear Family,

From _____ to _____, our class will be collecting canned food to share with others.

Peter's mother-in-law fixed Jesus food after He healed her from a fever. Also, Jesus fed more than 5,000 people with a little bit of food.

We want to tell these special things about Jesus, the Son of God. One way we can share about Jesus is by sharing our food.

Class_____

Teacher_____

Questions?
Call_____

NET WT. 10 OZ.

LITTLE BUNNY BOO-BOO!
(Tune: "I'm a Little Teapot")

Little Bunny Boo-boo helps my hurts,
With some ice so nice and cool.
But it's only Jesus, God's own Son;
Who heals our hurts and helps us run.

(Keep your egg or bag in the freezer. Place in the fold of the cloth back by bunny's tail when you have a "boo-boo." Say, "Thank You, Jesus, God's own Son.")

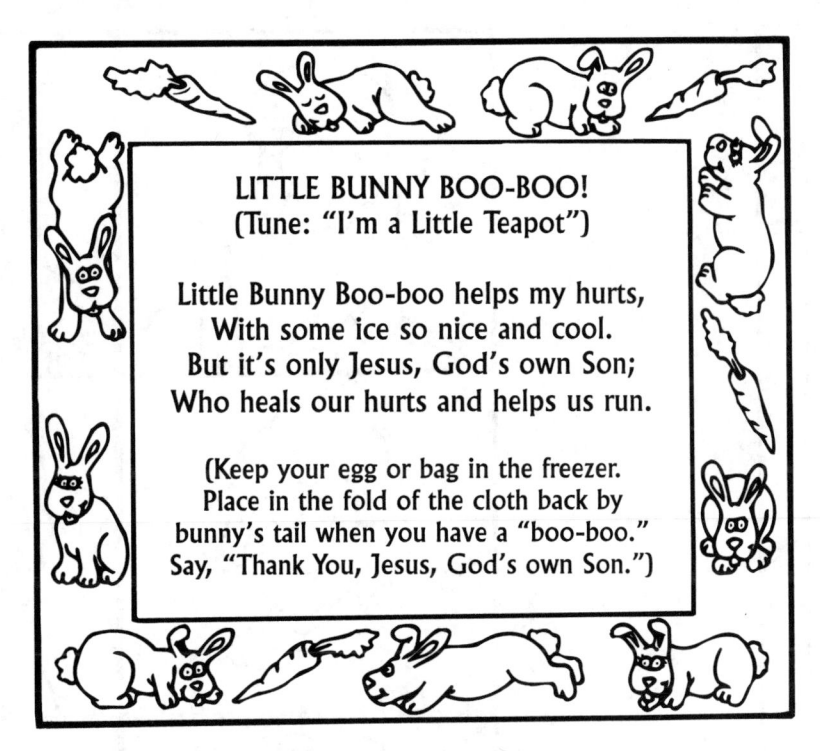

Instructions for making Bunny:

1. Fold opposite corners to center.

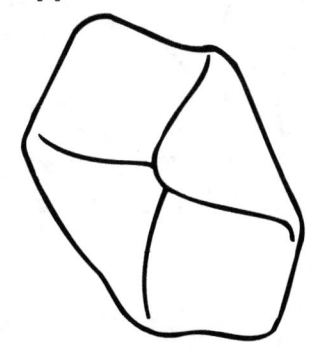

2. Roll folded edges to center.

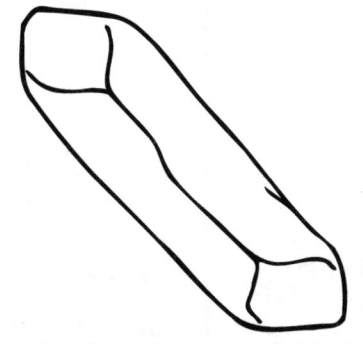

3. Fold roll in half with open edge up.

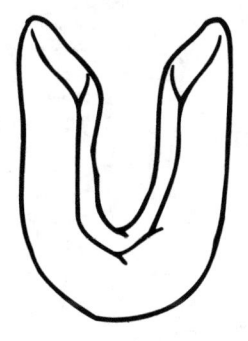

4. Fold ears back and secure folded end with rubber band.

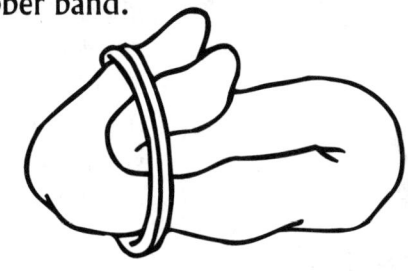

5. Add eyes, nose, and tail.

6. When you have a "boo-boo," place your frozen egg or bag in the fold of the cloth back by bunny's tail.

Basket cover

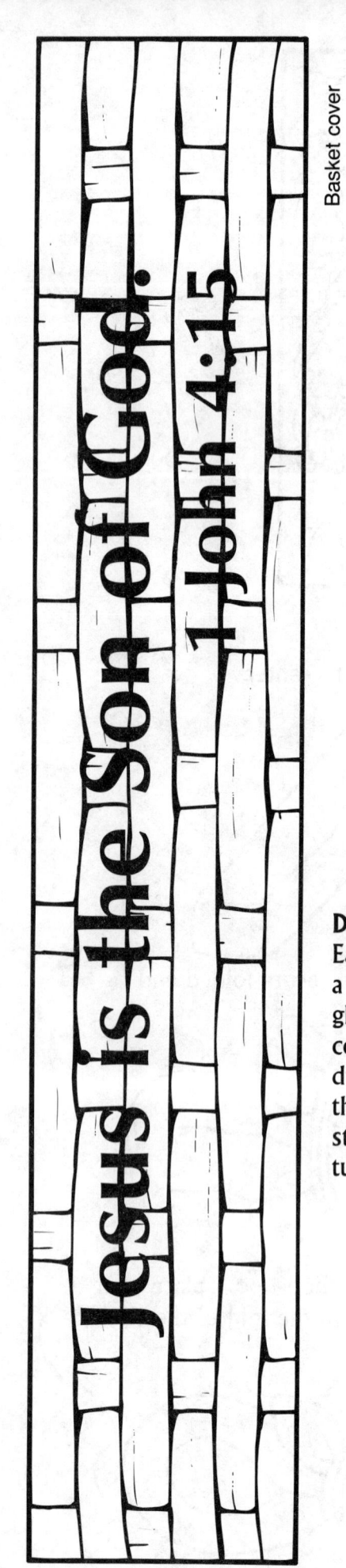

Jesus is the Son of God.
1 John 4:15

Telling Tube cover

DIRECTIONS:
Each child will need a margarine tub with a slit in the bottom, a craft stick, scissors, glue, markers or colored pencils, and a copy of the food and basket. Have children color the food and basket. Cut out the food and glue it to the top of the craft stick. Glue the basket to the side of the tub. Insert stick into tub and slit.

Food

157

158

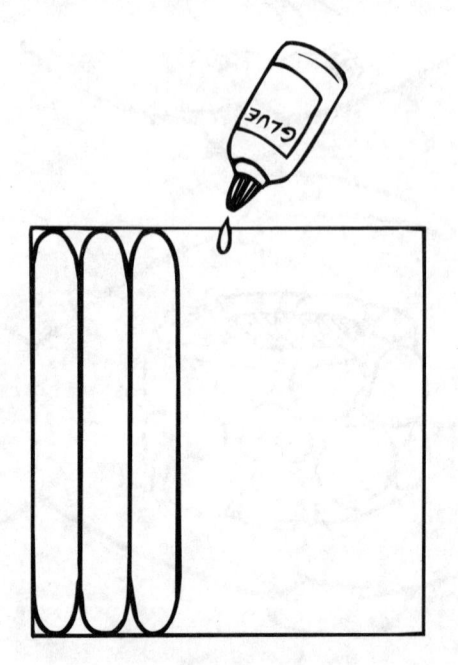

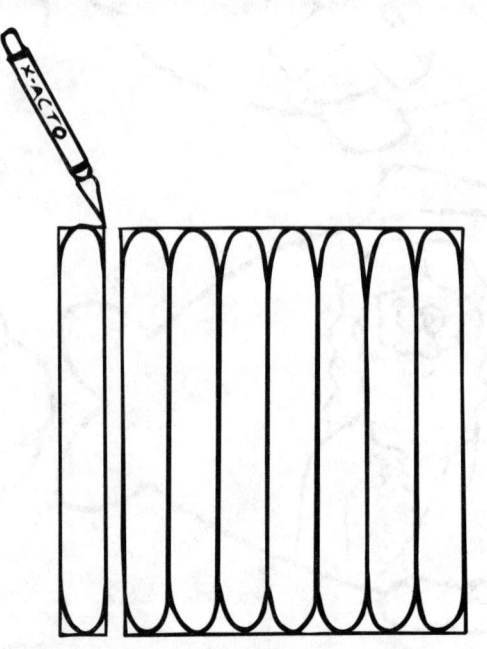

Unit 7
Lessons 27-30

Jesus Teaches Us

◆◆◆◆◆

By the end of this unit, the children and leaders will . . .
Know Name four ways to follow Jesus.
Feel Feel able to follow Jesus.
Do Follow Jesus by doing what He teaches.

Unit Bible Words for Memory
"I follow the example of Christ"
(1 Corinthians 11:1, NIV).

◆◆◆◆◆

Unit Lessons

Lesson 27
Jesus Taught Us to Pray
Luke 11:1-4; Matthew 6:5-13
Children will learn what Jesus taught His followers about prayer, and they will examine the prayer that Jesus prayed as an example.

Lesson 28
Jesus Taught Us to Share
Luke 12:13-21
Children will hear a story Jesus told about a rich farmer who selfishly kept everything for himself.

Lesson 29
Jesus Taught Us to Help
Luke 10:30-37
Children will learn a story Jesus told about a Samaritan who helped a hurt man when other people passed him by.

Lesson 30
Jesus Taught Us to Be Thankful
Luke 17:11-19
Children will hear how Jesus healed ten lepers, and only one returned to thank Him.

◆◆◆◆◆

Why Teach This Unit to Four-Year-Olds—Six-Year-Olds?

Jesus taught people in ways that children can understand. He taught through His example and through the stories He told. The stories in this unit give four examples of ways to follow Jesus' example that children can easily do. Jesus told us how to pray; children can pray as Jesus taught. Jesus said we should share and not keep everything for ourselves; children can share. Jesus said we should help those who need it, whether they are our friends or enemies; children can help others. And Jesus said we should thank Him for what He has done for us; children can thank Jesus.

◆◆◆◆◆

Bible Time Line

The stories for this unit are pictured on the time line, pages 316 and 317.

Provide the time line page for children who arrive early, or plan time at the end of the Bible story during each session for children to color the time line and look for the hidden pictures.

See page 6 in this book for suggested time-line projects.

◆◆◆◆◆

Materials

All Lessons
 a Bible
 markers, colored pencils, crayons
 white paper, construction paper, poster board
 tape, masking tape
 Plasti-Tak
 glue
 scissors
 a stapler
 paper hole punch
 yarn or string

Lesson 27
 several toy telephones or disconnected real telephones and a book about manners (optional)
 a video camera and blank tape or a Polaroid camera and film
 props for the situations in Activity 2: a candy bar, a playground ball, and a children's game
 small pads of paper, small sharpened pencils

Lesson 28
 sandpaper
 a large cardboard box, wrapping paper, tissue paper, ribbon, and artificial flowers
 a cupcake paper for each child and a box of oatmeal
 several extra toys on hand for children who were not in class last week or who forgot to bring a toy
 five index cards
 macaroni shells (suitable for stringing), cereal with holes in each piece, or plastic beads; bowls; and stiff string or plastic lacing
 a bag of M&M's and a tray with sides
 extra candy if needed for Wrap-up, and sandwich bags

Lesson 29
 clean cloths, Bible-times containers (small bottles with stoppers, small clay containers), strips of cloth for bandaging, cups. If you don't have any bottles with stoppers, use an empty medicine bottle with a cork or a piece of cloth stuffed in the top for a stopper.
 small envelopes
 an empty two-liter pop bottle
 four empty two-liter bottles and a ball. You may wish to fill the bottles partway (dry beans, sand, gravel) to make them more stable.

Lesson 30
 strips of white cloth
 a large bag with a piece of children's clothing, a can of food, a pillow, a picture of a house, a picture of a family, and other items that represent things your children might be thankful for
 puffy paint (equal parts flour, salt, and water, and liquid tempera paint), plastic squeeze bottles such as mustard or ketchup containers, cardboard squares or heavy paper
 fabric scraps or ribbon and a small treat such as candy or gum

◆◆◆◆◆

The Beginner's Bible™ Resources

Jesus and the Children Stickers, Standard Publishing, #22-01035, call 1-800-543-1353

Jesus and the Children Floor Puzzle, Standard Publishing, #28-02717, call 1-800-543-1353

Jesus and the Children Inlay Puzzle, Standard Publishing, #28-02703, call 1-800-543-1353

The Beginner's Bible™ New Testament GeoSafari Bible Pack, Standard Publishing, #14-24002, call 1-800-543-1353

The Beginner's Bible™ Bible Lessons GeoSafari Bible Pack, Standard Publishing, #14-24005, call 1-800-543-1353

Unit 7
Lesson 27

Jesus Taught Us to Pray
(Luke 11:1-4; Matthew 6:5-13)

Most children are delighted to find out that God really wants them to talk to Him. They are also beginning to learn that there are certain guidelines that go along with most privileges. They should easily grasp the idea that Jesus gave His followers an example of how to talk to God.

Bible Words

"I follow the example of Christ" (1 Corinthians 11:1).

Goals

Name a way to follow Jesus. (Pray.)
Feel able to pray as Jesus taught us.
Follow Jesus by praying to God.

♦♦♦♦

Activity 1—Let's Talk

You will need several toy telephones or disconnected real telephones and a book about manners (optional).
Whom do you talk to on the telephone? What do you say when you answer the telephone? Do you have any rules at your house about answering and talking on the telephone? Let children share, then demonstrate using the telephone. Answer the telephone correctly, talk with a proper volume, and say good-bye before you hang up. Encourage the children to practice these skills with the toy telephones you have provided. **We have learned the correct way to talk on the telephone. There is also a correct way to talk to God, or to pray. Jesus taught us the way to pray. Today in our Bible Time, we will find out what Jesus said.**

I Will Follow Him Each Day
(Tune: "The Muffin Man")

Jesus teaches me to pray.
The Bible tells me what He thought.
I will follow Him each day.
I'll do what Jesus taught.

Jesus teaches me to share.
The Bible tells me what He thought.
I will follow Him each day.
I'll do what Jesus taught.

Jesus teaches me to help.
The Bible tells me what He thought.
I will follow Him each day.
I'll do what Jesus taught.

Jesus teaches me to thank.
The Bible tells me what He thought.
I will follow Him each day.
I'll do what Jesus taught.

Leaders' Evaluation

	Great!	OK!	More!	Oops!	Suggestions
Activity 1					
Activity 2					
Bible Time					
Application					
Bible Memory					
Craft					
Snack					
Game					
Wrap-up					

ACTIVITY 2—Candid Camera

You will need a video camera and blank tape or a Polaroid camera and film. You will also need props for the situations you choose. Props for the situations below might include a candy bar, a playground ball, and a children's game.

Tell children that they will play the starring roles in acting out some situations. During Application, the children will watch the video or look at the pictures and decide how the child in the situation should pray. Following are some suggested situations, but come up with ideas that fit your group of children.

1. A child is at the grocery store with his mom. He asks for a candy bar. She says, "No!" The child looks longingly at the candy bar and starts to reach for it.

2. A group of children are playing on the playground. One friend shoves or elbows another child. Then the friend helps the child up and says, "I'm sorry. I shouldn't have done that."

3. A little brother or sister asks a child to play with him or her. The child says, "Go away. I don't want to play with you."

4. A mom is talking to a child and says, "We can't go to grandma's house right now. She is very sick."

◆◆◆◆

BIBLE TIME—Teach Us to Pray

You will need a Bible and a toy telephone.

Hold up the toy telephone. **Earlier we learned a good way to talk on the telephone.** Have children tell you what they learned. **Jesus taught His followers a good way to talk, too. But Jesus didn't teach them how to talk on the telephone. He taught them something much more important—how to talk to God. Talking to God is also called prayer or praying to God. Some people in Jesus' time stood in crowds of people and prayed to God loudly like this.** Hold your arms in the air and look up to Heaven as you say loudly, "God, please hear my prayer." **Those people wanted everyone to think they were**

leader around the room. The leaders can walk in different paths, they can do different motions (wave, hop, skip, wiggle, swing, and so on), and they can make different noises (giggle, hoot, whisper, hum, and so on). **You are choosing to follow only your group's leader! We are choosing to follow Jesus.**

◆◆◆◆

WRAP-UP—Prayer Pictures

You will need the Prayer Pictures posters made during the Craft.

Tell children that you will give them secret messages. They must listen closely. Call children up one at a time or in pairs and whisper an instruction concerning cleaning the room to them. Continue until the room is cleaned up, then gather children in a large group.

You listened closely and followed my instructions! You are good followers. How will you follow Jesus by praying this week? Give children their Prayer Pictures posters and have them draw the first picture on their pad of paper, reminding them of a time when they will pray this week.

Teach children the first verse of "I Will Follow Him Each Day" from page 8 of this session. Sing the song several times. Then close with prayer, thanking God for listening to us every time we talk to Him.

NOTE: Send a note home with the children, asking them to choose a toy to give for a sharing basket next week.

important and special to God. But God doesn't need us to show off our prayers, or to talk loudly for Him to hear us. Jesus said that when we pray, we should talk quietly to God by ourselves like this. Ask children to bow their heads with you as you quietly say a prayer, "Father, please help us to learn how You want us to pray."

Some people in Jesus' time also tried to pray very long prayers. They almost acted like they were in a prayer contest, to see who could pray the longest. They talked on and on and on. But Jesus said we don't need to use many words. God knows what we need before we even ask Him for it!

Then Jesus showed His followers how they should pray to God. He said a prayer for them. Jesus' prayer helps us learn the kinds of things we should say to God when we pray. Many people call Jesus' prayer "The Lord's Prayer." Have you ever heard of "The Lord's Prayer"? Let children share. Here are the words of Jesus' prayer:

"Our Father in Heaven, may your name always be kept holy. Your kingdom come and Your will be done here on earth, just like it is in Heaven.

Please give us what we need for today.

Forgive us for what we have done wrong, just like we forgive others who do wrong to us.

Please keep us from being tempted to do wrong things, and save us from Satan, when he tries to get us to do wrong.*"

Let's see what Jesus' prayer teaches us about talking to God. When you start talking on the phone, you say, "Hello! How does Jesus begin His prayer? He calls God "our Father in Heaven." Why do we call God "our Father"? Even though God is so big and powerful, Jesus said that because God loves us, we are like God's children, and God is our Father. Jesus says we should pray that what God wants will happen. What are some things that we know God wants to happen on earth? He wants everyone in the world to know Jesus. He wants everyone to obey and love Him.

When we pray for what God wants, that is called praying for God's will.

Lesson 27

ACTIVITY TIME

Do as many activities as time permits.

Craft—Prayer Pictures Poster

You will need copies of page 177, markers or crayons, small pads of paper, glue or tape, small sharpened pencils, yarn or string, and a stapler.

Give children copies of page 177 and ask them to color the pages. Then help the children glue or tape a small pad of paper in the blank area on the lower-right corner of the page. Cut small lengths of yarn or string and tape a pencil to the end of each piece. Then staple the other end of the yarn or string to the page, so that children will have a pad of paper and pencil readily available to draw their prayer pictures.

Drawing prayer pictures can help us remember to talk to God like Jesus taught us. We can draw pictures of things we need. What things that we need do you see on the page? Warm bed, food. We can draw pictures of things we are thankful for. What pictures on this page are you thankful for? What else are you thankful for? We can draw pictures of wrong things we want God to forgive. We can draw pictures of reasons we love God. What could you draw to show you love God?

Snack—Our Daily Bread

Provide a loaf of warm bread, margarine and jam or jelly, and water or juice to drink.

Pray to thank God for giving you what you need every day. Then allow children to eat the bread with margarine and/or jelly and drink their juice.

Game—Jesus' Followers

In this unit, we are learning to be followers of Jesus. What does it mean to follow someone? You do what they do. Let's practice being followers. Divide the children into groups and provide a leader for each group. Ask the groups to follow the

Unit 7

Then Jesus said we should ask God for what we need for that day. What are some things we need every day? Food, a warm place to stay, something to wear. That doesn't mean we should ask God for a lot of new toys, or chocolate chip cookies to eat for every meal. Jesus asks God only for what we need.

Next, Jesus says we should ask God to forgive us for what we have done wrong. Have you ever done anything wrong? Let children respond. **We all do wrong things every single day. Jesus said that when we ask God to forgive us, we should also remember to forgive people who do wrong things to us. What are some wrong things someone might do to us?** Allow children to respond. A friend could say something mean to them; another child might make fun of them or push them; a little brother or sister might hit them; a parent might get angry at them for something they didn't do. Jesus said we need to forgive those people, just like God forgives us.

Then Jesus says that we should ask God to keep us from being tempted. Do you know what it means to be "tempted"? It means wanting to do something wrong. Often Satan is the one who tries to get us to do wrong things. We need to ask God to help us choose right, even when we really want to do wrong.

How did Jesus end His prayer? The words about being tempted are the end of the prayer. What do we usually say to end our prayers? In Jesus' name, amen. Jesus told His followers in another place that they should always ask God for **things in His name! So when we pray, we ask for things "in Jesus' name,"** just like He told us.

Talking to God is one of the wonderful things about following Jesus, because God has promised that He always listens to us. **Let's read Jesus' prayer again.** Slowly read the words of the prayer again.

*NOTE: In some Bible versions, there is a section added on at the end of the prayer: "For yours is the kingdom and the power and the glory forever. Amen."

APPLICATION—Prayer Videos

You will need the video or photographs made in Activity 2, a piece of poster board, and a marker.

Show the videos made in Activity 2. Stop the video after each situation and ask the children what the child could pray. **One thing that the Bible promises us is that God always hears our prayers, and God always answers our prayers.**

Have children call out things for which they would like to pray to God. Write their prayer requests on the poster board. Then lead children in a prayer to God, mentioning the items they named.

◆◆◆◆◆

BIBLE MEMORY—Bible-verse Pull

You will need copies of page 180, scissors, yarn or string, tape, and crayons or markers (optional). Before class, cut out several copies of the figures on page 180. Color them if desired. Cut several long pieces of yarn or string and attach the Bible words figures in order at varying distances along each string. Make a Bible-words string for every three or four children in your class. Hide the string around your classroom, stretching out each string so that children will have to search for each Bible-words figure.

Divide the children into groups of three or four and ask them to find a string and search to its end, finding the words of the Bible verse along the way. When all groups have found the strings, gather them together. **The words on our strings are the words to our Bible verse.** Have a volunteer help you find the highlighted words in your Bible. Point to them as you read them to the children: **"I follow the example of Christ" (1 Corinthians 11:1).** Ask the children to say the words with you several times. They can look at the shapes on their strings to help them remember the words of the verse.

Unit 7
Lesson 28

Jesus Taught Us to Share
(Luke 12:13-21)

Today's Bible story illustrates that sharing is often difficult for people of any age. Young children can often talk about a good plan for sharing, but acting upon that plan is something entirely different. The man in the crowd and his brother were both having trouble sharing. Jesus showed them that sharing happens when one's heart is right with God

Bible Words

"I follow the example of Christ" (1 Corinthians 11:1).

Goals

Name a way to follow Jesus. (Share.)
Feel able to share as Jesus taught us.
Follow Jesus by sharing.

◆◆◆◆

ACTIVITY 1—Bigger Barns

You will need copies of page 178, scissors, crayons, sandpaper, and glue.

Give children copies of page 178. Ask them to cut out the barn on the solid lines and fold on the dotted lines. Help them with the folding as needed. Then ask them to color the bigger barn; then fold up the page and color the smaller barn. They may cut sandpaper "rocks" and glue them on the barn to add texture. **Show me which barn is smaller. Which barn could hold more grain? Which barn do you like best? The man in a story Jesus told wanted bigger barns. We'll find out what Jesus said about his barns.** Ask children to save their barns to take with them to the Bible Time.

--- fold ---

I Will Follow Him Each Day
(Tune: "The Muffin Man")

Jesus teaches me to pray.
The Bible tells me what He thought.
I will follow Him each day.
I'll do what Jesus taught.

Jesus teaches me to share.
The Bible tells me what He thought.
I will follow Him each day.
I'll do what Jesus taught.

Jesus teaches me to help.
The Bible tells me what He thought.
I will follow Him each day.
I'll do what Jesus taught.

Jesus teaches me to thank.
The Bible tells me what He thought.
I will follow Him each day.
I'll do what Jesus taught.

ACTIVITY 2—A Sharing Box

You will need a large cardboard box, wrapping paper, tissue paper, ribbon, artificial flowers, scissors, a stapler, and glue.

Today we are going to learn how we can follow Jesus by sharing. We are going to make a sharing box. Later, we will put the toys we brought to share in our box. Right now, let's decorate the sharing box. Encourage children to use their imaginations to decorate the box. They can make tissue-paper flowers or cut out tissue-paper shapes. They can tie ribbon in bows or tie ribbon around the box. They can cover the box with wrapping paper. They can staple artificial flowers on the box. Help them with the gluing and stapling.

BIBLE TIME—The Rich Fool

You will need the barns made during Activity 1, a cupcake paper for each child, and a box of oatmeal.

Once a man came to Jesus. He asked Jesus to make his brother share with him. Jesus knew that both brothers needed to learn how to share. So Jesus told a story.

Jesus' story was about a rich farmer. The farmer probably had a house, plenty of wonderful food and clothes, many servants, and many animals. Jesus told us in His story that the **rich man had barns.** Have the children hold up the barns they made in Activity 1. The barns should all be folded to show the smaller barns. **The rich man's barns probably looked a little different from our barns. His barns were big storage bins for holding grain and other crops.**

One year at harvesttime, the farmer's fields produced a wonderful crop. He had more grain than he had ever had before. Pour oatmeal into cupcake papers for the children and ask them to hold the papers. **The farmer looked at his harvest. He looked at his grain. "My barns are not big enough to hold all of this grain," he said.**

— fold —

sharing again. I am going to give each of you some candy. With whom will you share your candy? How much candy will you give that person? Encourage children to think of a friend, parent, or sibling with whom they could share. Talk about ways of dividing the candy.

Lead the children in prayer, asking God to help them follow Jesus by sharing. Let volunteers pray as well. Close by singing the first two verses of "I Will Follow Him Each Day" from page 8 of this session.

Leaders' Evaluation

	Great!	OK!	More!	Oops!	Suggestions
Activity 1					
Activity 2					
Bible Time					
Application					
Bible Memory					
Craft					
Snack					
Game					
Wrap-up					

Now the farmer could have done several things. He could have taken some of the grain and given it to poor, hungry people. But he did not do that. He thought, "That grain is all mine! I'm not giving any away." Take back some of the cupcake papers.

The farmer could have sold some of the grain and given the money to help poor people. But he did not do that. He thought, "That grain is all mine! I'm not selling any to help others." Take back some more cupcake papers.

He even could have had a big party and invited all of his neighbors over to have a good time and eat plenty of food. But he did not do that. He thought, "That grain is all mine! I'm not letting anyone else eat it." Take back the rest of the cupcake papers.

What do you think the farmer decided to do? Let children guess. He decided to tear down his little barns. He decided to build much bigger barns for storing the grain. Ask the children to unfold their barns. He decided to keep all the grain for himself. He thought he would be able to enjoy the grain for many, many years.

He was wrong. Jesus said that the farmer didn't enjoy his grain, because the selfish farmer died that very night.

The farmer in Jesus' story tried to keep everything for himself, instead of sharing with others. Because of his selfishness, we don't call him the "rich farmer." Instead, we call him the "rich fool."

◆◆◆◆

APPLICATION—Toys to Share

You will need the sharing box decorated in Activity 2 and the toys the children brought to class to share. Have several extra toys on hand for children who were not in class last week or who forgot to bring a toy.

Have the children sit in a circle with the box in the middle. **Last week, we learned that we can follow Jesus by praying like He taught us. This week, we learned that we can follow**

Lesson 28

Divide the popcorn evenly among the children. You may wish to have several children help you share the popcorn. Then pour the juice.

Ask volunteers to pray and thank God for the snack. **Thank You for the food we eat. We want to follow Your example by sharing. We love You, Jesus.**

Game—Sharing Relay

You will need a bag of M&M's® and a tray with sides.

Divide the children into two groups. Have the groups form two lines, facing each other. Pour the candy onto the tray. Have the first child in one line carry the tray over to the first child in the second line and share a piece of candy. Then that child carries the tray back to the other line and shares, and so on, until everyone has had a piece.

Be sure each child takes only one or two pieces of candy. Save the leftover candy to use during the Wrap-up.

◆◆◆◆

WRAP-UP—What Can You Share?

You will need the leftover candy from the game, extra candy if needed, and sandwich bags.

OPTION: Provide sheets of stickers for the children to take home and share.

One of the best things to share with a friend is work. Let's share the work of straightening our room. When the room is clean, ask the children to gather in a large group.

What have you shared today? They shared toys, beads for necklaces, popcorn, and candy. **You are following Jesus by sharing. Jesus is happy when you share. Can you think of some things you can share at home, at the playground, and at school?** Help children think of things they can share, such as crayons, toys, snacks, balls, and so on. **With whom can you share your toys? Your crayons? A snack?** Children can share with their friends, their brothers and sisters, their neighbors, their parents. **You are going to have a chance to follow Jesus by**

Unit 7

Jesus by sharing. Let's share our toys and promise Jesus that **we will follow Him.** Ask the children to come up one at a time and put their toys in the box. As each child puts the toy in the box, he should say, "I will follow Jesus," or "I will share like Jesus taught."

When all the toys have been gathered, teach children verse 2 of "I Will Follow Him Each Day" from page 8 of this session. Sing the song several times. Then ask children to think of other things they can share at home, at church, at the playground, and at school. Sing the song again, changing the third line to name some of the things the children will share.

"Jesus teaches me to share.
The Bible tells me what He thought.
I will share my playground ball.
I'll do what Jesus taught."

◆◆◆◆

BIBLE MEMORY—Mix a Verse

You will need a Bible with the memory verse highlighted and marked, five index cards, a marker, tape, and five toys from the sharing box. Before class, print the words of the memory verse on the five cards. Divide the words of the verse between the five cards as follows: I, follow, the example, of Christ, 1 Corinthians 11:1. Tape one card to each toy.

Set the toys up in order and have the children say the words of the verse with you. Have a volunteer find the marked verse in your Bible, and point to the words of the verse as the children say them.

Then mix up the toys and have the children put them in order. Mix up the toys several times and have the children put them in order. You may wish to time the children to see how quickly they can put the verse in order.

If you have time, tape the index cards to five different toys and play the game again.

What does it mean to "follow the example of Christ"? Following Christ's example means doing what He did, acting

like He acted, loving like He loved, doing what He told us to do. **We follow Christ's example when we share with other people like He taught us.**

ACTIVITY TIME

Do as many activities as time permits.

◆◆◆◆

Craft—Sharing Necklaces

You will need macaroni shells (suitable for stringing), cereal with holes in each piece, or plastic beads; bowls; and stiff string or plastic lacing. Before class, put the beads or other objects for stringing in bowls. Put enough in each bowl for two or three children to make a necklace. Cut the string or lacing into pieces long enough to make children's necklaces and tie a knot in the end of each piece.

Give each child a piece of string or plastic lacing. Then ask them to work in groups of two or three. Each group will share a bowl. Tell the children that they are going to make sharing necklaces. The children in their group will share the objects in the bowl. They should decide how they should share between them to make the necklaces.

When the children have finished their necklaces, help them tie the ends together. **When you shared with your friends, you were following Jesus. I am proud of you for doing what Jesus taught us.**

Snack—Fair Share

You will need a large bowl of popcorn, a pitcher of juice, several different-sized bowls, and cups.

Begin your snack time by placing a different-sized bowl in front of each child.

Would you like me to serve the popcorn in these bowls? Would that be fair? Let children respond. **What if I use a cup to measure the same amount of popcorn for each person? When we want to share food, we can usually find a fair way to do it.**

Unit 7
Lesson 29

Jesus Taught Us to Help
(Luke 10:30-37)

The story of the Good Samaritan hits home with children and adults alike. Most of us can recall more than one time when we wonder whether we should have or could have helped if we had taken the time or the risk to get involved. Children need to find concrete ways that they can help.

Bible Words

"I follow the example of Christ" (1 Corinthians 11:1).

Goals

Name a way to follow Jesus. (Help.)
Feel able to help as Jesus taught us.
Follow Jesus by helping others.

◆◆◆◆

Activity 1—A Bible-times Doctor

You will need clean cloths, Bible-times containers (small bottles with stoppers, small clay containers), strips of cloth for bandaging, cups. If you don't have any bottles with stoppers, use an empty medicine bottle with a cork or a piece of cloth stuffed in the top for a stopper.

What does your mom do when you are sick or when you get a cut? She gives you medicine, makes you rest, makes you drink lots of water, washes your scrapes, puts ointment and Band-Aids on your cuts. In Bible times, they did some of the same things to care for sick people that we do today. Doctors still made sick people rest, and they probably gave them drinks of cool water. When they had cuts, they washed and bandaged them. Let's pretend to be Bible-times people taking care of

---

I Will Follow Him Each Day
(Tune: "The Muffin Man")

Jesus teaches me to pray.
The Bible tells me what He thought.
I will follow Him each day.
I'll do what Jesus taught.

Jesus teaches me to share.
The Bible tells me what He thought.
I will follow Him each day.
I'll do what Jesus taught.

Jesus teaches me to help.
The Bible tells me what He thought.
I will follow Him each day.
I'll do what Jesus taught.

Jesus teaches me to thank.
The Bible tells me what He thought.
I will follow Him each day.
I'll do what Jesus taught.

someone who is sick. Children can work in groups of two or three. One child can be the sick person. The other children can pretend to wash their wounds and pour medicine on them. Then they can bandage them. They can give the sick person a drink of water and help them rest. Let children take turns pretending to be the sick person.

A man in our Bible story was hurt and bleeding. He needed someone to take care of him. Listen to see how a man helped the hurt man.

ACTIVITY 2—We Can Help!

Before class, check with your church about a project your children could do to help. The project should be something that can be done in a fairly short amount of time. Some possibilities include sharpening pencils, washing dishes, sorting used clothing for the food and clothing pantry, picking up trash in the parking lot or grounds. Provide the materials necessary for the children to complete the project.

Have children repeat the memory verse with you: "I follow the example of Christ." **Today we are going to help at church. I follow the example by helping. You are big enough to help at church.**

Explain the helping project that the children will be doing. Then go to the area where you will complete the project and assign tasks as needed. As the children work, praise them for their help and encourage them to think of other areas where they can help.

What are some other ways that you could help at church? Pick up trash when you see it, help clean up the Sunday-school room, help pick up and weed outside, and so on. **What are some ways that you help at home?** Allow children to share chores they do at home. **Can you think of other ways that you could help at home?** Children can set the table, clear the table, dust the furniture, make their beds, take out the trash, pick up toys, pick up trash in the yard.

2   Unit 7

What are some of the ways we named? How will you help this week? Allow children to share and remember the many ways to help that have been discussed. As the children tell the ways they will help, use Band-Aids to attach their armbands around their arms. **These armbands say that you are a "Helper." You are following Jesus' example. I know Jesus is proud of you when you help like He taught.** Close with prayer, thanking God for your children and their help.

Until parents come, play a game. Ask children to squat down. Name people they could help and have them jump up if they can name a way to help that person. The first person to stand can name a way to help. People to name include: teacher, mom, dad, grandma, grandpa, little brother or sister, big brother or sister, neighbor, friend, grocery store clerk, and so on.

Leaders' Evaluation

	Great!	OK!	More!	Oops!	Suggestions
Activity 1					
Activity 2					
Bible Time					
Application					
Bible Memory					
Craft					
Snack					
Game					
Wrap-up					

Lesson 29   7

BIBLE TIME—A Helpful Stranger

You will need the cloths, medicine bottles, and bandages used to care for sick people in Activity 1.

Tell the story with everyone standing, or with children sitting on chairs low enough for their feet to reach the floor. **I want you to use your feet to help me tell this story. Make your feet do what my feet do.**

Jesus once told this story to teach a man to be a helpful neighbor.

Walk slowly in place. **Once a man was taking a trip. He was on a lonely road. Suddenly he heard something!** Run in place. **Robbers! Stop.**

The robbers grabbed the man. They beat him up. They stole everything he had—even his clothes! Then they left him alone. Walk quickly in place.

The poor man lay on the ground, too hurt to move. Then he heard something. Walk slowly in place. **A priest was walking by.** Walking. Walking. Walking. Speed up your feet. **The priest did not stop to help the man! Poor, poor man.**

A little later, the man heard something else. Walk slowly in place. **More footsteps! A temple helper was walking by.** Walking. Walking. Walking. Speed up your feet. **The temple helper did not stop to help. Poor, poor man.**

Even later, the man heard something again. Walk slowly in place. **More footsteps!** Stop walking. **The footsteps stopped. The priest had not stopped. The temple helper had not stopped. Who had stopped?**

The hurt man must have been very surprised. The man who stopped to help was a stranger and a Samaritan. The hurt man was a Jew. Jews and Samaritans didn't like each other. The hurt man probably closed his eyes and waited to hear the Samaritan man walk away. But the Samaritan did not.

The Samaritan went to the hurt man. He cleaned his cuts and sores. Hold up a cloth and pretend to wipe at a sore on your arm. **He poured medicine on them.** Pretend to pour medi-

Lesson 29

---

healthy. **Eating healthy foods will help our bodies grow and be strong.** Ask a volunteer to pray, thanking God for the healthy snack. Then children can spread peanut butter on the fruit slices and drink their juice.

Game—Helper Bowl

You will need four empty two-liter bottles, four pieces of paper, a marker, tape, masking tape, and a ball. Before class, print a way to help on each of the pieces of paper (hugs, kind words, kind acts, a smile) and tape each paper around a two-liter bottle. You may wish to fill the bottles partway (dry beans, sand, gravel) to make them more stable. Line the bottles up at one end of the room. Make a masking-tape line a distance away from the bottles, behind which the children will stand.

Ask children to stand behind the masking-tape line. They will take turns rolling the ball at the bottles. When they knock over bottles, they will name to whom they could give the help described on the bottles. Give each child a chance to play.

NOTE: You may wish to divide the children into two teams and give points for the bottles that are knocked over and the people to help that are named.

WRAP-UP—Helping Bandages

You will need Band-Aids and the armbands made during the Craft time.

Assign children helping tasks to do as they clean the room. Then ask them to gather in a large group.

What does our Bible verse say? Say the words of the verse together. **When you pray as Jesus taught, you are following His example. When you share, you are following Jesus' example. When you help clean the room, when you help a friend, when you help at church, you are following Jesus' example!** Lead children in singing the first three verses of "I Will Follow Him Each Day" from page 8 of this session.

We have talked about many, many ways that you can help.

Unit 7

cine from one of the bottles on your arms. He bandaged his cuts. Wrap a bandage around your arm. **Then the Samaritan put the man on his donkey.** Begin to walk. **He took him to an inn.** Stop walking. **He took him inside and took care of him. The next day he left money for the innkeeper to use to care for the hurt man.**

The priest and the temple helper didn't stop to help the hurt man. But the Samaritan helped the hurt man! Jesus told this story to show us that we should help others like the Samaritan man did.

APPLICATION—First-Aid Kit

You will need copies of the Band-Aids on page 179, scissors, crayons or markers, and small envelopes.

Give children the copies of the Band-Aids and ask them to color and cut them out.

Tell about a time when you were hurt and had to wear a Band-Aid. Allow children to share. **Sometimes people aren't hurt on the outside, but they hurt on the inside. They might be sad or angry or upset about something. The pictures on these band-aids show how we can help our friends who are hurting. How do the pictures show that we can help?** Kind words, kind acts, a hug, and a smile. **Let's practice.** Ask children to take turns pretending to be crying or hurt while another child helps. The children can hug the friend, say kind things (I'm sorry you're sad. What can I do to help you? I love you. I'm glad you're my friend.), give their friend something to help them feel better (a tissue, share a piece of candy), and, once their friend feels better, give them a smile.

Give children the envelopes and ask them to put their Band-Aids in the envelopes to make first-aid kits. They can put their names on the envelopes and take them home to remind them of ways to help their friends.

BIBLE MEMORY—Spin and Say

You will need an empty two-liter pop bottle.

Have the children sit in a circle. Review the words of the memory verse. Set the pop bottle in the center of the circle and spin it around. When the bottle stops, say the memory verse again, inserting the name of the person to whom the bottle is pointing. "Ashley follows the example of Christ." Then have the child tell a way she will help. Give suggestions as needed. Continue until every child has had a turn. If you wish, children may take turns spinning the pop bottle.

ACTIVITY TIME

Do as many activities as time permits.

Craft—Helper Armbands

You will need copies of the armband on page 179, scissors, and crayons or markers.

Give the children copies of the armband and ask them to cut them out.

What is a way you can help someone this week? You can think of a way to help someone who is hurt. Or you can think of a way to help at home, or church, or school. Help children think of ways they can help. Then ask them to draw a picture of the way they can help on their armbands. They can color and decorate the rest of the armband.

When the children are finished decorating the armbands, help them print their names on the back of the bands. Keep the armbands to use during Wrap-up.

Snack—Healthy Helping

You will need fruit slices (apple, banana), peanut butter, and juice in small cups.

If we are going to help people, we need to keep our bodies

Unit 7
Lesson 30

Jesus Taught Us to Be Thankful
(Luke 17:11-19)

It may be possible to be thankful without saying thank-you, but the Bible story today indicates that expressing thanks is important. The Bible does not say that Jesus removed the blessing of healing from the nine who did not give thanks, but He was disappointed. How many times each day do we forget to say thank-you to our Provider, Sustainer, and Redeemer?

Bible Words

"I follow the example of Christ" (1 Corinthians 11:1).

Goals

Name a way to follow Jesus. (Say thank-you.)
Feel able to be thankful as Jesus taught us.
Follow Jesus by saying thank-you.

Activity 1—Ten Lepers

You will need several copies of page 181 on heavy paper, scissors, crayons, red markers or crayons, strips of white cloth, and tape or glue. Before the session, cut out 11 figures from the copies of page 181. Save one figure to use during the Bible Time. **Leprosy is a terrible skin disease. Today, we can cure leprosy. But in Bible times, there was no way to get rid of it. Lepers in Bible times had to live away from their family and friends. They weren't allowed to touch other people. They were alone! There are ten lepers in our Bible story today. We are going to make figures of ten lepers.** Give children ten of the figures that you cut out before class. Ask each child or pair of children to color a figure of a leper and make red spots to

---

I Will Follow Him Each Day
(Tune: "The Muffin Man")

Jesus teaches me to pray.
The Bible tells me what He thought.
I will follow Him each day.
I'll do what Jesus taught.

Jesus teaches me to share.
The Bible tells me what He thought.
I will follow Him each day.
I'll do what Jesus taught.

Jesus teaches me to help.
The Bible tells me what He thought.
I will follow Him each day.
I'll do what Jesus taught.

Jesus teaches me to thank.
The Bible tells me what He thought.
I will follow Him each day.
I'll do what Jesus taught.

represent leprosy on the leper's face, legs, and arms. They can wrap strips of cloth around the spots and tape or glue them in place to bandage them.

ACTIVITY 2—Thank-you Sack

You will need a large bag with a piece of children's clothing, a can of food, a pillow, a picture of a house, a picture of a family, and other items that represent things your children might be thankful for.

Our Bible story today is about a man who said thank-you to Jesus. We are going to say thank-you too! Ask the children to come up one at a time and draw out one item. Talk about specific things they are thankful for.

You drew out a children's shirt. Do you have a favorite shirt or dress that you are thankful for? This house has a big front yard for children to play. What part of your house are you thankful for? A big play room? A warm bedroom? A bathtub with bubbles and toys?

Lead children in prayers of thanksgiving for the specific things they name after each item is drawn. Set the items out in the Bible-story area.

BIBLE TIME—One Remembers, Nine Forget

You will need the ten lepers made during Activity 1 and the one figure you saved, which has no leprosy spots. Before class, place the figure you saved outside the room.

One day when Jesus was traveling, He met ten men. The men had a bad skin disease called leprosy. Hold up the ten figures the children made. What did we learn about leprosy? The men couldn't live with their families. They couldn't touch other people. There was no cure for their disease.

The men knew they weren't supposed to get very close to anyone else, but they had heard some special things about

child to say a short thank-you prayer to God.

Until parents arrive, sing the fourth verse of "I Will Follow Him Each Day," inserting things the children name for which they are thankful.

"Jesus teaches me to thank.
The Bible tells me what He thought.
I will thank Him for my mom.
I'll do what Jesus taught."

Other suggestions are: my brother, my church, my school, His love, every day, my warm bed.

Leaders' Evaluation

	Great!	OK!	More!	Oops!	Suggestions
Activity 1					
Activity 2					
Bible Time					
Application					
Bible Memory					
Craft					
Snack					
Game					
Wrap-up					

Jesus. They really wanted to get close enough to talk to Him. They cried out, "Jesus, please help us."

Jesus knew what the ten men wanted. They wanted to be well. Jesus said, "Go show yourselves to the priest." The priest had to look at the men and say that their skin was clean before they could see their families again.

The men believed that Jesus was going to make them well. They hurried off to see the priest. Remove the ten figures from the room. Make rejoicing noises. "Look at me! Look at my hands. Look at my feet. Tell me what you see." Look back inside.

Do you want to know what happened? What do you think the men saw? Let children tell you what they think happened. As the men were going to see the priest, they looked down. Their skin was no longer covered with sores. They didn't hurt anymore. They were well. They must have been so excited! They couldn't wait to see the priest and go home to their families and friends. Pause.

All except one! Reenter the room carrying the one well figure. One man had to do something before he went to the priest. Go back to the story area. That man went back to see Jesus. When he found Jesus, he fell at Jesus' feet and thanked Him. He praised God that Jesus had made him well.

Jesus was pleased that one man had remembered to say thank-you. But He was sad that nine men forgot!

◆◆◆◆

APPLICATION—Puffy Paint Pictures

You will need puffy paint (equal parts flour, salt, and water; and liquid tempera paint), plastic squeeze bottles such as mustard or ketchup containers, cardboard squares or heavy paper, pencils. Before class, make several colors of puffy paint by mixing equal parts flour, salt, and water in a bowl. Then add the desired amount of liquid tempera paint and pour into plastic squeeze bottles.

Earlier we remembered to say thank-you to God. What are

Lesson 30

3

What disease did the men in the story have? How many men asked Jesus to heal them? Where did Jesus tell the men to go? What happened on the way to the priest? What did one man remember to tell Jesus?

Game—Scavenger Hunt

This game may be played inside or outside. Before class, make a list of items of ten that the children can find in the area in which you play. For example, they could find ten blades of grass, ten leaves, ten crayons, ten blocks, ten stones, ten cups, ten paper towels, and so on.

Have children work in groups of three or four. Assign each group an item to find. They should find and bring you ten of that item. When they have brought you ten of the item you chose, they should take nine items back and leave one with you.

How many lepers did Jesus heal? How many returned to tell Jesus thank-you?

◆◆◆◆◆

WRAP-UP—Thankful Followers

You will need the paintings made during Application. Assign children jobs to do to clean up the room. Then ask them to gather in a large group.

Say the Bible words together. When have you followed Christ's example by praying? Helping? Encourage children to share how they have been following the example of Jesus. Sing all four verses of "I Will Follow Him Each Day" from page 8 of this session.

Today we learned that another way to follow Jesus is to say thank-you. Whom will you thank this week? What will you tell that person? Have children show the pictures made during Application. They should tell whom their picture is for, and what they will tell that person when they give them the picture. Saying thank-you is another way we can follow Jesus. Let's say thank-you to God right now. Close with prayer, asking each

Unit 7

some things that we thanked God for? Remind children of things they mentioned in Activity 2. One way we can follow Jesus' teaching about saying thank-you is by thanking the **people who help and care for us. When we thank our parents, our teachers, and our friends, we are following Jesus. Who are some other people who help us?** Help children think of people they could thank, such as a bus driver, a mail carrier, an older brother or sister, and so on. **Whom would you like to thank? What would you like to thank that person for? Let's draw pictures to say thank-you.** Give each child a cardboard square or piece of heavy paper on which to paint. If children wish, they may sketch with pencil, then squeeze the paint over the lines. Or they may simply squeeze their paint design onto the paper. When children are finished, help them print their names on their paintings. Set the paintings aside to dry until Wrap-up. The paint will harden in a puffy shape.

BIBLE MEMORY—Memory Twist

You will need five copies of page 180, a sheet of paper, a pencil, a paper clip, and tape. Before class, use masking tape to make a rectangular grid on the floor with twenty squares in it. Cut out five sets of memory-verse objects from page 180 and randomly tape them in the squares in the grid. Draw a spinner circle on the paper and divide it into four sections. Label the sections right foot, left foot, right hand, left hand. Use the pencil and paper clip as the spinner, or have a child flip a penny onto the paper, and use the section on which the penny lands. Review the words of the verse with the children. Then allow them to take turns playing a memory game, similar to the game "Twister." Let one child at a time stand on the grid. Spin the spinner, and the child places the body part chosen on the "I" space. Continue spinning until the child has completed the memory verse with the sections "follow," "the example," "of Christ." Then have that child stay in position and add another child. See how many children can stay on the grid at one time.

When the grid becomes too crowded, have the children clear out and continue the game with a clear grid.
OPTION: For younger children, you may wish to simplify the game. Have them start at one end of the grid and hop on the words of the verse in order.

ACTIVITY TIME

Do as many activities as time permits.

Craft—Pocket Picture

You will need copies of page 182, crayons or markers, fabric scraps, glue, a stapler, and a small treat such as candy or stickers. Give children copies of page 182. Ask the children to color and decorate their pictures. Help them fold up the bottom part of the page where indicated and staple it in place. They can glue fabric scraps onto the folded up part of the page to decorate it. As they work, discuss ways they have learned to follow Jesus. **What ways to follow Jesus do you see on the page? How will you follow Jesus this week?** When the children have completed their work, give each child seven small treats to place in the pocket. **Each day you choose to follow Jesus, take a treat from the pocket.**

Snack—Thank-you Salad

You will need an assortment of fruits, a large bowl, a knife, paper cups, and plastic spoons.

Let children wash hands before you begin. Let the children assist you in peeling and slicing the fruit. For example, they could peel bananas and wash and pick off grapes. As you work together, talk about the different fruits God made. Finish the salad by squeezing the juice of an orange over the fruit. Divide the fruit salad into individual cups. Before the children eat, say a prayer of thanks, allowing each child to name a fruit or food for which he is thankful. As the children eat, review the Bible story.

PRAYER PICTURES

177

Fold back

Fold up

HELPER

179

I follow the example of Christ

181

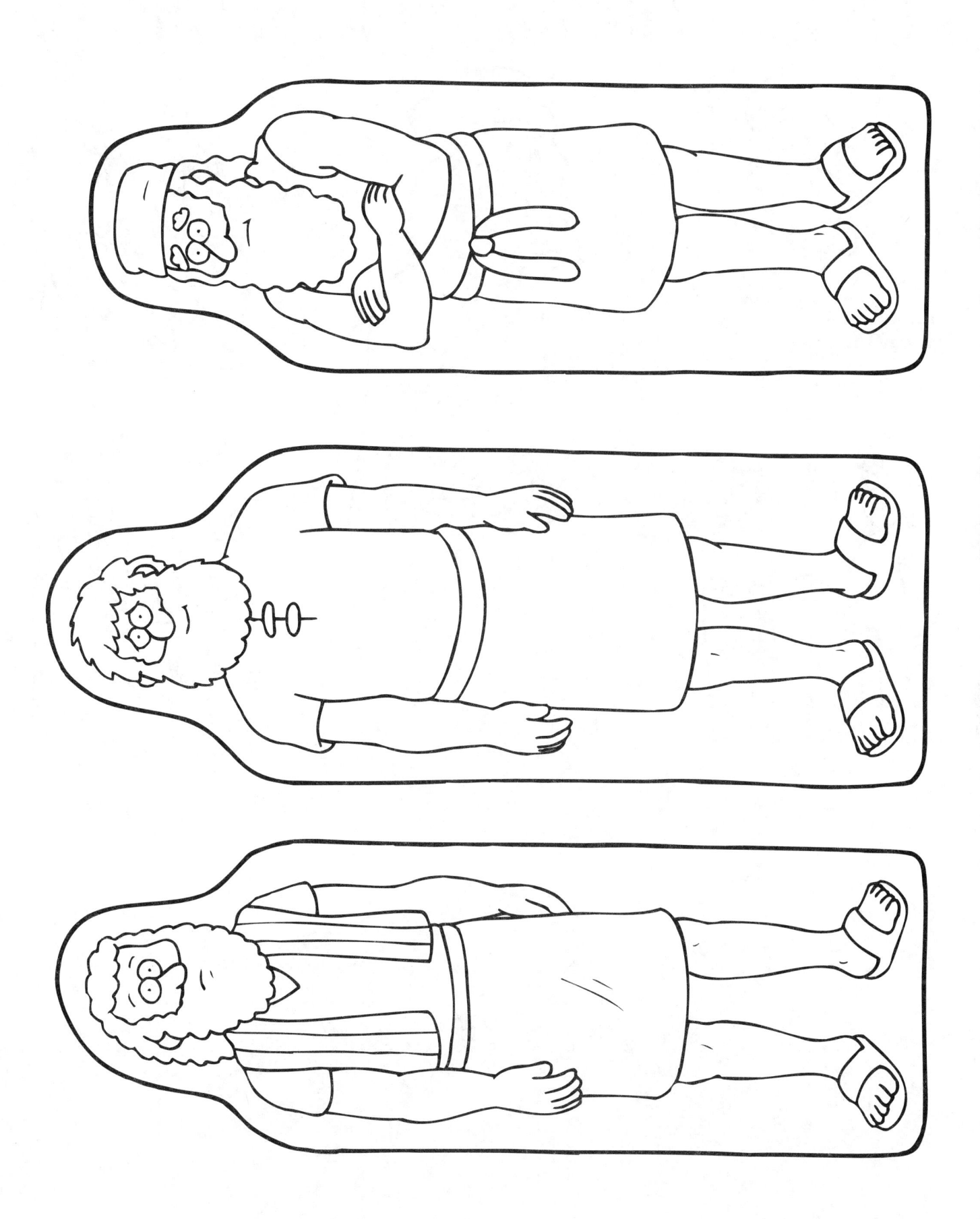

I follow the example of Christ

Fold up

Unit 8
Lessons 31-35

Jesus Is Alive

◆◆◆◆◆

By the end of this unit, the children and leaders will . . .
Know Name people who know Jesus is alive.
Feel Feel excited that Jesus is alive.
Do Celebrate Jesus' resurrection.

Unit Bible Words for Memory
"'I know that you are looking for Jesus, who was crucified. He is not here; he has risen'" (Matthew 28:5b-6a, NIV).

◆◆◆◆◆

Unit Lessons

Lesson 31
Jesus Is Praised
John 12:12-19; Matthew 21:1-11
Children will see how people waved palm branches and praised Jesus as their earthly king when He entered Jerusalem riding on a donkey before the feast of Passover.

Lesson 32
Jesus Is Alive!
John 18:1–20:18
Children will learn how the same people who praised Jesus asked for Him to die on a cross. Then they will hear the good news: Jesus did not stay dead in the tomb. He came back alive three days later!

Lesson 33
The Disciples See Jesus
John 20:19-31; Luke 24:36-43
Children will discover how the disciples and then Thomas saw that Jesus really was alive!

Lesson 34
Breakfast with Jesus
John 21:1-14
Children will hear how Jesus helped His followers catch fish and then cooked them breakfast.

Lesson 35
Jesus Returns to Heaven
Acts 1:1-14; Matthew 28:16-20
Children will hear how Jesus returned to Heaven.

◆◆◆◆◆

Why Teach This Unit to Four-Year-Olds—Six-Year-Olds?

This unit contains the reason for our faith, the heart of the good news about Jesus. Children will not question the facts, but will simply accept the incredible truth. Jesus really did die on the cross. And He really did come back alive three days later! By teaching them these facts, you will build a foundation of faith that they will rely on as they continue to grow and learn.

◆◆◆◆◆

Bible Time Line

The stories for this unit are pictured on the time line, pages 317 and 318.

See page 6 in this book for suggested time-line projects.

Materials

All Lessons
- a Bible
- markers, colored pencils, crayons
- white paper, construction paper, poster board
- tape, masking tape
- Plasti-Tak
- glue
- scissors
- a stapler
- paper hole punch
- yarn or string

Lesson 31
- green crepe paper, empty paper-towel rolls or strips of cardboard, and a small fan (optional)
- old newspapers, several spray bottles of water, and various colors of tissue paper
- a blindfold

Lesson 32
- several large blankets, a large trash bag, and old newspapers
- plastic Easter eggs, a basket, a cassette player, and cassette of praise songs
- plastic eggs and a small treat, such as stickers or erasers
- thinned yellow tempera paint, paintbrushes, paint smocks, paper towels for cleanup
- plastic eggs and spoons

Lesson 33
- a funnel, a teaspoon, baking soda, several balloons, a half-cup of vinegar and an empty two-liter bottle
- a typewriter, butcher paper folded to look like a newspaper, old teaching pictures or cards with Easter events pictured
- tagboard, fabric glue or a stapler, and a pair of old knit gloves
- a toy microphone
- three or four balloons
- a cassette of music and a cassette player
- Easter grass
- a balloon for each child

Lesson 34
- a number of items children can use to pretend to make breakfast: toy dishes; egg cartons; play food; spatulas; empty cereal boxes; a play kitchen
- old teaching pictures showing miracles that Jesus performed (e.g., healings, feeding 5,000, calming the storm)
- 153 goldfish crackers in a jar
- a length of mural paper
- straws
- a large number of Lego® blocks, a child's empty wading pool, and two empty potato sacks with the labels removed

Lesson 35
- powdered laundry detergent (preferably not concentrated), a bowl
- empty egg cartons
- craft sticks
- tempera paint, paper plates or pie tins, paintbrushes, paint smocks

The Beginner's Bible™ Resources

Jesus and the Children Stickers, Standard Publishing, #22-01035, call 1-800-543-1353

Jesus and the Children Floor Puzzle, Standard Publishing, #28-02717, call 1-800-543-1353

Jesus and the Children Inlay Puzzle, Standard Publishing, #28-02703, call 1-800-543-1353

The Beginner's Bible™ New Testament GeoSafari Bible Pack, Standard Publishing, #14-24002, call 1-800-543-1353

The Beginner's Bible™ Bible Lessons GeoSafari Bible Pack, Standard Publishing, #14-24005, call 1-800-543-1353

Unit 8
Lesson 31

Jesus Is Praised
(John 12:12-19; Matthew 21:1-11)

When Jesus entered Jerusalem riding on a donkey, crowds of people followed Him. They sang songs, waved palm branches, and hailed Him as a king.

Bible Words

"'I know that you are looking for Jesus, who was crucified. He is not here; he has risen'" (Matthew 28:5b-6a).

Goals

Tell who sang to Jesus.
Feel excited that Jesus is alive!
Celebrate Jesus' resurrection.

◆◆◆◆

Activity 1—Palm Branches

You will need green crepe paper, scissors, empty paper-towel rolls or strips of cardboard, tape, and a small fan (optional). Before class, cut strips of green crepe paper, several for each child.

Give children the empty cardboard tubes and green crepe paper. Show children how to tape the ends of the crepe paper strips inside one end of their paper-towel tubes (or on the end of a strip of cardboard). You might turn a small fan on low speed, and show children how the crepe paper floats in the air as they wave their "branches."

In our story today, many people cut branches off palm trees and waved them in the air to praise Jesus the King. Let's pretend that these are palm branches that we can wave in the air for Jesus.

Hosanna to the King of Kings!
(Tune: "Jesus Loves Me")

Hosanna to the King of Kings.
He is Lord of everything.
Wave your branches; praise His name.
Thank You, God, that Jesus came.

Jesus is King!
Jesus is King!
Jesus is King!
He's Lord of everything!

Oh, Jesus Is My King!
(Tune: "Did You Ever See a Lassie?")

Oh, Jesus is my King, my King, my King.
Oh, Jesus is my King
He is alive!

Jesus died on a cross, a cross, a cross.
Jesus died on a cross.
But now He's alive!

We celebrate on Easter, on Easter, on Easter.
We celebrate on Easter.
He is alive!

Jesus went to Heaven, to Heaven, to Heaven.
Jesus went to Heaven.
He is alive!

He will come back soon, back soon, back soon.
He will come back soon.
He is alive!

Sing "Hosanna to the King of Kings!" from page 8 of this session several times as the children make and play with their "branches."

ACTIVITY 2—How to Praise

◆◆◆◆

Have children sit in a circle. Explain to them that you are going to say things to praise one of them, and the others should guess who you are talking about.

When you praise someone, it means that you tell good things about him. Can you guess who I am praising? Some examples of praising statements follow: She has pretty, long black hair. She smiles all the time and always shares toys with her friends. She is a good big sister to her baby brother. When children guess correctly, start describing another child until each has been praised.

I know Someone we should praise more than anybody else. **He is bigger and stronger than anyone or anything! He is kind and loving. Who is He?** God. Let children think of things to say to praise God: Thank You for making the world. You are greater than anyone. I'm glad you made me. Thank You for loving us.

In our story today, many people had a parade just to praise Jesus! We can praise Jesus every day.

BIBLE TIME—A Parade for Jesus

◆◆◆◆

Children will need the palm branches that they made in Activity 1. Explain to them that they should hold the branches still except when you say the word "praise."

Do you know what it means to praise? Let children respond. Remind them of the praise you gave them in Activity 2. **I can praise you by telling you what a good job you are doing sitting and listening. When we say and do nice things for someone, we are praising them. We all like to be praised, and so**

WRAP-UP—The Cleanup March

◆◆◆◆

As we clean up the room, let's march and sing like we are in a parade for Jesus. Lead children in singing "Hosanna to the King of Kings!" and marching as they straighten up the room. When the room is clean, gather children together to review the story and memory verse.

What special holiday is coming? Easter. **Next week we will talk about the very first Easter.**

Until parents arrive, have a "Follow the Leader" Parade. Have children line up with their palm branches. You stand in the front as the first leader. Begin marching around the room and doing different motions—waving the palm branch above your head, sticking the palm branch under your arm, shaking the palm branch near the floor, waving the palm branch in figure eights in front of you, and so on. Children volunteers may also take turns being the leader.

Leaders' Evaluation

	Great!	OK!	More!	Oops!	Suggestions
Activity 1					
Activity 2					
Bible Time					
Application					
Bible Memory					
Craft					
Snack					
Game					
Wrap-up					

does God. When we praise Jesus, we tell Him how good and special He is. Our story today is about a time when some people praised Jesus.

When you hear me say the word "praise," then you wave your palm branches to praise Jesus. Let's practice. In church and at home, we like to praise (wave branches) Jesus. Jesus likes to hear us praise (wave branches) Him. Good! Now listen carefully to the story, so you will know when to wave your branches.

There was going to be a big feast with lots and lots of people in the big city of Jerusalem. Jesus and His disciples were going to go to the feast. It was going to be a very important feast and a very important week. Jesus knew that this would be His last trip on earth to Jerusalem. He knew that in just a few days crowds of angry people would ask for Him to be put to death. But right now, the crowds weren't angry at all. They were excited about their King, Jesus, because they thought He was going to stay here on earth as their King and get rid of the awful Romans that ruled their country.

While they were traveling, Jesus said to two of His disciples, "Go into the town near here. When you get there, you will see a donkey with her colt tied up. Bring them to me. If anyone asks what you are doing, tell him that the Lord needs the animals."

The disciples did exactly what Jesus said to do. They brought the donkey to Jesus. Then they laid their coats on the donkey and Jesus sat on them. As Jesus was riding the donkey into Jerusalem, a huge crowd of people came to praise Him (wave branches). They took big branches off the palm trees and waved them in the air. The people shouted and sang, "Hosanna in the highest! Praise (wave branches) Jesus!" Many people spread their coats and branches from the trees in the road for Jesus. It must have looked like a big parade. The people knew that Jesus was a king, and they wanted to praise (wave branches) Him!

Next week (insert appropriate time) is Easter Sunday. Do you know why we celebrate Easter? Jesus died and came back

Lesson 31

OPTION: If you have time, provide enough materials for children to make two cross necklaces. They can keep one necklace and give the other to a friend or family member to remind them that Jesus died and came back alive on Easter. **When you tell others about Jesus, you are celebrating Easter.**

Snack—Easter Eggs

You will need eggs, crackers, cheese, and washable markers. Before class, boil and refrigerate enough eggs so each child can have one.

Give children the eggs and markers. Children can decorate their eggs with any design they choose. When the eggs are decorated, lead children in prayer. Show them how to peel their eggs, then join them in their snack. Serve the eggs with crackers and cheese.

What special holiday is coming? Easter. **It is fun to decorate eggs at Easter time. Do you know why we celebrate this holiday? Do we celebrate so we can color eggs and wait for the Easter bunny?** No. We celebrate Easter because Jesus died and rose again.

Game—Pinup Branches

You will need the palm branch pattern from page 205, brown and green paper, scissors, tape or Plasti-Tak, and a blindfold. Before class, cut out a simple brown tree trunk and hang it on a wall at the children's level. Also enlarge and cut out a large number of green palm branches, using the pattern on page 205. Place a piece of tape or Plasti-Tak on the back of each branch.

Take turns blindfolding the children, turning them around several times, and having them "pin" the branches on the palm tree.

Who used palm branches to praise Jesus? Many people. What did they shout? Hosanna; praise Jesus!

Unit 8

alive on Easter. The Sunday before Easter is also a special day. It is called Palm Sunday. Do you know why? Allow children to respond. That day is called Palm Sunday because of what we learned in today's story. On Palm Sunday, we remember that crowds of people waved palm branches and praised Jesus as their King.

◆◆◆◆

APPLICATION—Praise Him!

You will need the palm branches made in Activity 1 and used in Bible Time. Before class, check with a few other classes about the children "parading" through their rooms. If the weather is nice, it would be fun to "parade" outside. Line children up with their branches.

What can we do to praise Jesus? Sing, dance, clap, pray. **Let's sing a song right now to praise Jesus.** Review the song "Hosanna to the King of Kings!" from page 8 of this session that the children learned in Activity 1. Repeat the song several times. If the children are not comfortable with all the words of the song yet, simply sing the chorus of the song during your parade. You may also sing other familiar praise songs to Jesus.

Let's have a parade for Jesus like the people in our story did. We can wave our branches, sing our song, and shout "Hosanna! Praise Jesus! He's our King!" Practice waving, singing, and shouting several times. Then lead children in the parade.

◆◆◆◆

BIBLE MEMORY—Role Play

You will need a Bible and a bookmark. Before class, mark Matthew 28:5, 6 in your Bible with a bookmark.

Do you know what special holiday is coming? Easter. **We have Easter so we can remember and praise Jesus because He died for us and came back to life again. Our Bible verse can help us to remember that.**

Have a child open your Bible to Matthew 28:5b–6a. Point out the highlighted verses in your Bible to the children and read the words to them. Have the children repeat the verse with you several times.

Show the women how to search for Jesus and be afraid when the angel appears. Then encourage the "angel" to say the Bible words to the women, who are then very happy!

An angel said these words to some women who were looking for Jesus' body after He was killed and put in a tomb. But Jesus' body was not there! He had risen! Have the children take turns pretending to be the women and the angel at the tomb. Show the women how to search for Jesus and be afraid when the angel appears. Then encourage the "angel" to say the Bible words to the women, who are then very happy!

◆◆◆◆

ACTIVITY TIME

Do as many activities as time permits.

Craft—Cross Necklaces

You will need the cross pattern from page 205, heavy paper, scissors, yarn, a paper hole punch, old newspapers, several spray bottles of water, and various colors of tissue paper. Before the session, cut crosses from heavy paper using the pattern on page 205. Using a paper hole punch, put a hole at the top of each cross. Also, cut a length of yarn for each child's necklace. Cut various colors of tissue paper into small squares (experiment to make sure you have thin tissue that will bleed when wet). Fill a couple of spray bottles with water.

We are celebrating a special day, Easter. We have Easter because Jesus died on a cross and came back alive again. Let's make a cross necklace to remind us why we have Easter.

Show children how to lay their crosses on newspaper, then cover them with squares of tissue paper. Let the children spray their crosses with water. After several minutes, have the children remove the wet paper, leaving painted designs on the crosses. When the crosses are dry, put pieces of yarn or string through the holes in the tops of the crosses and tie the ends together to make necklaces.

Unit 8
Lesson 32

Jesus Is Alive!
(John 18:1–20:18)

After being tried and falsely accused, Jesus was led away to be crucified. His friends laid His body in a new tomb. On the first day of the week, an angel rolled the stone away from the tomb and Jesus rose from the dead.

Bible Words

"'I know that you are looking for Jesus, who was crucified. He is not here; he has risen'" (Matthew 28:5b-6a).

Goals

Tell who saw Jesus die and come back alive.
Feel excited that Jesus is alive!
Celebrate Jesus' resurrection.

Activity 1—A Cave Tomb

You will need several large blankets, a large trash bag, and old newspapers.

Before class, cover a table in your classroom with large blankets to make a "cave." Make sure the sides hang down to the floor. Leave an opening on one side of the "cave." Place a large trash bag full of crumpled newspapers in front of the opening. You may want to let the children make the "stone" themselves by helping to crumple newspapers and stuffing them in the large trash bag.

In our Bible story today, we will be talking about Jesus' crucifixion and resurrection. *Crucifixion* means that Jesus died on a cross. *Resurrection* means that Jesus came back to life again! At Easter, we celebrate when Jesus came back alive.

Hosanna to the King of Kings!
(Tune: "Jesus Loves Me")

Hosanna to the King of Kings.
He is Lord of everything.
Wave your branches; praise His name.
Thank You, God, that Jesus came.

Jesus is King!
Jesus is King!
Jesus is King!
He's Lord of everything!

Oh, Jesus Is My King!
(Tune: "Did You Ever See a Lassie?")

Oh, Jesus is my King, my King, my King.
Oh, Jesus is my King
He is alive!

Jesus died on a cross, a cross, a cross.
Jesus died on a cross.
But now He's alive!

We celebrate on Easter, on Easter, on Easter.
We celebrate on Easter.
He is alive!

Jesus went to Heaven, to Heaven, to Heaven.
Jesus went to Heaven.
He is alive!

He will come back soon, back soon, back soon.
He will come back soon.
He is alive!

When Jesus died, His friends put His body in a tomb or cave. Let's pretend this is the cave. Here is a stone to put in front of the door.

Show children the cave. Let them crawl inside and see how dark it is. Let children take turns being the angel that rolled away the stone and sat on it. Encourage the "angel" to say the Bible words when the other children look in the cave.

ACTIVITY 2—The First Easter

You will need photocopies of the picture cards from page 206, scissors, crayons or markers, plastic Easter eggs, a basket, a cassette player, and cassette of songs. Before class, color and cut out the picture cards from page 206. Fold each card and put it into a plastic Easter egg. Then put all the eggs in a basket.

Have all the children sit in a circle and pass the basket around as music is played. When the music stops, the person holding the basket can draw out an egg and open it. Have the child hold the picture up for the class to see. Encourage the child to tell whether he thinks the picture is a part of the first Easter or not. Continue the game until all the eggs have been opened.

We are excited because of Easter. What special things do we do at Easter time? Color eggs; get candy. These are fun things, but the most important part of Easter is that Jesus died and is alive again!

BIBLE TIME—Jesus Is Alive!

Have children gather at the table that has been made into a cave. Put the stone over the entrance to the cave.

Do you know what special holiday we are celebrating? Easter. **What do we do on Easter?** Go to church; get candy; color eggs. **People didn't do any of these things on the very first Easter. Let me tell you the story about what happened on the first Easter morning.**

Easter. **How can you celebrate Easter because Jesus is alive?** Sing praises to Him; tell others He is alive. Lead children in prayer and sing, "Oh, Jesus Is My King!"

Until parents come, sing praise songs from the cassette used in Application. Let volunteers take turns leading the group in motions to the songs. They can wave their arms, step side-to-side, turn around, clap their hands, march in place, bend down and up, and so on.

Leaders' Evaluation

	Great!	OK!	More!	Oops!	Suggestions
Activity 1					
Activity 2					
Bible Time					
Application					
Bible Memory					
Craft					
Snack					
Game					
Wrap-up					

Jesus had come to the city of Jerusalem. There was a parade when He came. People sang, "Hosanna! Praise the King!" But there were other people who did not like Jesus. They said that He was not really a king. They told lies about Him and wanted to kill Him.

These bad people told the soldiers to arrest Jesus. The soldiers laughed and made fun of Jesus. They hit Him and spit on Him. They even put a crown made out of thorns on His head. Then they made Him carry a heavy cross up a hill called Golgotha. There they put Him on a cross between two robbers. Do you think that Jesus was mad at these people? No, He still loved these mean people and prayed for them!

When Jesus died, His friends were very sad. Some of them took His body and put it in a tomb like this one. Point to the cave. There was a big stone in front of the door. Point to the stone. Some Roman soldiers stood at the tomb to guard it.

On Sunday morning, some of Jesus' friends came to the tomb very early in the morning. They were still very sad. They may have been talking about Jesus and crying as they came to the tomb of their friend. But when they got there, what do you think they found? Let children share. They didn't find any Roman guards, and they didn't find Jesus either. Instead, the heavy stone was pushed away, and the tomb was empty! Where was Jesus? Push the stone away and have the children look into the empty tomb.

The other women ran right away to tell some of Jesus' followers what they had found. But Jesus' friend, Mary Magdalene, stayed at the tomb. She was sad because she thought someone had stolen Jesus' body. She sat by the tomb and cried. Suddenly, she saw someone standing in front of her. He said, "Why are you crying, Mary?" She looked up. It was Jesus! He was alive!

Mary was so happy that she ran and told all of Jesus' friends the good news about what she had seen. She said, "Jesus is alive! I have seen Him!"

Lesson 32

Snack—Remember Jesus!

For this snack, you will need to provide saltine crackers and/or another type of unleavened bread, such as pita bread, and grape juice in small cups. Explain to the children that when people become Christians, they take communion during the church service.

Before Jesus died, He had a last supper with His disciples. He told them a way to remember Him. Christians today still remember Jesus the way He told His followers. They eat bread and drink juice to remind them that Jesus died for them. When a person becomes a Christian and is baptized, she takes communion at church to remember how Jesus died for our sins.

Lead children in prayer, then encourage them to enjoy their snack.

Game—Egg-citing Relays

You will need plastic eggs and spoons.

Gather children into two or three groups for relays. In the first relay, have the children carry plastic eggs on spoons back and forth without dropping them. In the second relay, have the children roll the plastic eggs across the floor with their noses. Help the children encourage one another.

We color and hunt for eggs to celebrate Easter. What happened on the first Easter? Jesus rose from the dead.

❖❖❖❖❖

Wrap-up—Joyful Cleanup

Let's skip and tell the good news that "Jesus is alive!" while we clean up the room today. Show children how to happily straighten up the room.

When the children are finished with cleanup, have them gather for review. **Who came back to life again?** Jesus. **How did Jesus die?** On a cross. **What did the angel say at the tomb?** Have children say the words of the memory verse together. **What special day do we celebrate because Jesus is alive?**

Unit 8

APPLICATION—The Tomb Is Empty!

You will need a cassette of praise songs your children enjoy singing and a cassette player. If possible, choose songs that talk about Jesus' death and resurrection.

Everyone dies some time. But we know that we do not need to be afraid, because God is stronger than death. Jesus rose again! There are some people who do not know that Jesus is alive. There are some people who do not know why we have Easter. We should tell them that the tomb is empty!

Have children come up one or two at a time to look inside the tomb. Ask them if there is anything inside. No, the tomb is empty.

Let's say a prayer together: Thank You, God, for Easter. Thank You that Jesus died on the cross for us. Thank You that the tomb is empty, and Jesus is alive!

Lead children in singing "Hosanna to the King of Kings!" and "Oh, Jesus Is My King!" from page 8 of this session. Then use the cassette of praise songs to sing to Jesus. Even if children don't sing all of the words, encourage them to become involved in the songs through movement. Clap, wave your arms above your head, sway back and forth, and so on.

BIBLE MEMORY—Hot/Cold Search

You will need plastic eggs and a small treat, such as stickers or erasers. You may wish to avoid using candy as a treat, since many children will receive other candy Easter treats. Before class, fill the plastic eggs with the treats.

Gather children together. Practice saying the Bible verse together several times. Send one child at a time from the room (or have him face the wall and cover his eyes) while you hide an egg. When the child comes back, have the children give directions to help him find the egg. If the child is close, the children will say he's getting warmer. If he's going away from the egg,

the children will say that he is cold. When the egg is found, have the child say the Bible verse, then he can open the egg to get the treat inside. Continue until every child says the verse and receives a treat.

An angel said these words to some women who were looking for Jesus. What happened to Jesus? He arose. Why do we celebrate Easter? Jesus is alive!

ACTIVITY TIME

Do as many activities as time permits.

Craft—An Empty Tomb

You will need dark-colored construction paper, brown or black crayons, thinned yellow tempera paint, paintbrushes, paint smocks, paper towels for cleanup, and the pattern of the empty tomb on page 208.

Before class, make a sample picture and experiment with the tempera paint to make the right consistency. The paint should not stick to the crayon.

The soldiers at Jesus' tomb said they saw a bright flash of light; then Jesus was gone and the tomb was empty. He had come back alive. Let's draw a picture to remind us that Jesus came back alive!

Give children the construction paper and brown or black crayons. Show children how to draw a simple picture of the empty tomb. You can show them the empty tomb pattern on page 208 as an example. If children need help, trace a simple empty tomb on their papers and have them color it in with the crayons. Make sure children press down hard with their crayons. Give each child a paint smock, then have them paint lightly over their whole paper with thinned yellow tempera paint. Then set the pictures aside to dry. **Who died on a cross?** Jesus. **Where did Jesus' friends put His body after He died?** Cave; tomb. **What happened on Easter morning?** Jesus arose!

Unit 8
Lesson 33

The Disciples See Jesus
(John 20:19-31; Luke 24:36-43)

After Jesus arose, He appeared to the disciples, but Thomas was absent. Thomas could not believe that Jesus was alive until he touched Him and saw His wounds. Jesus blessed those who, unlike Thomas, have faith to believe without seeing Him.

Bible Words

"'I know that you are looking for Jesus, who was crucified. He is not here; he has risen'" (Matthew 28:5b-6a).

Goals

Tell who saw that Jesus is alive.
Feel excited that Jesus is alive!
Celebrate Jesus' resurrection.

❖❖❖❖

Activity 1—Is Air There?

You will need a funnel, a teaspoon, baking soda, several balloons, a half-cup of vinegar and an empty two-liter bottle. Before class, prepare to do a couple of science experiments. Be sure to practice your experiments beforehand, so that they go smoothly. Using a funnel, put a couple teaspoons of baking soda in two balloons (do not blow the balloons up). Have a couple other balloons ready to use. Pour a half-cup of vinegar into the bottom of an empty two-liter bottle.

Gather children and talk about the air around them. Can they see it? How do they know that it is there? Have them watch while you put the mouth of a balloon over the neck of the two-liter bottle, letting the baking soda fall into the vinegar. The balloon will inflate. Do the experiment again.

— fold —

Hosanna to the King of Kings!
(Tune: "Jesus Loves Me")

Hosanna to the King of Kings.
He is Lord of everything.
Wave your branches; praise His name.
Thank You, God, that Jesus came.

Jesus is King!
Jesus is King!
Jesus is King!
He's Lord of everything!

Oh, Jesus Is My King!
(Tune: "Did You Ever See a Lassie?")

Oh, Jesus is my King, my King, my King.
Oh, Jesus is my King
He is alive!

Jesus died on a cross, a cross, a cross.
Jesus died on a cross.
But now He's alive!

We celebrate on Easter, on Easter, on Easter.
We celebrate on Easter.
He is alive!

Jesus went to Heaven, to Heaven, to Heaven.
Jesus went to Heaven.
He is alive!

He will come back soon, back soon, back soon.
He will come back soon.
He is alive!

Blow up a balloon with your mouth and then let it go without tying it. Do this several times, discussing how you know the air is there even though you cannot see it.

The air in the balloon is like God. We cannot see Him, but we know that He is here with us. This is called faith. In our story today, one of Jesus' friends said that he would not believe that Jesus was alive, unless he saw and touched Jesus. Jesus said we are special, because we believe even though we have not seen and touched Him. We have faith.

♦♦♦♦♦

ACTIVITY 2—Front-page News

You will need a large piece of butcher paper, a typewriter, pencils and pens, markers, paper, tape, scissors, old teaching pictures or cards with Easter events pictured. Before the session, fold the butcher paper to look like a newspaper.

What is the good news about Easter? Jesus died, but rose again! **Our newspapers have news, but no news is this big! No one can come back to life after they are dead. Only God has power over death. Let's pretend to be reporters and make a newspaper that tells the big news that Jesus is alive!**

Let children pretend to type and write the "news," then tape the reports into the big newspaper. Other children can pretend to take photos (draw pictures) and tape them in as well. Children can also cut out pictures from old teaching pictures or cards to tape in the newspaper.

♦♦♦♦♦

BIBLE TIME—Jesus Visits His Friends

You will need photocopies of page 207, tagboard, crayons or markers, fabric glue or a stapler, and a pair of old knit gloves. Before the story, prepare the puppets of Jesus and Thomas from page 207. Photocopy the puppets on tagboard, color and cut them out, then glue or staple the head and arms to a pair of old knit gloves. The heads of the puppets should be fastened to the

2 Unit 8

---

going to tell that Jesus is alive? Let children share.

Lead the children in prayer, then sing "Hosanna to the King of Kings!" and "Oh, Jesus Is My King" from page 8 of this session.

Until parents come, play a variation of the game played with balloons and music during Bible Memory. Have children hit the balloons in the air to each other while the music is playing. When the music stops, the children holding balloons tell whom they will tell about Jesus coming back alive or what they will tell. If the children need help knowing what to tell, refer them to the news they reported during Application.

Leaders' Evaluation

	Great!	OK!	More!	Oops!	Suggestions
Activity 1					
Activity 2					
Bible Time					
Application					
Bible Memory					
Craft					
Snack					
Game					
Wrap-up					

Lesson 33 7

three middle fingers, and the arms to the thumbs and pinky fingers. Wear both glove puppets to tell the story.

Last week we talked about the very first Easter. Nobody colored eggs or gave each other candy. **What special thing happened?** Jesus arose.

Jesus' friends were sad, because He had died on a cross and been buried in a cave tomb. But on Easter Sunday morning, an angel rolled the big stone away from the door of the cave, and Jesus came back to life again!

One evening the disciples, some of Jesus' friends, were together inside a house. They were sad and afraid, so they locked the doors. Suddenly, there was Jesus standing in the middle of them! Show the puppet of Jesus. Jesus said, "Peace be with you!" The disciples were scared at first. They thought He might be a ghost. But Jesus said, "Do you have anything to eat?" They gave Him some fish to eat. The disciples were very excited that Jesus was alive!

One of Jesus' disciples, Thomas, was not with them when Jesus came to visit. Show the puppet of Thomas. The other disciples said, "We have seen Jesus!" But Thomas would not believe it! He said, "I won't believe unless I can touch Jesus. I won't believe until I see the nail marks in Jesus' hands."

A week later, all of the disciples were together again. Thomas was there too. Suddenly Jesus stood among them again. Show both puppets. Jesus said to Thomas, "Touch me. Put your finger here. See the nail marks in my hands. You should believe!" Have the Jesus puppet hold out his hands and the Thomas puppet touch them. Thomas knew it was Jesus and he believed. Jesus told Thomas, "You had to see me to believe. But how special are those people who believe in me without seeing!"

OPTION: Allow children to make their own glove puppets. You can purchase knit gloves at a store for a low price. Children can use their puppets to tell each other the story about Jesus' dying and coming back alive.

Give children small, new paintbrushes. Let them decorate their cookies by painting them with the colored whipping cream. They may also decorate their cookies with colored sugar or sprinkles.

Why do we celebrate Easter? To remember that Jesus died and came back to life. **Let's make these cookies to celebrate, because Jesus is alive!**

Lead children in prayer, thanking God that Jesus is alive! Join them in eating the snack.

Game—Alive, Alive!

Gather children together. The teacher should start out being the "angel." Have the children sit down and cover their eyes like they are crying. Make sure the children are spread out, so that the "angel" can walk between and around them. The "angel" can walk among the children, tapping one at a time on the head and saying, "Jesus is alive!" When a child is tapped, he should jump up and say, "Alive, Alive!", then follow the angel until all the children are in line. Try the game several times, letting the children take turns being the "angel."

Who rolled the stone away from Jesus' tomb? An angel. **Why was the stone rolled away?** Jesus was alive! **What special day do we celebrate because Jesus is alive?** Easter.

♦♦♦♦

Wrap-up—Whom Can You Tell?

You will need a balloon for each child.

While you are cleaning up today, think of someone to whom you can tell the good news about Easter. Say a prayer for that person.

Encourage the children to straighten and clean up the room. Give each child a specific task to do. When the task is completed, give the child one of the balloons to take home.

When everyone has a balloon, have all the children gather together to review the story. **Who arose on Easter?** Jesus. **Who saw that Jesus is alive?** Thomas; disciples; Mary. **Whom are you**

APPLICATION—Sharing the Big News

You will need a toy microphone and the newspapers made in Activity 2.

Hold up the newspaper that the children made earlier. Talk about the different pictures and "reports." Ask the "reporters" to tell what they wrote and took pictures of for the news. Let each child stand up and "report" the news individually. Children will enjoy pretending to speak into a microphone. Use a toy microphone or any sticklike toy that resembles one. The teacher may need to ask questions to help out.

Jesus' death and resurrection is the biggest news ever! Jesus wants us to tell the news to others. Whom can you tell? Encourage children to name specific family members or friends that they could tell about Jesus. **Let's thank God for Jesus. Let's praise and thank God because He is stronger and bigger than death.**

Lead children in prayer, then sing all verses of "Oh, Jesus Is My King!" from page 8 of this session together.

◆◆◆◆

BIBLE MEMORY—Balloon Pass

You will need a Bible with the memory verse marked and highlighted, three or four balloons, a cassette of music, and a cassette player.

Have a volunteer help you find the highlighted verse in your Bible. Read the verse as you point to the words. Then have the children say the verse with you several times. Have them sit in a circle and pass three or four balloons around, while music is played. When the music stops, the children holding the balloons should stand up and recite the Bible verse together. Repeat the game several times, so that all children have a chance to review the verse.

Do you remember who spoke these words? An angel. **To whom was the angel speaking?** Women looking for Jesus' body.

This happened on the morning of the very first Easter. **Who saw Jesus after He arose?** Mary; disciples; Thomas.

◆◆◆◆

ACTIVITY TIME

Do as many activities as time permits.

◆◆◆◆

Craft—Easter Stencils

You will need the stencil patterns from page 208, tagboard, scissors, light-colored construction paper, colored pencils, markers or watercolors, glue, and Easter grass. Before class, prepare Easter shapes by cutting out several of each pattern (cross, empty tomb, palm branch, flower) found on page 208. Use tagboard to make the stencils. Complete a sample Easter picture to show the children.

Give each child a piece of construction paper. Children can trace the stencil shapes onto their construction paper to make an Easter picture. Then they can color or paint them with watercolors. They could also glue Easter grass to the bottom to finish the picture.

What do we celebrate at Easter? Jesus died and rose again. **Who saw that Jesus was alive again?** Disciples; Thomas. **You can use your picture to tell someone about the real story of Easter.**

OPTION: Make a photocopy of page 208 for each child in your class. Children can color and cut out the shapes on the page, arrange them on their paper, and glue them in place to make an Easter picture.

Snack—Cutout Sugar Cookies

You will need sugar cookies in Easter shapes (eggs, crosses, flowers), a pint of whipping cream, food coloring, four small bowls, new paintbrushes, and colored sugar and sprinkles (optional). Before class, purchase or make sugar cookies in Easter shapes. Divide a pint of whipping cream between four small bowls. Color the cream with the food coloring, making four different pastel colors (pink, green, blue, yellow).

Unit 8
Lesson 34

Breakfast with Jesus
(John 21:1-14)

The disciples had fished all night without catching anything. When Jesus appeared on the shore, they threw the net in again as He told them to. The enormous catch of fish was a miracle, and the disciples knew that it was Jesus waiting for them with breakfast ready.

Bible Words

"'I know that you are looking for Jesus, who was crucified. He is not here; he has risen'" (Matthew 28:5b-6a).

Goals

Tell who saw that Jesus is alive.
Feel excited that Jesus is alive.
Celebrate Jesus' resurrection.

Activity 1—Let's Make Breakfast!

You will need a number of items children can use to pretend to make breakfast. These could include toy dishes; egg cartons; play food; spatulas; empty cereal boxes; a play kitchen.

In our story today, Jesus appears to some of His friends after they have been fishing all night long. Jesus made breakfast for His friends. Let's pretend to make breakfast for our friends.

Lead children in pretending to set the table, pour coffee, fry eggs, and so on. Talk about the differences between their breakfast and the one Jesus made for His friends.

Do you think that Jesus made pancakes for His friends for breakfast? No, He made fish. He cooked it over a fire on a beach. Would you like to eat fish for breakfast?

Hosanna to the King of Kings!
(Tune: "Jesus Loves Me")

Hosanna to the King of Kings.
He is Lord of everything.
Wave your branches; praise His name.
Thank You, God, that Jesus came.

Jesus is King!
Jesus is King!
Jesus is King!
He's Lord of everything!

Oh, Jesus Is My King!
(Tune: "Did You Ever See a Lassie?")

Oh, Jesus is my King, my King, my King.
Oh, Jesus is my King
He is alive!

Jesus died on a cross, a cross, a cross.
Jesus died on a cross.
But now He's alive!

We celebrate on Easter, on Easter, on Easter.
We celebrate on Easter.
He is alive!

Jesus went to Heaven, to Heaven, to Heaven.
Jesus went to Heaven.
He is alive!

He will come back soon, back soon, back soon.
He will come back soon.
He is alive!

ACTIVITY 2—What Is a Miracle?

Before class, gather a number of old teaching pictures showing miracles that Jesus performed (e.g., healings, feeding 5,000, calming the storm). Or photocopy time-line pages 316 and 317 from this book and have children act out miracles pictured on those pages. If you use the time-line pages, be sure to make enough copies so that each group can have a copy. The miracles pictured are: Jesus heals Peter's mother-in-law, brings a widow's son back from the dead, feeds 5,000, heals ten lepers, heals a blind man.

Show children the pictures you have gathered and have them tell you what miracle is shown in each scene. After discussing miracles, explain to the children that they will get to act out some miracles of Jesus. Divide children into groups and give each group one of the pictures. The children can talk about and practice acting out the story they will perform. Some groups may need a teacher's assistance. Let each group take a turn acting out the story on their picture, while the other children guess which miracle of Jesus it is.

A miracle is a special act of God. It is something that people cannot do. Could you or I do a miracle? No. Jesus did lots of miracles while He was on the earth. In our story today, Jesus does a miracle. He helps the disciples catch lots and lots of fish!

BIBLE TIME—A Big Catch!

Before class, count out 153 goldfish crackers and place them in a jar. Set the jar on the table in front of the children.

What do I have in my jar? Let children guess. Goldfish. How many fish do you think are here? Let children guess. In our story today, the disciples go fishing. Listen and find out how many fish they catch.

After Jesus rose from the dead, some of the disciples were in a boat fishing. They did not fish with fishing poles. They used

— fold —

Lead children in prayer, then sing "Oh, Jesus Is My King!" from page 8 of this session.

Until parents arrive, play a celebration game. Have the children sit on the floor. Call out ways to celebrate Easter. If you call out a way to celebrate that Jesus is alive, the children should jump to their feet. If the way to celebrate doesn't have anything to do with Jesus, the children should lie back flat on the floor. Some ways to celebrate could be: color Easter eggs, sing praises to Jesus, find an Easter basket, go to church on Easter morning, visit the Easter bunny, have an Easter egg hunt, read or listen to the Easter story in the Bible, tell someone "Jesus is alive!", eat lots of Easter candy.

Leaders' Evaluation

	Great!	OK!	More!	Oops!	Suggestions
Activity 1					
Activity 2					
Bible Time					
Application					
Bible Memory					
Craft					
Snack					
Game					
Wrap-up					

a big net to catch fish. All night long they stayed out in the boat! They threw their net into the water. Pretend to throw a net on the left side of your chair. **How many fish did they catch? None!** They threw their net in again. Throw your net in again. **How many fish did they catch? Zero! They did not catch any fish all night long!**

Early in the morning, Jesus came and stood on the beach. He called out to the disciples (cup your hand around your mouth), "Friends, did you catch some fish?"

The disciples called back, "No, we didn't!"

So Jesus said, "Throw your net on the right side of the boat, and you will find some fish." The disciples listened and threw their net on the right side of the boat. Pretend to throw a net out on your right side. When they did, their net caught so many fish they could not pull it out of the water. Pretend to pull at a heavy net.

Peter said, "That's Jesus on the beach!" So he jumped out of the boat and swam all the way to shore. Make swimming motions. When the other disciples landed the boat on shore, Peter grabbed the heavy net and pulled it (tug at your net) out of the water. **Do you know how many fish were in the net?** Hold up the jar of fish. **There were 153 fish! That's a lot of fish!** The disciples knew that Jesus had helped them catch all those fish.

Jesus had breakfast ready for His friends. He had made fish and bread over a fire. The disciples sat down and ate with Jesus. They were happy to be with their Friend again. They were happy that Jesus was alive!

♦♦♦♦

APPLICATION—A Celebration Song

You will need a length of mural paper, tape, a marker, and crayons or colored pencils. Before the activity, attach the mural paper to the wall or lay it out on the floor and gather the children around it.

How did the disciples know that it was Jesus on the beach?

Lesson 34

---

small paper cups. Let children put several gummy fish or small fish crackers to swim in the water. Lead children in prayer, then join them in eating their snack.

Who went fishing in our story today? Disciples. **Whom did the disciples see on the shore?** Jesus. **The disciples were very happy that Jesus was alive again!**

Game—Catching Fish

You will need a large number of Lego® blocks, a child's empty wading pool, and two empty potato sacks with the labels removed. Before class, spread the blocks out in the pool. If you do not have a pool, use any large container that the children can "fish" from, such as a large cardboard box.

Divide children into two teams. Line them up on opposite sides of the pool. Tell them that they will see how many "fish" their team can catch. At your signal, the first child in each team will take the potato sack net, run to the pool, and grab a handful of "fish" to throw in the net. They should continue until every child has had a turn. Then let the teams count up their catch of fish.

♦♦♦♦

Wrap-up—Swim Up!

Encourage children to clean up the room together. Let's pretend to be a school of fish swimming together and cleaning up. Assign different "fish" to do various things as they "swim" around the room.

When the classroom is straightened, have children gather in a circle. **Why do we have Easter?** Jesus died and rose again. **Who saw Jesus after He came back to life again?** Disciples; Thomas; Mary. **Whom can you tell about why we have Easter?** Mom and dad; friends; neighbors. Turn to the child next to you and say, "Why are you happy at Easter, Jane?" The child answers, "Because Jesus is alive!" Then Jane asks the same question of the child next to her. Continue around the circle until all the children have a chance to tell why they are happy at Easter.

Unit 8

They knew because He did a miracle. They knew, and we know, that only God and His Son, Jesus, can do miracles. **We are happy just like the disciples, because we know that Jesus is alive! We are going to write a song to show we are happy Jesus is alive.**

Ask children to choose a familiar tune to use to write their song. The tune could be a children's song, such as "London Bridge," or it could be the tune to a chorus they sing at church, such as "God Is So Good." Then guide children to choose new words to the tune that praise Jesus because He is alive. Give them some suggestions to choose from: Jesus is alive; we love Jesus; we will celebrate Jesus; we praise You, Jesus; and so on. As you decide on the words of the song, print them in one line across the length of mural paper. Practice singing the words of the song together.

Then give children crayons and colored pencils and have them illustrate the words of the song. They can draw pictures of Jesus, of the empty tomb, of the boat and the disciples catching fish, or any other picture that praises Jesus. When they are finished, post the mural on the wall and sing the song of praise together.

Keep the mural to use during next week's session.

♦♦♦♦

BIBLE MEMORY—Something Fishy!

You will need a cassette of children's songs and a cassette player.

Gather children and practice saying the Bible verse together several times. Then have children join hands and make a circle. When music is played, have children in the "net" raise their arms with hands still joined. Choose one child to be the "fish" and pretend to swim in and out under the arms of his friends. When the music stops, the children in the circle should lower their arms, trying to catch the fish inside the circle. If the fish is caught, he joins in the circle net. Continue until everyone has had a chance to be a fish.

The disciples went fishing all night. Whom did they see on the shore? Jesus. **They were happy because Jesus was alive!**

ACTIVITY TIME

Do as many activities as time permits.

♦♦♦♦

Craft—Fisherman Flip Card

You will need photocopies of the flip cards on page 209, scissors, index cards, tape, and pencils or straws. Before class, make a sample flip-card picture and demonstrate it for the children.

Give each child a set of flip cards and two index cards. The children should cut out the two flip-card pictures and tape each one to an index card. Then they should tape a straw or pencil securely to the back of one of the cards, and then tape the other card on top of that, so that the two cards are back to back, with the straw between them. Children should tape the tops and sides of the cards together, so they are securely fastened. When children hold the straw in their hands and roll it back and forth, the picture should look as if it is moving.

Who went fishing in our story today? Disciples. **How many fish did they catch?** None until Jesus came, then 153. **Who cooked fish for breakfast?** Jesus.

Snack—Swimming Fish

You will need instant vanilla pudding, milk, blue food coloring, and several empty baby food jars. Divide a package (or more, depending on the size of your class) of vanilla pudding between several empty baby food jars. Add the proper portion of milk and a few drops of blue food coloring to each. Screw the lids on tightly, then let the children take turns shaking them as you sing "Oh, Jesus Is My King!" and "Hosanna to the King of Kings!" from page 8 of this session.

When the pudding has thickened, divide the "water" into the Bible verse with any other caught fish.

If the fish is caught, he stays in the net and practices saying the Bible verse with any other caught fish. If the fish is not

Unit 8
Lesson 35

Jesus Returns to Heaven
(Acts 1:1-14; Matthew 28:16-20)

Jesus returned to Heaven before the eyes of His disciples. Before leaving, He told the disciples to tell others about Him and to make new disciples. Jesus will return to earth in the same manner He left.

Bible Words

"'I know that you are looking for Jesus, who was crucified. He is not here; he has risen'" (Matthew 28:5b-6a).

Goals

Tell who saw Jesus go up to Heaven.
Feel excited that Jesus is alive and in Heaven!
Celebrate Jesus' resurrection.

◆◆◆◆

Activity 1—Cloudy Skies

You will need a large sheet of blue paper or individual pieces of blue construction paper, powdered laundry detergent (preferably not concentrated), a bowl, and paper towels for cleanup. Before class, cover a table with a large sheet of blue paper, or you may choose to give children individual pieces of blue construction paper.

Tell the children that you need their help mixing up a bowl of clouds. Pour the laundry detergent in a bowl and add water slowly. Let the children help stir the clouds until they are smooth like fingerpaint. Show children how to paint clouds with their fingers on the blue paper "sky." Then allow children to wash their hands. Set aside their cloud paintings to dry as you discuss clouds.

---fold---

Hosanna to the King of Kings!
(Tune: "Jesus Loves Me")

Hosanna to the King of Kings.
He is Lord of everything.
Wave your branches; praise His name.
Thank You, God, that Jesus came.

Jesus is King!
Jesus is King!
Jesus is King!
He's Lord of everything!

Oh, Jesus Is My King!
(Tune: "Did You Ever See a Lassie?")

Oh, Jesus is my King, my King, my King.
Oh, Jesus is my King
He is alive!

Jesus died on a cross, a cross, a cross.
Jesus died on a cross.
But now He's alive!

We celebrate on Easter, on Easter, on Easter.
We celebrate on Easter.
He is alive!

Jesus went to Heaven, to Heaven, to Heaven.
Jesus went to Heaven.
He is alive!

He will come back soon, back soon, back soon.
He will come back soon.
He is alive!

Where are clouds? In the sky. Who made the clouds? God. In our story today, Jesus returns to His home, Heaven. Jesus goes up into the sky and a cloud hides Him from the disciples.

♦♦♦♦

ACTIVITY 2—Caterpillars and Cocoons

You will need several empty egg cartons, scissors, markers, construction paper, glue, tape, and paper towels. Before class, cut up egg cartons to make caterpillars. Cut the egg cartons into fourths, so that each caterpillar has three sections.

Give children the caterpillars and let them decorate their caterpillars with markers. Then they can cut scraps of construction paper to glue on for antennae, eyes, and spots. When the caterpillars are finished, have children wrap their caterpillars in cocoons, using paper towels and tape. Make sure names are written on the outside of each cocoon.

Caterpillars wrap themselves in tight cocoons for a long time. When they come out of their cocoons, they are new and different! Do you know what they turn into? Butterflies or moths. **At Easter we remember that Jesus rose again. We can have new life, too, if we believe in Him.**

Set the cocoons aside to use at Craft Time.

OPTION: Also provide the book *The Very Hungry Caterpillar*, by Eric Carle, and read it to the children as they hold their caterpillars in their laps.

♦♦♦♦

BIBLE TIME—Jesus Goes to Heaven

Follow the instructions in the Application section to make a picture of Jesus going into the clouds to use as you tell the story. If possible, take the class outside to tell the story. If weather does not permit, sit by a large window, where children can see up into the sky.

Have the children lay back and look up into the sky. Ask questions about the sky. **What do you see? What color is it?**

Jesus, you are celebrating Easter. Whom will you tell that Jesus is alive? Encourage children to name a person they will tell.

Lead children in prayer. Refer children to the song mural they made during the last session, and sing the song they wrote several times. Then sing "Hosanna to the King of Kings!" and "Oh, Jesus Is My King!" from page 8 of this session.

Be sure children have their cloud pictures, their pictures of Jesus from Application, and their butterflies as they leave.

Leaders' Evaluation

	Great!	OK!	More!	Oops!	Suggestions
Activity 1					
Activity 2					
Bible Time					
Application					
Bible Memory					
Craft					
Snack					
Game					
Wrap-up					

How big is the sky? Who made the sky?

Have the children sit up and listen. We have talked about how Jesus was crucified by angry men. But after He was buried, He came back alive again. He visited lots of people, including His disciples. He ate with His disciples. He helped them catch fish. He made them breakfast.

But soon it was time for Jesus to return to Heaven to be with His father, God. One day Jesus met His disciples on the top of a mountain. Show children the picture of Jesus with His disciples. The figure of Jesus should be attached to a craft stick and inserted in the slit on the picture. He said, "It is time for me to go back to live in Heaven with my Father. But don't worry. I will send the Holy Spirit to live inside of each of you." Jesus made sure His followers knew what to do after He was gone. He said, "Go everywhere in the world. Tell all people the good news about me."

Then Jesus rose up into the clouds right before the disciples' eyes! Use the craft stick to raise the figure of Jesus up behind the cloud on the page. The disciples kept looking up into the sky, hoping to see Jesus again. Look into the sky; shield your eyes.

Suddenly there were two angels standing with the disciples! The angels said, "Why are you standing here looking into the sky? Jesus will be back. He will come down from Heaven, just like He went up."

The disciples were excited to know that Jesus would be coming back. They went and did His work just like Jesus told them to, because they knew that Jesus is alive.

◆◆◆◆

APPLICATION—Jesus Is Coming

You will need photocopies of the scene on page 209 and photocopies of the cloud and figure of Jesus on page 210, scissors, crayons, tape, and craft sticks. When you photocopy the scene on page 209, place a piece of paper over the flip cards and illustrations at the top of the page, so that it remains blank on the copy.

Lesson 35

Let children squeeze whipped cream on their crackers to look like clouds. They can sprinkle colored sugar on their clouds. Lead children in prayer, then join them in their snack.

Where are clouds? In the sky. When Jesus went up into Heaven, a cloud hid Him from the disciples. Who spoke to the disciples? Two angels. When will Jesus come back? Anytime. How will He come? Just like He left.

Game—Easter Pictionary

You will need a chalkboard and chalk or poster board and a marker.

Have children sit in front of a large chalkboard. Draw one picture at a time on the board and have the children guess what it is and tell what it has to do with the Easter story. Ideas of things to draw include: cross(es) on a hill; cave tomb; palm branch; boat on water; fish and net; angels; mountain; cloud; donkey; angel. OPTION: Older children may also want to take turns drawing, while the other children guess.

Why do we have Easter? Jesus died and rose again. Who saw that Jesus was alive? Mary; disciples. Who saw Jesus go up to Heaven? Disciples.

◆◆◆◆

Wrap-Up—Walking on Clouds

You will need the song mural made last week.

Let's pretend that we are walking on clouds while we clean up the room today. Show children how to tiptoe or walk softly as they put toys away and push in chairs.

Gather children together to review the Easter story and unit Bible verse. We have learned all about Easter, and the wonderful things that Jesus has done for us. Jesus died on a cross, but He did not stay in the grave. He arose! He is in Heaven, but He promised that He will return someday. Have children say the Bible verse with motions learned during Bible Memory. You can tell your friends and family the same thing the angels told. Jesus is not in the tomb. He is alive! When you tell about

Unit 8

Where is Jesus now? In Heaven with God. When will Jesus be back? We don't know, but we do know He is coming back. **We are going to make a special picture to remind us that Jesus left, but He is coming back.**

Help children cut out the cloud and figure of Jesus. Children can color the scene on page 209 and the figures. Children should also tape the cloud in the blank area in the top half of the page. Children should tape only the sides of the cloud, so that the bottom is free to allow the figure of Jesus to be slid beneath it. Children should also tape a craft stick to the back of the figure of Jesus. Cut a slit in each child's page where indicated. Children can place the craft stick figure in the slit, so that Jesus is talking to His followers. Then they can raise the figure up and slide it beneath the cloud to show Jesus going into Heaven.

Lead children in prayer, then sing "Oh, Jesus Is My King!" from page 8 of this session. As children sing the last verse of the song, they can use the craft stick to raise the figure of Jesus up into the clouds.

BIBLE MEMORY—Action Words

Gather children together to review the Bible verse. Say the verse several times together. Then discuss actions to put with the words to help the children remember.

"I (point to self)
know (point to forehead)
that you (point to others)
are looking (put hand up to eyes)
for Jesus (point to heaven),
who was crucified (stretch arms out wide).
He is not (shake head)
here (point to ground);
He has risen (stand up; arms above the head)."

Practice the verse several times with the motions, until the children are comfortable with them.

An angel said these words to women who were looking for Jesus' body. Did they find His body? No. **Why didn't they find His body?** He had come alive again! **What special day do we celebrate because Jesus is alive?** Easter.

ACTIVITY TIME

Do as many activities as time permits.

Craft—Beautiful Butterflies

You will need the butterfly pattern from page 210, white construction paper, scissors, tempera paint, paper plates or pie tins, paintbrushes, paper towels for cleanup, paint smocks, the cocoons made in Activity 2, and a stapler or tape. Before the session, fold the construction paper in half horizontally. Place the dotted line of the butterfly pattern on the fold, trace it, and cut it out. Make a butterfly for each child.

Pour a small amount of each color of paint onto a paper plate or pie tin. Make sure each child has a paint smock. Give the children the butterflies and ask them to decorate only one wing of the butterfly with splotches of paint. Then help them close the wings and rub them together. When the butterfly wings are opened, there should be matching designs on them. Put away the paint and use paper towels to clean up before proceeding to the next step.

Let the children open the cocoons made in Activity 2 and take out the caterpillars. Glue or staple the caterpillars to the center of the butterfly wings. Discuss what happens to the caterpillars in their cocoons.

What do caterpillars turn into? Butterflies. **What do we celebrate at Easter?** Jesus died and rose again. **Where did Jesus go?** Heaven. **We can have new life through Jesus, and one day we will live with Him in Heaven.**

Snack—Whipped Cream Clouds

You will need graham crackers, whipped cream in a can, and colored sugar (optional).

205

206

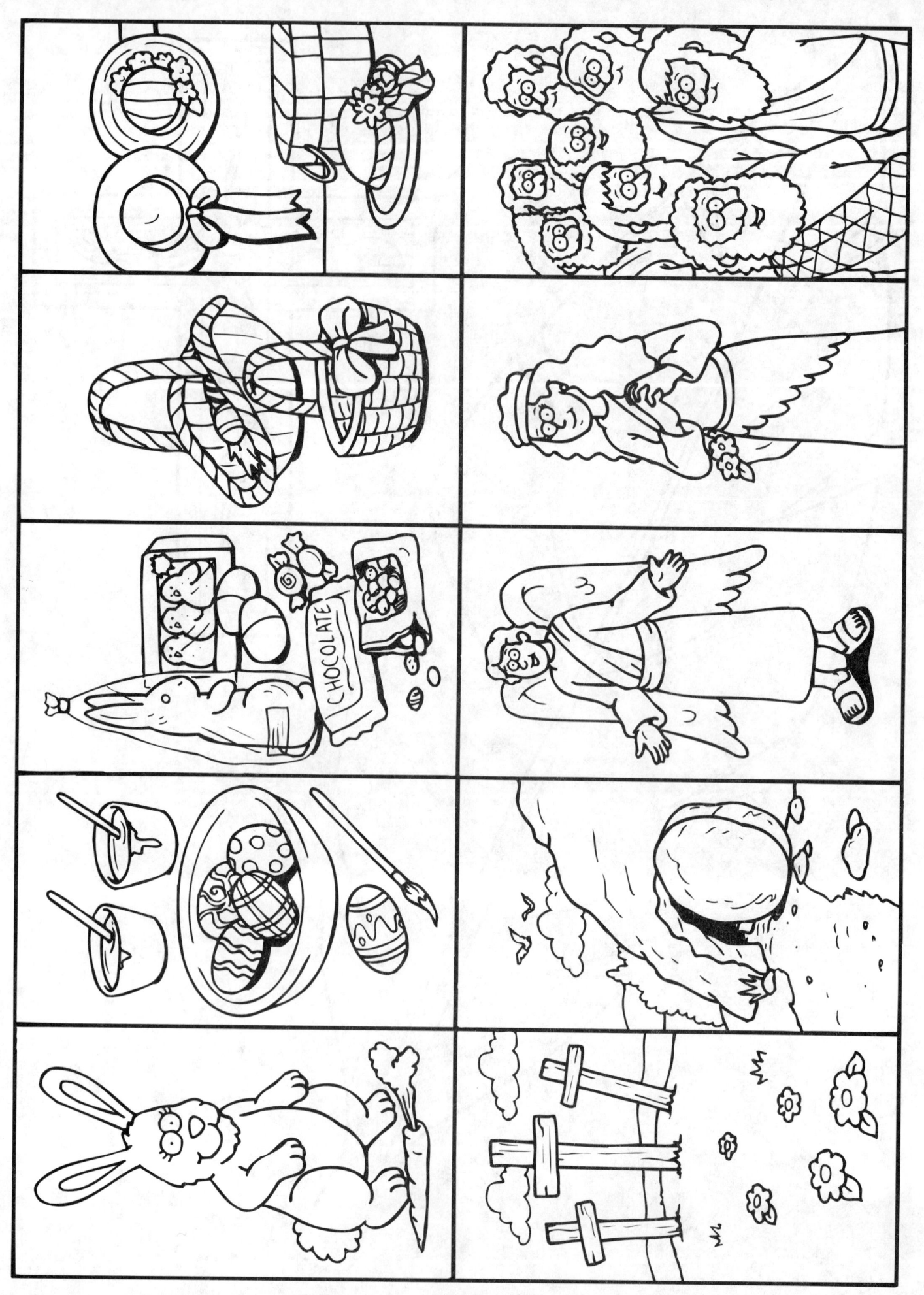

207

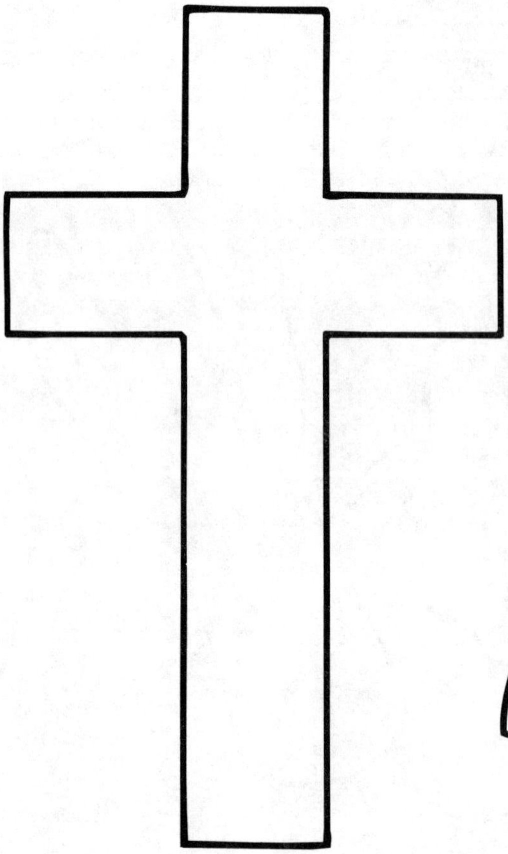

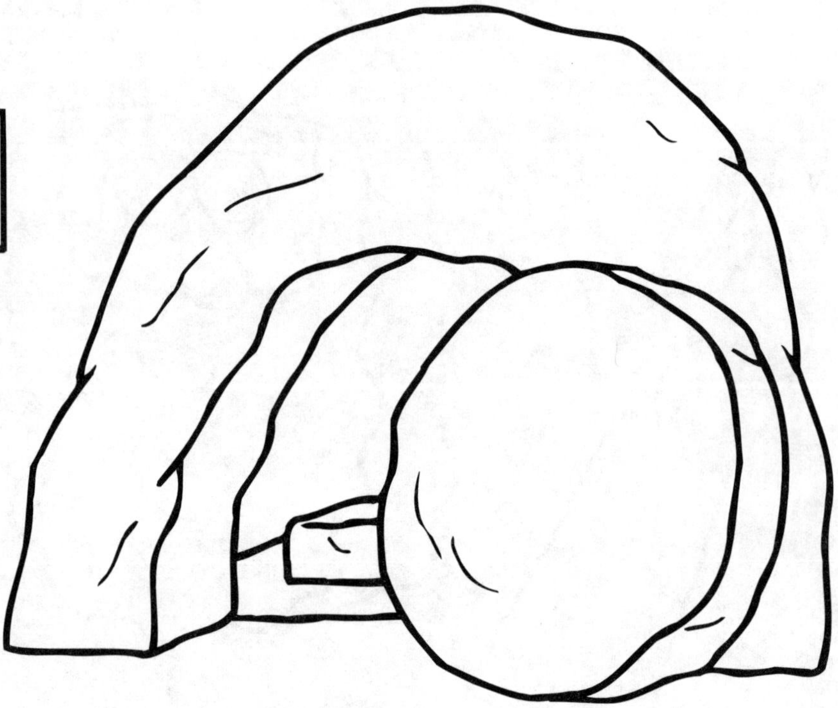

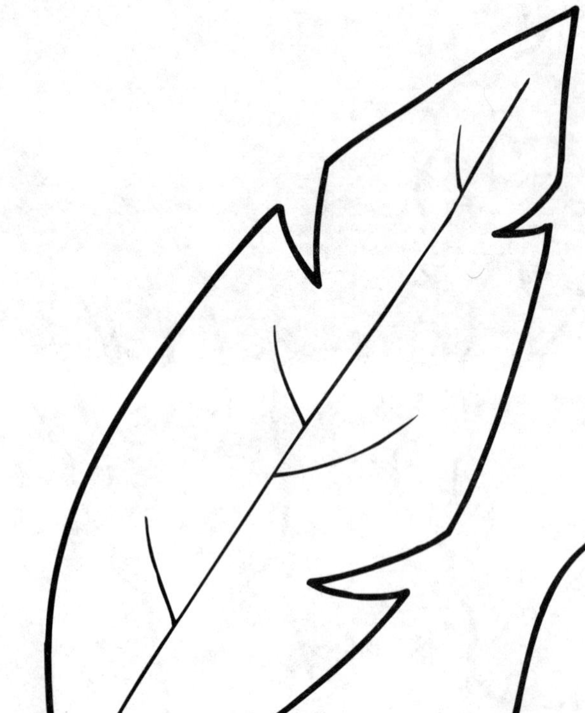

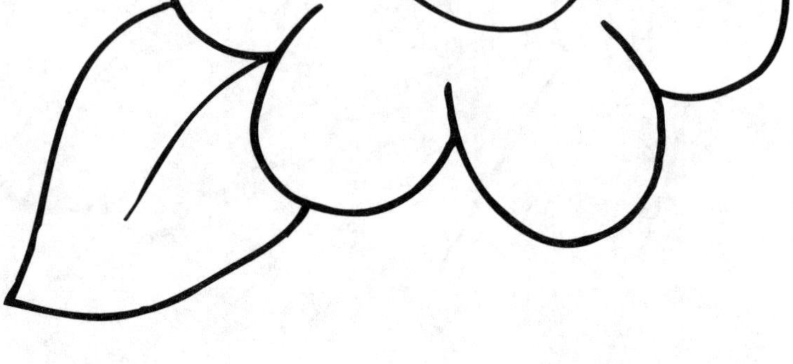

209

Unit 9
Lessons 36-39

Tell About Jesus

◆◆◆◆◆

By the end of this unit, the children and leaders will . . .
Know Name people in the first church who told the good news about Jesus.
Feel Feel confident telling about Jesus.
Do Follow the church's example of telling about Jesus.

Unit Bible Words for Memory
"They never stopped teaching and proclaiming the good news that Jesus is the Christ" (Acts 5:42, NIV).

◆◆◆◆◆

Unit Lessons

Lesson 36
Peter Tells About Jesus
Acts 2
Children will discover what happened when God sent the Holy Spirit on the day of Pentecost and Peter first told people about Jesus.

Lesson 37
Peter and John Tell About Jesus
Acts 3; 4:22
Children will learn how Peter and John healed a lame man in the temple and told about Jesus.

Lesson 38
Philip Tells About Jesus
Acts 8:4-40
Children will hear how the Holy Spirit sent Philip to help a man from Ethiopia understand God's Word and to tell the man about Jesus.

Lesson 39
Paul Tells About Jesus
Acts 9–28
Children will learn how Paul traveled and told everyone he met the good news about Jesus.

◆◆◆◆◆

Why Teach This Unit to Four-Year-Olds—Six-Year-Olds?

Children have an enthusiasm and boldness for telling about Jesus. If they begin telling now, the habit will grow with them. This unit gives them four examples of people in the early church who told about Jesus. Your children can tell about what Jesus did like Peter. They can tell about times Jesus has helped them like Peter and John did at the temple. They can use their Bibles to tell about Jesus like Philip did. And they can tell every person they see about Jesus like Paul did.

◆◆◆◆◆

Bible Time Line

The stories for this unit are pictured on the time line, pages 316 and 317. The time line will be used throughout all units in this book.

Provide the time-line page for children who arrive early, or plan time at the end of the Bible story during each session for children to color the time line and look for the hidden pictures.

See page 6 in this book for further instructions on using the time line and for suggested time-line projects.

Materials
All Lessons
  a Bible
  markers, colored pencils, crayons
  white paper, construction paper, poster board
  tape, masking tape
  Plasti-Tak
  glue
  scissors
  a stapler
  paper hole punch
  yarn or string

Lesson 36
  1½" strips of tagboard in lengths to fit around children's heads
  a craft stick
  a small stool or other item safe for standing on and items that represent different ways to tell about Jesus: toy telephones; paper, pens, and envelopes; a bike helmet; and a school book bag
  a blank cassette, a cassette player
  a large piece of butcher paper, a blindfold
  Optional: two 1½" rubber bands and four 18" strips cut from crepe-paper rolls for each child

Lesson 37
  a wheelchair or scooter board, a cane or a walker (optional)
  Post-it® notes
  a craft stick
  "O"-shaped cereal
  small safety pins and glitter
  a cassette of praise songs your children enjoy and a cassette player

Lesson 38
  craft sticks
  children's Bibles (such as The Beginner's Bible™)
  small envelopes and scraps or fabric or ribbon, glitter, or sequins (optional)
  ribbon

Lesson 39
  a grocery bag, a stack of letters, a piece of chalk, a book bag, a rake or other yard tool, a preschool toy, a jacket and purse, a pair of glasses, and props for any other people you will include in Activity 2
  a toy boat or a picture of a boat, a pair of handcuffs, and a pair of shoes
  calendar sheets from a planner
  a bean bag or other small object
  margarine tub lids or lids from 12-ounce frozen juice cans, self-adhesive magnets
  Optional: tops from polystyrene egg cartons, plastic drinking straws cut in two pieces, a 5" piece and a 3" piece
  at least one balloon for each child

The Beginner's Bible™ Resources
Jesus and the Children Stickers, Standard Publishing, #22-01035, call 1-800-543-1353
Jesus and the Children Floor Puzzle, Standard Publishing, #28-02717, call 1-800-543-1353
Jesus and the Children Inlay Puzzle, Standard Publishing, #28-02703, call 1-800-543-1353

The Beginner's Bible™ New Testament GeoSafari Bible Pack, Standard Publishing, #14-24002, call 1-800-543-1353
The Beginner's Bible™ Bible Lessons GeoSafari Bible Pack, Standard Publishing, #14-24005, call 1-800-543-1353

Unit 9
Lesson 36

Peter Tells About Jesus
(Acts 2)

After Jesus went to live in Heaven, His followers began meeting regularly. One day, a large crowd gathered and Peter told everyone there the good news of Jesus. On that day 3,000 people came to believe that Jesus is the Son of God. This is how the church began.

Bible Words

"They never stopped teaching and proclaiming the good news that Jesus is the Christ" (Acts 5:42).

Goals

Name a person who told the good news about Jesus

Feel confident telling about Jesus.

Follow Peter's example of telling about Jesus.

◆◆◆◆

ACTIVITY 1—Flame Headband

You will need copies of the flame from page 229; scissors; tagboard; red, yellow, and orange markers or crayons; tape; and a stapler. Before class cut 1½" strips of tagboard in lengths to fit around children's heads.

Give each child a flame and ask them to color the flames red, yellow, and orange. Then help each child attach the colored flame to the center of a tagboard headband. Fit the headband to each child's head and staple the two ends together.

How do you think it would feel to have a fire on your head? Some people in our Bible story today had flames of fire on their head. But they didn't get burned or hurt. Instead, they received a very special gift!

---fold---

We Will Tell!
(Tune: "If You're Happy and You Know It!")

Peter told about Jesus. He's God's Son. (We will tell!)
Peter told about Jesus. He's God's Son. (We will tell!)
Peter told about Jesus. Peter told about Jesus.
Peter told about Jesus. He's God's Son. (We will tell!)

Philip told about Jesus. He's God's Son. (We will tell!)
Philip told about Jesus. He's God's Son. (We will tell!)
Philip told about Jesus. Philip told about Jesus.
Philip told about Jesus. He's God's Son. (We will tell!)

Paul told about Jesus. He's God's Son. (We will tell!)
Paul told about Jesus. He's God's Son. (We will tell!)
Paul told about Jesus. Paul told about Jesus.
Paul told about Jesus. He's God's Son. (We will tell!)

We will tell about Jesus. He's God's Son. (We will tell!)
We will tell about Jesus. He's God's Son. (We will tell!)
We will tell about Jesus. We will tell about Jesus.
We will tell about Jesus. He's God's Son. (We will tell!)

ACTIVITY 2—Tell the News

Before class, prepare a list of ways important news is spread. Your list might include talking on the telephone, talking to a friend, watching television, using the Internet or e-mail on a computer, riding a bike to a friend's house to tell him, writing a letter, listening to a teacher or parent, reading a newspaper.

Play a simplified version of Charades to illustrate the many ways good news can be spread. Demonstrate the way to play this game by acting out one method. Tell students you will whisper an idea to those who wish to act it out. Allow volunteers, one at a time, to stand in front of the group and pantomime one action. The remaining children can make guesses.

BIBLE TIME—Wind and Fire

You will need the Peter figure from page 229, markers, scissors, a craft stick, tape, and the headbands made in Activity 1. Before class, color and cut out the figure of Peter. Fold the figure and attach it to a craft stick.

After Jesus died on the cross, His body was placed in a tomb. But Jesus did not stay dead. On the third day, God made Him live again. Jesus walked on the earth and talked with people for forty more days. Then He rose to Heaven.

After Jesus returned to Heaven, the people who had listened to Jesus teach and who believed Jesus was the Son of God gathered each day for prayer. Hold up the figure of Peter, sad side forward. But they were sad. They missed Jesus, their friend. They were lonely without Him, and they weren't sure what they should do now that He was gone. Jesus had told them to wait in Jerusalem for a special gift that He would send them. But His followers didn't know what gift Jesus was talking about or when He would send the gift to them. They sat and prayed and waited and wondered.

Several weeks after Jesus had left, the Jews celebrated a

WRAP-UP—I Can Tell Like Peter

Sit in a circle and lead children in this familiar finger play. "Here is the church, here is the steeple. Open the doors, and see all the people." Explain that the church is more than a building. The church is people. The people who lived many years ago and heard Peter tell the good news began meeting to learn more about God's love. They started the church.

Who in today's story told the good news about Jesus? Peter. **Whom could you tell about Jesus?** Encourage children to name people. **What could you tell that person about Jesus?** Sing the first and fourth verses of "We Will Tell!" from page 8 of this session.

Leaders' Evaluation

	Great!	OK!	More!	Oops!	Suggestions
Activity 1					
Activity 2					
Bible Time					
Application					
Bible Memory					
Craft					
Snack					
Game					
Wrap-up					

special day called Pentecost. Visitors had come to Jerusalem from many different countries to celebrate the feast of Pentecost. Jerusalem was filled with people from all over the world!

On the day of Pentecost, Jesus' followers were all in one place praying. Suddenly they heard a sound like a strong wind blowing. Can you sound like the wind? Encourage children to make appropriate sounds. They may have checked the weather outside, but there was no wind blowing outside. The followers looked around, wondering what was happening. What they saw no one had ever seen before. It looked like a flame of fire was above each person's head. Ask children to put on the flame headbands they made earlier. But it wasn't a real fire. No one was hurt. God was with His people in a new way. He had sent the Holy Spirit.

The Holy Spirit was the special gift Jesus had promised His followers. The Holy Spirit helped them not to be afraid to tell people about Jesus. He helped them not to feel sad that Jesus had gone back to Heaven. Suddenly, Jesus' followers were excited. They couldn't wait to tell everyone about Jesus. Turn the figure of Peter over, so that the happy side is up.

People came running when they heard the sound of the blowing wind. A crowd gathered, a crowd of people from many different countries and of people that lived in Jerusalem. "What's going on?" the crowd of people asked.

With the Holy Spirit helping him, Peter stood up in front of the crowd and told them the good news about Jesus Christ. He said that Jesus was the Messiah, the one God had promised to send.

"Tell us more!" the people said.

Peter told everyone, "God sent Jesus to teach people about God's love. Jesus was killed on a cross. But God brought Him back to life again. He is the Lord and Christ."

Many people believed what Peter was saying. They said, "What should we do?"

Peter said, "You must tell God you are sorry for your sins and be baptized. Then God will forgive you, and you also will

Lesson 36

3

— fold —

Snack—Letter Breadsticks

You will need a one-pound loaf of frozen white bread dough for each group of eight to ten children, a knife, and a greased cookie sheet. Before the session, thaw the frozen dough in the refrigerator overnight.

One way we can tell about Jesus is writing. Let's make letters from dough to remind us of one way we can tell about Jesus.

Cut the dough into pieces, 1/2" wide. Give one piece of dough to each child and ask him to roll the dough into a "snake." Then help the children shape the long piece of dough into a letter and place on a greased cookie sheet. Bake at 400 degrees for 10-12 minutes. One 1-pound loaf makes 8 to 10 breadsticks. You may wish for children to shape the dough into the first letter of their name, of someone who tells others about Jesus, or to spell out a word in today's Bible story or memory verse.

Game—Happy Birthday to the Church

You will need a large piece of butcher paper, a blindfold, markers, tape or Plasti-Tak, scissors, and construction paper. Before the session, draw a large birthday cake on a piece of butcher paper. Hang it on a bulletin board or mount it on the wall. Cut a paper candle for each child. Have a marker and roll of masking tape on hand when it is time to begin the game.

Print each child's name on a candle before the game begins. Place a rolled piece of masking tape on the back of the candle. One at a time, each child tries to put a paper candle on top of the cake. Ask children to close their eyes, turn them around if you wish, and point them in the direction of the cake. (Make sure there is nothing in the way that might trip a child.) See how many candles make it to the top of the cake. Talk about Pentecost being the birthday of the church.

OPTION: Provide two 1 1/2" rubber bands and four 18" strips cut from crepe paper for each child. Place one rubber band on the wrist of each child and slip two crepe paper strips under each rubber band. Have children line up and lead them around the room, doing hand motions, as you sing "Happy Birthday" to the church. Children can take turns being the leader.

Unit 9

215

6

receive the gift of the Holy Spirit." That day, over 3,000 people believed Peter and were baptized. They began meeting together to worship God. We call that special day Pentecost and celebrate it as the birthday of the church.

◆◆◆◆◆

APPLICATION—Tell Like Peter

You will need the flame headbands used in Bible Time, a small stool or other item safe for standing on, and items that represent different ways to tell about Jesus: toy telephones; paper, pens, and envelopes; a bike helmet; and a school book bag.

Let children take turns pretending to be Peter. Peter will wear a flame headband and stand on a stool as he tells about Jesus. Suggested things that Peter can tell include: Jesus died on a cross, but He came back alive. Jesus is God's Son. Jesus is alive in Heaven today. Tell God you are sorry and be baptized. Jesus loves you.

The other children can be the crowd. Suggested things the crowd can say include: Tell us more about Jesus. What do we need to do? We are sorry for what we have done. We want to follow Jesus.

You can tell about Jesus like Peter did. Let's practice telling our friends and people we know about Jesus.

Let children work in groups of two or three and practice telling about Jesus. They can use the props you brought to practice different ways of telling: on the phone, printing a letter or drawing a picture, riding to a friend's house to tell, telling on the school bus or at school. Children can take turns being the person in the group to tell about Jesus. If they need help, give children suggestions of things to tell about Jesus. They can tell the same things that Peter told, and they can also tell other things that Jesus did.

◆◆◆◆◆

BIBLE MEMORY—Record and Proclaim

You will need a blank cassette, a cassette player, and a Bible with Acts 5:42 marked and highlighted.

Hold up your Bible and ask the children to help you find the verse. Point to the words of the verse as you read them to the children. Then ask the children to say the verse with you.

Be sure to explain what the word "proclaiming" means. ("Proclaim" means to publicly announce or officially declare.) Repeat the verse again with the children several times. Vary the speed and volume at which you speak to keep the children's attention. When most of the children can say the verse, tape-record each child or pair of children repeating it. Announce each child's name on tape before he says the verse. Say, "Ryan tells the good news." If the entire verse is too long for young children to remember, have them repeat just the last phrase. The teacher can say, "They never stopped teaching and proclaiming the good news," and the children can add, "that Jesus is the Christ."

◆◆◆◆◆

ACTIVITY TIME

Do as many activities as time permits.

Craft—Tell About Jesus Megaphones

You will need copies of the megaphone from page 230 on heavy paper, scissors, crayons or markers, and tape.

Give each child a megaphone. Have children color the design and cut on the dark line. Help children roll the megaphone and tape in place.

What are some things Peter told about Jesus? He is the Son of God. He died on the cross, but He came back alive. He is the Lord and Christ. **We can tell the same things about Jesus.** Encourage children to use their megaphones to tell about Jesus like Peter did. If the physical arrangement of the classes in the church permits, walk in the halls spreading the good news.

Unit 9
Lesson 37

Peter and John Tell About Jesus
(Acts 3; 4:22)

Peter and John healed a crippled man sitting at the temple gate. When people saw the healed man walking and running and praising God, they wondered what had happened to him. Peter and John used this opportunity to tell the people about Jesus, God's Son.

Bible Words

"They never stopped teaching and proclaiming the good news that Jesus is the Christ" (Acts 5:42).

Goals

Name two people who told the good news about Jesus.
Feel confident telling about Jesus.
Follow Peter and John's example of telling about Jesus.

Activity 1—If I Couldn't Walk

If possible, bring a wheelchair or scooter board to class. (A scooter board is a square of plywood, approximately 12", to which four wheels are attached. A person sits cross-legged or on knees and moves along using his hands.) You might also bring a cane or a walker.

OPTION: If you do not have access to any of these devices, have the children take turns trying to move around without using their legs. They could drag themselves on the floor, or have other children carry them.

Use the hallway or open area for children to take turns in one of the devices you brought to class. Talk about what it would be like not to be able to walk.

We Will Tell!

(Tune: "If You're Happy and You Know It!")

Peter told about Jesus. He's God's Son. (We will tell!)
Peter told about Jesus. He's God's Son. (We will tell!)
Peter told about Jesus. Peter told about Jesus.
Peter told about Jesus. He's God's Son. (We will tell!)

Philip told about Jesus. He's God's Son. (We will tell!)
Philip told about Jesus. He's God's Son. (We will tell!)
Philip told about Jesus. Philip told about Jesus.
Philip told about Jesus. He's God's Son. (We will tell!)

Paul told about Jesus. He's God's Son. (We will tell!)
Paul told about Jesus. He's God's Son. (We will tell!)
Paul told about Jesus. Paul told about Jesus.
Paul told about Jesus. He's God's Son. (We will tell!)

We will tell about Jesus. He's God's Son. (We will tell!)
We will tell about Jesus. He's God's Son. (We will tell!)
We will tell about Jesus. We will tell about Jesus.
We will tell about Jesus. He's God's Son. (We will tell!)

What would you do when you came to stairs? To a curb? How would you pick up something you'd dropped? Where would you sit in church with the chair or walker? Have children try to pick up something off the floor, or go up or down a step, while dragging one leg. They could use a cane or walker to help, or they can try without any helps.

The man in our story today could not walk, but he didn't even have a wheelchair to help him get around. He probably had someone carry him to the gate of the temple every day. He sat at the gate, begging people for money. Listen to find out what Jesus' power did for the man.

◆◆◆◆

ACTIVITY 2—Telling How Jesus Helps

You will need Post-it® notes and pencils or pens.

In today's story, Peter and John tell everyone how Jesus helped a man who could not walk. One way we can let other people know about Jesus is by telling them how Jesus has helped us and our friends and families.

Ask the children to think of times that Jesus has helped them or someone they know. These could be times when someone was sick and got better, when someone was sad or scared and Jesus helped them feel better, when someone was in need and Jesus provided what they needed. As the children name things, give them Post-it® notes and ask them to print or draw a picture of the time Jesus helped that they named. Be sure each child names at least one time that Jesus helped. If some children cannot think of a time Jesus has helped, ask questions about the situations mentioned above to prompt their thinking. You may wish to think ahead of a few situations in your own life when Jesus helped, and ask children who cannot think of a situation to draw a picture of one of the times Jesus helped you or someone you know.

Ask the children to keep the Post-it® notes to use during Application.

2

Unit 9

---

notes home and put them on a refrigerator, mirror, or other prominent place to remind them of what they can tell about how Jesus helped. Say a prayer, asking Jesus to give the children courage to tell and the right words to tell. Then sing verses 1 and 4 of "We Will Tell!" from page 8 of this session. Encourage children to enthusiastically call out "We will tell!" at the end of each line of the song.

NOTE: Tell children to be sure to bring their children's Bibles next week. You may wish to send a note home with parents, asking them to remind the children to bring their Bibles.

Leaders' Evaluation

	Great!	OK!	More!	Oops!	Suggestions
Activity 1					
Activity 2					
Bible Time					
Application					
Bible Memory					
Craft					
Snack					
Game					
Wrap-up					

Lesson 37

7

BIBLE TIME—A Leaping Lame Man

You will need the figure of the lame man from page 231, markers, scissors, tape, a craft stick, and the figure of Peter from page 229 used during last week's Bible Time. Before class, color and cut out the figure of the lame man. Fold it and glue it to a craft stick.

One day, two of Jesus' helpers were going to the temple to pray. Hold up the figure of Peter. One of the men was Peter. Do you remember what Peter did in last week's story? He told a large crowd of people about Jesus. The other man was named John. As Peter and John entered the temple, they passed a man who could not walk. Hold up the figure of the lame man, with the crippled side forward.

Because the man could not walk, he sat on the ground by the temple gate calling out to people asking them for money. When he saw Peter and John walk past, he called to them. Peter stopped and turned to the lame man. Peter said to the lame man, "Look at us."

The man turned and looked, thinking Peter would give him some money.

But Peter said, "We don't have any money, but what we do have, we will give to you."

The man who could not walk must have wondered, "If they don't have any money, what could they have that I would want?"

Peter said, "In the name of Jesus Christ, walk." Then Peter helped the man stand. At once he could walk! Turn the figure of the man around, so that the walking side is forward. The man went into the temple, walking and jumping and praising God because he was able to walk.

The people in the temple were surprised. They knew this man had never been able to walk. For nearly forty years he had sat by the temple gate asking for money. Yet here he was, walking with Peter and John.

Peter explained, "By the name of Jesus this man was

Lesson 37

3

Snack—Edible Necklace

You will need the necklaces made in Bible Memory, extra cereal, milk, and cups.

Pour milk in the cups one at a time. Hand a cup of milk to the first child and say, "They never stopped teaching and proclaiming." The child should take the cup and say, "The good news that Jesus is the Christ." Continue with each child.

When everyone has a cup of milk, offer a prayer of thanks. Then children may eat the cereal from their necklaces. Have extra cereal on hand.

Game—Walking and Jumping and Praising God

You will need a cassette of praise songs your children enjoy and a cassette player.

Play this game in an open area. Ask the children to stand in a circle. Begin by asking children to demonstrate ways they might act out their praise to God. Ideas include raising hands overhead or cupping hands at mouth and saying, "Praise God." Agree on one motion for the class to use in this game.

Play the music and have the children walk in a circle. When the music stops, children are to jump and praise God. When the music resumes, children should walk about again. Repeat the game several times, using different music and different motions of praise each time.

WRAP-UP—Tell How Jesus Helps

Encourage children to clean up the room, then gather together in a large group.

If the pins made during the Craft time have dried, let each child wear hers home. As you are pinning them on, ask, "Whose name is this? Tell me someone with whom you can share the good news of Jesus."

Whom will you tell about Jesus this week? What will you tell that person about Jesus? Remind children of what they discussed during the Application. Ask them to take their Post-it®

Unit 9

6

219

healed." Peter and John told all the people more about Jesus. They told the people that Jesus had died and come back alive, and that now He was in Heaven. They told everyone the good news that Jesus is the Christ.

If your class is familiar with the song "Peter and John Went to Pray," sing it together as a class with the slap, clap, clap rhythm on the verse (slap your legs with your hands once, then clap twice) and with motions (walking, leaping, raising hands in air for "praising God") on the chorus. Sing the song through slowly at first, then gradually get faster as you sing it through several more times.

◆◆◆◆

APPLICATION—Tell How Jesus Helped

You will need the Post-it® note pictures made in Activity 2, a poster board, and a marker. Before class, print a large title on the poster board: We Tell How Jesus Helped Us.

Earlier in our session, we talked and drew pictures about ways Jesus has helped us and people we know. Let's listen to all the ways Jesus has helped us. Encourage children to bring their notes forward one at a time and stick them to the poster board. Children can add new notes, if they think of other situations.

Wow! Look at all the times Jesus has helped us. These are a lot of things that we can tell people we know about Jesus. Whom could you tell about how Jesus has helped us? You could tell someone who is sick how Jesus has helped your sick friends. You could tell someone who is sad or scared how Jesus has helped you and loves you. You could tell someone who just doesn't know about Jesus about how Jesus died and came back alive. Encourage children to come back up and choose a Post-it® note from the poster board that shows what they will tell about how Jesus helped. They should share whom they will tell about how Jesus helped.

◆◆◆◆◆

BIBLE MEMORY—Memory-verse Necklaces

You will need a Bible with the memory verse marked and highlighted, "O"-shaped cereal, tape, and yarn. Before class, cut the yarn into lengths for necklaces. Wrap one end of each piece of yarn with tape. Tie a knot in the opposite end.

Let volunteers help you find the verse in your Bible. Point to the highlighted words as you read them to the children. Then review the verse by saying it aloud several times with the children.

Give the children the pieces of yarn and the cereal. They should string a piece of "O" cereal onto the yarn for each word of the verse that they say. Encourage them to repeat the verse several times, until their necklace has lots of cereal on it. When the necklaces are complete, tie the ends together and allow children to wear them until Snack time.

◆◆◆◆

ACTIVITY TIME

Do as many activities as time permits.

Craft—Jesus Pins

You will need copies of the Jesus Pin from page 229 on tagboard or other stiff paper, scissors, glue or tape, colored pencils, small safety pins, and glitter.

Have children color the letters with colored pencils and cut them out. You may need to cut out the pins for younger children. Glue or tape a safety pin to the back. The teacher can run a line of glue through the center of each letter and let the children sprinkle on glitter. (If children apply the glue, the letters may not be readable.)

You can use your pin to help you remember to tell about Jesus. What will you tell others about Jesus when you wear your pin? You can tell about a time when Jesus helped you.

Unit 9
Lesson 38

Philip Tells About Jesus
(Acts 8:4-40)

Philip, one of the seven deacons chosen to distribute food in the early church, went to Samaria to tell the good news of Jesus. Crowds followed Philip because of the miracles he performed and people he healed. They believed what he said about the kingdom of God and were baptized. Philip also explained the Scripture to an Ethiopian who believed and was baptized.

Bible Words

"They never stopped teaching and proclaiming the good news that Jesus is the Christ" (Acts 5:42).

Goals

Name a person who told the good news about Jesus.
Feel confident telling about Jesus.
Follow Philip's example of telling about Jesus.

◆◆◆◆

Activity 1—Scrolls

You will need copies of page 232, scissors, crayons or markers, glue, and craft sticks. If you have younger children in your class, cut out and tape the strips together before class.

Give each child a copy of page 232 and ask the children to color the pictures. Then they should cut the page in half lengthwise on the solid line and tape the two halves together to form one long strip. The strip showing Philip talking to a group of people should be first. The strip showing Philip running alongside a chariot should be second. Tape or glue a craft stick to each end of the picture strip and help the children roll the ends of the strip to the middle to make a scroll.

— fold —

We Will Tell!
(Tune: "If You're Happy and You Know It")

Peter told about Jesus. He's God's Son. (We will tell!)
Peter told about Jesus. He's God's Son. (We will tell!)
Peter told about Jesus. Peter told about Jesus.
Peter told about Jesus. He's God's Son. (We will tell!)

Philip told about Jesus. He's God's Son. (We will tell!)
Philip told about Jesus. He's God's Son. (We will tell!)
Philip told about Jesus. Philip told about Jesus.
Philip told about Jesus. He's God's Son. (We will tell!)

Paul told about Jesus. He's God's Son. (We will tell!)
Paul told about Jesus. He's God's Son. (We will tell!)
Paul told about Jesus. Paul told about Jesus.
Paul told about Jesus. He's God's Son. (We will tell!)

We will tell about Jesus. He's God's Son. (We will tell!)
We will tell about Jesus. He's God's Son. (We will tell!)
We will tell about Jesus. We will tell about Jesus.
We will tell about Jesus. He's God's Son. (We will tell!)

What does your Bible look like? Their Bibles are books. They may have pictures in them, or they may have lots of words. **In Bible times, their books looked like these scrolls.** Show children how to unroll and roll the different edges of the scroll to use them. You may wish to give Bibles to children who don't have children's Bibles, so that they can use them at home to tell about Jesus. Or offer parents the opportunity to purchase children's Bibles.

Let them practice using their scroll to find the pictures in order. **The man in our Bible story today used a scroll to tell about Jesus.**

◆◆◆◆◆

ACTIVITY 2—My Bible Tells About Jesus

You will need children's Bibles (such as The Beginner's Bible™). Provide enough Bibles, so that each child can have one. Encourage children who remembered to bring their own Bibles to use them. You may wish to give Bibles to children who don't have children's Bibles, so that they can use them at home to tell about Jesus. Or offer parents the opportunity to purchase children's Bibles.

Last week, Peter and John told about Jesus by talking about how He helped a lame man walk again. We found out some ways that Jesus helped us that we could tell people. Did any of you tell someone how Jesus helped you? Allow children to share their experiences. Share your own personal experience as well.

In today's story, Philip uses the Bible, God's Word, to tell a man about Jesus. **We can use the Bible to teach people about Jesus, too. Let's find some ways we can use our Bibles to tell about Jesus.**

Have the children open their Bibles to about the middle of the book. Tell them that the stories about Jesus will be in the back part of the book. Then call out stories about Jesus and have children try to find them in their Bibles. Some stories to include are: Jesus' birth; Jesus and the children; Jesus calms a storm; Jesus feeds 5,000; Peter and John heal a lame man through Jesus' power. Ask children to find other stories about Jesus that they could tell their friends.

What stories about Jesus did you find in your Bible? What stories about Jesus? Children can hang mobiles over their doorknobs or bedposts to help them remember to tell.

Sing verses 1, 2, and 4 of "We Will Tell!" from page 8 of this session. To vary the song, have children shout "We will tell!" on one verse, whisper it on the next, and then shout it again on the third.

Until parents come, have the children use their children's Bibles to look for other stories about Jesus. If they need direction, call out other stories about Jesus for them to find: Jesus heals a blind man; Jesus tells the story of the Good Samaritan; Jesus heals ten lepers; Jesus rides into Jerusalem on a donkey.

Leaders' Evaluation

	Great!	OK!	More!	Oops!	Suggestions
Activity 1					
Activity 2					
Bible Time					
Application					
Bible Memory					
Craft					
Snack					
Game					
Wrap-up					

story could you tell a friend about Jesus? When could you show your friend that story about Jesus?

BIBLE TIME—Philip Tells About Jesus

You will need the scrolls made in Activity 1.

Today the first thing you did was to make a scroll. Hold up a scroll. Ask children to roll their scroll to the first picture. As you tell the story, continue to roll out different pictures on the scroll and have children follow your lead with their own scrolls. In our Bible story today, Philip uses a Bible scroll to tell a man about Jesus.

Philip was a helper in the early church. His job was to make sure people in the church at Jerusalem had enough to eat. Then there came a time when the early Christians had to leave their homes and move. Philip traveled to Samaria and told people there that Jesus was the Son of God. Unroll and point to the first picture on the scroll. Philip also helped the people in Samaria. He healed men and women, boys and girls. People who could not stand or walk were able to after Philip blessed them. Because of the miracles Philip performed, many people wanted to hear what Philip had to say. He told people the good news about Jesus.

While Philip was in Samaria, God's angel spoke to him. Roll the scroll to the second picture. The angel said, "Go to the road that leads to Gaza." Philip did as the angel said.

Roll the scroll to the third picture. A very important man from Ethiopia was riding down the road to Gaza in a chariot. He was reading from a scroll that had part of God's Word on it. The scroll was the book of Isaiah from the Bible. Even though Isaiah lived many years before Jesus, he told about Jesus' birth. Roll the scroll to the fourth picture. When Philip saw the man riding in his chariot and reading the scroll, he ran alongside the chariot. He saw that the man was reading from God's Word. Philip asked the Ethiopian, "Do you understand what you are reading?"

Lesson 38

Snack—Peanut Butter and Jelly Roll Sandwich

You will need a jar of alternating peanut butter and jelly, bread, and a knife.

Let children spread a thin layer of the peanut butter and jelly onto one slice of bread. (Remove the crust if you like.) Help children to roll the sandwich. Enjoy eating the PBJ roll along with a discussion of how the Old Testament was first written on scrolls. Explain that scrolls were made from leather or paper and rolled to close.

Game—Gallop to Gaza

You will need a construction-paper sign that says "Gaza." Before the activity, set up a simple path or course from one side of the room to the other by setting up chairs to weave in and out of, tables to go around, and so on. If weather permits, you may wish to set up your path outside.

Tell the children that they will be a team of horses galloping to Gaza. You be the first team leader. The children should line up behind you and follow you as you gallop through the path you have set up to get to Gaza. When you have completed the path once, choose a volunteer to be the next leader. Children may choose to skip, hop, waddle, spin, baby-step, or march to Gaza as they play again.

WRAP-UP—Whom to Tell About Jesus

On your last trip to Gaza, guide different children to gallop over and clean up areas along the way. When the room is clean, gather in a large group.

Whom will you tell about Jesus this week? What Bible story will you show that person about Jesus? Encourage children to use their Bibles to show you the story about Jesus that they will share. To whom will you give your card about Jesus? What will you say to that person when you give them the card? Be sure children have their cards to take home with them. Where will you hang your mobile to help you remember to tell about

Unit 9

"How can I unless someone explains it to me?" was the man's reply. Roll the scroll to the fifth picture. Philip climbed into the chariot and looked at the scroll. The man was reading something in Isaiah about Jesus. Philip told the man from Ethiopia all about Jesus, about Jesus' birth, about His teaching and healing, and about how Jesus had died and come back alive. He told the man what he needed to do if he wanted to follow Jesus.

The man was so excited that he wanted to follow Jesus right away. He pointed to the side of the road. "Look! Here's some water. I want to be baptized right away." Turn the scroll to the sixth picture. So Philip and the man stopped right there beside the road, and Philip baptized the man from Ethiopia. He had decided to follow Jesus because Philip used God's Word to tell him about Jesus.

APPLICATION—Good News Cards

You will need the Jesus pictures from page 231; construction paper; scissors; glue; crayons or markers; small envelopes; and scraps of fabric or ribbon, glitter, or sequins (optional). Before class, fold the construction paper into fourths to make a card for each child.

Ask children to color the pictures from page 231 and cut them out. Give each child a construction-paper card. On the front of the card, they should glue the picture of Jesus that says, "Guess what I know about Jesus!" They can choose which pictures about Jesus to glue on the rest of their card. They may glue on scraps of fabric or ribbon, glitter and sequins if you wish. Help each child place the card in a small envelope.

Whom will you tell about Jesus this week? Write their name on the front of the card. Help children as needed.

BIBLE MEMORY—Echo Verse

You will need a Bible with the memory verse marked and highlighted.

Let a volunteer find the verse in the Bible. Show children the highlighted words as you say the verse together.

Let the class echo the Bible verse after you. Divide the class into two groups. The teacher should say a short phrase from the verse and have the first group repeat it, then the second group. If you wish, have each group say the verse a little quieter, getting softer just as an echo does. Say the verse several times, varying which group goes first. As the children learn the verse, have them repeat longer phrases until they can say the entire passage.

ACTIVITY TIME

Do as many activities as time permits.

Craft—Tell People Everywhere Wall Hanging

You will need the mobile pieces from page 233, scissors, crayons or markers, ribbon, and a stapler.

Ask children to color and cut out the shapes on the page. You may need to do the cutting in advance for very young children. Staple the pieces to a length of ribbon in the following order: megaphone, world, Jesus. Make a loop for hanging at the top of the ribbon and staple it in place. Make the loop large enough to be hung over a doorknob or bedpost.

Who are people you can tell about Jesus? Where are places you go that you can tell about Jesus? What will you tell about Jesus? If children need help remembering what to tell, review what Peter, John, and Philip told about Jesus. Encourage the children to take their wall hangings home and hang them on their door or bed to help them remember to tell about Jesus.

Unit 9
Lesson 39

Paul Tells About Jesus
(Acts 9–28)

Paul, a persecutor of the early church, was blinded on the road to Damascus. When his sight was restored, he began traveling the world, telling people everywhere the good news that Jesus is the Christ. Paul told everyone he met, including his jailer and the soldiers guarding him, about Jesus.

Bible Words

"They never stopped teaching and proclaiming the good news that Jesus is the Christ" (Acts 5:42).

Goals

Name a person who told the good news about Jesus.
Feel confident telling about Jesus.
Follow Paul's example of telling about Jesus.

◆◆◆◆◆

Activity 1—Finger Puppet

You will need copies of the Paul puppet from page 234 on heavy paper, scissors, and markers or crayons. If you have younger children in your class, cut out the puppets before class. Ask children to color and cut out the Paul puppets. As each child finishes the puppet, cut out the finger holes for him. Show children how to put their index and middle finger through the two holes and walk the puppet.

The name of your puppet is Paul. Can you make your Paul puppet walk? Run? Tiptoe? Kneel? Paul walked and traveled many places telling about Jesus. Keep your Paul finger puppet and we will learn more about Paul's travels and how Paul told about Jesus in today's Bible story.

— fold —

We Will Tell!

(Tune: "If You're Happy and You Know It!")

Peter told about Jesus. He's God's Son. (We will tell!)
Peter told about Jesus. He's God's Son. (We will tell!)
Peter told about Jesus. Peter told about Jesus.
Peter told about Jesus. He's God's Son. (We will tell!)

Philip told about Jesus. He's God's Son. (We will tell!)
Philip told about Jesus. He's God's Son. (We will tell!)
Philip told about Jesus. Philip told about Jesus.
Philip told about Jesus. He's God's Son. (We will tell!)

Paul told about Jesus. He's God's Son. (We will tell!)
Paul told about Jesus. He's God's Son. (We will tell!)
Paul told about Jesus. Paul told about Jesus.
Paul told about Jesus. He's God's Son. (We will tell!)

We will tell about Jesus. He's God's Son. (We will tell!)
We will tell about Jesus. He's God's Son. (We will tell!)
We will tell about Jesus. We will tell about Jesus.
We will tell about Jesus. He's God's Son. (We will tell!)

ACTIVITY 2—Preach Like Paul

You will need a grocery bag (grocery store clerk), a stack of letters (mail carrier), a piece of chalk (teacher), a book bag (friend at school), a rake or other yard tool (neighbor), a preschool toy (little sister or brother), a jacket and purse (babysitter), a pair of glasses (grandma or grandpa), and props for any other people you will include in the activity, such as Mom and Dad, aunts and uncles, friends next door, and so on.

The man in our story today was so excited about Jesus' good news that he told everyone he met about Him. We can tell everyone we meet about Jesus too. Let's practice. Tell the children that you will pretend to be some of the people they see every day. They will pretend to tell that person about Jesus. Hold up or wear the different props and tell the children who you are pretending to be, then have them tell you about Jesus. They could tell stories they know about Jesus. For example, they could tell the grocery store clerk how Jesus helped His friends catch lots of fish. They could tell the teacher how Jesus taught a crowd of over 5,000 people and then fed them with five loaves of bread and two fish. They could tell a little brother or sister how Jesus took time to play with children. Offer suggestions to the children as needed. Praise them for telling about Jesus.

BIBLE TIME—Paul Tells About Jesus

You will need a Paul finger puppet from Activity 1, a toy boat or a picture of a boat, a pair of handcuffs, and a pair of shoes.

The people in the early church did not always have an easy life. Sometimes they were treated badly because they believed Jesus is the Christ. There was one man, named Paul (Put on finger puppet.)**, who was so sure the Christians were wrong that he threw them in jail. He asked permission to travel to different towns looking for believers. "When I find them, I'll throw them in jail," he said.**

Then we will burst these balloons to remind us that we are bursting with good news about Jesus. Ask children to hold their planner pages made during Application and stand in a circle. Begin a prayer time, and ask each child who desires to promise God that he will tell about Jesus this week. When all the children have had an opportunity to pray, let them burst the balloons. If you wish to keep the noise level down, blow up the balloons without tying them closed, and let children release them. Then enthusiastically lead the children in singing all verses of "We Will Tell!" from page 8 of this session.

Close your time together by praying Psalm 67:1-2: "May God be gracious to us and bless us and make his face shine upon us; that your ways may be known on earth, your salvation among all nations."

Leaders' Evaluation

	Great!	OK!	More!	Oops!	Suggestions
Activity 1					
Activity 2					
Bible Time					
Application					
Bible Memory					
Craft					
Snack					
Game					
Wrap-up					

(Walk finger puppet.) But one day while Paul was traveling to one of the towns, a bright light flashed in the sky in front of him. A voice said, "Why do you torture me?"

Paul fell to the ground. (Make puppet lay down.) "Who is talking?" he asked.

The voice said, "I am Jesus, the one you are trying to make people stop believing in. Now go to the city and wait until you are told what to do."

The men traveling with Paul heard the voice but they did not see anyone. They helped Paul to the city. (Walk puppet.) For three days Paul was blind. He could not see.

Then God sent a man named Ananias to heal Paul. Ananias placed his hands on Paul, and God made Paul able to see again.

Paul began telling everyone in that city what had happened to him. But he didn't stay in one city for very long. He had such good news to tell he wanted everyone to know. Paul began traveling the whole world, telling people wherever he went the good news that Jesus is the Christ.

Hold up the shoes. Paul walked many, many miles on dusty roads to tell people about Jesus.

Hold up the boat or picture. Paul traveled on many boats, across many waters to tell new people about Jesus.

Hold up the handcuffs. Paul was even put in jail many times for telling about Jesus. But Paul was so excited about Jesus that he told his jailer about Jesus. He told the soldiers that guarded him about Jesus.

It didn't matter where Paul was or who he was with, he talked about Jesus, God's Son.

◆◆◆◆

APPLICATION—A Telling Planner

You will need calendar sheets from a planner and pens or colored pencils. You can purchase planner sheet packs at most stores that have an office supply section. Purchase the type of calendar sheets that have blank squares, rather than lines, so that the children can draw pictures.

Christians were cautious about Paul at first. They did not think they could trust him. But Paul proved he was truly a believer. He traveled everywhere telling people the good news of Jesus.

Game—"Far and Near" Missionary Journey

You will need masking tape. Before class, mark starting and turnaround points for each team with a piece of masking tape on the floor.

Remind children that after Jesus spoke to him, Paul traveled everywhere telling people that Jesus is the Christ. Paul traveled far from home and to those countries nearby. If Paul went far away, he traveled by boat. If he went nearby, he walked.

Play this simple relay game. Divide the children into two or three groups and ask them to line up behind the masking-tape starting line you made before class. Ask the children to determine an action that symbolizes riding in a boat. Perhaps taking sliding steps while pretending to row a boat. At your signal the first child on each team moves to the turnaround point using the boat action and returns walking. When the first child crosses the starting line, the next child starts on the missionary journey. The first group to finish the "journey" wins the game. Play several more times if time permits.

◆◆◆◆

WRAP-UP—Bursting with Good News

You will need at least one balloon for each child. Before this activity, blow up the balloons.

Guide children to clean up the areas of the room. When they are finished, ask them to gather in a large group.

Hold up the balloons. Paul didn't tell about Jesus every once in a while. He didn't tell one or two people about Jesus. Paul was so excited about Jesus that he was bursting with the good news. He told people everywhere he went about Jesus. We can be like Paul. We can tell about Jesus everywhere that we go. **Let's promise Jesus that we will tell about Him—everywhere!**

Show the children a calendar sheet. Have any of you seen your moms or dads or other adults use a calendar or a planner to help them remember what to do and where to go? Let children share their experiences.

We are going to make a planner sheet today to help us remember whom we can tell about Jesus. Give each child a planner sheet and ask the children to draw pictures of the people they see each week that they will tell about Jesus. Refer back to the people mentioned in Activity 2 if they need suggestions. Encourage them to fill as many of the spaces as possible with pictures of people they will tell.

Paul told people everywhere he went about Jesus. You can tell people everywhere about Jesus, just like Paul did. Your planner sheet will help you remember whom you can tell about Jesus.

♦♦♦♦

BIBLE MEMORY—Toss the Bean Bag

You will need a Bible with the memory verse marked and highlighted and a bean bag or other small object.

Ask children to sit in a circle on the floor. Review the memory verse by saying it with the children several times, until they are comfortable with the words of the verse. Have a volunteer help you find the verse in your Bible and point to the words as the children say them.

Then hold up the bean bag (or other small object). Explain that you will say the first part of the verse and toss the bean bag to someone in the circle. The child who catches the bean bag (or to whom it lands the closest) is to complete the verse. That child begins the verse and tosses the bean bag to another child who says the rest of the verse. You may wish to have children work in pairs.

OPTION: If you have older children, have them toss the bean bag and say one word of the verse.

Unit 9

4

ACTIVITY TIME

Do as many activities as time permits.

♦♦♦♦

Craft—Memory-verse Magnet

You will need copies of the magnet on page 234, scissors, crayons or markers, margarine-tub lids or lids from 12-ounce frozen juice cans, self-adhesive magnets.

Ask children to color and cut out the magnet from page 234. They should glue the magnet to the inside of a margarine-tub or juice-can lid. Give each child a strip of self-adhesive magnet to attach to the back of the lid. (Make sure it is long enough to hold the weight of the lid.)

To whom will you give your magnet? What will you tell that person about Jesus?

OPTION: Make a boat to remind children that Paul traveled everywhere, telling the good news about Jesus. For each child you will need a top from a polystyrene egg carton, a plastic drinking straw, construction paper, crayons or markers, scissors, and masking tape. Cut each straw in two pieces, a 5" piece and a 3" piece. Cut two right triangles from construction paper for each child. Make one 4" triangle and one 2 1/2" triangle. These will be the sails. Children can decorate the sails with crayons or markers. Use masking tape to secure one drinking straw "mast" inside each end of the egg carton. The boats will float.

Snack—Traffic Signals

You will need graham crackers, peanut butter, and M&Ms.

Break a graham cracker into four sections. Have children spread a layer of peanut butter on top of the cracker. Add three M&Ms down the center of the cracker. Put a red candy on top, a yellow in the middle, and a green one on the bottom.

Talk about the meaning of the three colored lights on a traffic signal. **What made Paul stop putting Christians in jail?** Being blinded by a light. **What did Paul do after he could see again?** He told people the good news of Jesus. **Some of the early**

Lesson 39

228

5

229

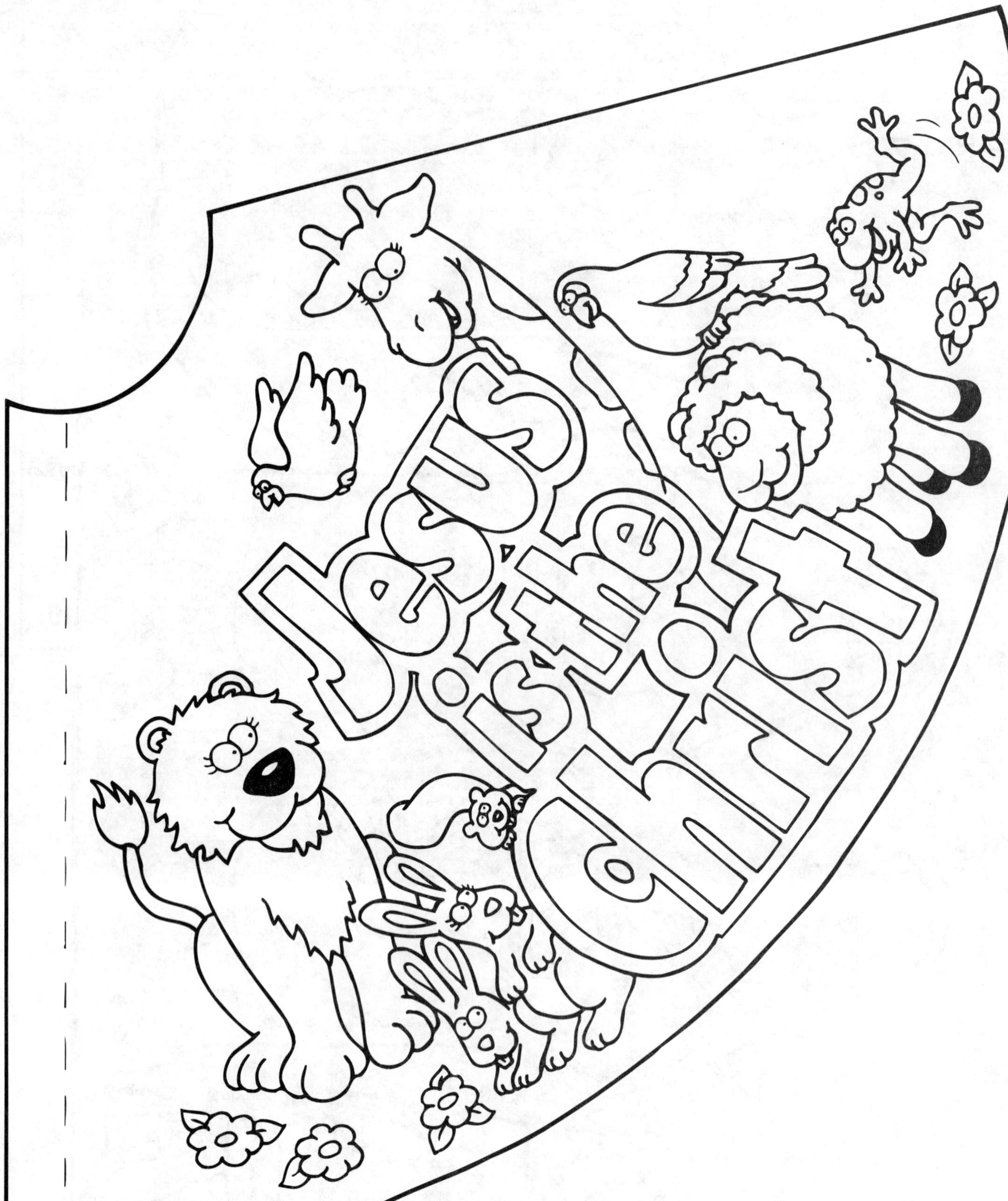
Jesus is the Christ

He died and came back alive.

He loves you!

He made a lame man walk.

Guess what I know about Jesus!

232

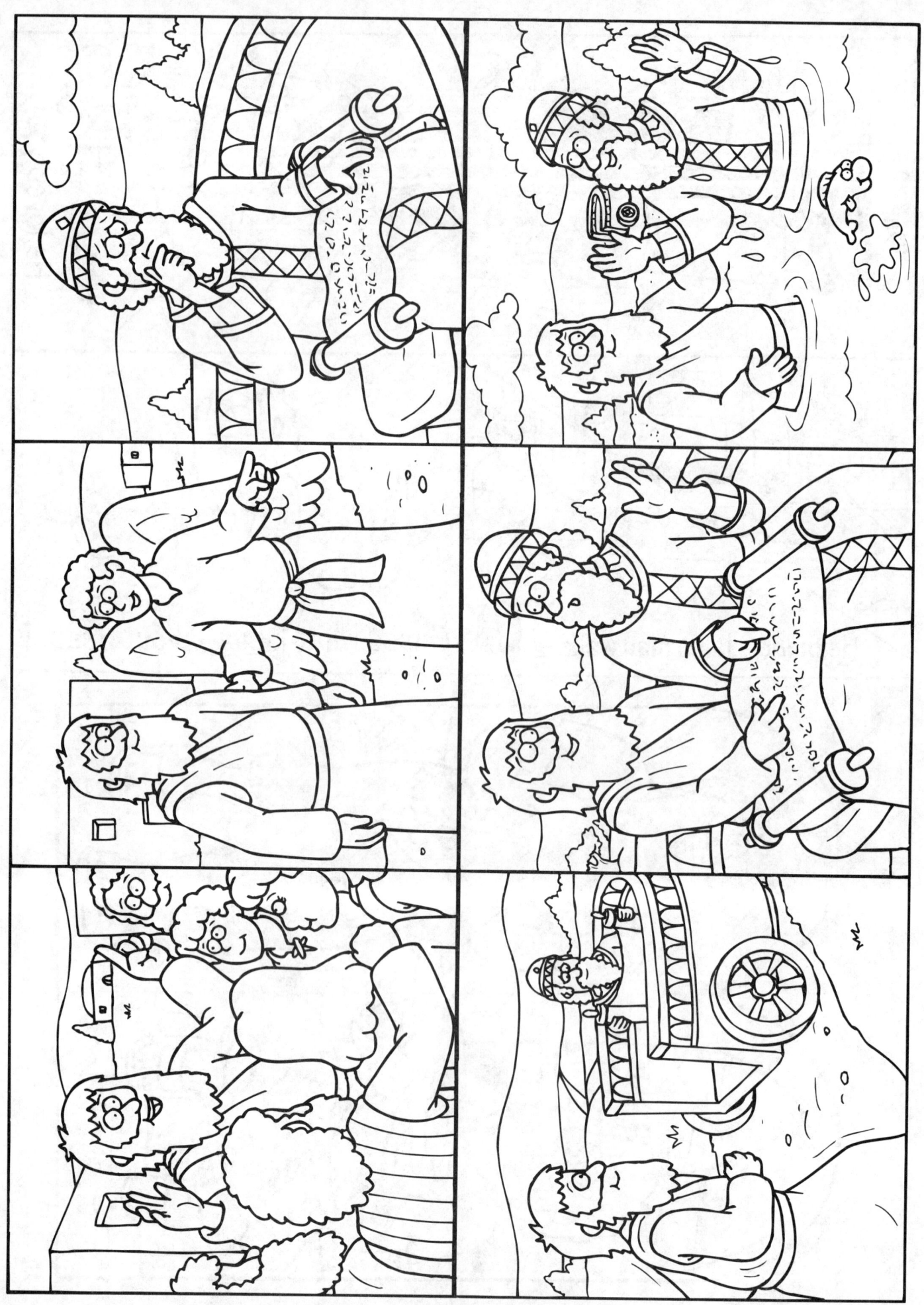

ABOUT JESUS

EVERYWHERE

TELL PEOPLE

234

Unit 10
Lessons 40-44

God Is Powerful

◆◆◆◆◆

By the end of this unit, the children and leaders will . . .
Know Tell how God showed five Bible people He is powerful.
Feel Feel amazed at God's great power.
Do Worship God because He is powerful.

Unit Bible Words for Memory
"Lord, there is no one like you. You are great. Your name is great and powerful" (Jeremiah 10:6, ICB).

◆◆◆◆◆

Unit Lessons

Lesson 40
God's Power Feeds Elijah
1 Kings 17:1-6
Children will discover that God sent ravens to feed Elijah.

Lesson 41
God's Power Feeds a Widow
1 Kings 17:7-16
Children will learn how God fed Elijah, a widow, and her son with a little flour and a little oil.

Lesson 42
God Shows the People His Power
1 Kings 18:20-39
Children will see how God showed His power to His people when Elijah had a contest with the prophets of Baal. God sent down fire from Heaven to show that He is God.

Lesson 43
God's Power Makes a Boy Live Again
2 Kings 4:8-37
Children will learn how the prophet Elisha asked God to use His power to bring a little boy back to life again.

Lesson 44
God's Power Heals Naaman
2 Kings 5:1-14
Children will hear how Naaman traveled to Israel to be cured of his leprosy by the prophet Elisha. When Naaman washed seven times in the Jordan River, God's power healed him.

◆◆◆◆◆

Why Teach This Unit to Four-Year-Olds—Six-Year-Olds?

Your children will enjoy the fascinating facts contained in the Bible stories for this unit—birds bring food, fire falls from Heaven, a sick man rinses in a river and becomes well. These examples of God's power can fill your children with a sense of excitement that will lead them to worship.

◆◆◆◆◆

Bible Time Line

The stories for this unit are pictured on the time line, pages 313 and 314.

See page 6 in this book for further instructions on using the time line.

◆◆◆◆◆

Materials

All Lessons
a Bible
markers, colored pencils, crayons
white paper, construction paper, poster board
tape, masking tape
Plasti-Tak
glue
scissors
a stapler
paper hole punch
yarn or string

Lesson 40
pictures from nature magazines of a lion, frog, fish, whale, raven (bird), donkey, hornet, worm, ram
a fairly thick paperback book for each child
items to use to decorate a picture (clear plastic for water, sand for the ground, cloth for Elijah)
spring-type clothespins, assorted feathers, and magnet strips
an offering plate

Lesson 41
1 cup of flour, 3 tablespoons oil, 3 tablespoons water, a mixing bowl, spoon, a rolling pin, wax paper, and an electric skillet
a cassette of the song "Awesome God" from Rich Mullins' album *Winds of Heaven . . . Stuff of Earth* and a cassette player, or a recording of another worship song about God's power that your children enjoy singing
craft sticks, cooking oil, and cotton balls
a blindfold

Lesson 42
a balance beam or anything that the students can walk along with the heel-to-toe method and is no wider than four inches (a piece of wood, a curb, a masking-tape outline)
a megaphone or a loudspeaker with a microphone—something to magnify your voice
a bag of penny candy
a paperweight-sized stone for each child, a permanent black marker, paintbrushes, poster paints, and paint shirts
24 small stones (or plastic or wooden blocks), six glasses of water, and two dishpans

Lesson 43
stickers
a picture of a Bible-times house and items to make Elisha's room: a blanket or sleeping bag and pillow to make a bed, a small table, a chair, an oil lamp or candle
a roll of 30" wide wrapping paper

Lesson 44
a bar of soap, laundry spot remover, carpet spot remover or floor cleaner, glass cleaner, a tub of water, a garment with a spot, a small mirror, and paper towels
a variety of U.S. and foreign coins and bills
rhythm instruments
aluminum foil, coins of various sizes, paper plates, rubber cement, and paper towels
two plastic cups, two 12" pieces of string or ribbon, and two flat washers (purchase at a hardware store)

◆◆◆◆◆

The Beginner's Bible™ Resources
God's Amazing Animal Stickers, Standard Publishing, #22-01064, call 1-800-543-1353
God's Sea Creatures Stickers, Standard Publishing, #22-01065, call 1-800-543-1353
The Beginner's Bible™ Old Testament GeoSafari Bible Pack, Standard Publishing, #14-24001, call 1-800-543-1353
The Beginner's Bible™ Bible Lessons GeoSafari Bible Pack, Standard Publishing, #14-24005, call 1-800-543-1353

Unit 10
Lesson 40

God's Power Feeds Elijah
(1 Kings 17:1-6)

After Elijah delivered God's message that there would be no rain in Israel, he went to the Kerith Ravine to hide. Here, God used His awesome power to send ravens to feed Elijah.

Bible Words

"Lord, there is no one like you. You are great. Your name is great and powerful" (Jeremiah 10:6).

Goals

Tell how God showed Elijah He is powerful.
Feel amazed at God's great power.
Worship God because He is powerful.

◆◆◆◆

Activity 1—Animals That Helped God

You will need pictures of the following animals: lion, frog, fish, whale, raven (bird), donkey, hornet, worm, ram. Look for pictures in nature magazines or old Sunday-school materials. Distribute the pictures among the children. Each child or pair of children should think of a clue that will help the rest of the class guess the name of his or her animal. Clues could include words that rhyme with the animals' names or noises and actions that the animals make.

The Bible tells us about some animals that did things they don't usually do. Let's see if we can guess some of these animals. Have children give their clues.

Each one of these animals did something unusual in the Bible. Each of these animals showed God's great power because they did something animals don't usually do! Today,

— fold —

Jeremiah 10:6
(Tune: "Three Blind Mice")

Lord, there is
no one like You.
You are great. You are great.
Your name is great and powerful.
Your name is great and powerful.
There's no one like You.
Jeremiah 10:6

Lord, there is
no one like You.
You are great. You are great.
You sent the ravens to feed Elijah.*
Your name is great and powerful.
There's no one like You.
Jeremiah 10:6

*Other verses:
3. You gave a widow flour and oil.
4. You sent down fire from Heaven.
5. You made a little boy live again.
6. You healed a leper named Naaman.

237

we'll find out what some ravens did that showed God's power. Show the picture of the raven.

◆◆◆◆◆

ACTIVITY 2—A Trick or a Miracle?

You will need the pictures of Bible animals that were used in Activity 1.

How many of you have a pet? What kind of animal is your pet? Many animals can be trained to do tricks. Lions can be trained to jump through rings of fire. Whales can be trained to play catch. **Have you trained your pet to do any tricks?** Let children talk about their pets.

What would you think if your pet talked? Maybe he would say, "Good morning. How are you today?" You'd be amazed because that is something animals don't usually do. **What would you think if your pet went to the grocery store and brought home some meat and bread?** Again, you'd be amazed because that is something animals can't do.

God's Word tells us about many animals that did things that animals don't usually do. I'll show a picture of each one and tell you what it did. You tell me if what the animal did was a trick or a miracle.

A group of hungry lions refused to eat Daniel. A bunch of frogs moved in with the Egyptians. A large fish swallowed Jonah and then spit him out several days later unharmed. A donkey talked to his master. A swarm of hornets cleared the way for God's people. A worm ate a tree. A ram saved Isaac from being sacrificed. All are miracles.

God's Word tells us why these animals were able to do these things. God worked miracles; the animals could do these things because of God's power. The actions of these animals showed God's power to the people they helped. Their actions showed God's power because their actions were things that animals don't do.

— fold —

that pleases God when we leave this room neat and clean for the next group who will use it.

As children finish their tasks, have them bring their letters to God and their ravens to the circle. We've learned about God's power today. **How did God show His power to Elijah?** God sent ravens to feed Elijah. **Show me your ravens. Show me your letters to God. We are going to ask our ravens to help us deliver our letters to God. What do our letters to God say?** Have students "read" their letters aloud. **Put your letter in your raven's mouth.** Then pass the offering plate. Instruct students to open their ravens' mouths and drop their letters in the plate. Close by teaching the children the second verse to "Jeremiah 10:6" from page 8 of this session. Then sing both verses together.

Leaders' Evaluation

	Great!	OK!	More!	Oops!	Suggestions
Activity 1					
Activity 2					
Bible Time					
Application					
Bible Memory					
Craft					
Snack					
Game					
Wrap-up					

BIBLE TIME—No Rain or Dew

You will need a fairly thick paperback book for each child. Instruct students to place the spine of the book in the palm of their left hand and close their hand around the book. Instruct students to rub the thumb or index finger of the right hand across the pages of the book to make a flapping sound. This sound will resemble the sound of a flock of birds flying. Have children practice fanning the pages of the book. At your signal during the story, students will use the paperback books to make the flocking sound.

God's prophet, Elijah, had some bad news for the king of Israel. It was news that the king probably wouldn't believe until, of course, it happened. And when Elijah's news happened, it would make the king very angry at Elijah.

Elijah's news for the king was a message from God. Since Elijah was God's prophet, he spoke God's messages. So when Elijah delivered the news to the king, he said, "I serve the Lord, the God of Israel. As surely as the Lord lives, I tell you the truth. No rain or dew will fall during the next few years unless I command it."

Now King Ahab was a wicked king who did not honor or obey God. He probably thought that Elijah was crazy. But just as Elijah said, the dew and the rain stopped. And King Ahab was angry at Elijah. He was so angry, he sent men to look for Elijah to kill him.

Meanwhile, God told Elijah to leave Israel and to go to a special hiding place by a brook called Kerith. Here, Elijah could safely hide from King Ahab. Here, God took care of His servant Elijah. In the morning, God sent ravens to feed Elijah. Have children fan their books. Here come the ravens with bread and meat for Elijah. Elijah drank water from the brook. Again, in the evening, God sent the ravens to feed Elijah. Have children fan their books. Here come the ravens with bread and meat for Elijah. Day after day, God sent the ravens to feed Elijah. Have children fan books. Elijah stayed hidden in

Snack—The Ravens Brought Bread

You will need the ravens made during the craft, crackers, a cracker dip, and water.

Set up a "hiding place" in the room. Gather the students and their ravens in the hiding place. Place a plate of crackers in the center of the students. **We're going to pretend that we are Elijah. We are in God's special hiding place and it's time to eat. Our ravens are going to bring us our bread.** Have students use their ravens' "mouths" to pick up a cracker, dip it in the cracker dip, and eat it.

What do you think Elijah thought when he saw the ravens bring him bread and meat? Discuss. I'm sure Elijah was reminded of God's great power.

Game—Bring Elijah's Supper

You will need two ravens made during the craft. Play the following version of "Run for Your Supper."

Remember how God showed His power through the ravens? Yes, the ravens delivered bread and meat to Elijah. We're going to be the ravens and bring Elijah's supper to him. Have students sit in a circle. Choose one student to be Elijah. Put the ravens in the center of the circle. Elijah walks around the outside of the circle and chooses two students who are sitting beside each other. He touches them on their heads and says, "Bring Elijah's supper." Elijah remains in that spot. The chosen two race to the center of the circle, pick up a raven, and run in opposite directions around the circle. The first one to return to the starting place and touch Elijah becomes the new Elijah. Return the ravens to the center of the circle. After each round, ask, **How did God show Elijah His power?** God sent the ravens to feed Elijah.

WRAP-UP—An Offering of Worship

You will need the letters from Bible Memory, the ravens from the Craft time, and an offering plate.

Instruct children to clean up the room. We are acting in a way

this special place until the brook dried up because there was no rain. Next week, we'll find out where Elijah went when the brook dried up and how God's power continued to help him.

♦♦♦♦

APPLICATION—God Is Powerful

You will need copies of the letter on reproducible page 257, markers, glue, scissors, items to use to decorate the picture (clear plastic for water, sand for the ground, cloth for Elijah, and so on), and the paperback books from Bible Time.

I'm going to name some things that happened in today's Bible story. If it was something that showed God's power, fan your books and say, "God is powerful." If it wasn't something that showed God's power, then sit quietly.

1. King Ahab did not obey God. (No.) 2. Elijah told King Ahab some bad news from God. (Yes.) 3. King Ahab was angry. (No.) 4. The rain and the dew stopped when Elijah said it would stop. (Yes.) 5. No one could find Elijah in God's hiding place. (Yes.) 6. Elijah was hungry. (No.) 7. Ravens brought food to Elijah. (Yes.)

What did the ravens do? They brought bread and meat for Elijah to eat. **Is this something that the ravens usually do?** No. **Is this something that the ravens were trained to do?** No. **How were the ravens able to bring bread and meat to Elijah both morning and evening?** God told them what to do. **How did the ravens show God's power to Elijah?** They did something that they don't usually do—they fed Elijah.

Give each child a copy of page 257. Explain that they are going to make a picture and learn a verse to help them worship God for His power. **When we draw a picture about God's power, we are worshiping Him for His power.** Children may color the picture of Elijah and the ravens, and cut and glue items on the picture to decorate it. Save the pictures to use during Bible Memory.

BIBLE MEMORY—A Letter to God

You will need copies of the Bible-verse letter that the children worked on during Application and crayons.

Let's worship God because He is powerful. Our Bible verse will help us. Look at your papers. Here is our Bible verse: **"Lord, there is no one like you. You are great. Your name is great and powerful"** (Jeremiah 10:6). Have children "read" the verse with you several times. Sing the first verse of "Jeremiah 10:6" from page 8 of this session to help children learn the words of the verse. Sing the song several times, until the children are comfortable with it. Then have children complete the letters to God that they started in Application. They may use crayons to trace the letters of the verse and sign their names at the bottom. Fold the letters in half to form a card. As time permits, have students color the outside of the cards.

♦♦♦♦

ACTIVITY TIME

Do as many activities as time permits.

♦♦♦♦

Craft—Raven Clothespins

You will need one spring-type clothespin and a copy of the raven on page 258 for each child, assorted feathers, scissors, glue, and magnet strips. If you have younger children in your class, cut out the ravens before the session.

Help children cut out and glue the raven to the clothespin so that the snap opening will serve as the raven's mouth. Allow students to decorate their ravens with feathers. Attach a magnet strip to the bottom side of each clothespin.

How did God show His power to Elijah in today's story? God sent ravens to feed Elijah. **Why does this show us God's power?** Ravens don't usually bring food to people or even come near people.

Unit 10
Lesson 41

God's Power Feeds a Widow
(1 Kings 17:7-16)

No rain in Israel soon meant no food in Israel. God showed His power to Elijah and the widow at Zarephath by feeding them when there was no food. God did this by keeping a jar of flour and a jug of oil from running empty.

Bible Words

"Lord, there is no one like you. You are great. Your name is great and powerful" (Jeremiah 10:6).

Goals

Tell how God showed Elijah and a woman He is powerful.
Feel amazed at God's great power.
Worship God because He is powerful.

◆◆◆◆

Activity 1—Gathering Sticks

You will need at least one stick (pencil) for each child, slips of paper, a pen, and tape. Before class, write the following phrases on separate slips of paper and draw a simple picture of each one. Following is a list of phrases and suggested pictures: no rain (raindrops with an X through them), widow (from page 260), son (Bible-times boy), jar of flour (from page 260), jug of oil (from page 260), bread (loaf of bread), water (cup of water), Elijah (from page 260), and several slips with the words "God's power" (a flexed arm). Attach each slip of paper to a stick. Add to the list if needed so that each child will have a stick. Lay the sticks around the room.

A woman in today's Bible story was gathering sticks. Let's help her. Find one stick (pencil) in this room. When all the

---

Jeremiah 10:6
(Tune: "Three Blind Mice")

Lord, there is
no one like You.
You are great. You are great.
Your name is great and powerful.
Your name is great and powerful.
There's no one like You.
Jeremiah 10:6

Lord, there is
no one like You.
You are great. You are great.
You sent the ravens to feed Elijah.*
Your name is great and powerful.
There's no one like You.
Jeremiah 10:6

*Other verses:
3. You gave a widow flour and oil.
4. You sent down fire from Heaven.
5. You made a little boy live again.
6. You healed a leper named Naaman.

sticks have been found, gather the children in a circle. **Let's look at the pictures and try to read what is written on our sticks.** Have children guess what the pictures mean. Then help them read the words on their sticks. **All of these things are a part of today's Bible story. We know that something exciting happened because God's power was a part of the story!**

◆◆◆◆

ACTIVITY 2—Flour and Oil Make Bread

You will need 1 cup of flour, 3 tablespoons oil, 3 tablespoons water, a mixing bowl, spoon, a rolling pin, wax paper, and an electric skillet.

God showed His power to Elijah and a widow by keeping them supplied with flour and oil. **Why were the flour and oil important?** The flour and oil are mixed together to make bread. **We are going to use flour and oil to make bread.** Explain each step of making the bread as you go along. Ask volunteers to help as needed. Mix the three ingredients together until the mixture forms a ball. Divide the mixture in half and use a rolling pin to flatten each half. Cook in the skillet at 300-350 degrees for two minutes on each side. Cool and break into pieces. One cup of flour will make about three dozen bite-sized pieces.

What happened to our flour and oil? We used it to make bread, and we used it up. **The widow in today's story used flour and oil to make bread too. She used the flour and oil, but the flour and oil were never used up. How does this show God's power?** Making bread should have used up the flour and oil, but God kept the flour and oil from being used up.

◆◆◆◆

BIBLE TIME—Flour and Oil

You will need one copy of the jar and the jug from page 259. You will also need separate copies of the flour and oil areas from the jar and jug (dashed lines). Make the flour copies on white paper and the oil copies on yellow paper. Each child should

2 Unit 10

◆◆◆◆

WRAP-UP—A Powerful God

You will need the sticks from Activity 1. Distribute the sticks around the room. God is powerful. One way that we can worship our powerful God is to make sure our room is neat for those who will use it next. While you are cleaning the room, gather one stick and then join me in a circle. Ask each child to tell something about the person or thing that is written on his stick. Then offer prayers of praise, thanking God for His power. Close by singing the first three verses of "Jeremiah 10:6" from page 8 of this session.

Leaders' Evaluation

	Great!	OK!	More!	Oops!	Suggestions
Activity 1					
Activity 2					
Bible Time					
Application					
Bible Memory					
Craft					
Snack					
Game					
Wrap-up					

Lesson 41 7

Snack—No Rain in the Land

You will need dried banana and apple snacks as well as fresh bananas and apples. Cut the fresh fruit into slices. Put the dried snacks and the fresh snacks in separate containers.

After Elijah announced that there would be no rain in the land, he went to hide by a brook. **What happened to the brook where Elijah had been hiding?** It dried up. **Why did the brook dry up?** There had been no rain in the land. **What was the land of Israel like in today's story?** Dry. **Why was the land dry?** There was no rain.

Our snacks today will help us understand what it was like in Israel without rain. Look at this fresh fruit. **How does it look?** Juicy and good. Now look at this dried fruit. **How does it look?** Shriveled and dry. **Which one of these containers of fruit hasn't had any rain? Which one looks like a land without rain?** The dried fruit. All the water has been removed from this dried fruit.

The water had been removed from the land of Israel; it was dry and shriveled up. **What did this do to the food supply in Israel?** Food was hard to find. Without rain, crops couldn't grow. **How did God show His power when there had been no rain in Israel?** He fed Elijah, a widow, and the widow's son by not letting their flour and oil run dry. Say a prayer of praise for God's power, then serve the snack.

Game—Put the Oil in the Jug

You will need the jar and jug and the flour and oil pieces used during Bible Time, a blindfold, and pencils.

Redistribute the flour and oil pieces to the students. **Our God is powerful. God showed His power in today's story. What did God do?** He gave Elijah and the widow bread every day. The flour in the jar did not run dry and the oil in the jar was not used up.

Have students trace the sentence on their papers. Then take turns having students either pin the flour in the jar or the oil in the jug while blindfolded. Before each student takes his turn, ask him to "read" the words on his flour or oil piece.

---

have either a flour or an oil piece. Attach a piece of tape to the back of each flour and oil piece. Post the jar and the jug on a bulletin board or a wall. Tape a flour piece in the jar and an oil piece in the jug. Create pairs of children—one with a flour piece and one with an oil piece. Assign each pair a number. At your signal during the story, each pair will place their flour and oil pieces in the outlines of the jar and jug.

Elijah had been hiding by a brook where the ravens had been feeding him. Since there had been no rain in the land, the brook dried up. So God told Elijah to go to Zarephath to find a certain widow. Elijah obeyed.

When Elijah arrived at Zarephath, he saw the widow that God had sent him to find. She was gathering sticks. Elijah asked the widow to bring him a drink of water. Elijah also asked her for a piece of bread.

"I'm sorry," said the widow. "I don't have any bread. I only have a handful of flour in a jar and a little oil in a jug." Show jar and jug pictures. The widow was gathering sticks so that she could build a fire to make the flour and oil into bread. It was going to be the widow and her son's last meal because there was no more food.

Elijah must have surprised the woman with what he said next. "Don't be afraid. Go home and do what you have planned to do. But first, make me some bread and bring it to me. Then make some bread for you and your son. Do this because the Lord God of Israel says, 'The jar of flour will not be used up and the jug of oil will not run dry.'"

The widow went home and did what Elijah told her to do. She used the flour and the oil to make some bread for Elijah. Remove flour and oil from the jar and jug. When she did, she still had enough flour and oil to make some more bread. Have pair #1 put their flour and oil patterns on the jar and jug. **The widow made some more bread.** Remove flour and oil. **And flour and oil remained in the jug.** Have pair #2 put their flour and oil in the jar and jug. Continue this until every child has had a turn to replace either the flour or oil. **The jar of flour was not used up and the jug of oil did not run dry—just as the Lord** had said through His prophet Elijah. This happened until God sent rain to the land of Israel.

◆◆◆◆

APPLICATION—Awesome God

You will need a cassette of the song "Awesome God" from Rich Mullins' album *Winds of Heaven . . . Stuff of Earth* and a cassette player. If you do not have this song, choose another worship song about God's power that your children enjoy singing. The song will be used in the rest of the lessons in this unit. Adapt the discussion below to fit the words of the song you choose.

Discuss the following before singing the song. **The title of the song we are going to sing is "Awesome God." What does the word *awesome* mean?** Discuss with the children—fearful, powerful, great, amazing, wonderful. **Why is God awesome?** Answers will vary. This song praises God for His power. **What powerful things has God done?** Discuss. **How did God show His power to Elijah and the widow?** God gave them bread to eat by not allowing the flour and oil to be used up. **How did God show His power to Elijah when Elijah was hiding by a brook?** Help children recall last week's story. **When I think of God's power, I am amazed. There is no one like God.**

This song will help us praise God for His power. Discuss the words to the chorus. Then have students listen to the verses of the song and sing along on the chorus.

◆◆◆◆

BIBLE MEMORY—Choral Prayer

Lead the children in saying the Bible verse several times. Sing "Jeremiah 10:6" from page 8 of this session to help children review the verse. Then divide the children into three groups. Each group should be seated together. Assign group one the first sentence of the verse. Give group two the second sentence. Group three will recite the third sentence.

What does our Bible verse tell us about God? There is no one like God; He is great and powerful. **Our Bible verse helps us worship God for His power. God's power is amazing. Let's name two ways God showed His power to Elijah.** God sent ravens to feed Elijah. God provided bread for Elijah by keeping a widow supplied with flour and oil. **God has shown His power to us too. Let's bow our heads and say our Bible verse as a prayer to God.** Lead each group to say their sentence in order. Close by saying amen together.

◆◆◆◆

ACTIVITY TIME

Do as many activities as time permits.

Craft—Oil Rubbings

You will need the pictures of Elijah and the widow and the jar of flour and jug of oil from page 260, crayons, craft sticks, white glue, cooking oil, and cotton balls. Cover the work area with newspaper. Provide wet wipes to clean oily fingers.

Show the bottle of cooking oil. **Most of us have oil like this at home. Your moms and dads use it to cook. We learned today that oil and flour make bread. God used some oil and flour to show His power. How did God show Elijah and the widow He is powerful?** He provided food for them by keeping the widow's flour and oil from being used up. Give children the pictures of Elijah with the widow. **We are going to use our oil to help us make a picture of Elijah and the widow and of the jar and jug that God used to feed them. The picture will remind us that God is powerful.**

Instruct students to use crayons to color their pictures. If time is limited, children may choose one picture to complete. When they are finished, have children use an oil-soaked cotton ball to rub oil over their pictures. When dry, the pictures will have a transparent look. Glue a craft stick frame around each picture. Encourage students to hang their pictures in a window at home.

Unit 10
Lesson 42

God Shows the People His Power
(1 Kings 18:20-39)

God showed His power to the prophets of Baal and to the people of Israel when He sent fire to burn up Elijah's sacrifice.

Bible Words

"Lord, there is no one like you. You are great. Your name is great and powerful" (Jeremiah 10:6).

Goals

Tell how God showed the prophets of Baal and the people He is powerful.
Feel amazed at God's great power.
Worship God because He is powerful.

◆◆◆◆

Activity 1—Wavering

You will need a balance beam. If a balance beam is not available, use a substitute balance beam such as a long narrow piece of wood or a strip of masking tape placed on the floor. If the weather permits, a curb or a parking rail would work. Anything that the students can walk along with the heel-to-toe method and is no wider than four inches would work.

Give all the children a chance to walk the balance beam. Spot them as needed so no one falls off and gets hurt. **Was it hard to keep your balance on the balance beam? Most of you wavered back and forth from side to side in order to keep your balance. In today's story, the people of Israel were like that. They were wavering back and forth. They weren't trying to keep their balance on a balance beam; they were trying to decide who is God. First they thought God was God. Stand on balance beam

---

Jeremiah 10:6
(Tune: "Three Blind Mice")

Lord, there is
no one like You.
You are great. You are great.
Your name is great and powerful.
Your name is great and powerful.
There's no one like You.
Jeremiah 10:6

Lord, there is
no one like You.
You are great. You are great.
You sent the ravens to feed Elijah.*
Your name is great and powerful.
There's no one like You.
Jeremiah 10:6

*Other verses:
3. You gave a widow flour and oil.
4. You sent down fire from Heaven.
5. You made a little boy live again.
6. You healed a leper named Naaman.

245

and lean to one side. Then they thought a false god named Baal was God. Lean to the other side. They wavered back and forth between God and Baal. Waver back and forth between the two sides of the beam. We're going to find out what caused the people to stop wavering and to know that God is God.

◆◆◆◆

ACTIVITY 2—Powerful God

You will need the song "Awesome God" or other worship song used in lesson 41, and a megaphone or a loudspeaker with a microphone—something to magnify your voice.

We're going to have a contest. The contest will be between two teams. Divide the children into two teams. Choose only one child for team A. Choose a confident, outgoing child. The rest of the class will be team B. Tell the children that they will have a yelling contest to discover which team can say "God is powerful" the loudest. Ask children to guess which team will win. Children should predict that the larger team will win.

Have the large group shout first. Then join the solo child and shout through the megaphone or loud speaker—whatever it takes to be louder than the large group.

In today's story, Elijah had a contest against 450 prophets of Baal. It looked like the prophets of Baal would win. After all, there were 450 of them. But Elijah had something that the prophets of Baal didn't have. Elijah had God, and God wanted to show His power. God showed His power by sending fire. God is awesome and powerful. Play the song "Awesome God" and have children sing along on the chorus.

◆◆◆◆

BIBLE TIME—The Contest on Mt. Carmel

Choose one child to be Elijah. The rest of the group will be prophets of Baal. Allow children time to practice. Have Elijah practice saying, "O Lord, answer me." Have the prophets of Baal practice saying, "O Baal, answer us."

2 Unit 10

WRAP-UP—Bible-verse Messages

You will need the candy messages from Bible Memory. Arrange with other class teachers for your group to come in at the end of class and deliver the messages. If you meet just before a worship time, children may stand in a foyer area and hand out the messages to passersby.

Give children a few minutes to straighten the room, then gather them together. Distribute the candy messages among them. We are going to deliver these messages to the people of our church. When you hand a message to someone, say, "The Lord is God." When we do this, we will be worshiping God for His power by telling others about His power. Say a prayer and lead the children to where they will be handing out the messages.

Leaders' Evaluation

	Great!	OK!	More!	Oops!	Suggestions
Activity 1					
Activity 2					
Bible Time					
Application					
Craft					
Snack					
Game					
Wrap-up					

Lesson 42 246 7

Three years had passed since Elijah announced to King Ahab that there would be no rain in the land of Israel. Elijah had been hiding—first in the Kerith Ravine where God sent ravens to feed him. Then, when the brook dried up from the lack of rain, Elijah visited a widow and her son. God fed Elijah and the widow and her son by keeping the widow's flour and oil from being used up. Now it was time for Elijah to visit King Ahab.

Elijah said, "Tell the people of Israel and the prophets of Baal to meet me on Mt. Carmel." When everyone arrived on Mt. Carmel, Elijah said, "How long will you waver between God and Baal. If the Lord is God, follow Him. If Baal is God, follow him." But the people did not answer him.

So Elijah said, "Let's have a contest. I will sacrifice to the Lord. The prophets of Baal will sacrifice to Baal. Neither of us will set fire to the sacrifice. Instead, the prophets of Baal will call on Baal, and I will call on the Lord. The god who answers by setting fire to the sacrifice is God."

The people liked Elijah's idea. Baal had 450 prophets. God had one prophet. It didn't look good for Elijah—four hundred and fifty prophets of Baal to one prophet of God.

So the contest began. The prophets of Baal prepared their sacrifice and began to pray to Baal. Prophets of Baal say, "O Baal, answer us." There were 450 prophets praying to Baal. Prophets of Baal say, "O Baal, answer us." They were loud. Prophets of Baal say, "O Baal, answer us." They cried to Baal all day. Prophets of Baal say, "O Baal, answer us." But Baal did not answer.

Now it was Elijah's turn. He used twelve stones to build an altar. He laid wood on the altar. He laid the sacrifice on the altar. He had twelve large jars of water poured over the sacrifice, the wood, and the altar. The sacrifice was soaked with water. It was time. Elijah stepped forward and prayed. Have Elijah pray, "O Lord, answer me." Elijah also prayed, "Let these people know that You, O Lord, are God."

Then the fire of the Lord fell from Heaven and burned up Elijah's sacrifice as well as the wood, the stones, and the water,

used them to build an altar. Elijah's stones were a lot bigger than ours. **How many stones did Elijah use?** Twelve. **Why did Elijah build an altar?** He was building it so that God could show He is powerful. **How did God show He is powerful?** He sent fire to burn up Elijah's sacrifice. Our stones will remind us that **God is powerful.** Distribute stones and have children paint them. Set them aside to dry.

Snack—It Happened at Mt. Carmel

You will need caramel dip (purchased or homemade), apple slices and toothpicks.

Where did the contest between God's prophet and the 450 prophets of Baal take place? Mt. Carmel. Our caramel dip reminds us of what happened at Mt. Carmel. **How did God show His power to the prophets of Baal and to the people?** He sent fire from Heaven to burn Elijah's sacrifice. Mt. Carmel was an exciting place because God's power showed the people of Israel that **God is God!** Ask a child to thank God for His power and for the snack. Instruct children to use the toothpicks to pick up an apple slice and dip it into the melted caramel.

Game—Build the Altar

You will need 24 small stones (or plastic or wooden blocks), six glasses of water, and two dishpans.

Divide the children into two teams. Determine a starting point and place the dishpans across the room. Assign each team a dishpan. Give each team twelve stones and three glasses of water. Teams will run a relay race to build an altar in the dishpan and cover it with water. This will mean fifteen trips by each team to the dishpan. Several children on each team may have to run twice.

When the game is over, gather the students around the dishpans. **Look how much water we poured over the stones! Will this burn?** No! **Did Elijah's sacrifice burn?** Yes! It had a lot of water poured over it. **Why did it burn?** God's power caused it to burn. **When the people saw Elijah's sacrifice burn, what did they say?** "The Lord is God. The Lord is God."

When the people saw this, they fell to their knees and onto their faces and cried, "The Lord is God! The Lord is God!" The contest was over. One prophet of God stood against 450 prophets of Baal and won! God is powerful.

◆◆◆◆◆

APPLICATION—The Lord Is God!

You will need copies of the responsive reading written below.

Before the contest between God and Baal, what did the people think about God? Maybe He was God. What did the people think about Baal? Maybe he was God. The people weren't sure who was God; they wavered between God and Baal. When the contest was over, what did the people think about God? God is God. What did the people think about Baal? Baal is not God. What did the people do when they saw the fire of God burn up Elijah's sacrifice? They fell down with their faces to the ground and cried, "The Lord is God! The Lord is God!"

We will read a responsive reading to worship God for His power. Distribute the reading and assign the solo parts to different children. Help them with their parts as needed.

Solo: Praise be to the name of God forever and ever.
All: The Lord is God.
Solo: Wisdom and power are His.
All: The Lord is God.
Solo: God made the earth by His power.
All: The Lord is God.
Solo: God made the world by His wisdom.
All: The Lord is God.
Solo: He is the One who performs miracles.
All: The Lord is God.
Solo: He shows His power to His people.
All: The Lord is God.
Solo: What god is so great as our God?
All: The Lord is God.
Solo: There is no one like our God.
All: The Lord is God.

Solo: His name is great and powerful.
All: The Lord is God.
OPTION: If you have younger children in your class, you read the solo parts, and have the group repeat, "The Lord is God!"

◆◆◆◆◆

BIBLE MEMORY—Send Word Throughout the Land

You will need a bag of penny candy, copies of the Bible-verse strips from page 258, scissors for each child, and white glue or cellophane tape.

Lead children in reciting the Bible verse. Sing "Jeremiah 10:6" from page 8 of this session to help children review the verse. **How does our verse say that the Lord is God?** There is no one like you. **What else does our Bible verse tell us about God?** He is great and powerful. **How did God show His power to Elijah and the people at Mt. Carmel?** He sent fire from Heaven and burned up Elijah's sacrifice. **Word was sent throughout all of Israel inviting people to the contest between God and Baal. Now let's send word to the people that "The Lord is God."** Give each child one section of Bible-verse strips and a handful of candy. Children cut the strips apart and glue or tape a piece of candy to each one. Do as many as time permits. Children will deliver the messages during Wrap-up.

◆◆◆◆

ACTIVITY TIME

Do as many activities as time permits.

Craft—Elijah Took Twelve Stones

You will need a paperweight-sized stone for each child, a permanent black marker, paintbrushes, poster paints, and paint shirts. Before class, wash the stones and allow to dry completely. Use a black permanent marker to write the following words on each stone: God Is Powerful.

What did Elijah do with some stones in today's story? He

Unit 10
Lesson 43

God's Power Makes a Boy Live Again
(2 Kings 4:8-37)

God showed His power to the woman from Shunem when she had a son as Elisha had promised. Then God showed His awesome power again when He brought her son back to life after he died.

Bible Words

"Lord, there is no one like you. You are great. Your name is great and powerful" (Jeremiah 10:6).

Goals

Tell how God showed a boy and his mother He is powerful.
Feel amazed at God's great power.
Worship God because He is powerful.

◆◆◆◆◆

Activity 1—Amazing Gifts!

You will need the box pattern from page 262, the story pictures from page 261, stickers, and markers. Prepare one box and one set of pictures for each student. Keep the pictures separate from the boxes, and do not show them to the children.

Show the children the boxes you have made. **In a few minutes, I am going to put a gift inside each one of these boxes. Why do people give each other gifts?** We give gifts to celebrate something, to show appreciation for someone, and to help someone. Allow students to choose a box and use markers or stickers to decorate the box. Print each child's name on his box.

In today's story a woman from the town of Shunem gave

—fold—

Jeremiah 10:6
(Tune: "Three Blind Mice")

Lord, there is
no one like You.
You are great. You are great.
Your name is great and powerful.
Your name is great and powerful.
There's no one like You.
Jeremiah 10:6

Lord, there is
no one like You.
You are great. You are great.
You sent the ravens to feed Elijah.*
Your name is great and powerful.
There's no one like You.
Jeremiah 10:6

*Other verses:
3. You gave a widow flour and oil.
4. You sent down fire from Heaven.
5. You made a little boy live again.
6. You healed a leper named Naaman.

God's prophet Elisha a gift. Her gift couldn't be put in a box. Her gift was the size of a room—in fact, it was a special room where Elisha could stay when he visited. Later, Elisha gave the woman an even more special gift. We will find out about the gift in the Bible story. Before the Bible story, place a set of six pictures in each box, stacked in order from one to six.

ACTIVITY 2—Elisha's Room

You will need a picture of a Bible-times house and items to make Elisha's room—a blanket or sleeping bag and pillow to make a bed, a small table, a chair, an oil lamp or candle.

In today's story, a woman from Shunem made a room on her roof where Elisha stayed when he visited. **Let's make a room like the one the woman made.**

Show children the picture of the Bible-times house. Explain that Elisha's room was on the roof of the house. Show children where they will build the room. It might work best to build in a corner of your room. Children may furnish the room with a bed, table and chair, and a lamp.

BIBLE TIME—Restored to Life

You will need the story boxes prepared for Activity 1 and the room made in Activity 2.

Have children sit around the room to listen to the story. Give each child one of the story boxes from Activity 1 and instruct them to remove the lids. The gift in these boxes is a story about God's power. Take each picture out of your box when I tell you to look at it.

Look at picture one. God's prophet, Elisha, often visited the town of Shunem. Whenever Elisha was in Shunem, he stopped to eat with a well-to-do woman and her husband. The woman knew that Elisha was God's prophet.

WRAP-UP—Gifts of God's Power

You will need one set of story pictures.

Instruct children to give the next group who uses the room a gift by cleaning and straightening the room. Then gather children in a circle. **Several gifts were given in today's story. Let's name them.** The Shunammite woman built a room for Elisha. Elisha promised the woman a son. God brought the son back to life after he died. **What gift did we receive today?** The gift of a story that shows us God's power. Show the pictures from the story. **Let's thank God for His power.** Ask children to repeat the following prayer after you. **Dear Lord, You are powerful. Thank You for showing us that You are powerful. In Jesus' name, amen.** Close by singing "Awesome God" or another praise song about God's power, used in the last two sessions.

Leaders' Evaluation

	Great!	OK!	More!	Oops!	Suggestions
Activity 1					
Activity 2					
Bible Time					
Application					
Bible Memory					
Craft					
Snack					
Game					
Wrap-up					

One day, the woman asked her husband to build Elisha a room on the roof of their house. In the room, she put a table, a chair, and a lamp. Point to each of the items in your room as you mention it. Look at picture two. Elisha was thankful for the gift that the Shunammite woman and her husband had given him. The room was very nice! Elisha wanted to do something for the woman.

Elisha asked his servant Gehazi, "What can I do for her?" Gehazi said, "She has no son and her husband is old."

So Elisha promised the woman that she would have a son. At first the woman didn't believe Elisha because she had never been able to have children. Look at picture three. But the next year, the woman gave birth to a son—just as Elisha had promised.

The child grew, but one day, he got sick and died. Look at picture four. His mother picked him up and took him to Elisha's room on the roof. She laid her son on Elisha's bed. The woman left immediately to find Elisha. She traveled to Mt. Carmel where Elisha was staying. The woman told Elisha what had happened to her son. Elisha gave his staff to his servant Gehazi. Look at picture five.

Elisha told Gehazi to hurry to the boy and to lay his staff on the boy's face.

Gehazi did just as Elisha told him to do, but nothing happened. When Elisha reached the house, he found the boy lying dead. He shut the door to his room and prayed. He walked back and forth in the room. He prayed. Take picture six out of the box. Then the boy sneezed seven times and woke up. How did God show the woman that He is powerful? God brought the boy back to life after being dead.

◆◆◆◆◆

APPLICATION—God's Amazing Power!

Students will need their story boxes and pictures used in Bible Time. Ask them to put their pictures in order, one through six. Tell them to hold up each picture one at a time as you ask a

Lesson 43

— fold —

---

work folded until everyone is finished.

How did God show a woman and her son that He is powerful? He brought the boy back to life after he was dead. God is powerful. What did the boy do just before he woke up? He sneezed seven times. Have children unfold their craft. Each of our paper chains has seven boys—one boy for each time the boy in the story sneezed. Our chains will help remind us that God is powerful. He brought a boy back to life.

Snack—The Gift of a Son

Use a boy-shaped cookie cutter to cut out shapes from a package of tortillas. Cover each shape with shredded cheese and broil until the cheese bubbles. (Or provide any boy-shaped snack such as gingerbread or frosted sugar cookies).

Our snack is shaped like a boy. Who was the boy in today's story? He was the Shunammite woman's son. What happened to the boy? He died. How did God show the boy and his mother that He is powerful? He made the boy live again after he had died.

Game—Power Concentration

You will need one set of story pictures for each child. Group children in groups of two or four. Shuffle their story box pictures together and lay them on the floor facedown in a grid pattern. Each child takes a turn choosing two pictures to turn over. If the two pictures are a match, the child says, "God is powerful," and removes the match. Play until all the pictures have been paired. If four children play in a group, there will be two pairs of each picture.

OPTION: For younger children, you may wish to divide the pictures into two matching groups. Lay one group on the floor, faceup, in a grid pattern. Shuffle the other pictures. Have children take turns drawing a picture, finding the matching picture in the grid, and laying the picture on top. Play until all the pictures in the grid are matched.

Unit 10

question about the story. After each question, they will answer, "God is powerful!" Practice saying the phrase together several times.

What did the prophet Elisha know about God when he promised the Shunammite woman a son? What did he know about God when her son was brought back from the dead? God is powerful.

What did God show the woman and her son in Elisha's room? God is powerful.

What did the Shunammite woman know about God when He gave her a son as Elisha promised? God is powerful.

What did the Shunammite woman learn about God when He brought her son back to life? God is powerful.

What did Gehazi, Elisha's servant, know about God? God is powerful.

What did the son of the Shunammite woman learn about God when he was brought back to life? God is powerful.

Tell children that the gift Elisha gave the Shunammite woman was amazing! **Ask them to show you what it looks like to be amazed! What does it mean when something is amazing?** Something is amazing when we wonder about how it was made or how it happened. We may be surprised by something that is amazing.

What are some things you know that are amazing? Allow children to respond. Many things in nature are amazing—thunderstorms, birds that fly south in the winter, how the sun rises each day. Sometimes the things people do are amazing, like a person who sings well or plays basketball well. The most amazing things are the things that God made and the things that God does. Even the amazing things that people do are possible because of how God made us.

Let's make a list of amazing things. Then we will pray to thank God for His amazing power! List things children name that God made or that God made people able to do. Then lead children in prayer, thanking God for the amazing things. Ask for volunteers to pray.

4 Unit 10

— fold —

BIBLE MEMORY—No One Like You

The Shunammite woman knew that God is powerful. Why? God gave her a son when she didn't have any children. God brought her son back to life after he died. **I think our Bible verse tells us what the Shunammite woman must have thought about God.** Sing the verses of "Jeremiah 10:6" from page 8 of this session to help children review the words of the verse. Then have children make up motions to go with the words of the verse. Following are suggested motions, but encourage children to decide their own motions.

Lord (reach hand up to Heaven),
there is no one like you (shake head from side to side).
You are great (stretch arms high and wide above your head)
Your name (reach hand up to Heaven)
is great (stretch arms high and wide above head)
and powerful (make fists and flex arms at sides).

ACTIVITY TIME

♦♦♦♦

Do as many activities as time permits.

Craft—Seven Sneezes

You will need the pattern of the boy from page 258, a roll of 30" wide wrapping paper, scissors, pencils, and cellophane tape. Before class, use tagboard to make the patterns of the boy. Prepare strips of wrapping paper 5 inches high by 30 inches wide. Fold each piece of wrapping paper in half, then in half again, and in half again. Then unfold each paper and fold it again accordion-style. Cut off one folded panel, so that only seven folded panels remain.

Give each child a strip of folded paper and a boy pattern. Show children how to place the pattern along the fold and trace around it. Then show children how to cut out the pattern and to leave the folded edge uncut. Have students keep their finished

Lesson 43   5

252

Unit 10
Lesson 44

God's Power Heals Naaman
(2 Kings 5:1-14)

Because of his incurable disease, Naaman was doomed to a life of isolation, with little chance of recovery. The complete healing of his skin disease was an awesome demonstration of God's power.

Bible Words

"Lord, there is no one like you. You are great. Your name is great and powerful" (Jeremiah 10:6).

Goals

Tell how God showed Naaman He is powerful.
Feel amazed at God's great power.
Worship God because He is powerful.

◆◆◆◆

Activity 1—Spot Removers

You will need the following spot removers: a bar of soap, laundry spot remover, carpet spot remover or floor cleaner, glass cleaner. You will also need a tub of water, a garment with a spot, a small mirror, and paper towels.

Show children the spot removers. **Have you seen your mom use one of these to clean spots in your house? Do you help your mom clean spots in your house?** Hold up the glass cleaner and ask children if they know what it is used for. Then use the glass cleaner to clean a mirror.

Hold up the bar of soap and ask what it cleans. Then use the soap and wash hands in the tub of water. Hold up the carpet cleaner and ask what it is used for. Then use carpet (or floor) cleaner to clean a spot on the carpet (floor). Finally, hold up the

—fold—

Jeremiah 10:6
(Tune: "Three Blind Mice")

Lord, there is
no one like You.
You are great. You are great.
Your name is great and powerful.
Your name is great and powerful.
There's no one like You.
Jeremiah 10:6

Lord, there is
no one like You.
You are great. You are great.
You sent the ravens to feed Elijah.*
Your name is great and powerful.
There's no one like You.
Jeremiah 10:6

*Other verses:
3. You gave a widow flour and oil.
4. You sent down fire from Heaven.
5. You made a little boy live again.
6. You healed a leper named Naaman.

253

laundry spot remover and ask what it is used for. Then apply the remover to a spot on a garment and rinse in the tub of water.

All of these spot removers remove spots. The man in our Bible story today had a spot he wanted to remove. But it was a spot that none of these spot removers could clean. It was a spot that only God could clean. He had a spot of leprosy. Leprosy is a skin disease. In Bible times, leprosy couldn't be cured by men. Only God could cure leprosy.

◆◆◆◆◆

ACTIVITY 2—God's Power Is Greater

You will need a variety of U.S. and foreign coins and bills. Show children the various types of money. Ask them to guess where the different types of money come from. Tell them what country each kind of money is from.

What do you use money for? They may use money to buy toys, candy, or clothes. **What do your parents or other people you know use money for?** To buy food and clothes, to pay for the things they need to live, like a house. Many people think that money is powerful because money can buy them anything they want. Some people use money to buy themselves honors and awards. They may buy time with an important person.

The man in today's lesson, Naaman, thought money had power. He took gifts of money and clothing to the king of Israel to buy the cure for his skin disease—leprosy. But Naaman could not buy the power to cure leprosy. Only the power of God could heal Naaman.

◆◆◆◆◆

BIBLE TIME—Seven Dips in the River

You will need the story strip from page 260 and frame from page 261 for each child, scissors, crayons, and tape. Before class, prepare the visuals by cutting the viewer and the slits in the viewer along the dotted lines. Cut out the story strips.

—fold—

WRAP-UP—Drawing God's Power

You will need the drawings made in Application and cellophane tape. Prepare an area on a bulletin board or wall to display the drawings.

Tell the children to clean up the room, just as Naaman cleaned himself in the river.

When the children are finished, gather them in a circle. Give each one an opportunity to post his drawing and to say a prayer of praise for God's power. **God shows us His power in many ways. We know that God is strong enough to take care of us. God's power is amazing! We are thankful for God's power.** Close by singing "Awesome God" or another song of praise for God's power used the last four sessions.

254

Leaders' Evaluation

	Great!	OK!	More!	Oops!	Suggestions
Activity 1					
Activity 2					
Bible Time					
Application					
Bible Memory					
Craft					
Snack					
Game					
Wrap-up					

Distribute the visuals to the children and ask them to color their story strips. Then help them thread the strips through the slits in their viewers and tape the ends together to form a circle. Help the children move their strips so the first picture is showing in the viewers. Determine a signal such as a beep to tell students when to turn their story strips to the next scene.

NOTE: If time is limited, thread the story strips through the viewers and tape them in place before class.

This is Naaman. He was a very important man in the country of Aram. He was the commander of Aram's army. But he had leprosy—a terrible skin disease for which there was no cure. *Beep.*

Naaman's wife had a servant girl who was from Israel. She knew about God's prophet Elisha. She knew that God could heal Naaman's leprosy. The servant girl told Naaman about Elisha. *Beep.*

So Naaman went to the king of Aram and asked for permission to go to Israel. The king said okay. So Naaman left for Israel. With him, he took 750 pounds of silver, 150 pounds of gold, and ten sets of clothing! Whew! Naaman was serious about getting rid of his leprosy. He was willing to spend a lot of money to be healed. *Beep.*

When Naaman arrived in Israel, he went to see the king of Israel. Naaman asked the king of Israel to heal him of his leprosy. The king of Israel was shocked. He was so upset he tore his robes. The king said, "I am not God. I cannot heal leprosy!" *Beep.*

God's prophet Elisha heard that the king had torn his robes. Elisha told the king to send Naaman to him. When Naaman arrived at Elisha's house, Elisha sent a messenger to tell Naaman, "Go, wash yourself seven times in the Jordan, and you will be healed." At first Naaman was mad. He did not believe that the Jordan River could heal his leprosy. He also thought that a man of his importance with all his money deserved a personal visit by the prophet Elisha. But Elisha didn't want Naaman's money or gifts. He wanted Naaman to see God's power. *Beep.*

---

in separate containers: chocolate, strawberry, caramel, marshmallow, sprinkles, crushed M&Ms®, crushed nuts. NOTE: Be sure to check with the children for any food allergies.

Why was the number seven important to Naaman? Elisha told Naaman to wash seven times in the Jordan to rid himself of leprosy. **What happened when Naaman dipped himself seven times?** He was healed of his leprosy. **How did God show His power to Naaman?** God healed him of an incurable disease. **We have seven kinds of toppings for our bananas. Dip your bananas seven times!** Slice the bananas into bite-sized pieces. Children may skewer a banana piece with a toothpick. Encourage them to dip the banana pieces seven times—once in each topping. They may dip seven pieces of fruit each in a different topping. They may dip three pieces in any combination of the seven. They may dip one piece in all the toppings!

Game—Wash and Be Clean

You will need two plastic cups, two 12" pieces of string or ribbon, and two flat washers (purchase at a hardware store). Make a bolero game. Tie the string or ribbon through the washer. Poke a hole in the bottom of the cup and tie the other end of the ribbon to it. Secure with tape.

Divide the class into two teams. Team members line up side by side. Player one begins by trying to flip the washer into the cup. He gets one try and passes the cup to the next player. Each player tries once until the team receives seven points. A point is earned when a player successfully flips the washer into the cup. The first team to receive seven points wins.

What did Naaman think when Elisha told him to wash in the Jordan River? He was angry and wouldn't do it. **What happened then?** Naaman's friends helped him change his mind and do what he was told. **How many times did Naaman dip in the Jordan?** Seven. **To play our game, we have to be like Naaman. We have to dip the washer in the cup seven times before we can win the game.** Naaman had to dip in the Jordan seven times before he won! **What did Naaman win when he obeyed?** He won his health and his life.

Naaman finally decided to do what Elisha had told him to do. He dipped himself seven times in the Jordan River. His leprosy was gone. His skin was clean! Naaman knew that it wasn't the Jordan River that healed him of his leprosy; it was God. Naaman knew that it wasn't money that healed him; it was God. Naaman said, "Now I know that there is no God in all the world except in Israel!" Naaman saw God's power.

◆◆◆◆

APPLICATION—God Is Powerful Drawings

You will need markers and drawing paper.

God is powerful. **How did God show Naaman He is powerful?** God healed Naaman of his leprosy. **How does God show us He is powerful?** Answers will vary and may include Bible stories learned the last five weeks, events in nature, and ways God cares for us (giving us food, clothing, shelter, healing us when we are sick, comforting us when we hurt).

Let's worship God because He is powerful. We will each draw a way that God shows us He is powerful. When children are finished, ask each one to tell about his drawing about God's power. After each child has shared, lead the class to say in unison, "God is powerful."

◆◆◆◆

BIBLE MEMORY—A Bible-verse Band

You will need rhythm instruments.

Lead the children in singing the verses of "Jeremiah 10:6" from page 8 of this session. Sing the verses several times, until children are comfortable with the words. Sing the verses several times while playing the instruments.

◆◆◆◆

ACTIVITY TIME

Do as many activities as time permits.

◆◆◆◆

Craft—Coin Rubbings

You will need aluminum foil, markers, coins of various sizes, paper plates, rubber cement, and paper towels. Before class, cut the foil into two-inch squares. Glue coins to paper plates using rubber cement glue to make the coins easy for the children to work with. After the activity, the coins can be easily removed from the plates and the rubber cement can be rubbed off the coin.

Give each child several foil squares and the coins on the paper plates. Instruct them to lay the foil over a coin and rub across it with a marker. Washable markers will resist the foil. Use the paper towel to rub the color. The rubbing will look like the coin and be slightly colored.

When Naaman left his country to find the man of God, what did he bring with him? Money and clothes—gifts.

Why did Naaman bring gifts with him? He wanted to pay someone to cure his leprosy. Being cured of leprosy was worth a lot of money to Naaman.

Why did God cure Naaman of his leprosy? Did God want Naaman's money? No. **Did Elisha want Naaman's money?** No. **What did God and His servant Elisha want?** They wanted Naaman to turn his heart to God. God wanted Naaman to love and worship Him.

What did Naaman think about God after he was cured of leprosy? Naaman said, "There is no God in all the world except in Israel." God's power showed Naaman that He is God.

Snack—Dip Seven Times

You will need bananas, toothpicks, and the following toppings Naaman He is powerful? God healed Naaman of his leprosy. After Naaman was healed of his leprosy, he praised God for His power. Naaman learned that God is great and powerful. When we say our Bible verse, we worship God because He is great and powerful. Distribute the rhythm instruments. Have

Lord, there is no one like you.

Lord, there is no one like you. You are great. Your name is great and powerful.
Jeremiah 10:6

Lord, there is no one like you. You are great. Your name is great and powerful.
Jeremiah 10:6

Lord, there is no one like you. You are great. Your name is great and powerful.
Jeremiah 10:6

Lord, there is no one like you. You are great. Your name is great and powerful.
Jeremiah 10:6

God is Powerful

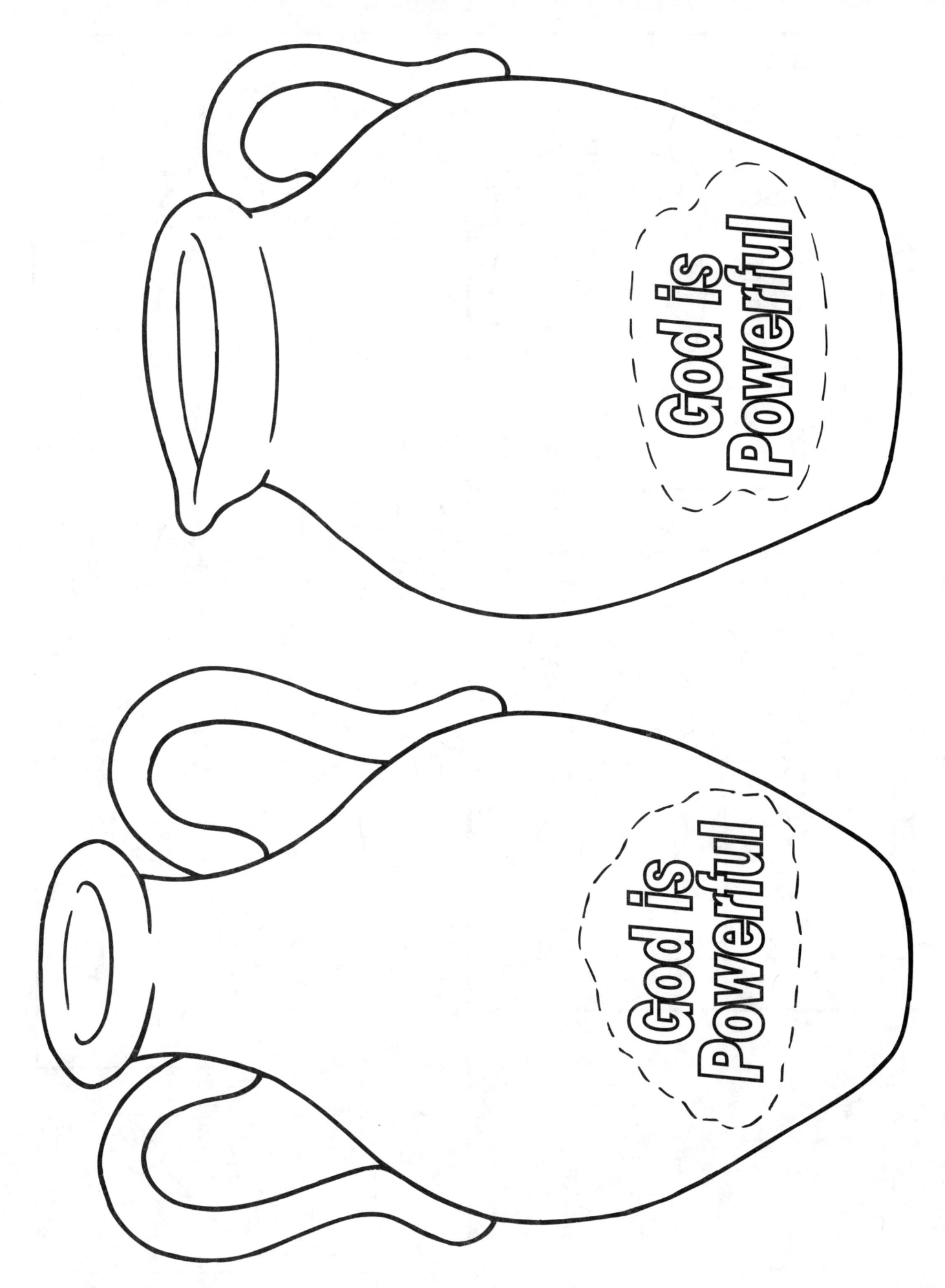

God is Powerful

259

260

GOD IS POWERFUL

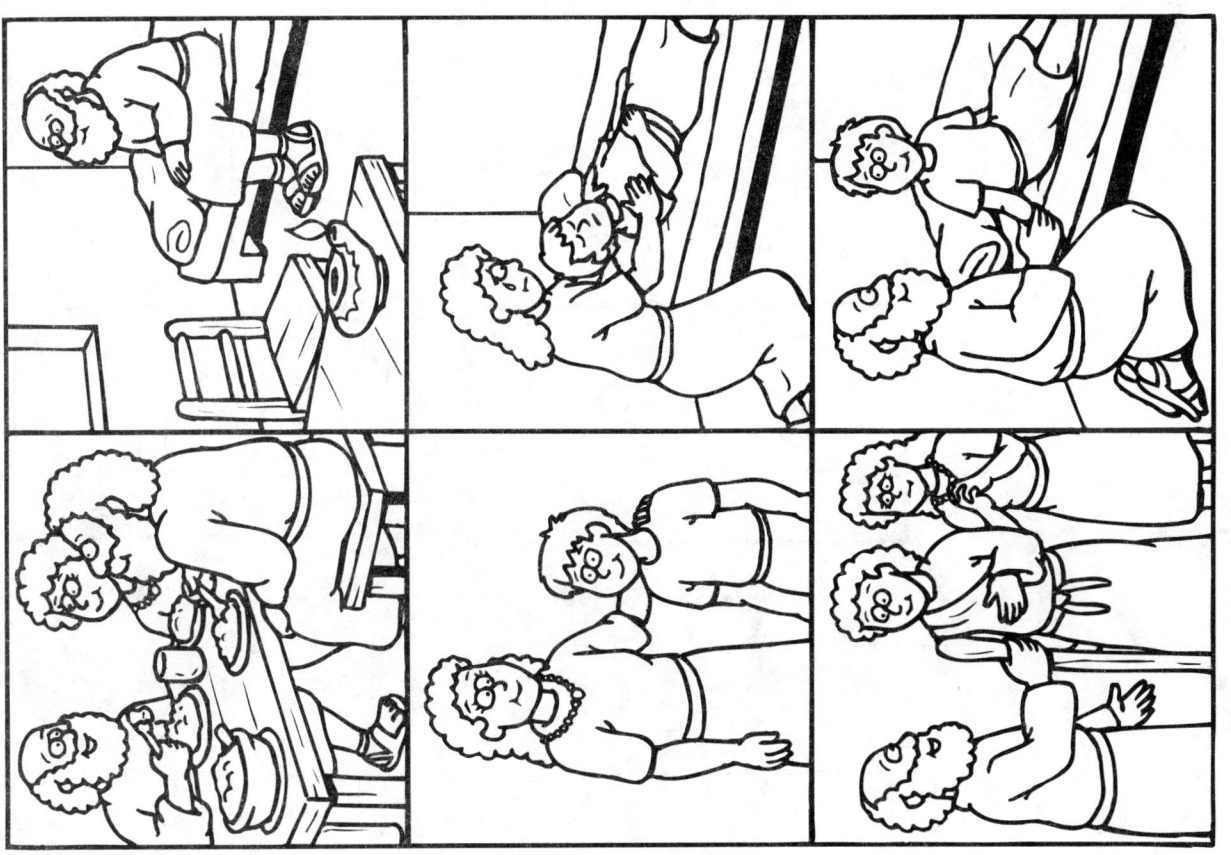

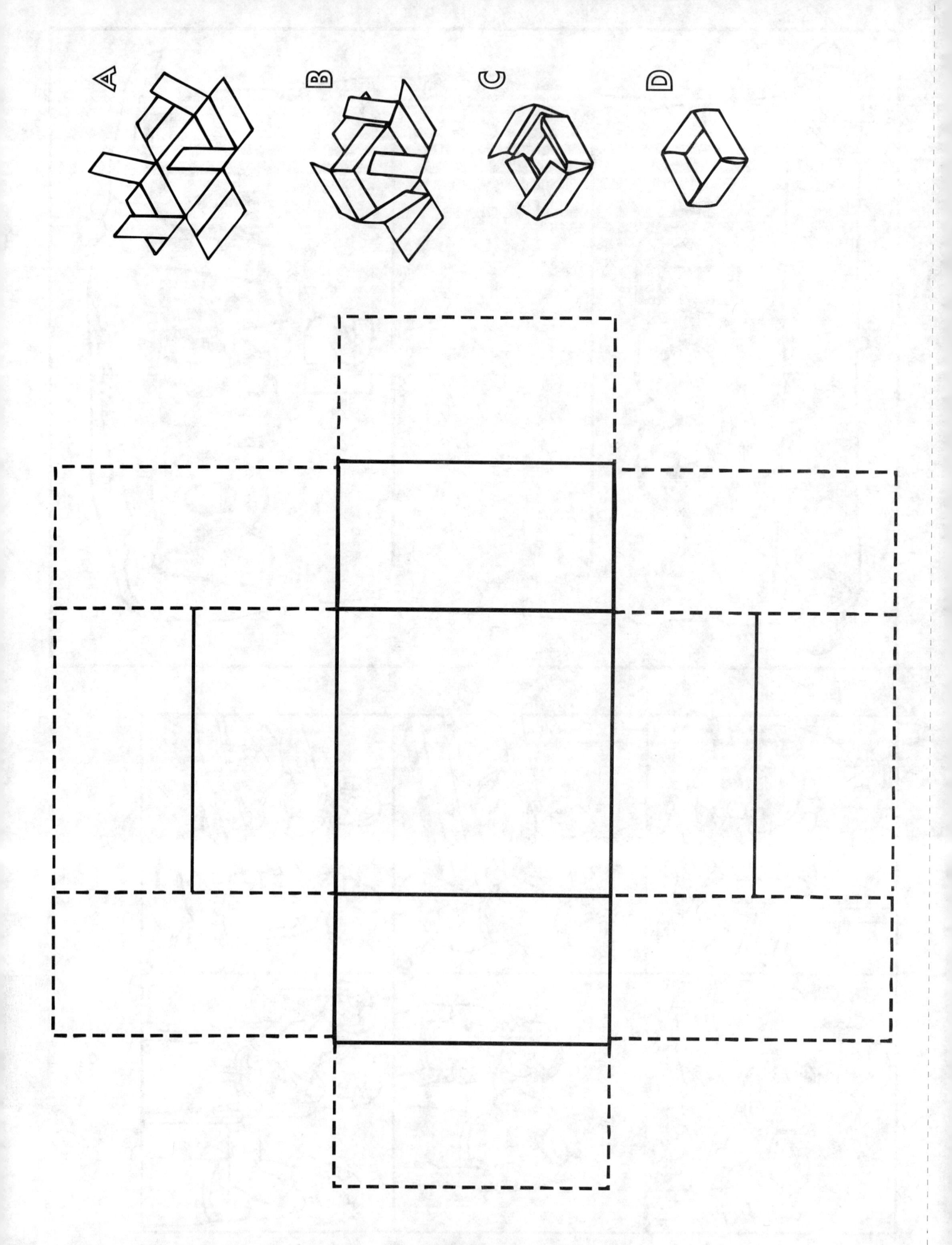

Unit 11
Lessons 45-48

God Hears Our Prayers

◆◆◆◆◆

By the end of this unit, the children and leaders will . . .
Know Tell four Bible people who prayed to God.
Feel Feel confident that God hears prayers.
Do Pray to God.

Unit Bible Words for Memory
"Never stop praying. Give thanks whatever happens"
(1 Thessalonians 5:17, 18a, ICB).

◆◆◆◆◆

Unit Lessons

Lesson 45
Solomon Prays to Choose Right
1 Kings 3:4-14; 4:29-34
Children will discover what Solomon asked for when God told him he could ask for whatever he wanted.

Lesson 46
Hezekiah Prays to Be Healed
2 Kings 20:1-11
Children will hear what happened when Hezekiah was sick with a boil and asked God to heal him.

Lesson 47
Manasseh Prays When He Is Sorry
2 Chronicles 33:1-20
Children will learn that Manasseh disobeyed God and did many bad things. But when Manasseh asked God to forgive him, God heard his prayer.

Lesson 48
Jehoshaphat Prays When He Is Thankful
2 Chronicles 20:1-21, 30
Children will hear how Jehoshaphat and the people thanked God when they went to battle.

◆◆◆◆◆

Why Teach This Unit to Four-Year-Olds—Six-Year-Olds?

Children learn well by example, and the Bible people who prayed in this unit's Bible stories can encourage them in their prayers to God. They can ask God for help in choosing right like Solomon. They can pray for healing for those who are sick like Hezekiah. They can tell God they are sorry when they do wrong like Manasseh. And they can thank God for what He has done like Jehoshaphat. Children can feel confident that God will hear their prayers, just as He heard the Bible people.

◆◆◆◆◆

Bible Time Line

The stories for this unit are pictured on the time line, page 313. The time line will be used throughout all units in this book.

Provide the time-line page for children who arrive early, or plan time at the end of the Bible story during each session for children to color the time line and look for the hidden pictures.

See page 6 in this book for further instructions on using the time line and for suggested time-line projects.

Materials
All Lessons
a Bible
markers, colored pencils, crayons
white paper, construction paper, poster board
tape, masking tape
Plasti-Tak
glue
scissors
a stapler
paper hole punch
yarn or string

Lesson 45
old dress-up clothes, such as fancy dresses, costume jewelry, capes (large pieces of fabric or twin size flat sheets), and suit coats, large safety pins for helping the clothes fit, crowns (make from paper, glue, and glitter) and scepters (using cardboard or paper-towel tubes with foil for covering), a throne (a bed sheet draped over a chair)
small envelopes
a cassette of children's songs and a cassette player
"fun" stickers (see resources below)

Lesson 46
items to set up a pretend doctor's office: a toy phone, chairs, bathroom scale, measuring tape, tongue depressors, flashlight, bandages, stethoscope, clipboards, pencils, and paper
paper plates and paper fasteners
two paper lunch bags
a clock with movable hands
an old blanket, sleeping bag, or old comforter, and a small sofa pillow
clear adhesive-backed paper
bright sunlight or a spotlight (i.e., bright lamp without lampshade)

Lesson 47
the following props: two paper cups, a bell, dishes, books, and toy cars
a small area for a worship center with a table in it and the following items to put on the table: a Bible, a seasonal decoration from nature, a picture of Jesus and/or a cross, and a tablecloth
a cassette of worship songs and cassette player (optional)
9" paper plates and ribbon
two tapes of music (one happy and lively, the other sad and slow)

Lesson 48
a cassette player and cassettes of worship songs
a blank cassette
colored cellophane
a blindfold

The Beginner's Bible™ Resources
God's Amazing Animal Stickers, Standard Publishing, #22-01064, call 1-800-543-1353

God's Sea Creatures Stickers, Standard Publishing, #22-01065, call 1-800-543-1353

The Beginner's Bible™ Old Testament GeoSafari Bible Pack, Standard Publishing, #14-24001, call 1-800-543-1353

The Beginner's Bible™ Bible Lessons GeoSafari Bible Pack, Standard Publishing, #14-24005, call 1-800-543-1353

Unit 11
Lesson 45

Solomon Prays to Choose Right
(1 Kings 3:4-14; 4:29-34)

King Solomon asks God for wisdom. This pleases God. Solomon becomes the wisest man in the world.

Bible Words

"Never stop praying. Give thanks whatever happens" (1 Thessalonians 5:17, 18a).

Goals

Tell what Solomon prayed. (Please help me do right.)
Feel confident that God hears prayers.
Pray to ask God to help you do right.

◆◆◆◆

ACTIVITY 1—King and Queen for a Day

You will need old dress-up clothes, such as fancy dresses, costume jewelry, capes (large pieces of fabric or twin-size flat sheets), and suit coats. Large safety pins for helping the clothes fit. Make crowns (using paper, glue, and glitter) and scepters (using cardboard or paper-towel tubes with foil for covering). Make a throne using a bed sheet draped over a chair.

Let the children dress up like kings and queens. Discuss what a king or queen does. Talk about why it is important for kings and queens to do what is right. Use this activity to introduce the four kings whose stories are told in this unit. Explain why the Bible says that some kings were bad and some were good. (Bad kings did not obey or worship God. Good kings did.) **If you were a queen (or king) in Bible times, tell one thing that you would do.** Encourage children to answer. Let one boy stay dressed as a king to be King Solomon during the story.

Who Did Pray?
(Tune: "This Is the Day")

Who did pray? Who did pray?
For w-is-dom. For w-is-dom.
(Repeat first two lines.)
Solomon prayed for w-is-dom.
Solomon prayed for w-is-dom.
Who did pray? Who did pray?
For w-is-dom.

Who did pray? Who did pray?
When he was sick. When he was sick.
(Repeat first two lines.)
Hezekiah prayed when he was sick.
Hezekiah prayed when he was sick.
Who did pray? Who did pray?
When he was sick.

Who did pray? Who did pray?
When he was sorry. When he was sorry.
(Repeat first two lines.)
Manasseh prayed when he was sorry.
Manasseh prayed when he was sorry.
Who did pray? Who did pray?
When he was sorry.

Who did pray? Who did pray?
When he was thankful. When he was thankful.
(Repeat first two lines.)
Jehoshaphat prayed when he was thankful.
Jehoshaphat prayed when he was thankful.
Who did pray? Who did pray?
When he was thankful.

ACTIVITY 2—Make Good Choices

You will need the sticker pictures on page 281, crayons or washable markers, and small envelopes. Prepare the stickers ahead of time by brushing a coat of the following mixture on the back of the pictures: one part vinegar, two parts white glue, a few drops of peppermint extract.

Distribute the stickers. For this activity, you will need only the six pictures at the top of the page. Ask the children to color the stickers. While they are coloring, discuss the choices the children in the pictures have made. (A child picking up toys, setting the table, praying, listening to teacher, brushing teeth, and two children playing together.) Describe each picture and ask why that choice would have been a good choice. Then ask the children to tell what a bad choice would have been in each situation. (A child leaving toys scattered, not wanting to help, forgetting to talk to God, talking while the teacher is talking, forgetting to take care of his teeth or body, and children fighting or arguing over toys.) **Whom can we ask to help us make good choices?**

Put each child's stickers in a small envelope and write the child's name on it. Save these stickers for use during the Application activity.

◆◆◆◆

BIBLE TIME—
Solomon Prays for Help to Choose Right

You will need a copy of the "Solomon" stickers on page 281. Prepare the stickers as directed in Activity 2. Color and cut them out. Make a paper crown. Use the stickers to decorate the crown as directed in the story. You will need the boy dressed like a king chosen during Activity 1.

Use the child dressed as a king from Activity 1. Have the child stand beside you as you tell the story. Place the crown upon the child's head and add the stickers to the crown as indicated. **When King David died, his son Solomon became the new**

WRAP-UP—Good Choice Stickers

You will need extra "fun" stickers. See unit page 264 for suggested stickers.

Gather the children. Each child should wear his crown. Ask them to look around the classroom for something that needs to be put away, or straightened, or picked up and put in the trash. Send them out to help clean up the classroom. Walk around observing their choices. Reward each child making a good choice with a "fun" sticker placed on her crown.

When the room is clean, gather the children around you. Review with them the good choice King Solomon made. Tell a good choice you observed each child making during today's class. Reward each child with another "fun" sticker for his crown. Say a closing prayer.

While children wait for their parents to pick them up, sing the first verse of "Who Did Pray?"

Leaders' Evaluation

	Great!	OK!	More!	Oops!	Suggestions
Activity 1					
Activity 2					
Bible Time					
Application					
Bible Memory					
Craft					
Snack					
Game					
Wrap-up					

king of Israel. Solomon knew that to be a good king, he would need to be wise. Being wise is more than being smart. A wise person makes good choices and does what is right. Solomon wanted to be a wise king. He wanted to do right always.

Soon after Solomon became the new king of Israel, he wanted to show his love for God by offering sacrifices. The smell from the burning of Solomon's sacrifice went up to God like a prayer. In those days the smell of burning sacrifices was very pleasing to God.

Later that night, while Solomon was sleeping, he had a dream. In the dream God spoke to him. He said, "Solomon, I will give you anything you want. Just ask me for it!"

This was a very important decision. Solomon wanted to make a good choice. He was a new king. There were a lot of things he needed. Israel was a big land with a lot of people. Solomon must have thought carefully about his request.

Let's think about some of the things that he could have asked God to give to him. How about asking for lots of money? Show the money sticker. If Solomon were the richest king, everyone would think he was the most important. He could have asked for a big army. Show the army sticker. To be the strongest and most powerful country, a king needs a big army. What if he asked God to help him live a long time? Show the sticker of an old king. Being king for a long time would make him famous. Everyone would hear about a king who ruled for a long, long time. What else do you think he might have asked God to give him? Let the children respond. Other responses might be a big palace, fancy clothes, a gold throne, fast horses, special food, etc. As the children name items that are pictured on the stickers, show those stickers.

Solomon thought about all the ways God had helped his father, King David. He also remembered that because of God's kindness he had been chosen to be the next king. Solomon knew he did not know everything a king needed to know. He knew it was important for a king to make good choices, to obey God's laws, and do what God said to do.

Finally, Solomon prayed to God and asked for wisdom. Do

beginning this evening. The Sunday ring is the last ring. (*Adjust the rings to your time frame.)

Tonight after you say your bedtime prayer, take the "Sunday" (or whatever the day is) ring off at the bottom of the chain. Each night this week after you pray take off another ring. When only the praying hand is left, bring it back to me and you will receive a prize.

Snack—The Royal Jewels

Prepare several different colors of finger gelatin using the "Jiggler" recipe found on most boxes of flavored gelatin. Follow the directions for preparing, chilling, and serving. Cut the gelatin into different jewel shapes. Serve each child a variety of shapes and colors.

Pray with the children before they eat. While they are eating, review the story of King Solomon. Would you like to have been King Solomon? Why? Why not? What do you think it would have been like to live in a palace? What kind of clothes would you have worn? Would you have worn a crown all the time?

Game—Musical Crown

You will need the crown used in the Bible story, a cassette of children's songs, and a cassette player. Place a chair for each child in a circle.

Pass the crown of King Solomon around the circle while music is being played. Stop the music. The child holding the crown has to name something God gave Solomon because He was pleased that Solomon asked Him for wisdom. (Money, clothes, big army.)

What was the good choice Solomon made? How did God show Solomon that he had made a good choice? When we make good choices, it makes us feel good. Our parents are pleased with our good choices. How do you know that your mommy or daddy is pleased with your choices?

you know why? Solomon wanted to be a good ruler over God's special people. He wanted to know the difference between right and wrong. Solomon chose wisdom because he wanted to do what was right.

God was very pleased. Asking for wisdom was the right choice. God gave Solomon great wisdom. Lick and stick the "WISDOM" sticker in the middle of the front of the crown. No one before Solomon had ever had so much wisdom and no one after Solomon would be as wise as he was. Then God said that because Solomon had not asked for lots of money or a powerful army, He was going to give him those things and more. Describe each sticker as you choose a child to lick and stick the sticker on King Solomon's crown. The only thing God told Solomon to do was to obey His laws and commands. If he did this, God would also give him a long life. Have a child place the sticker picturing an "old king" on the crown.

Solomon became known as the wisest man in the world. He helped people solve their problems by telling them the right things to do. He even taught the people about plants, animals, birds, bugs, and fish. People came from all over the world to listen to Solomon's wisdom. God kept His promise. No man has ever been as wise as Solomon.

◆◆◆◆

APPLICATION—Choose to Do Right

You will need a construction-paper crown for each child, the stickers the children colored in Activity 2, and a stapler. **What did Solomon pray for?** He prayed for wisdom. **Was that a good choice? Who heard Solomon's prayer?** God did! **Who hears us when we pray?** God hears our prayers too.

Pass out the blank crowns and the stickers from Activity 2. Review the choices pictured on the stickers. Now let the children decorate their crowns with the stickers. Fit and staple each crown for each child. Gather the children wearing their crowns in a circle. Teach them the first verse of "Who Did Pray?" from

page 8 of this session. Then pray with the children asking God to help them make the right choices.

◆◆◆◆

BIBLE MEMORY—Crown Relay

You will need Solomon's crown used in the story. Place two chairs about ten feet apart. On one chair place the crown. Line up the children behind the other chair. (If you have a large group, set up two chairs and a crown for every group of ten children.) Help the children memorize the first sentence, "Never stop praying." Each child runs from the starting chair to the chair with the crown. The child picks up the crown and says, "Never stop praying." The child puts the crown back on the chair, returns to the starting chair and taps the next child in line.

Discuss what "never stop praying" means. Explain that it means to remember to pray always. It also means that you can pray anywhere and anytime. Ask the children to suggest times and places they can pray.

◆◆◆◆

ACTIVITY TIME

Do as many activities as time permits.

◆◆◆◆

Craft—Handy Prayer Chain

You will need a copy of the praying hands on page 282 for each child. Copy the praying hands on card stock if possible. Cut these out before class time. Provide crayons, glue, a stapler, and seven construction paper strips, 8" x 1", for each child.

Let the children color their praying hands. Demonstrate how to glue the days of the week onto the strips. Staple the Saturday* ring to the bottom of the hands. Then staple the other rings together in the correct order forming a chain. The rings should be stapled in order, so that the child can tear off a ring each day,

Unit 11
Lesson 46

Hezekiah Prays to Be Healed
(2 Kings 20:1-11)

Good King Hezekiah becomes very sick and is about to die. He prays and asks God to heal him. God hears Hezekiah's prayer, and he is healed.

Bible Words

"Never stop praying. Give thanks whatever happens" (1 Thessalonians 5:17, 18a).

Goals

Tell what Hezekiah prayed. (Please help me get well.)
Feel confident that God hears prayers.
Pray to ask God for healing.

◆◆◆◆

Activity 1—The Doctor Is In

Set up a pretend doctor's office. You will need a toy phone, chairs, bathroom scale, measuring tape, tongue depressors, flashlight, bandages, stethoscope, clipboards, pencils, and paper. Use an adult to play the doctor. The children can play the parts of the staff (nurses and receptionists) and the patients. **Let's pretend this area in our classroom is a doctor's office. Help me put all the things a doctor will need in the right place.** Step back and let the "experts" on the hows and whys of a doctor's office go to work. When everything is set up, assign roles and begin "seeing" patients. Weigh and measure the patients. Check for sore throats. Put bandages on cuts and scrapes. After a while, begin telling the children about sick King Hezekiah. **The Bible tells about a good king named Hezekiah. One day King Hezekiah became very sick. He was so sick he

---

Who Did Pray?
(Tune: "This Is the Day")

Who did pray? Who did pray?
For w-is-dom. For w-is-dom.
(Repeat first two lines.)
Solomon prayed for w-is-dom.
Solomon prayed for w-is-dom.
Who did pray? Who did pray?
For w-is-dom.

Who did pray? Who did pray?
When he was sick. When he was sick.
(Repeat first two lines.)
Hezekiah prayed when he was sick.
Hezekiah prayed when he was sick.
Who did pray? Who did pray?
When he was sick.

Who did pray? Who did pray?
When he was sorry. When he was sorry.
(Repeat first two lines.)
Manasseh prayed when he was sorry.
Manasseh prayed when he was sorry.
Who did pray? Who did pray?
When he was sorry.

Who did pray? Who did pray?
When he was thankful. When he was thankful.
(Repeat first two lines.)
Jehoshaphat prayed when he was thankful.
Jehoshaphat prayed when he was thankful.
Who did pray? Who did pray?
When he was thankful.

269

thought he was going to die. Hezekiah couldn't go to a doctor like you do when you are sick. Instead, a messenger from God came to see Hezekiah. The messenger's name was Isaiah. At Bible story time, we will hear the message that God gave Isaiah for King Hezekiah. Now let's pretend that one of you is King Hezekiah. How would you feel if no doctor could make you well?

◆◆◆◆

ACTIVITY 2—Time for Prayer

You will need paper plates, poster board, scissors, markers or crayons, and paper fasteners. Before class, cut out a pair of clock hands (long and short hand) for each child. Print "Time to Pray" on each paper plate. If you have younger children in your class, also print the numbers on each paper plate to make the clock face. Make a sample clock.

Give each child a paper plate. Show the children the sample clock you made. Help them print the numbers on their paper plates to make a clock. Help as needed. Then help the children attach the hands to the clock with paper fasteners. Demonstrate how to turn the hands to show the time. Help them use their clocks to show familiar times of the day. (Wake up at 7:00, lunch at 12:00, naptime at 1:00, playtime at 3:00, bedtime at 8:00, etc.)

Hold up the sample clock. **Our clocks say, "Time to Pray." Let's say that together. Today's Bible story is about a good king who took time to pray. The good king's name was Hezekiah. Let's say that name together.**

◆◆◆◆

BIBLE TIME—Hezekiah Prays When He Is Sick

You will need the puppets of Hezekiah and Isaiah on page 283 and two paper lunch bags. Color and assemble the puppets. Place the puppets on your hands and hide them behind you. **After King Solomon there were many kings that ruled over God's people. Some worshiped God and were good kings.**

2 Unit 11

Discuss with the children what they eat when they are sick. Pursue in detail if a child says he eats soup. Before eating, ask a child to thank God for the healthy snack.

◆◆◆◆

Game—Shadow Tag

You will need bright sunlight to make shadows to play this game. If there is no sun to make shadows, use a spotlight (i.e., bright lamp without lampshade).

Choose a child to be "the 'germs' that made Hezekiah sick" and another child to be "Isaiah." The rest of the children are "Hezekiah" and they are to keep their "shadows" from being stepped on by "germs." When "germs" steps on a child's shadow, the child must stop and freeze with hands folded in prayer. The frozen child is "sick" and must wait for "Isaiah" to come and tag her. Once the child is tagged, she is "well" and can run again.

◆◆◆◆

WRAP-UP—Shadow Copies

Divide the children into pairs. Send each pair to an area of the room that needs to be cleaned and straightened. When they return after completing their job, gather the children still in pairs around you as you sing verses one and two of "Who Did Pray?"

Have the pairs of children face each other. Tell one partner to act out something that Hezekiah did in the story. (Felt sick, cried, prayed.) Have the other partner copy as if he were the person's shadow. Now that partner should act out something Isaiah did in the story. (Told a sad message from God, told a happy message from God.) Have the other partner copy. Change partners and repeat. Do this as long as they are interested or until parents arrive.

270

Lesson 46 7

Some worshiped idols (false gods made of stone, wood, or metal) and were bad kings. This is a story about one of the good kings named Hezekiah.

Hezekiah became king when he was a young man. He trusted in God and did what was right. When he became king, there were many places in the land where people worshiped false gods. Hezekiah tore down the false gods and the places where the false gods were worshiped. God was pleased that Hezekiah obeyed all His commands. Many good things happened to Hezekiah, but one day King Hezekiah became very sick.

With one hand hold up the Hezekiah puppet.

Hezekiah: I am so sick. I don't think I will get well. I think I am going to die.

Teacher: God's messenger, Isaiah, came to see King Hezekiah.

With the other hand, hold up the Isaiah puppet.

Isaiah: **God has sent me to tell you that you will not get well. You need to give orders to all those who will take over your kingdom. You are going to die from this sickness.** Isaiah exits.

Teacher: Hezekiah did not want to die. He wanted to get well, so he prayed.

Hezekiah: (Bow his head.) Dear God, Please help me get well. I have always obeyed You. I have done everything you said was right. Amen.

Teacher: Hezekiah was so upset he cried very loudly.

Hezekiah: (Make loud crying sounds.) I don't want to die! (Cry some more.)

Teacher: As Isaiah was about to leave the king's home, God spoke to him again. He told Isaiah to go back to Hezekiah and gave Isaiah another message. This time the message was good news! Isaiah puppet returns.

Isaiah: **Hezekiah, God has heard your prayer and seen your tears. In three days He is going to heal you. You will live for fifteen more years. God also said He is going to save you and Jerusalem from your enemy.**

Lesson 46

3

---

to the next person who says the second word. Continue around the circle. Change directions and go around the circle again. The teacher should always say the book, chapter, and verse each time the verse is said. Do not expect the children to say this part yet.

Hezekiah didn't stop praying when he was sick. Even when Isaiah told him he was going to die, he still prayed. We should always pray too.

◆◆◆◆◆

Activity Time

Do as many activities as time permits.

Craft—Prayer Reminders

You will need copies of the wristbands on page 284, crayons or markers, tape, scissors, and clear adhesive-backed paper. Before the session, cut out a set of wristbands for each child.

Let the children color their wristbands. **Whom do you know that is sick?** If the children don't know anyone, have names of sick people from your church office ready. Write the person's name on the child's wristband. Write the child's name on the sick person's wristband. Then place the wristbands on a large piece of clear, adhesive-backed paper and place another sheet of the paper on top. Cut out the wristbands. Tape each child's wristband to his wrist. Wearing this wristband will remind you to pray for the person while he or she is sick. **Who will hear our prayers? Yes, God will. He always listens to us pray.**

Ask children to give their other wristband to the person for whom they are praying. (Collect the ones whose names came from the office. Make sure those get delivered.) Lead the children in a general prayer for all who are sick. They will pray in detail before they go home.

Snack—Get-well Snack

Provide warm chicken noodle soup, crackers, and water to drink. You will need bowls, spoons, napkins, and cups.

Unit 11

271

6

Teacher: Then Isaiah took some figs (soft fruit that grows on trees) and smashed them so they looked like paste. He put this paste on the sore that was making Hezekiah so sick. Hezekiah wanted to know for sure if God was going to heal him. Listen to what he asked Isaiah.

Hezekiah: Isaiah, I want God to do something special so I will know He is going to make me well.

Isaiah: You can trust God to do what He says. Tell me, do you want the shadow on the steps to move forward ten steps or do you want the shadow to move back ten steps? (Verse 11 refers to the "stairway of Ahaz." This was a way to tell time using the shadow on steps. It was similar to a sundial.)

Hezekiah: The shadow on the steps always goes forward. That's easy! If God is really going to heal me, I want the shadow to move backward ten steps.

Teacher: Hezekiah knew that only God could move the step's shadow backwards. So Isaiah talks to God. Move the Isaiah puppet so that he is looking up.

Isaiah: God, Hezekiah wants to know if You are really going to heal him in three days. He wants You to prove it by making the shadow on the steps move backward ten steps.

Teacher: What do you think happened? Yes, God did make the shadow move backward ten steps. As the shadow moved backwards, so did the time of day go backwards. Only God could do that! God also answered Hezekiah's prayer. He healed Hezekiah. Hezekiah lived fifteen more years and ruled as the king over God's people.

◆◆◆◆

APPLICATION—Time to Pray

You will need a clock with movable hands. The children will also need the clocks they made in Activity 2. Help them use their clocks to copy the time shown on your clock.

NOTE: Ask the children who completed their prayer chains to share with the group and offer a small prize, such as gum or a book of stickers, to each one. See the craft from lesson 45 for

4 Unit 11

---

details on the prayer chain.

God wants us to be like Hezekiah. He wants us to pray. Hezekiah prayed when he was sick. Do you pray when you are sick? Do you pray when someone you know is sick? Discuss this and let the children tell about their experiences.

When Hezekiah was sick, he did not go to a special place to pray. He prayed right where he was. He was very sick, so he prayed right then. A wonderful thing happened! God heard his prayer and answered him.

God used the shadow made by the sun to prove He had the power to heal Hezekiah. God moved time backwards. No one but God could do that. Today we don't use a shadow to tell time. We use clocks, like this one. Show the clock. This is the way the hands on the clock move. Demonstrate moving the hands forward.

Let's think about different times in the day that we can pray. Set your clock at 7:00. **It is seven o'clock in the morning. Some of us wake up at this time. Is this a good time to pray? What could you pray for when you wake up?** Continue showing times of day and discuss the content of prayers at those times.

Do you think there is any time of day or night that you can't pray? No, God hears every prayer anytime. He hears prayers at night. He hears prayers during the daytime. Teach the second verse of "Who Did Pray?" from page 8 of this session.

◆◆◆◆

BIBLE MEMORY—Pass the Pillow

You will need an old blanket, sleeping bag, or old comforter. You will also need a small sofa pillow.

Spread out the blanket on the floor. Have the children sit in a circle on it. Tell them to pretend they are in bed just like they would be if they were sick. Review the first sentence of the Bible verse that was taught in the last lesson. Then teach the second sentence. Give the small pillow to one child and ask her to say the first word of the Bible verse. Ask the child to pass the pillow

Lesson 46 5

Unit 11
Lesson 47

Manasseh Prays When He Is Sorry
(2 Chronicles 33:1-20)

King Manasseh did not obey God and did many bad things. One day he prayed and told God he was sorry. God heard Manasseh's prayer and forgave him.

Bible Words

"Never stop praying. Give thanks whatever happens" (1 Thessalonians 5:17, 18a).

Goals

Tell what Manasseh prayed. (I'm sorry for what I have done.)
Feel confident that God hears prayers.
Pray to tell God you are sorry.

◆◆◆◆

Activity 1—Choices: Bad Ones! Good Ones!

You will need the following props: two paper cups, a bell, dishes, books, and toy cars.

Use these four negative situations to help the children think about good choices. The children can act these out or you can ask some adults or teens to do the acting. They should use the props provided to help them act out the situations.

1. Austin and Nathan are sitting next to each other at snack time. Austin drinks his juice. His empty cup rolls off the table. Nathan sees the cup on the floor and smashes it with his foot.

2. The teacher rings a bell. It is time to put the toys away. Libby and Ashley have been playing in the Home Living Center. Libby starts putting the dishes away. Ashley walks over to the

---

made during Application. Lead children in a prayer, asking them to silently tell God they are sorry. They can use their drawings to help them think about what to pray. Close by singing the first three verses of "Who Did Pray?"

Until parents arrive, do an activity with the Rocking Faces made during the Craft time. Describe a situation in which a child has made a wrong choice or a right choice. Ask the children to decide if the face on the person in the situation is happy or sad and use their Rocking Faces to show how the person feels.

Who Did Pray?
(Tune: "This Is the Day")

Who did pray? Who did pray?
For w-is-dom. For w-is-dom.
(Repeat first two lines.)
Solomon prayed for w-is-dom.
Solomon prayed for w-is-dom.
Who did pray? Who did pray?
For w-is-dom.

Who did pray? Who did pray?
When he was sick. When he was sick.
(Repeat first two lines.)
Hezekiah prayed when he was sick.
Hezekiah prayed when he was sick.
Who did pray? Who did pray?
When he was sick.

Who did pray? Who did pray?
When he was sorry. When he was sorry.
(Repeat first two lines.)
Manasseh prayed when he was sorry.
Manasseh prayed when he was sorry.
Who did pray? Who did pray?
When he was sorry.

Book Center to look at books.

3. Kyle and Cody are playing with the toy cars. The boys are arguing over one particular car.

4. Jessica and Kimberly are lining up to go to the playground. The teacher asks Kimberly to be the line leader, but Jessica wants to be the leader. She runs to the front of the line before Kimberly gets there.

After each role play, ask: "What would have been a good choice?" Have the same people act out the role play again using the better choice. Discuss how good choices make you feel. Discuss how bad choices make you feel. **Today's Bible story is about a king who made bad choices. One day he decided to pray. He asked God to forgive him. What do you think God did? God will forgive you when you say you are sorry too.**

♦♦♦♦

ACTIVITY 2—Get Ready to Worship

You will need a small area for a worship center with a table in it and the following items to put on the table: a Bible, a seasonal decoration from nature, a picture of Jesus and/or a cross, and a tablecloth. Before class, place the items for the table in a bag.

Gather the children around the bag. **What is worship?** Showing God how special He is to us. We can worship by singing, reading the Bible, praying, giving an offering. **Where can we worship?** Usually we think about worshiping in a church building, but we can worship anywhere! **When can we worship?** We can worship on Sundays and we can worship any time or any day.

Point to the bag of items and tell children that it contains things they can use to help them worship. Tell them that they will use the items to make a place to worship in the classroom.

Take the children to the worship area and let them help set up the area using the items from the bag. They might enjoy adding their own ideas too.

Today's Bible story is about a king who chose to worship false gods instead of the Lord God. Do you know what a false

becomes a frown. First, ask the children to tell about things that make them smile and things that make them frown. Next, ask the children to tell about choices that make them smile and choices that make them frown. Finally, ask them to show how God's face looks when they say they are sorry for making a wrong choice. Pray and ask God's help in making good choices.

♦♦♦♦

Game—What's Your Attitude?

You will need two tapes of music. One should be happy and lively. The other needs to be sad or slow. Provide a tape player. If possible, use a dual cassette player to make switching the music easier.

Gather the children in an open space so they have room to move around as the music plays. Ask the children to listen carefully to the music and move the way the music makes them feel. At first, leave the same music on for a length of time. It may take the children a while to move to the tempo of the music. As they get better at moving to the tempo of the music, switch the music tapes a little faster. When they get tired of the change in tempos, stop the music and let them sit on the floor to rest. **How did the happy music make you feel? How did the sad, slower music make you feel?** This music reminds me of choices that we make. Good choices make me feel happy like I feel when I hear happy music. Wrong choices make me feel sad like I feel when I hear sad music. God wants us to make good choices. If we do make wrong choices, what should we say to God? Yes, we should say we are sorry. That's what King Manasseh did when he made a wrong choice.

♦♦♦♦

WRAP-UP—I'm Sorry Prayers

You will need the drawings from Application.

Ask children to choose an area of the classroom to clean up. Compliment them on making a good choice and send them to do their jobs.

Gather the children around you and give them their drawings

god is? A false god is a statue made of wood, stone, or metal. God wants us to worship Him, because He alone is the true God.

BIBLE TIME—Manasseh Prays "I'm Sorry"

You will need a Rocking Face made from the Craft project in today's lesson, markers, scissors, yarn, and glue. Before class, add a crown on both sides of the Rocking Face. Decorate both sides of the crown. Add a mustache and beard made of yarn to each side of the face.

Briefly review the prayers of Solomon and Hezekiah.

When King Hezekiah died, his twelve-year-old son, Manasseh, became the next king. King Manasseh ruled for a very long time—55 years. Show the sad face side. Set the folded paper plate on a table next to you. If a table is not available, set the visual on a book placed on your lap. Keep the attention of the children by occasionally tapping the side of the crown to make the face rock back and forth. **Most of that time Manasseh did what God said was wrong. Remember how King Hezekiah tore down places where people worshiped false gods? Well, his son did not obey or worship God. Instead, Manasseh built more places for the people to worship false gods. He even bowed down and worshiped the stars.**

All of these things were bad, Manasseh did something worse. He made a false god and put it in the temple. The temple had been built by King Solomon to honor God. It was a very special place. God was there! God was not pleased that a false god was worshiped in His temple.

Long before Manasseh's time, God had made a promise never to send His people away from their homeland. He said He would keep this promise as long as the people obeyed Him. But when King Manasseh put a false god in the temple and worshiped it, they disobeyed God.

God allowed the enemies of King Manasseh to capture him and take him away from Israel. Heavy chains were put around

Lesson 47

ACTIVITY TIME

Do as many activities as time permits.

Craft—Rocking Faces

You will need a copy of the happy and sad faces on page 284, 9" paper plates, scissors, markers or crayons, glue, yarn, and ribbon. Before the session, cut out the faces. Cut inside the black line so that the faces will not have an outline around them. Fold the paper plates in half.

Help the children glue a happy face on one side of the Rocking Face and a sad face on the other side. They can color the skin, the mouth, and the eyes. Cut and glue on pieces of yarn for hair. Use the ribbon to make bows for the girls to add to their hair.

Use your paper-plate face to show me how your face looks when you have made the wrong choice. How does your face look when you have made a good choice? How does your mother's face look when you have made a wrong choice? How does her face look when you have made a good choice? How does your friend's face look when you have been unkind to him? How does your friend's face look when you say you are sorry? When you say you are sorry, you please God. How do you think God's face looks when you say you are sorry?

Snack—Upside-down Snack

You will need round (2-3 inches in diameter) sugar cookies, a container of ready-made frosting, plastic knives, raisins for eyes, thin rope candy for mouth, and candy corn for nose.

Show the children how to frost their cookies. Then show them how to put the raisin eyes in place. Then put the candy corn nose between the eyes. Last, give each child two small pieces of the rope candy for the mouth. One piece goes below the nose in the shape of a smile. The other goes above the nose in the shape of a smile.

Show the children how to turn the cookie around so the smile

Unit 11

his arms. Manasseh was very sad and miserable. He thought about God. He decided to pray. He begged God to help him. He was sorry he had done so many bad things. God heard Manasseh's prayer.

God let Manasseh return to Jerusalem. He became king of God's people again. When these good things happened, Manasseh knew that the Lord God was the only true God. Turn the Rocking Face to the smiling side.

Now King Manasseh had a lot of work to do in God's city. First he rebuilt part of the wall around the city. This wall was used to keep out the enemy. He also made the wall higher. A higher wall would also make it hard for the enemy to try to capture God's city.

The best thing King Manasseh did was to tear down the places where the false gods were worshiped. He also took the false god out of God's temple. Then he and the people worshiped the one true and living God.

◆◆◆◆◆

APPLICATION—Let's Worship God

You will need drawing paper, crayons or colored pencils, and a cassette of worship songs and cassette player (optional).

Was God pleased when King Manasseh worshiped the false gods? Of course not! God was only pleased when Manasseh chose to tear down the places where the false gods were worshiped. God was very pleased when Manasseh said he was sorry. When you do something wrong, what should you do that would please God? Yes, you should tell God you are sorry for doing the wrong thing.

Let's be like Manasseh after he said he was sorry. Follow me to the worship area. Lead children to the worship area they prepared during Activity 2. Discuss worshiping only God. Discuss ways to worship God. You and your helpers should plan and participate in this lesson's worship time. In the next lesson the children will do the planning and participating. Following is a suggested worship time.

Sing verse 3 of "Who Did Pray?" from page 8 of this session and other worship songs that your children enjoy. Read 2 Chronicles 33:10-13 slowly several times. Give children drawing paper and ask them to draw a picture of what they hear described in the verses.

Ask children to turn their papers over and draw a picture of themselves telling God they are sorry, or a picture of a something they did that they need to tell God they are sorry for. Remind them of the situations from Activity 1 if they need guidance.

Keep the children's papers to use during Wrap-up.

◆◆◆◆◆

BIBLE MEMORY—Trading Cards

You will need copies of the trading card on page 285 on card stock, scissors, and markers or crayons. Before the session, cut out a card for each child.

During the Bible Time, have a helper hide a card for each child in a designated area. Do not make them hard to find. When you are ready to begin this activity, show the children one of the cards. Tell them that you have "lost" all the trading cards somewhere in the room. There is one card for each child. When a child finds a trading card, he is to bring it to you and say the Bible verse from memory. When you say "Go!", each child can begin looking for a missing card. After the child has found a card and said the verse, send him to a table to color the card. Give help as needed so that everyone finds a trading card. When everyone has found a card, ask the children if they have ever been lost. Let them share their experiences.

Do you remember how good it felt when your family found you? Do you remember how good it felt to see the faces of people you loved? I think King Manasseh might have felt that way when he got to go back home to Jerusalem after he told God he was sorry. I'm sure it felt good to see his city, his home, and friends again.

276

Unit 11
Lesson 48

Jehoshaphat Prays When He Is Thankful
(2 Chronicles 20:1-21, 30)

King Jehoshaphat was afraid of his enemies. He gathered all of the people and they prayed for God to keep them safe. The battle was won by singing praises!

Bible Words

"Never stop praying. Give thanks whatever happens" (1 Thessalonians 5:17, 18a).

Goals

Tell what Jehoshaphat prayed. (Thank you.)
Feel confident that God hears prayers.
Pray to thank God.

◆◆◆◆

Activity 1—Prayer Stickers

You will need copies of page 286, colored construction paper, scissors, markers or crayons, and a stapler.

Before class, prepare a booklet for each child by cutting a sheet of construction paper in half. Fold and assemble the two halves like a book and staple them together. Coat the backs of the stickers on the copies of page 286 with a mixture of one part vinegar, two parts white glue, and a few drops of peppermint extract. Make a sample book to show the children. If possible, enlarge the stickers on your sample to make them easier for the children to see.

Give each child a booklet and a copy of page 286 and ask them to cut out the stickers on the page. Show them how to lick

---

Who Did Pray?
(Tune: "This Is the Day")

Who did pray? Who did pray?
For w-is-dom. For w-is-dom.
(Repeat first two lines.)
Solomon prayed for w-is-dom.
Solomon prayed for w-is-dom.
Who did pray? Who did pray?
For w-is-dom.

Who did pray? Who did pray?
When he was sick. When he was sick.
(Repeat first two lines.)
Hezekiah prayed when he was sick.
Hezekiah prayed when he was sick.
Who did pray? Who did pray?
When he was sick.

Who did pray? Who did pray?
When he was sorry. When he was sorry.
(Repeat first two lines.)
Manasseh prayed when he was sorry.
Manasseh prayed when he was sorry.
Who did pray? Who did pray?
When he was sorry.

Who did pray? Who did pray?
When he was thankful. When he was thankful.
(Repeat first two lines.)
Jehoshaphat prayed when he was thankful.
Jehoshaphat prayed when he was thankful.
Who did pray? Who did pray?
When he was thankful.

and stick the words "God Hears Our Prayers" on the cover of the booklet. As you pass out each sticker, review the story about that king. **Here is King Solomon. What did he pray for? Why did he pray for wisdom? What happened after he prayed for wisdom?** Do the same with each king. Save the "Jehoshaphat" sticker for the end of the Bible story.

If there is time, the children may begin coloring their booklets. There will be time during the Wrap-up for more coloring.

◆◆◆◆

ACTIVITY 2—Worship Preparation

If you did not prepare the worship center in lesson 47, you will need to do it during this time. See lesson 47, Activity 2 for directions. Provide a cassette player and cassettes of worship songs in addition to the items needed to set up a worship center.

Today we will go again to our worship center after the Bible story. The last time the teachers were the worship leaders. Today some of you will be the worship leaders. Raise your hand if you have an idea for a song to sing during worship time. Make a list of songs and song leaders. This would be a good time to teach the fourth verse of "Who Did Pray?" from page 8 of this session. **What Bible verses can we read during worship?** Review past memory verses that the children can "read" from the Bible. **Would someone like to pray during our worship time?** Make a list of children who want to pray. If possible, use all the children who volunteer. If you have a lot of children, use some to form a choir. Form groups to recite Bible verses. Have your plan ready to use during the Application activity.

◆◆◆◆

BIBLE TIME—Jehoshaphat's Thank-you Prayer

You will need the sample booklet used in Activity 1, the sticker of Jehoshaphat, a blank cassette, and a cassette player. You will also need two male voices to make a tape recording of

— fold —

WRAP-UP—Four Ways to Pray

Line the children up. March around the room like King Jehoshaphat's soldiers. As you pass an area that needs to be cleaned up, assign some soldiers to stay there and straighten it up. Tell them you will be back to pick them up. Continue until everyone has a job. Then march back around the room picking up all the soldiers.

Gather the children around you for a closing prayer. Then pass out the glasses and the booklets. Let the children color their booklets while they wait for their parents to pick them up. Go around to each child and ask her about the different kings. Clear up any parts of the stories that she has confused. **Who hears and answers your prayers? Is there someone who is sick that you can pray for? Do you need to tell God you are sorry? What can you thank God for?** If possible, pray individually with the children.

Leaders' Evaluation

	Great!	OK!	More!	Oops!	Suggestions
Activity 1					
Activity 2					
Bible Time					
Application					
Bible Memory					
Craft					
Snack					
Game					
Wrap-up					

Jehoshaphat's prayer and Jahaziel's prophecy, printed in the Bible story below. Before class, have the two voices record their parts on the cassette. Jehoshaphat should speak first, followed by a short pause, and then Jahaziel. Cue the cassette to Jehoshaphat's prayer and have it ready to play when mentioned during the Bible story below.

Hold up the enlarged sample booklet made in Activity 1. As you point to each king, ask the children to tell the king's name and what he prayed for.

Now I am going to add King Jehoshaphat to my booklet. After you add Jehoshaphat to your booklet, show his picture as you tell the story.

Jehoshaphat was one of the best kings that ruled over God's people. One of the good things he did was to send special teachers to all of the towns in his kingdom. These teachers taught the people about God (2 Chronicles 17:7-9). They taught everyone how important it was to obey God and to trust Him when they needed help.

One day King Jehoshaphat needed God's help. Three powerful armies were on their way to fight Jehoshaphat's army. The king asked everyone in his kingdom to come to Jerusalem to pray. The news spread quickly. All of the men, women, and children came to Jerusalem. They even brought their babies with them.

King Jehoshaphat and all the people gathered in the temple. Then the king began to pray. Play the recording of Jehoshaphat's prayer as follows. "O God, You are the only God. You are powerful and mighty. No one is stronger than You. You gave us this land. Now our enemies are coming to take it away. We are standing here in this temple because we know You are here. Please help us and save us from our enemies. We do not know what to do, but we will keep our eyes on You." Turn off the cassette player.

When Jehoshaphat finished his prayer, another man, named **Jahaziel,** stood up to speak. He said (Play the next recording.), "God says, 'Don't be afraid of these large armies. You will not fight them. God will fight this battle! You are to stand and be

Lesson 48

3

---

sing? When is it a good time to read the Bible? I'm glad that you know how to "keep your eyes on God."

Snack—Sack Lunches

Prepare a small sack lunch for each child. Put small quantities in the sacks. Suggestions follow: one half of a peanut butter and jelly sandwich, cookies, slices of fruit, and juice boxes. Don't forget the napkins.

Did you know that when a soldier goes to war he has to take a backpack full of things he will need? Sometimes he has to take his sleeping bag. He always has to take food with him. There isn't time to go home and eat! Let's pretend we are King Jehoshaphat's soldiers. Here are our lunches. Let's carry our lunches until we can find a good spot to sit down and eat. Find a place where the children can sit on the floor and eat their sack lunches. Sing the song the singers sang during the battle. "Thank the Lord. His love never stops." (Tune: "God Is So Good.") Pray. While the children are eating, review what happened during the battle with the enemy.

Game—Who's Giving Thanks?

You will need a blindfold.

Before you play this game, review the song that the singers sang during the battle that the children learned during Bible Time. Sing it several times.

King Jehoshaphat knew that God was going to be with his army during the battle with his enemies. The singers sang a song that thanked God. We should always thank God too.

Have the children stand and form a circle. Choose one child to be blindfolded. This child must sit in the center of the circle. The standing children must walk slowly around the circle until the blindfolded child says, "Stop." The blindfolded child points to someone. That child must say or sing, "Thank the Lord. His love never stops." (If the child needs help, whisper the words in her ear, so that your voice is not heard by others.) Give the blindfolded child three chances to name the child who is singing or saying the song. Correct or not, the two children trade places.

Unit 11

strong. God is with you!" Turn off the cassette player. When they heard this, everyone bowed down and worshiped God. Then some people stood and praised God with loud voices. They were ready to go into battle and fight their enemies! No one was afraid!

The next morning King Jehoshaphat got his army ready. The king also chose some men to be singers. He told them, "Have faith in God. He will help you stand strong." King Jehoshaphat had the singers march in front of the soldiers. The singers sang praises to God. They sang a special song, "Thank the Lord. His love never stops." Pause and teach the children to sing these words to the tune "God Is So Good."

God kept His promise to fight the enemy. None of King Jehoshaphat's soldiers had to fight. The enemies fought each other! While the enemies were fighting each other, the king's singers kept singing. Have the children stand and sing the special song again. After that battle, King Jehoshaphat and God's people lived in peace. All of the other kings were afraid to fight against them.

Pass out the booklets made in Activity 1. Give each child a sticker of King Jehoshaphat to lick and stick in their booklets. The booklets can be colored during Wrap-up.

◆◆◆◆

APPLICATION—Let's Worship

Hold up the picture of Jehoshaphat again. **King Jehoshaphat prayed and thanked God for always helping His people. They "kept their eyes on God" and God kept them safe from their enemies. "Keeping our eyes on God" means to think about God every day and pray every day. How can we "keep our eyes on God"? Let's go to our worship center so we can "keep our eyes on God."**

Take the children to the worship center. Follow the plan the children made during Activity 2.

4 Unit 11

BIBLE MEMORY—1 Thessalonians 5:17 and 18a

This is the last time to teach this verse. Saying the name of the book, chapter, and verse may be too difficult for your children. However, you may want to try teaching this to kindergartners. They may enjoy the challenge!

Use the following motions to say the verse:

Never (Shake your head "no.")
stop (Raise your right hand as if saying "stop.")
praying. (Fold hands in prayer.)
Give (Place open hands at waist and then "give.")
thanks (Fold hands in prayer.)
whatever (Hold hands palms up; raise shoulders.)
happens. (Repeat the last motion.)

This verse reminds us to be like King Jehoshaphat and always "keep our eyes on God." Remember to tell God thanks—you just like King Jehoshaphat did.

◆◆◆◆

ACTIVITY TIME

Do as many activities as time permits.

◆◆◆◆

Craft—"Keep Your Eyes on God" Glasses

You will need copies of the glasses on page 285 on card stock, scissors, glue, colored cellophane, and crayons or markers. Cut out the glasses before class. Fold the arms and glue them onto the frames. Cut pieces of colored cellophane to fit the lenses of the glasses.

Give each child a pair of glasses to color. Use light colors so the words "Keep Your Eyes on God" can be seen. Then help the children glue colored cellophane behind the lenses of their glasses.

Help the children put on their glasses. **When we pray or sing praises or read the Bible, we are "keeping our eyes on God." Who can tell us a good time to pray? When is it a good time to**

Lesson 48 5

280

WISDOM

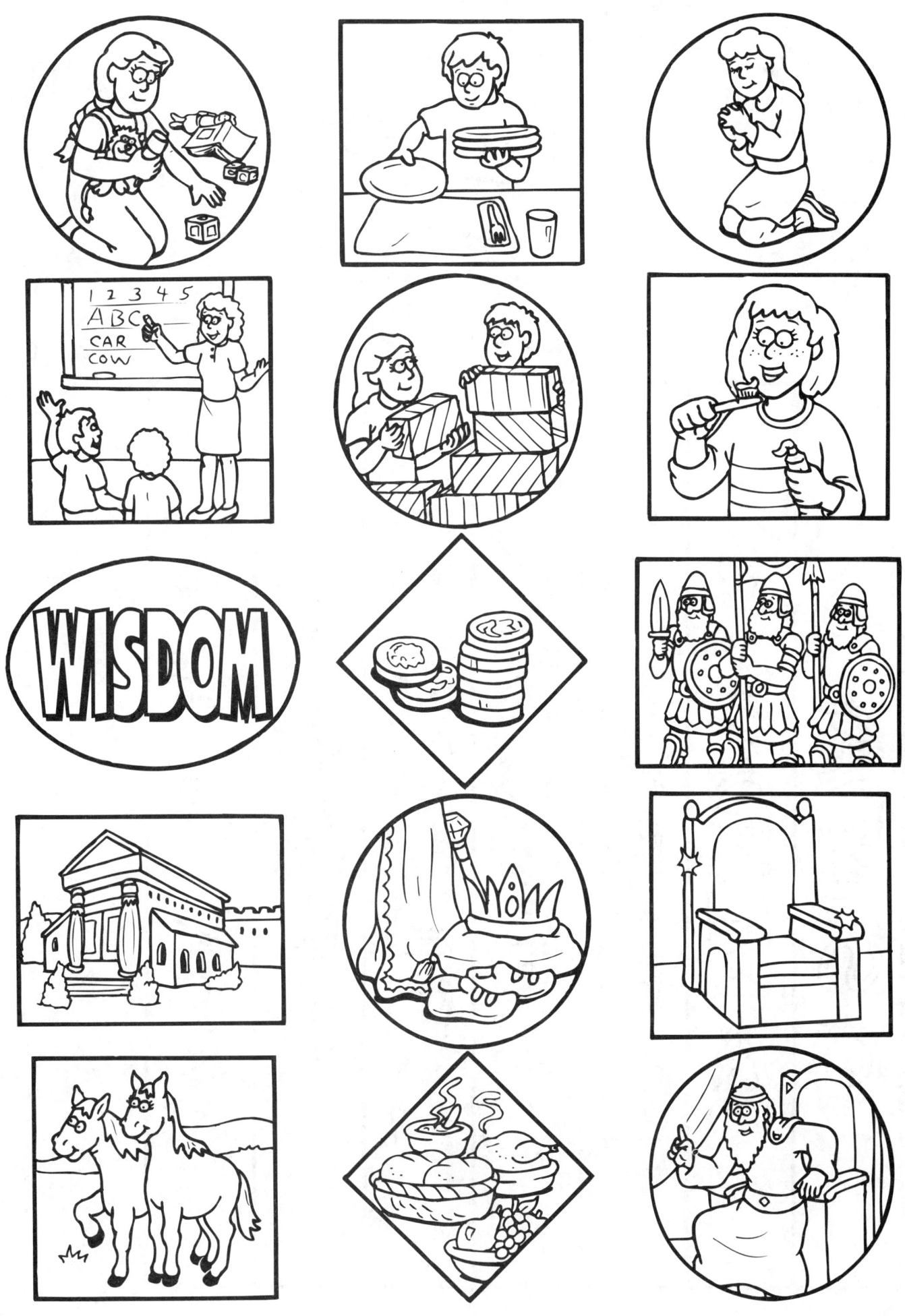

SUNDAY
MONDAY
TUESDAY
WEDNESDAY
THURSDAY
FRIDAY
SATURDAY

283

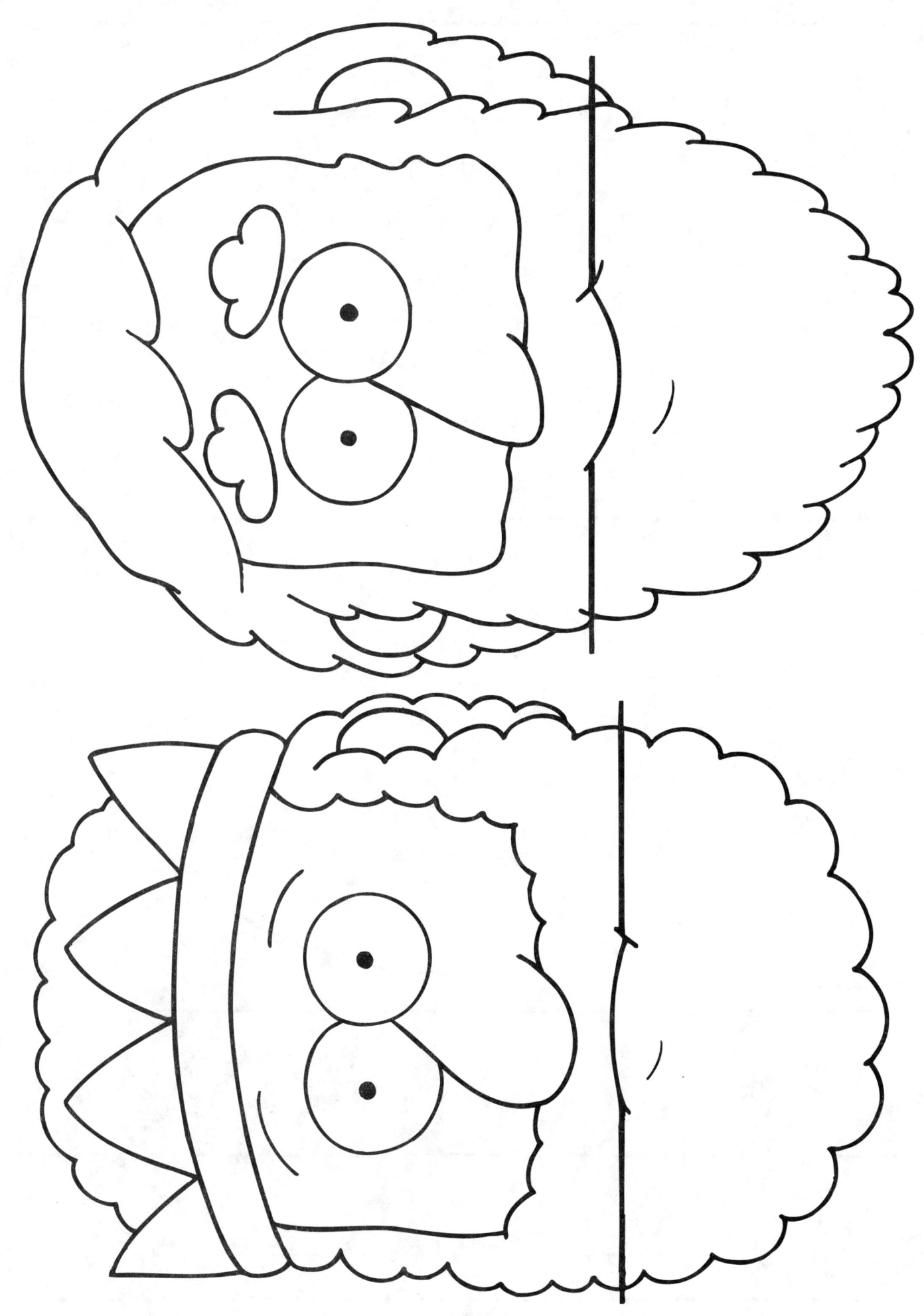

_____ is praying for you.

_____ is praying for _____

284

Never stop praying. Give thanks whatever happens.

1 Thessalonians 5:17, 18

Keep your eyes on God

God Hears Our Prayers

"Please help me do right."

"Please help me get well."

"I'm sorry for what I've done."

"Thank you, God."

Unit 12
Lessons 49-52

Do What Is Right

◆◆◆◆◆

By the end of this unit, the children and leaders will . . .
Know Name Bible people who made right choices.
Feel Desire to choose right.
Do Choose to do what is right.

Unit Bible Words for Memory
"Do what is right and good in the Lord's sight" (Deuteronomy 6:18, NIV).

◆◆◆◆◆

Unit Lessons

Lesson 49
Ezra and the People Learn God's Word
Nehemiah 8:1-12
Children will hear how the people listened all day as Ezra read God's Word.

Lesson 50
Josiah and the People Obey God's Word
2 Kings 22:1-13; 23:1-3, 21-23
Children will learn how a scroll of God's Word was found in the temple. When King Josiah and the people heard God's Word, they promised to obey.

Lesson 51
Micaiah Tells the Truth
1 Kings 22:1-37
Children will discover how Micaiah told the truth to King Ahab, even when 400 other false prophets lied.

Lesson 52
Samuel Chooses to Do Right All His Life
1 Samuel 2:18, 21, 26; 3:1-10, 19, 20; 4:1a; 7:15-17
Children will hear how Samuel chose to obey God as a little boy. He continued to obey when he grew up and became God's prophet.

◆◆◆◆◆

Why Teach This Unit to Four-Year-Olds—Six-Year-Olds?

Children can make choices that are pleasing to God, and this unit of lessons teaches four ways that children can obey and do right. They can listen to God's Word at home and at church like Ezra and the people. They can obey what God says like Josiah and the people. They can tell the truth, even when it is hard, like Micaiah. And they can do right as children, just like Samuel did.

◆◆◆◆◆

Bible Time Line

The stories for this unit are pictured on the time line, pages 312-314. The time line will be used throughout all units in this book.

Provide the time-line page for children who arrive early, or plan time at the end of the Bible story during each session for children to color the time line and look for the hidden pictures.

See page 6 in this book for further instructions on using the time line and for suggested time-line projects.

Unit 12

Materials

All Lessons
- a Bible
- markers, colored pencils, crayons
- white paper, construction paper, poster board
- tape, masking tape
- Plasti-Tak
- glue
- scissors
- a stapler
- paper hole punch
- yarn or string

Lesson 49
interlocking blocks, people, furniture, cars, and other building items

large blocks or carpet pieces, a step stool, and a storybook

items or pictures of items that might make children happy, such as snacks, movie videos, toys, hugging moms and dads, puppies or kittens, playground equipment, and so on

18" lengths of ribbon or yarn, and two empty toilet-paper tubes for each child, cotton swabs, and watercolor paints

stickers

Lesson 50
empty half-gallon milk cartons (optional)

water in spray bottles, old socks and towels, feather dusters, carpet sweepers and other cleaning tools

blocks (at least one block for each child)

fruit roll snacks (narrow strips, such as Fruit by the Foot, by Betty Crocker) and clear adhesive paper

ingredients for play dough (1 cup flour, 1/2 cup salt, 1 tsp cream of tartar, 1 cup water, 1 tbsp oil, food coloring, and peppermint extract), an electric skillet, and plastic bags

Lesson 51
several toy telephones, a cassette player, and a blank cassette

a cassette of familiar Bible songs

wire hangers, nylon hose, pom-poms

a basket or other container

Lesson 52
old socks or T-shirts, toothpaste, water, and small pieces of silver, such as silverware

large pieces of newsprint, tape measures, and rulers

a blanket and pillow

a cardboard box

all sizes and kinds of shoes: baby, child, tennis, tap, thong, adult boot, slipper, loafer, high heels, flats

several small cars

three hats, three big pairs of shoes, and three shirts or coats (If possible, choose sets of clothes, such as outfits for a nurse, a firefighter, a gardener, an airline pilot, a police officer, and so on.)

The Beginner's Bible™ Resources

The Beginner's Bible™ Old Testament GeoSafari Bible Pack, Standard Publishing, #14-24001, call 1-800-543-1353

The Beginner's Bible™ Bible Lessons GeoSafari Bible Pack, Standard Publishing, #14-24005, call 1-800-543-1353

Unit 12
Lesson 49

Ezra and the People Learn God's Word
(Nehemiah 8:1-12)

The people ask Ezra to read God's laws. They want to learn about God's Word. Nehemiah sees they are very sad because they have not been keeping God's Word, but he tells them to rejoice because now they are learning and this is a special day to God. They are to go home and celebrate.

Bible Words

"Do what is right and good in the Lord's sight" (Deuteronomy 6:18).

Goals

Tell who helped the people learn to do what is right.
Desire to choose right.
Choose to learn what is right.

◆◆◆◆◆

ACTIVITY 1—Listening Ears

You will need copies of the ears and pictures from page 305, scissors, 24" strips of construction paper or lengths of cash register tape, glue, tape, a stapler, and markers or crayons. If you have younger children in your class, cut out the ears and pictures before class.

Give each child a copy of page 305. Ask them to color and cut out the ears and pictures. Tape the ears to strips of construction paper or cash register tape to make a headband. Measure each headband to fit the child's head and staple it. Then ask children to glue the pictures on their headbands.

Gather 'Round, It's Bible Time
(Tune: "London Bridge")

Gather 'round, it's Bible time,
Bible time, Bible time;
Gather 'round, it's Bible time:
Time to learn.

The B-I-B-L-E

The B-I-B-L-E—
Yes, that's the book for me.
I stand alone on the Word of God,
The B-I-B-L-E.

I'll S-M-I-L-E
'cause God's Word teaches me.
I'll learn and listen every day.
I'll S-M-I-L-E.

Leaders' Evaluation

	Great!	OK!	More!	Oops!	Suggestions
Activity 1					
Activity 2					
Bible Time					
Application					
Bible Memory					
Craft					
Snack					
Game					
Wrap-up					

These pictures show us some Bible people who listened to what God says is right. **When are some times that we can listen and learn about what's right?** We listen to our teachers in Sunday school; we listen to our parents at home; we listen to God's Word when it is read. We will save our listening ears to wear during our Bible story.

◆◆◆◆

ACTIVITY 2—Church Building and Homes

You will need interlocking blocks, people, furniture, cars, and other building items.

Help the children use the blocks to build houses and churches. Add people, furniture and cars, and other items to complete the scene. **Where shall we put the baby cribs in our church? Can you build a slide for the playground? Let's put the sink and stove in the kitchen. Have you been to the church kitchen? Where does the choir sing in our church? Where will we put the kindergarten classroom?** Have children build their homes and talk about the people who live in them. **What do we do at home and church to learn about God and to do right?**

◆◆◆◆

BIBLE TIME—Ezra Reads God's Word

You will need large blocks or carpet pieces, a step stool, a storybook, a Bible, and a sample Bible-words scroll from the Craft time in this session. Before class, make a scroll, following the instructions in the Craft section of this lesson.

Have children help lay out blocks or carpet pieces to form a large square to sit in. Set the step stool in the center of the square. Sing "Gather 'Round, It's Bible Time" from page 8 of this session as children find a place to sit.

The people were gathered in the Jerusalem city square. We'll pretend this is our city square. They wanted Ezra to do something special. Help me pretend to call Ezra. I wonder what they wanted Ezra to do. Put on

Have children wear their Listening Ears as you tell them jobs they can do to clean up the room. Then have the children gather in a large group and praise them for using their listening ears. Give children their Bible-words scrolls and have them "read" the words. Then repeat the Bible-words rhythm learned in Bible Memory. Use a felt marker to write the names of who will help the child learn God's Word as they share with the class. **Who will read a Bible story to you? Who says prayers at your house? Has anyone helped you learn a Bible song or verse? Let's bow our heads and thank God for the people who will help us learn what is right. Dear God, thank You for the Bible. Thank You for families, friends and teachers that help us learn to do right.** Sing "The B-I-B-L-E" from page 8 of this session learned during Application.

Until parents arrive, help children practice finding things in their children's Bibles. Call out familiar Bible stories and have children try to find them in their Bibles. You may need to tell children if the story is found in the front of their Bibles (Old Testament) or the back of their Bibles (New Testament). Some familiar stories to include are: creation, Noah's ark, crossing of the Red Sea, David and Goliath, Daniel in the lions' den, Jesus' birth, Jesus calms a storm, Jesus feeds 5,000, Jesus heals a blind man, Jesus dies and comes back alive.

NOTE: Keep the Bible-words scroll to use in lesson 50. Keep the Listening Ears for use in lesson 51.

your listening ears as we find out what the people wanted Ezra to do.

"Ezra, Ezra," the people called to the preacher/priest. "I wonder what all those people want," thought Ezra the preacher/priest. Then he heard them ask for a very special thing. What do you think the people asked Ezra? Let's try to guess. Give several children an opportunity to answer. Give the following clues: hold up a storybook, Bible, scroll. **What do we do with books?** Look. Read. Listen. Yes, the people asked Ezra the preacher/priest to bring out God's Word. Ezra brought out the special scroll with God's Word written on it. Ezra climbed high up on a platform and began unrolling the scroll. Hold your scroll and climb up on the step stool. **What do you think all the people did when they saw Ezra open the scroll?** Give time for answers. To show they loved God and wanted to listen to God's Word, they all stood up. Can you all stand up? Ezra started reading early in the morning when the sun came up. Ezra kept reading. The people kept listening. Ezra kept reading until it was lunchtime and the people kept listening. They wanted to learn all about God's Word. As Ezra praised God, the people lifted their hands and said, "Amen, Amen." Have children repeat with you. Then they bowed down with their faces to the ground to show how much they loved God. Have children do so.

Then everyone sat down and the teachers/Levites helped them learn God's Word. As the people listened, they became sad. They felt so bad that they had not kept God's laws that they began to cry. "Stop crying," said Nehemiah the governor. "This is a special day to the Lord. You have listened and learned God's Word. Go home and celebrate. Be happy because you know God's Word and want to do it."

♦♦♦♦

APPLICATION—Be Happy!

You will need items or pictures of items that might make children happy, such as snacks, movie videos, toys, hugging moms

Lesson 49

Snack—Celebration Party

You will need colored cups, napkins, table covers, powdered lemonade, a pitcher, peanut butter, crackers, knives, and paper plates.

Let the children choose which job they will do to prepare their party. Some children can set the table with the table covers, cups, and napkins. Some children can measure, mix, and stir powdered lemonade. Another group will spread peanut butter on crackers.

What did Nehemiah tell the people? Stop crying and celebrate. He also told them to make sweet drinks and enjoy choice foods. They were to share their food with people who did not have any prepared. Name children and tell what job they choose. **Whom are you sharing with at your table, Tori? Jake, what job did you choose to help with?**

Ask for a volunteer to pray and thank God for the snack.

Game—Bring Out the Scroll

You will need the step stool and scroll used in Bible Time, and stickers.

Choose a child to hide the scroll while the other children bow down with their faces to the ground like the people did when they worshiped God. When the scroll is hidden, have the child stand on the stool and ask two or three children to, "Bring out the scroll." When the scroll is found, they will give it to "Ezra" and ask him to read it. Have all the children repeat the Bible words, "Do what is right and good in the Lord's sight. Deuteronomy 6:18." Choose a new Ezra and repeat until everyone has a turn to search. Place a Bible sticker on each child as he has a turn.

♦♦♦♦

WRAP-UP—Who Will Help You Learn?

You will need the Listening Ears made in Activity 1, the scrolls made during the Craft, and children's Bibles.

Unit 12

and dads, puppies or kittens, playground equipment, and so on; and a Bible.

I'm going to hold up some things that might make you happy. If it is something that makes you happy, I want you to give me a big smile! Hold up the items one at a time, and wait for the children's responses. Encourage them to share about favorite toys, pets, games, and other things that make them smile. At the end, hold up the Bible. **The people who listened to Ezra were glad to hear God's Word, because they knew obeying God's Word was the best way for them to be happy. Obeying God's Word makes us happy, too. In fact, God's Word is the best thing in the world to make us happy. We should all have big smiles on our faces for God's Word.** Sing "The B-I-B-L-E" from page 8 of this session. Teach children the words to the second verse, and ask them to sing it with big smiles on their faces.

When the children have learned the words to the verse, ask them to share some ways to learn about God's Word that they talked about in Activity 2. Sing verse 2 of the song, inserting ways the children name for the words "I'll learn and listen every day." An example follows:

I'll S-M-I-L-E
'cause God's Word teaches me.
When my Mom reads me Bible books,
I'll S-M-I-L-E.

Other phrases might include: I'll listen to my church teachers; I'll listen to my Mom and Dad; I'll pray to God every day; I'll read my Bible every day.

♦♦♦♦

BIBLE MEMORY—Rhythm Clap

You will need a Bible with Deuteronomy 6:18 highlighted and marked with a bookmark.

Help a volunteer help you find the highlighted verse in your Bible. Read the words to the children and ask them to say the words of the verse with you several times. When children are comfortable with the words of the verse, have them slap their legs and clap their hands with the words of the verse in the following rhythm:

Do what is right and good (slap, clap, clap, slap, clap, clap)
In the Lord's sight. (slap, clap, clap)
Deuteronomy 6:18. (clap, clap, clap, clap, slap, clap, clap)

If you have time, children may wish to create their own rhythm clap for the verse.

♦♦♦♦

ACTIVITY TIME

Do as many activities as time permits.

♦♦♦♦

Craft—Bible-words Scroll

You will need copies of the Bible-words scroll on page 306, blank paper, 18" lengths of ribbon or yarn, and two empty toilet-paper tubes for each child, tape, cotton swabs, and watercolor paints.

Before class, cut out the scrolls from the reproducible pages and cut extra lengths of blank paper to tape on either end of the scroll. The blank paper will be the part of the scroll that wraps around the toilet-paper tubes.

Give each child a scroll paper and help the children decorate the words of their scrolls with cotton swabs and watercolor paints.

As the scrolls dry, talk about the words on the scroll. **What do the words on our scrolls say?** Say the Bible words from Deuteronomy 6:18 aloud together. **How did Ezra do what is right and good? How can we do what is right and good like Ezra and the people?** We can listen to those who teach God's Word (our teachers and parents) and do what they say.

Give each child two toilet-paper tubes and help them tape them to each end of the scroll and roll it up. Help them tie their scrolls together with ribbon or yarn.

Unit 12
Lesson 50

Josiah and the People Obey God's Word
(2 Kings 22:1-13; 23:1-3, 21-23)

When King Josiah had the temple repaired, the workers found God's rules. King Josiah was sad because they had forgotten God's rules. He read God's rules to the people and the king and all the people promised to obey God's rules.

Bible Words

"Do what is right and good in the Lord's sight" (Deuteronomy 6:18).

Goals

Name the king who did right after he read God's rules.
Desire to choose right.
Choose to obey God's rules.

◆◆◆◆

ACTIVITY 1—Traffic Lights

You will need copies of page 307; scissors; black construction paper; glue or tape; red, yellow, and green markers; and empty half-gallon milk cartons (optional). If you wish to use milk cartons, cover them with black construction paper before class.

Give each child a copy of page 307 and a piece of black construction paper or a paper-covered milk carton. Ask the children to color the top light red, middle yellow, and the lower light green.

Traffic lights help us drive safely. What happens if people don't obey the lights? What do we do on the red light? Yellow? Green? Obeying traffic lights is very important. What words

— fold —

Gather 'Round, It's Bible Time
(Tune: "London Bridge")

Gather 'round, it's Bible time,
Bible time, Bible time;
Gather 'round, it's Bible time:
Time to learn.

The B-I-B-L-E

The B-I-B-L-E—
Yes, that's the book for me.
I stand alone on the Word of God,
The B-I-B-L-E.

I'll S-M-I-L-E
'cause God's Word teaches me.
I'll learn and listen every day.
I'll S-M-I-L-E.

Obey God and Do What Is Right
(Tune: "I Will Make You Fishers of Men")

Obey God and do what is right,
Do what is right, do what is right.
Obey God and do what is right
In the Lord's sight.

293

are on our traffic light? Do right and good. Obeying God's rules is important too. When we learn God's rules, they help us know how to live safely. Today in our Bible story, some people decided to obey God's rules.

◆◆◆◆

Activity 2—Housecleaning

You will need water in spray bottles, old socks and towels, feather dusters, carpet sweepers and other cleaning tools. Have children clean the room. Wash chairs, tables, doors, and shelves. Limit the children to three squirts with the spray bottle. King Josiah had the workers clean and fix their temple/church. You are working hard to clean our church room. How do you obey and help at home? While the workers were cleaning the temple/church, they found a special scroll/book that had been lost. It was the scroll/book of God's laws or rules.

◆◆◆◆

Bible Time—Lost and Found

You will need a sample traffic light made in Activity 1, two Bibles, the Bible-words scroll used in lesson 49, and blocks (at least one block for each child). Before class, use a bookmark to mark 2 Kings 22 in one Bible. Place the marked Bible and the scroll under a large pile of blocks.

Sing "Gather 'Round, It's Bible Time" from page 8 of this session to call the children to the story circle.

Compliment children on specific ways they have obeyed during the opening activities and cleanup time. Hold up a traffic light from Activity 1. Who knows what this is? What does the traffic light tell us? What would happen if we couldn't see the light? We could not obey or follow the signal.

Hold up a Bible. Who knows what this is? God's Word is like a traffic light. It gives us God's directions. God wants us to be kind to our friends, talk to Him in prayer, learn and obey

2 Unit 12

and clean up their plates, come when they are called. Watch for a traffic light on the way home and tell your family about King Josiah obeying God's rules. When we obey our parents, we obey God. God wants us to be good helpers at home. Obeying God's rules makes us happy. Sing the two verses to "The B-I-B-L-E" from page 8 of this session, encouraging children to smile as they sing.

Leaders' Evaluation

	Great!	OK!	More!	Oops!	Suggestions
Activity 1					
Activity 2					
Bible Time					
Application					
Bible Memory					
Craft					
Snack					
Game					
Wrap-up					

Lesson 50 7

294

His Word. If we could not see or hear about the Bible, we could not follow or obey God's directions.

King Josiah loved God, but God's rules had been lost. The people had forgotten God and did not take care of the temple/church. King Josiah sent workers to clean up and fix the broken temple/church. The workers found something very special while they were cleaning up the temple/church. "Look, look," they called to Hilkiah, the high priest, "look what we've found!" Have each child take a block from the pile you made before class and begin building a wall. We'll be like the workers fixing the broken temple. When a child finds the Bible and scroll, say. Look, look! Look what (child's name) has found. This is what happened in our Bible story. Choose a child to open the Bible to the place you have marked.

Hilkiah the priest said to Shaphan the secretary, "Look, look, I have found God's laws!"

Shaphan went to King Josiah and said, "Look, look, we have found God's laws!"

"Read them to me," said King Josiah. The king became very sad when he heard God's laws. King Josiah said, "We must read these to the people, so we all can obey."

"Look, look!" King Josiah may have said to all the people. "We have found God's laws. Come and listen." King Josiah promised to obey God's laws. All the people promised to obey God's laws. One of the first ways they obeyed was to celebrate the Passover dinner. King Josiah said, "Celebrate the Passover just as it is written in God's law. Always remember how God took care of His people."

The people said, "We promise to obey God's laws."

◆◆◆◆

APPLICATION—Do Right Roll-ups

You will need copies of the strips on page 306, scissors, tape, fruit roll snacks (long, narrow strips, such as Fruit by the Foot, by Betty Crocker), clear adhesive paper, and washable markers. If you have younger children in your class, cut out the strips,

Lesson 50

---

bags for children to take home. Let children wash and dry their hands before proceeding to the Snack time.

Snack—Haroset

You will need apples, nuts, cinnamon, white grape juice, small cups, spoons, and matzo crackers. Before the session, chop the apples and nuts. Mix with cinnamon and white grape juice to make haroset, a Passover food.

Serve the haroset in small cups. Set tables with spoons, matzo crackers, and water. This food was served at the Passover Dinner. The haroset mixture of apples and nuts reminded God's people of the mortar used with the bricks they built with in Egypt. God helped them leave Egypt and find a land where they would not be slaves. Having a Passover dinner to remember how God helped them was part of God's rules. Ask a volunteer to pray before the snack is served.

Game—Follow the Leader

You will need a construction paper crown.

Let children take turns choosing an action for the class to follow—hopping, sliding, jumping, galloping, walking backwards, hands up/down, swing arms, march slow/fast. Let the leader wear a crown like King Josiah.

When we follow someone, it is like obeying them. Follow the actions of the leader and you will be obeying. Who was the king who wanted to follow and obey God's rules? Who found God's rules? What did they do with them? What did the people promise?

◆◆◆◆

Wrap-up—Obey with a Smile

Give children instructions for cleaning up the room and praise them when they obey. Then have children gather together in a large group.

Ask children to share ways they will obey at home: feed the dog, pick up toys, set the table, go to bed on time, try new foods

Unit 12

tape them together, and cover them with clear adhesive before class.

Give children the copies of the strips and ask them to cut them out and tape them together. If time allows, children may use markers to color the strips. Help the children cover their strips with clear adhesive. (The fruit roll-up will stick to the paper.) Talk about the pictures on the strips.

What do our Bible words say? "Do what is right and good in the Lord's sight." **How did Josiah and the people do what was right and good in God's sight?** When they read and heard God's Word, they obeyed. **These strips show ways we can do what is right and good in God's sight. What are some ways to do right and good that you see on the strip?** Share crayons, pick up toys, set table, pray before bed, pray before meals, give God an offering of money, take food to those in need. **Let's sing about ways we can obey God.** Sing "Obey God and Do What Is Right" from page 8 of this session. Once the children are comfortable with the words of the song, substitute ways to obey. Other verses could include: Obey God by sharing your crayons; obey God by picking up toys; obey God by setting the table; obey God by praying at meals; obey God by praying in bed; obey God by giving to Him; obey God by giving some food.

When you are finished singing, help children measure out a fruit roll that is the same length as the strip. They can lay the fruit on their strip and roll it up. Help them tape their fruit rolls shut when they are done rolling them up. You may need to help younger children get started rolling their strip. **Take your fruit roll-up home. When you eat it, it will remind you how you can obey like Josiah and the people obeyed.**

◆◆◆◆

BIBLE MEMORY—Do Right and Good

You will need a Bible with Deuteronomy 6:18 marked and highlighted and the traffic lights made in Activity 1. Have a volunteer find the verse in your Bible. Say the highlighted words with the children several times. Then have children get their traffic lights. Ask for different groups of children to stand up and say the words on their lights. Have all the boys stand up, then all the girls. Have children with tie shoes, buckle shoes, and slip-on shoes stand up. Have children with red, yellow, green, black, and white on stand up.

King Josiah read God's laws so all the people could obey and do what is right and good in the Lord's sight. **You are doing right and good in God's sight by learning God's Word.**

◆◆◆◆

ACTIVITY TIME

Do as many activities as time permits.

◆◆◆◆

Craft—Make Play Dough

You will need ingredients for play dough (1 cup flour, 1/2 cup salt, 1 tsp cream of tartar, 1 cup water, 1 tbsp oil, food coloring, and peppermint extract), an electric skillet, and plastic bags. The play dough recipe makes 1/2 cup per child for six to eight children, so adjust ingredients according to the number of children in your class.

In class, let three different children put the flour, salt, and cream of tartar in the cold electric skillet. Let another child stir the dry ingredients together. Let other children add the water, oil, food coloring, and flavoring. Let children take turns stirring carefully while everyone repeats the Bible verse.

When we cook, there are rules we must obey. Before the skillet is plugged in, we will put our hand in our laps. Why is this a good rule to obey? What will happen to the skillet when it is turned on? Plug in and stir on medium heat until the dough is not shiny (like scrambled eggs). All moisture should be absorbed. Unplug skillet and dump dough on the table. Place skillet away from children. Give each child a lump to knead. **Can we flatten our dough out like a Bible or scroll? I'm glad you obeyed our safety rules. Whose rules did King Josiah read about? What did King Josiah promise?** Write names on plastic

Unit 12
Lesson 51

Micaiah Tells the Truth
(1 Kings 22:1-37)

Micaiah was a prophet of the Lord. Ahab, King of Israel, wanted King Jehoshaphat of Judah to go to battle. They consulted 400 false prophets and Micaiah. The 400 false prophets told the kings what they wanted to hear, "Go to battle." Only Micaiah told God's truth. Micaiah was put into prison for telling the truth.

Bible Words

"Do what is right and good in the Lord's sight" (Deuteronomy 6:18).

Goals

Name a man who did right by telling the truth.
Desire to choose right.
Choose to tell the truth.

◆◆◆◆

Activity 1—False Prophet Figures

You will need copies of page 308, scissors, and markers or crayons.

Give each child a copy of page 308 and ask the children to color and cut out the men on the page. These men were all prophets. What is a prophet's job? Allow children to respond. A prophet's job is to tell people the messages that God tells him or her to say. But these men were false prophets. They didn't tell people what God told them to say. Instead, they told people whatever they wanted to hear. In our Bible story today, these prophets all said the same thing: "Go to battle." Ask children to practice holding up their prophets and saying, "Go to battle."

Gather 'Round, It's Bible Time
(Tune: "London Bridge")

Gather 'round, it's Bible time,
Bible time, Bible time;
Gather 'round, it's Bible time:
Time to learn.

The B-I-B-L-E

The B-I-B-L-E—
Yes, that's the book for me.
I stand alone on the Word of God,
The B-I-B-L-E.

I'll S-M-I-L-E
'cause God's Word teaches me.
I'll learn and listen every day.
I'll S-M-I-L-E.

Obey God and Do What Is Right
(Tune: "I Will Make You Fishers of Men")

Obey God and do what is right,
Do what is right, do what is right.
Obey God and do what is right
In the Lord's sight.

Obey God and say what is true,
Say what is true, say what is true.
Obey God and say what is true
In the Lord's sight.

ACTIVITY 2—Talk and Listen

You will need several toy telephones, a cassette player, and a blank cassette.

We can all use our mouths to say right things or wrong things. What are some wrong things we might use our mouth for? Saying angry words, making fun of others, calling people names, telling lies. **What are some right things we can use our mouths for?** Saying nice things to others, singing and praying to God, telling people about Jesus. **Let's practice using our mouths to say right things!** Encourage children to use the telephone to pretend to call friends or family members and say right things. They can also record themselves on the cassette saying right things. Guide them if they need suggestions. They could call their friend to tell them something nice. They could record the Bible verse or a favorite praise song. They could record themselves telling a short Bible story.

You are all choosing to use your mouths for the right things. Micaiah the prophet had a hard job. He had to choose to use his mouth for right things too. Mean King Ahab wanted Micaiah to lie like all the false prophets. But Micaiah chose to tell the truth of God.

◆◆◆◆◆

BIBLE TIME—Micaiah Tells the Truth

You will need copies of page 309, scissors, markers, tape or Plasti-Tak, the prophets made in Activity 1, and the Listening Ears made in lesson 49. Before class, color and cut out the figures of Micaiah, King Ahab, and King Jehoshaphat. As you tell the story, attach the figures to a wall, poster board, or chalkboard.

Ask children to put on their Listening Ears as you prepare for the Bible story. Lead children in saying the memory verse, Deuteronomy 6:18. **Whom have we heard about in our Bible**

---

about saying right things and telling the truth like Micaiah. In the book of James, the Bible says that saying right things is one of the hardest things we can choose to do! Will you choose to tell the truth like Micaiah? Will you choose to tell the truth even though it is hard? Ask children to respond. Choosing right makes God happy, and it also makes you happy! Sing the second verse of "The B-I-B-L-E" with big smiles on your faces.

Until parents come, review the Bible story using the Micaiah masks. Let the children take turns coming up, holding their masks, and speaking for Micaiah. Micaiah, to whom did you talk? Two kings. Can you name one of them? What did King Ahab say to you? What did the messenger tell you to do? What did you tell the kings? What happened to you? What did you eat? Which king was killed? Which king came home? Were your words true?

Leaders' Evaluation

	Great!	OK!	More!	Oops!	Suggestions
Activity 1					
Activity 2					
Bible Time					
Application					
Bible Memory					
Craft					
Snack					
Game					
Wrap-up					

stories who did what is right and good? Ezra and the people, Josiah and the people. **How did Ezra, Josiah, and the people do right?** They listened to and learned God's Word. They obeyed God's Word. **Today we will hear about another person who did what is right and good. His name was Micaiah.** Ask children to say Micaiah's name aloud with you. One of the kings that Micaiah talked to has a hard name too. His name was Jehoshaphat. Ask the children to say Jehoshaphat's name with you.

King Ahab was the king of Israel. Tape or Plasti-Tak the figure of King Ahab to the board or wall. **King Ahab had a visit from Jehoshaphat, the king of Judah.** Attach the figure of Jehoshaphat to the board or wall. **King Ahab wanted King Jehoshaphat to help him fight a battle.** King Jehoshaphat said, "Let's ask God's prophet if we should go to battle." **King Ahab didn't want to know what God thought. He just wanted to go to battle. So King Ahab brought false prophets to see King Jehoshaphat. The false prophets lied to King Jehoshaphat because King Ahab wanted them to. What did the false prophets say?** Ask the children to say, "Go to battle," as they learned in Activity 1. Then ask them to bring their false prophets up and say, "Go to battle" as you attach them to the board or wall. **Look how many false prophets we have.** Count them together. **We have (number of prophets) false prophet figures on our board. But King Ahab had 400 false prophets that said, "Go to battle." That is many more prophets than we have here.**

King Jehoshaphat knew the false prophets were lying. He said, "Isn't there a prophet of the Lord we can ask?"

"Well, there is one prophet of the Lord named Micaiah," answered King Ahab, "but I hate him, because he always says something bad about me."

"Call Micaiah," said King Jehoshaphat. So King Ahab called Micaiah, the Lord's prophet. Attach the figure of Micaiah to the wall or board. All the false prophets were saying, "Attack, attack," when Micaiah came to the kings. Point to the large group of false prophets. Four hundred men wanted Micaiah to

Lesson 51

OPTION: Provide refrigerated bread sticks and a baking sheet. Before Bible Time, give each child a bread stick and help them twist it into whatever shape they want, then place it on the baking sheet. Have a helper bake the bread sticks and serve them during Snack time.

Game—Four Hundred and One Prophets

You will need the prophet figures made in Activity 1 and the Micaiah figure used during Bible Time. You may wish to color the Micaiah figure with a bright marker to distinguish him from the other prophets. Before the game, place all the figures in a basket or other container.

Place the basket in the front of the room. Have the children take turns going up in pairs or one at a time and drawing a prophet figure out of the basket. They should hold up the figure for the large group to see. If the figure is a false prophet, the group will say, "Go to battle." If the figure is Micaiah, the group should say, "God says, 'Don't go.'" Children who draw false prophet figures can keep them. Children who draw Micaiah should place him back in the basket. Continue until all the false prophet figures are gone.

The false prophets said what was easy. They thought it was okay to lie, because they told King Ahab what he wanted them to say. But in the end, only Micaiah (hold up the Micaiah figure) **was right because he told the truth.**

♦♦♦♦

Wrap-Up—Choose to Tell the Truth

You will need a Bible and the Micaiah masks made during the Craft.

Guide children as they clean up the room. Then ask them to gather in a large group.

Sing the first verse of "The B-I-B-L-E" from page 8 of this session. Then hold up your Bible and open it to the book of James. **We have chosen to learn and listen to God's Word, the Bible, like Ezra, Josiah, and God's people. God's Word tells us a lot**

Unit 12

lie and agree with them. King Ahab wanted Micaiah to lie. But Micaiah would not lie! Micaiah said, "I can only tell what the Lord says. King Ahab, you will be killed if you go to battle." "See, I told you," King Ahab said to King Jehoshaphat, "he never says anything good about me." One of the false prophets walked up and slapped Micaiah and made fun of him for telling the truth.

King Ahab said, "Take Micaiah to prison and feed him only bread and water until I come back safely from battle." The kings went to battle and King Ahab was killed, just like Micaiah said. Even when 400 other men lied, Micaiah told the true word of God.

◆◆◆◆

APPLICATION—Hard or Easy

You will need the recording of right things to say made in Activity 2.

Ask the children to sit in a circle. Play the recording of right things to say that the children made in Activity 2. **The right, true things that we recorded were all easy to say. But sometimes it is hard to choose right by telling the truth.** Tell the children that you are going to name some things that are hard and easy to say. If you say something easy, they should stay seated. If you say something hard, they should stand up. Following are suggestions. Say you love God. Say you broke a toy. Say you like hamburgers. Say you want to play with a friend. Say you played in the street. Say you hit your brother or sister. Say you love Jesus. Say you did not share.

When you are finished naming situations, ask the children to name some things that are hard or easy to say. **God wants us to always choose right and tell the truth even when it is hard or easy.**

Sing the two verses of "Obey God and Do What Is Right" from page 8 of this session.

BIBLE MEMORY—Pass the Phone

You will need a cassette of familiar Bible songs, a cassette player, and a toy telephone.

Play a familiar Bible song as children pass a telephone receiver. When the music stops, have the class say the words of the memory verse together. The child who is holding the phone should push the numbers 6, 1, and 8 on the phone when you say "Deuteronomy 6:18." Try to give every child a turn. Form two groups if your class is large.

◆◆◆◆

ACTIVITY TIME

Do as many activities as time permits.

Craft—Micaiah Mask

You will need wire hangers, nylon hose, scissors, glue, yarn, pom-poms, markers, and paper. Before class, bend a wire hanger into a diamond shape for each child. Place a nylon hose over the hanger and tie at the bottom. Trim any excess.

Give each child a covered hanger to use to make a Micaiah mask. They can color and cut out paper pieces to glue on Micaiah's face, and they can glue on yarn for hair. **Micaiah was a prophet of God who told the truth to the kings. King Ahab wanted Micaiah to lie and say it was good to go to battle. We want to be like Micaiah and choose always to tell the truth.**

Snack—Prison Food

You will need bread and water.

Let the children pass out the bread and water. **Who had only bread and water until the kings came back from battle? Where was Micaiah? Did the kings come back? Did Micaiah tell the truth?** Have the children give thanks for their mouths and ask God to help them always tell the truth.

Unit 12
Lesson 52

Samuel Chooses to Do Right All His Life

(1 Samuel 2:18, 21, 26; 3:1-10, 19, 20; 4:1a; 7:15-17)

As a young boy, Samuel lived and worked in the temple. As an older boy, he listened to God's Word. As a grown man, he taught other people God's Word. Samuel chose to do right all his life.

Bible Words

"Do what is right and good in the Lord's sight" (Deuteronomy 6:18).

Goals

Name a man who chose to do right all his life.
Desire to choose right.
Choose to do right—now and when I grow up.

◆◆◆◆

Activity 1—Polish Silver

You will need old socks or T-shirts, toothpaste, water, and small pieces of silver, such as silverware. If you do not have silver to clean, provide furniture polish, dust rags, glass cleaner, and paper towels. Let the children polish the furniture and clean the glass. You will need to assist the children in using the spray bottles.

Let the children use the toothpaste and cloths to clean and polish the silver. As the children work, praise them for their efforts. Discuss how Samuel might have helped in the temple. **You are helping to clean our church. The boy Samuel helped clean and take care of the items in the temple/church. He**

—fold—

Gather 'Round, It's Bible Time
(Tune: "London Bridge")

Gather 'round, it's Bible time,
Bible time, Bible time;
Gather 'round, it's Bible time:
Time to learn.

The B-I-B-L-E

The B-I-B-L-E—
Yes, that's the book for me.
I stand alone on the Word of God,
The B-I-B-L-E.

I'll S-M-I-L-E
'cause God's Word teaches me.
I'll learn and listen every day.
I'll S-M-I-L-E.

Obey God and Do What Is Right
(Tune: "I Will Make You Fishers of Men")

Obey God and do what is right,
Do what is right, do what is right.
Obey God and do what is right
In the Lord's sight.

Obey God and say what is true,
Say what is true, say what is true.
Obey God and say what is true
In the Lord's sight.

301

helped Eli the priest. Samuel chose to do right when he helped as a little boy.

ACTIVITY 2—Body Outlines

You will need large pieces of newsprint, pencils, markers, tape measures, and rulers. If possible, recruit extra adults to help with this activity.

Have each child lay on a large piece of newsprint as you outline his body. Provide tape measures and rulers for measuring. Let the children color their figures and add features. Look how big you are growing. Which child has the biggest hand? Which child is the tallest? Which child is the shortest? Do you have anyone in your family that is smaller or larger than you? Samuel was a young boy when he went to live in the temple/church. He always did right all his life.

◆◆◆◆

BIBLE TIME—A Boy and a Man Choose Right

You will need a blanket and pillow. Before the session, make a little bed on the floor with the blanket and pillow.

Sing "Gather 'Round, It's Bible Time" from page 8. Children can listen and tell about God. Teenagers can listen and tell about God. Grown-ups can listen and tell about God. Everyone can choose to do right, whatever age they are. I saw _____ (name of child) helping put the paints away. He chose the right thing to do. I saw _____ (name of child) helping clean up the silver and cloths. She chose the right thing to do. You are only _____ years old and are already choosing to do right.

As a young boy, Samuel worked in the temple. Let's stand up and reach up high as we pretend to polish the tall candlesticks in the temple/church. Now let's sit down and pretend we are listening to Eli the priest tell about God. Now let's lay down just like Samuel did in the temple. Let children take turns lying in Samuel's "bed." The other children can lie on the floor and pretend that they are Samuel, sleeping in his bed.

church as they clean up the room. Then gather the children together in a large group around the altar made during Application.

What are ways we can do right as children? Refer children to the pictures on the stones if they need help. Hold up the Bible. God's Word tells us everything we need to know about choosing right. Ezra knew God's Word was right. Josiah knew God's Word was right. Micaiah and Samuel knew God's Word was right. We can choose right just like they did. We can learn and study and obey God's Word. Have the children say the memory verse rhythm. Then sing the two verses of "The B-I-B-L-E" from page 8 of this session.

Until parents arrive, have children work on the time-line pictures for this unit from pages 312-314. Children can circle the hidden pictures and color the time line.

Leaders' Evaluation

	Great!	OK!	More!	Oops!	Suggestions
Activity 1					
Activity 2					
Bible Time					
Application					
Bible Memory					
Craft					
Snack					
Game					
Wrap-up					

One night, while Samuel was in his bed in the temple/church, the Lord called, "Samuel, Samuel." Samuel thought it was Eli and got up. Have children pretend to get up and walk to Eli's room.

"Go back to bed," Eli said, "I did not call you." So Samuel walked back to his bed and lay down. Have children go back to the area by Samuel's bed and lie down. **Again he heard a voice call, "Samuel, Samuel."** Have children sit up and listen. Samuel said, "Here I am." Again he walked into Eli's room. Get up and pretend to walk to Eli's room again. But Eli said, "Go back and lie down. I did not call."

Go back and lie down. Samuel lay down and heard the call a third time. "Samuel, Samuel." Again Samuel sat up and said, "Here am I" and walked into Eli's room. Do so with the children. Then Eli realized it was the Lord calling. "Go lie down, Samuel, and if He calls say, 'Speak, Lord, I am listening.'"

Go back and lie down by Samuel's bed. The Lord called "Samuel, Samuel." Samuel sat up (have children do so) and said (say his words with me), "Speak, Lord, for I am listening." Samuel did listen and learned and obeyed everything the Lord said.

As Samuel continued to grow, he always choose to do right. He helped other people learn God's Word so they could choose right. Samuel was a prophet of the Lord who traveled to different cities. Let's stand up and pretend to walk with a stick and travel like Samuel. In every city he visited, Samuel helped the people learn about God. When he came back home, he built an altar to thank God. All his life Samuel wanted to do right: when he was a boy, when he was a teenager, and when he grew to be a man.

◆◆◆◆

Application—Build an Altar

You will need a cardboard box, construction paper and tape or contact paper, markers, and scissors. Before class, cut stones out of construction paper or contact paper. Make enough stones for

Lesson 52

Snack—Trail Mix

You will need sandwich bags, teaspoons, and the following items in separate containers: raisins, sunflower seeds, mini-marshmallows, chocolate chips, pretzels, Cheerios, and dates.

Give each child a sandwich bag. Line up the items in containers and put a teaspoon in each one. Let children take one teaspoon of each of the items to put in their bags. Walk around the room and stop to have a snack. **Samuel traveled to all the cities to help the people learn about God. Let's say our Bible verse, "Do what is right and good in the Lord's sight"** (Deuteronomy 6:18). Walk to the water fountain or have a cup of water.

Game—Dress-up Relay

You will need three hats, three big pairs of shoes, and three shirts or coats. If possible, choose sets of clothes, such as outfits for a nurse, a firefighter, a gardener, an airline pilot, a police officer, and so on. Before the activity, place two chairs against the wall. Place a hat on each chair and a big pair of shoes under the chair. Place a shirt or coat on the back of the chair. OPTION: Adjust the number of items, according to the size of your class. There should be only five or six children in each group.

Form three lines at the opposite end of the room with only five or six children in each. At a given signal, the first child in line will run down and put the items on and run back, take them off and the next child will put them on. They will run to the chair, take off the clothes, and run back and touch the next child. If you have time, have groups switch lines and play again, trying on a different set of clothes. **Whether we are big or little, whether we are a nurse or firefighter or gardener, we can choose right!**

◆◆◆◆

Wrap-up—Always Do Right

You will need the altar made in Application, a Bible, time-line pages 312-314, and crayons.

Have children pretend to be like Samuel cleaning the temple/

Unit 12

the children in your class. Make the stones large enough to cover the cardboard box when they are all attached to the box.

Samuel did right as a little boy, and he did right even when he became an old man. We are never too little or too old to do right. We have decided that we will learn and listen to what God's Word says is right. What are some ways that we can choose right at home? At church? At school? With our friends? Encourage children to name many ways they can choose right. Then assign each child or pair of children a way to do right. They should draw a picture of that way to do right on a stone. Some ways children can do right: go to bed without complaining, pick up toys when asked, say kind things to a little brother or sister, listen when God's Word is read, say only kind things about other children, ask a child who is alone to play, let another child go first.

When the children have completed their pictures, ask them to come up one at a time, explain the way to do right, and attach their stone to the box.

In the Old Testament, when people worshiped God, they built an altar of stones and offered sacrifices to God. We are building an altar of stones and worshiping Him by telling Him that we will choose right.

When the altar is finished, have the children stand around it and sing "Obey God and Do What Is Right" from page 8 of this session. Then say a prayer. **Thank You, God, that we can choose right while we are children. Help us listen and learn and obey Your Word. Amen.** Let children word their own prayers if they would like.

♦♦♦♦

BIBLE MEMORY—Shoe Clap

Bring a variety of shoes to class, enough for one pair per child. Include all sizes and kinds: baby, child, tennis, tap, thong, adult boot, slipper, loafer, high heels, flats.

Let children choose a pair of shoes to put on their hands or fingers. Review the Bible-verse rhythm learned in lesson 49. As

— fold —

you say the Bible verse in rhythm, the children will clap shoes together.

Who could wear the shoes you have? Is there anyone in your family that could wear the ones you have? Do you think this person can choose right? Are they big or small?

♦♦♦♦

ACTIVITY TIME

Choose as many activities as time permits.

♦♦♦♦

Craft—On the Right Track

You will need copies of the track sections on pages 309 and 310, scissors, markers or crayons, and several small cars. If you have younger children in your class, cut out and fold the track sections before class.

Give children the copies of the three sections of the track. Ask them to color and cut out the track sections. Help them fold the sections on the dotted lines and tape them in order, 1-3. When the children have completed their tracks, discuss the pictures on the track.

How can you learn God's Word like Ezra and the people? Listen to God's Word when it is read; listen to my teacher; listen to my parents. **How can you obey God's Word like Josiah and the people?** When I learn what God's Word says, I do it—be kind, share, help, give. **When can you tell the truth like Micaiah?** When I do or say something wrong; when someone asks me about Jesus. **How can you do right when you are a child?** Do what I learn from God's Word and in church; obey my parents; tell others about Jesus.

Ask children to play a game in groups of three or four. They should take turns rolling a car down the track. They can tell a way that they can do the right thing on which the car stops. Children can take turns rolling from opposite ends of the track to be certain all four ways are discussed.

305

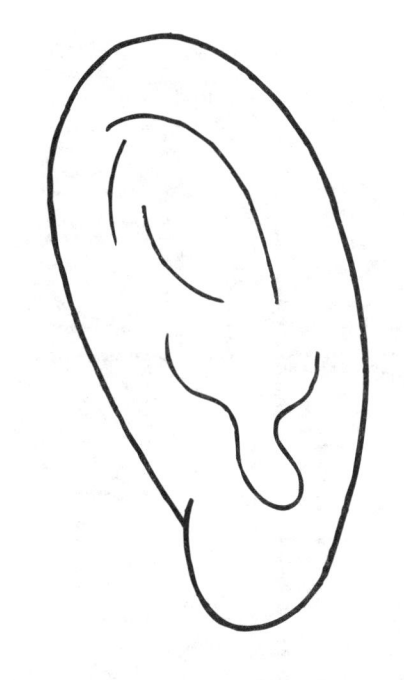

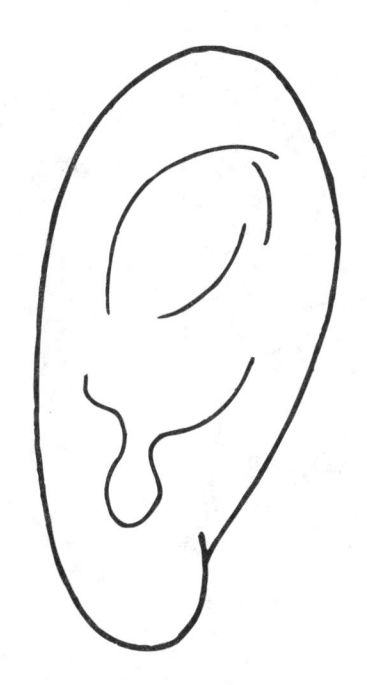

Do what is right and good in the Lord's sight.

Do Right Roll-up

Do what is right and good in the Lord's sight.

Bible Words Scroll

DO

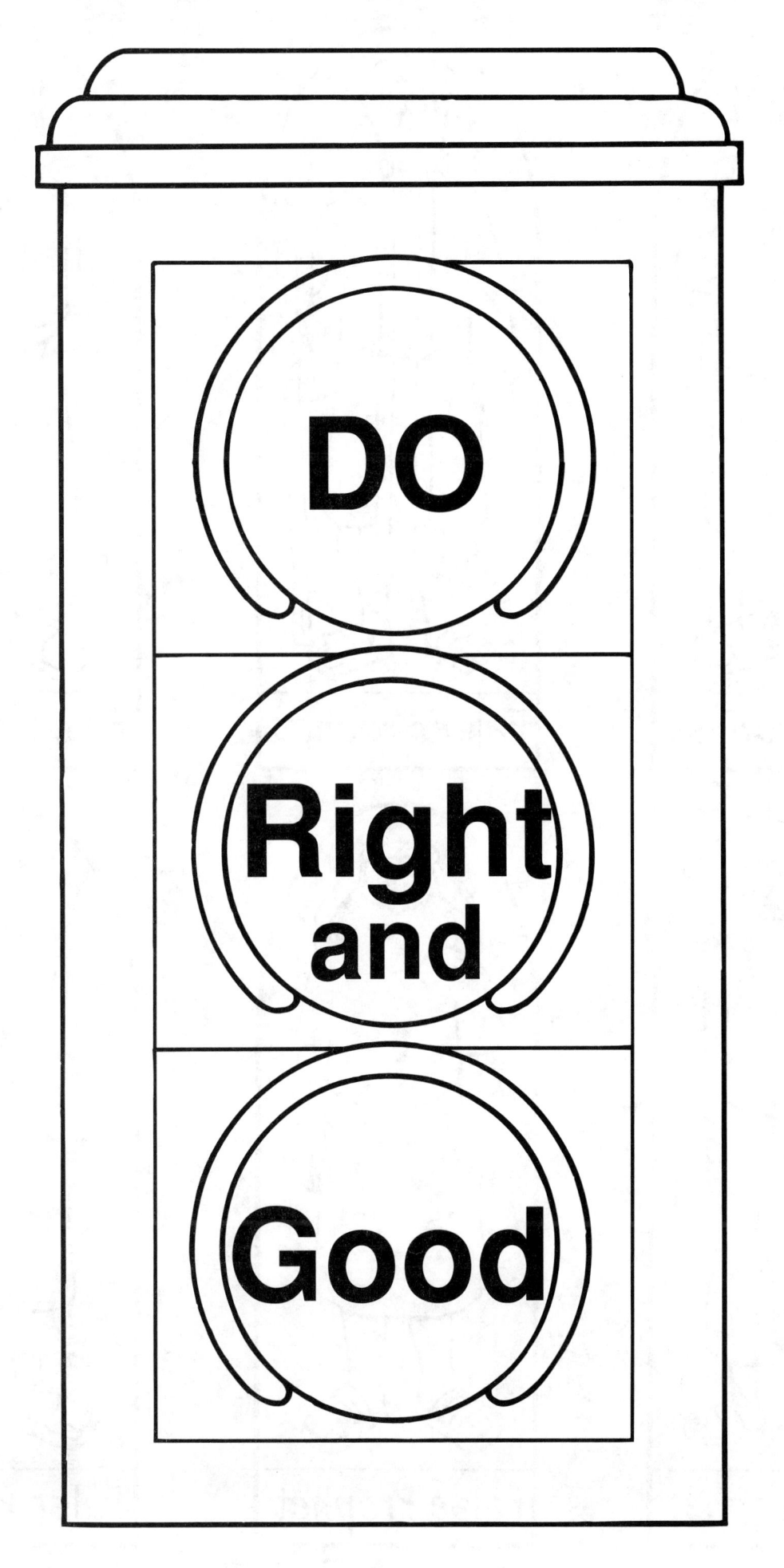

Right
and

Good

| False Prophet | False Prophet | False Prophet |

| False Prophet | False Prophet | False Prophet |

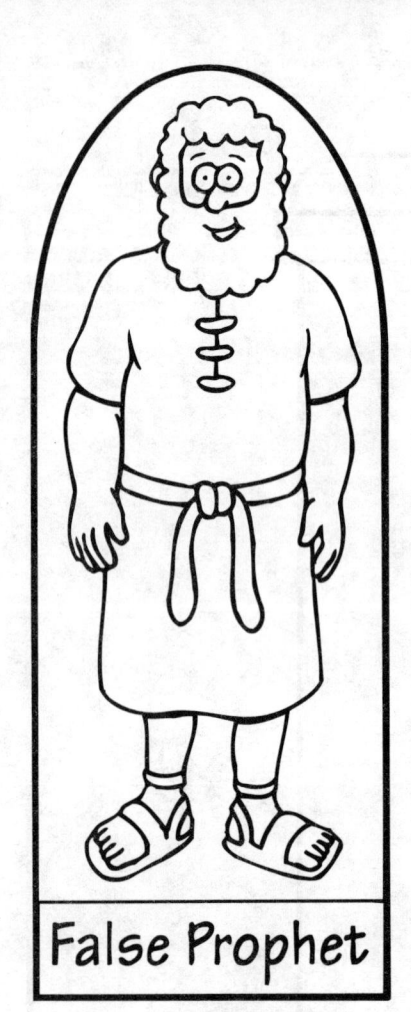

308

Jehoshaphat

Ahab

Micaiah

TAPE

309

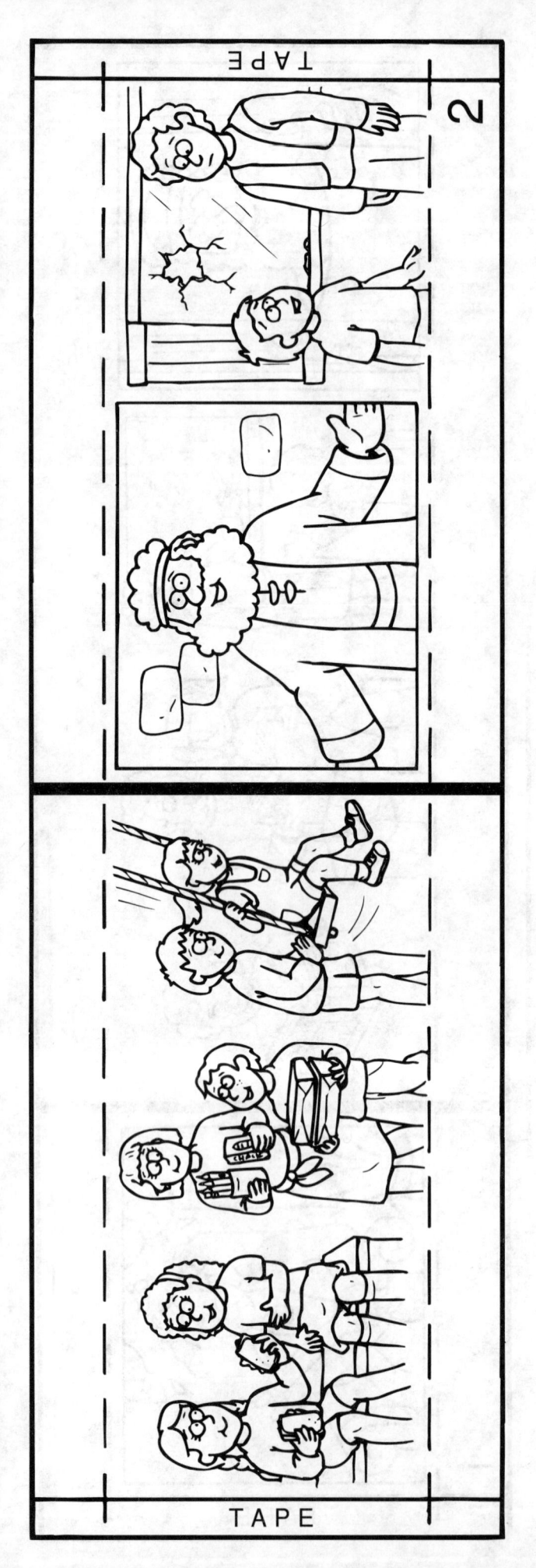

2

3

God Gives His People Food

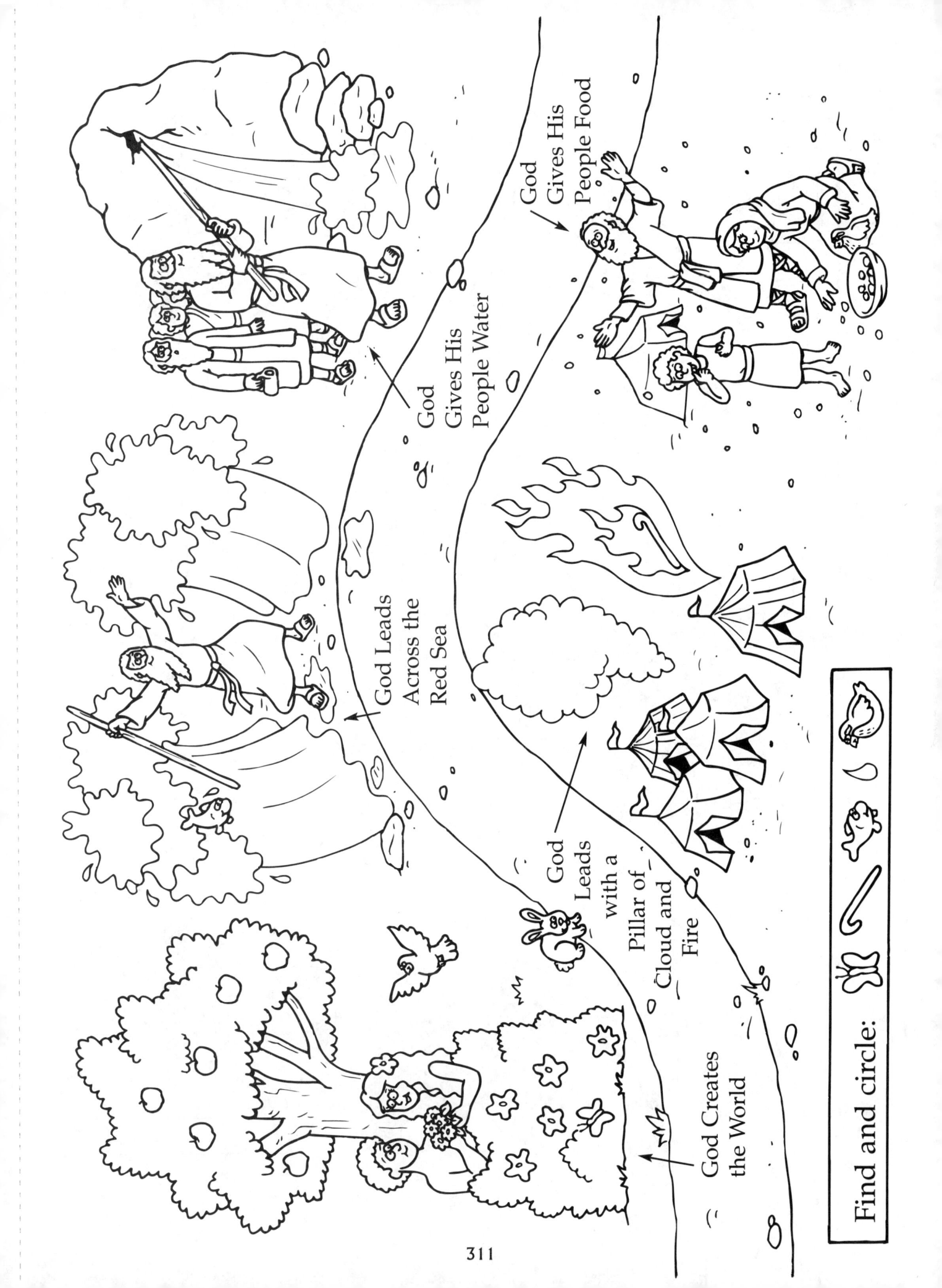

God Gives His People Water

God Leads Across the Red Sea

God Leads with a Pillar of Cloud and Fire

God Creates the World

Find and circle:

311

Find and circle:

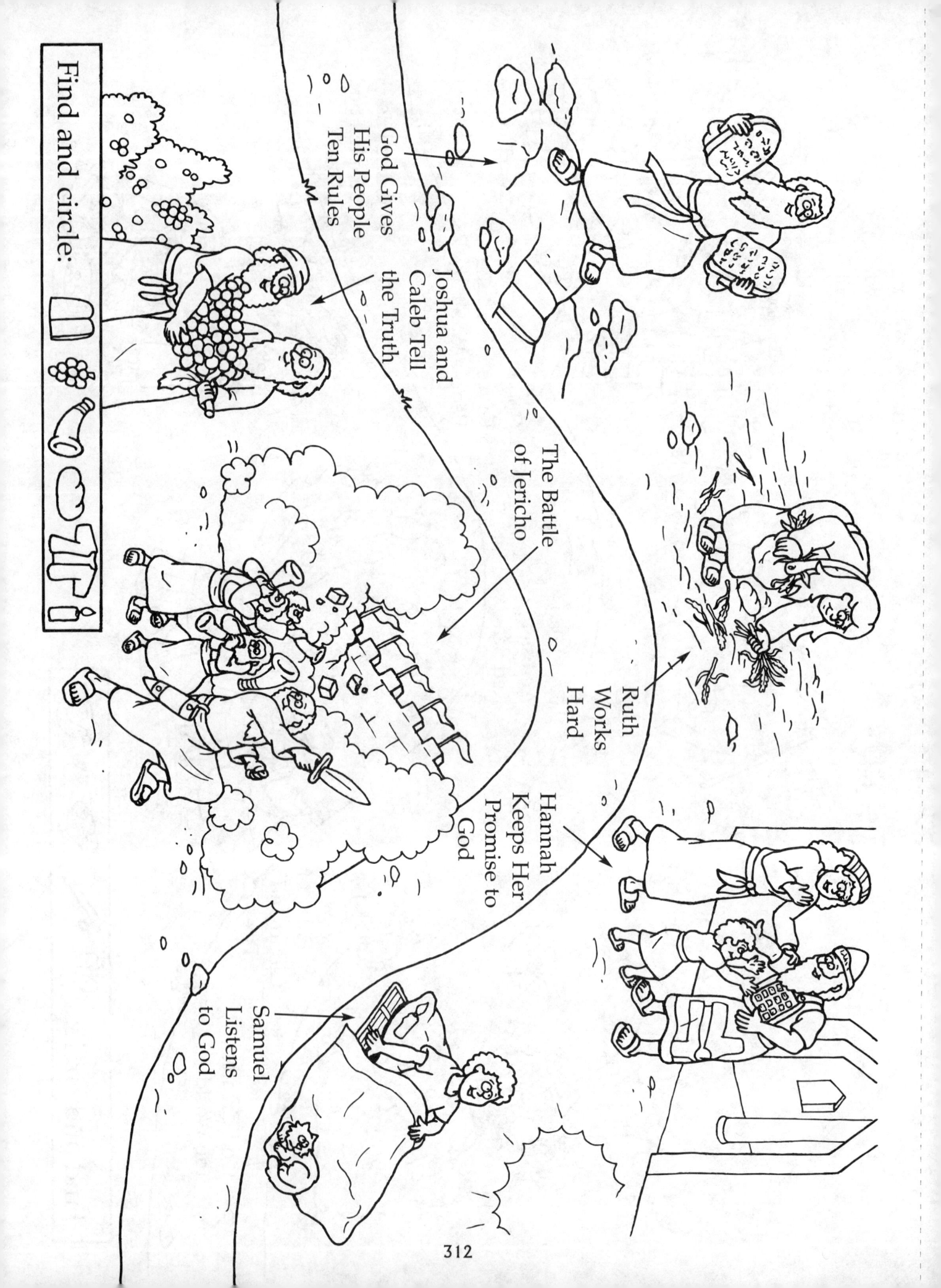

God Gives His People Ten Rules

Joshua and Caleb Tell the Truth

The Battle of Jericho

Ruth Works Hard

Hannah Keeps Her Promise to God

Samuel Listens to God

Micaiah Tells the Truth

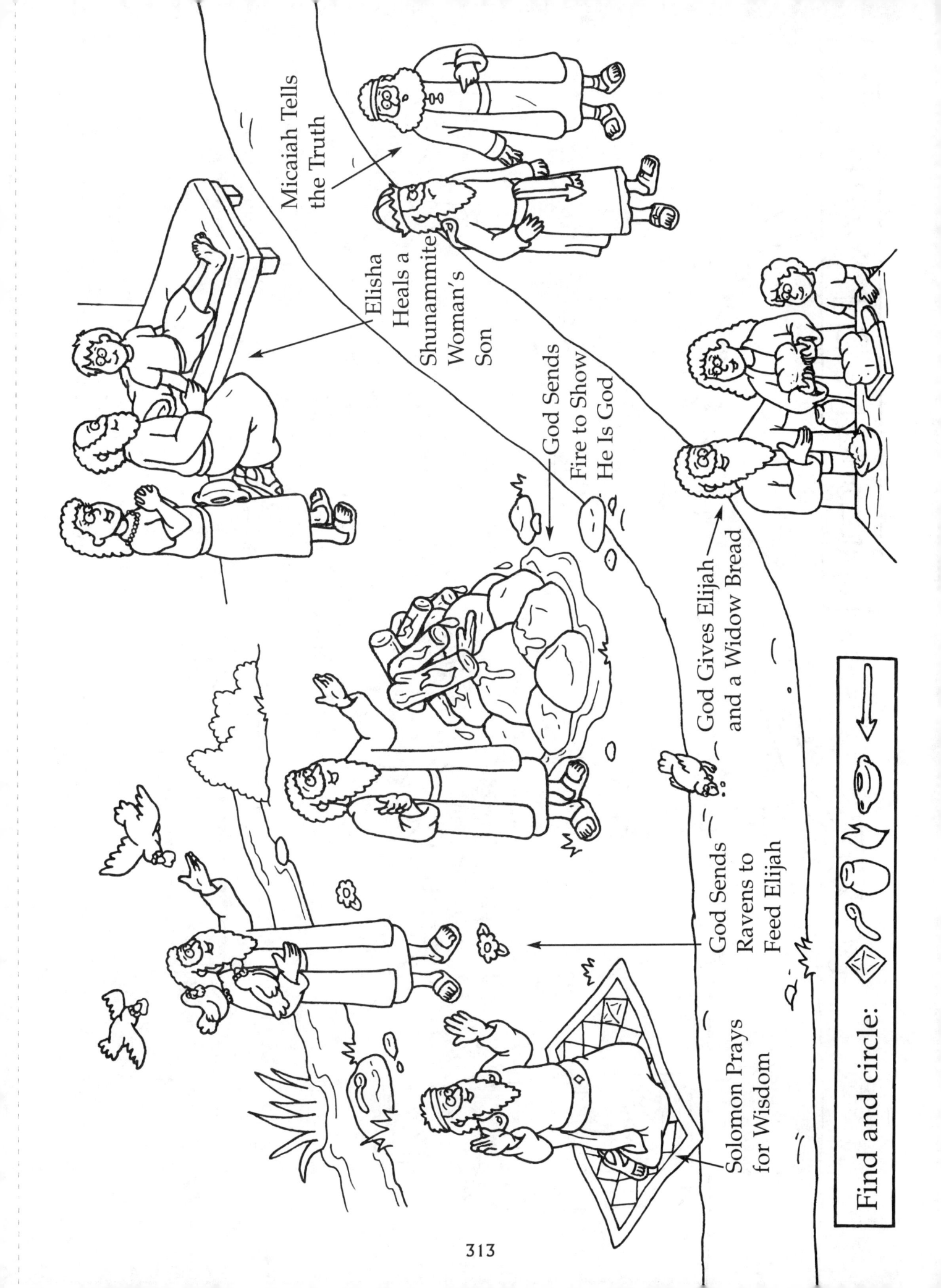

Elisha Heals a Shunammite Woman's Son

God Sends Fire to Show He Is God

God Gives Elijah and a Widow Bread

God Sends Ravens to Feed Elijah

Solomon Prays for Wisdom

Find and circle:

313

Find and circle:

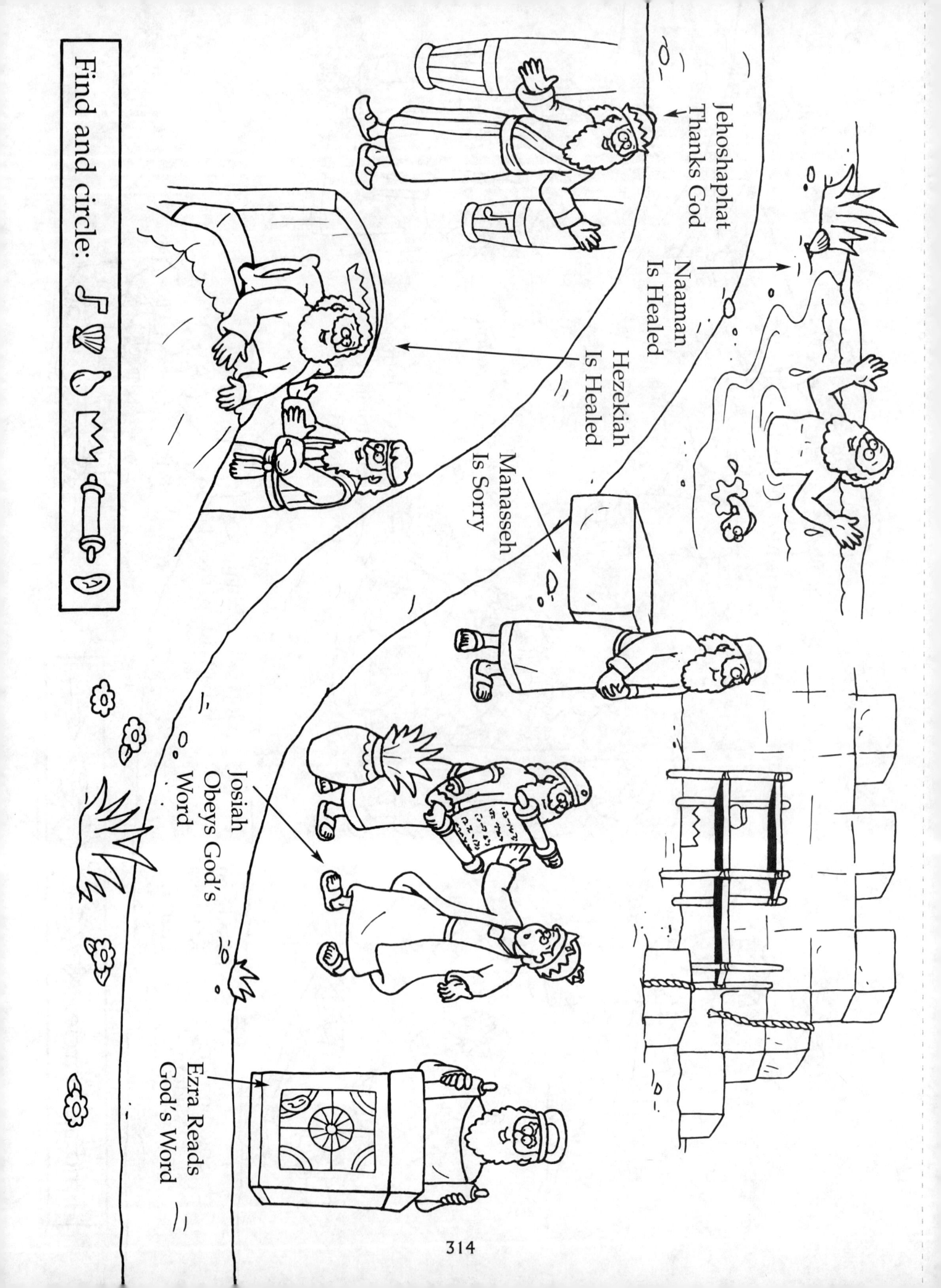

Jehoshaphat Thanks God

Naaman Is Healed

Hezekiah Is Healed

Manasseh Is Sorry

Josiah Obeys God's Word

Ezra Reads God's Word

314

Wise-men Visit Jesus

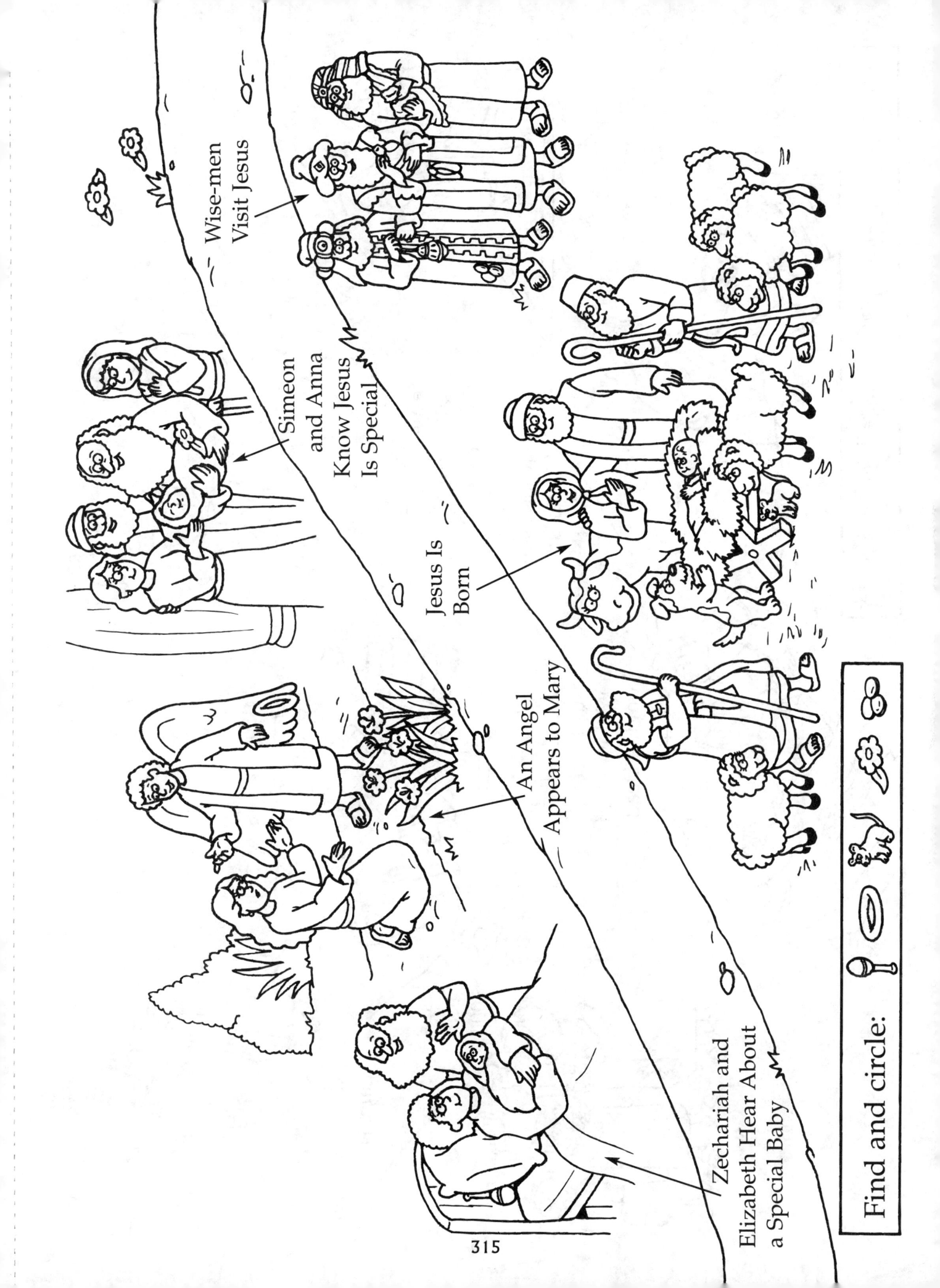

Simeon and Anna Know Jesus Is Special

Jesus Is Born

An Angel Appears to Mary

Zechariah and Elizabeth Hear About a Special Baby

Find and circle:

315

Find and circle:

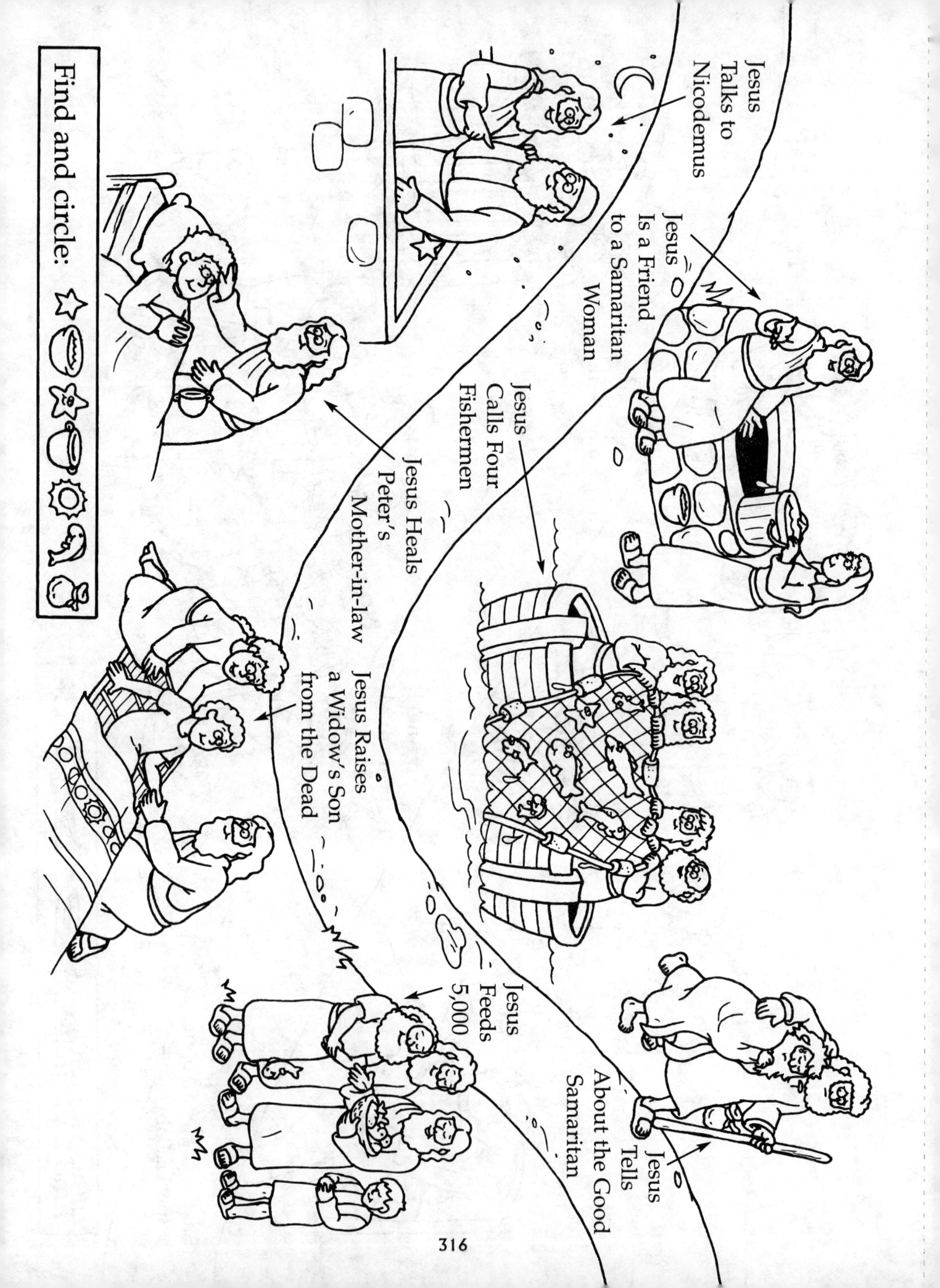

Jesus Talks to Nicodemus

Jesus Is a Friend to a Samaritan Woman

Jesus Calls Four Fishermen

Jesus Heals Peter's Mother-in-law

Jesus Raises a Widow's Son from the Dead

Jesus Feeds 5,000

Jesus Tells About the Good Samaritan

Jesus Rides Into Jerusalem

Jesus Dies and Lives Again

Jesus Heals Two Blind Men

Jesus Loves the Children

Jesus Heals Ten Lepers

Jesus Tells About the Rich Fool

Jesus Teaches Us to Pray

Find and circle:

317

Find and circle:

- Jesus Appears to His Followers
- Jesus Helps His Followers Catch Fish
- Jesus Returns to Heaven
- Jesus' Church Begins
- Peter and John Heal a Lame Man
- Philip Tells a Man from Ethiopia About Jesus
- Paul Tells About Jesus

Other children's product available!

THE BEGINNERS BIBLE

STANDARD PUBLISHING

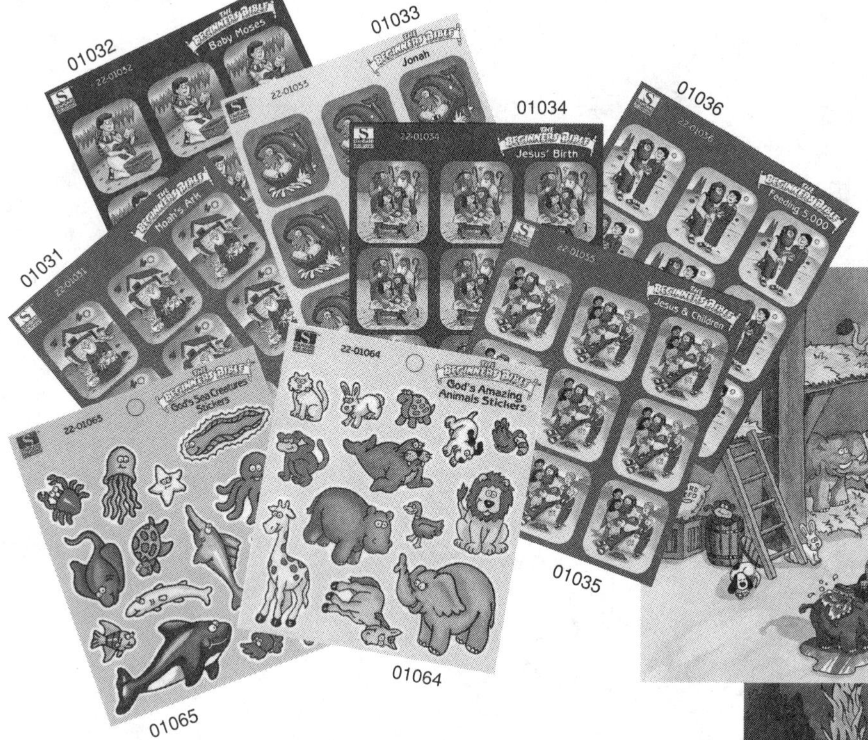

Stickers & Attendance Charts

Play-A-Sound Storybooks

Floor Puzzles

THE BEGINNERS BIBLE™

STANDARD PUBLISHING™

02715 — The First Christmas — 24 Large Easy-to-Use Pieces
02718 — Jesus and the Children — 24 Large Easy-to-Use Pieces
02716 — Noah's Ark — 24 Large Easy-to-Use Pieces — 2' x 3' Floor Puzzle
02717 — Jonah and the Great Fish — 24 Large Easy-to-Use Pieces — 2' x 3' Floor Puzzle

Inlay Puzzles

02702 — Jonah and the Great Fish
02704 — Jesus Is Born
02701 — Noah's Ark
02703 — Jesus and the Children
02700 — Adam and Eve

320